RETHINKING DEVELOP

RETHINKING DEVELOPMENT IN
LATIN AMERICA

edited by **Charles H. Wood and Bryan R. Roberts**

the pennsylvania state university press
university park, pennsylvania

Library of Congress Cataloging-in-Publication Data

Rethinking development in Latin America /
edited by Charles H. Wood, Bryan R. Roberts.
     p.   cm.
Papers of a conference entitled "Latin American sociology
and the sociology of Latin America" held in April 2001 at
the Center for Latin American Studies at the University of
Florida, Gainesville.
Includes bibliographical references and index.
ISBN 978-0-271-02894-1 (alk. paper)
1. Sociology—Latin America—Congresses.
2. Latin America—Social conditions—Congresses.
3. Political sociology—Latin America—Congresses.
4. Economic development—Latin America—Congresses.
I. Wood, Charles H., 1945–
II. Roberts, Bryan R., 1939–

HM477 .L29R47 2005
301′.098—dc22
2004023091

To the memory of Vilmar Faria,
SCHOLAR, COLLEAGUE, AND FRIEND

Contents

Acronyms

ANPOCS	Associação Nacional de Pesquisa e Pós-Graduação em Ciências Sociais
CAPES	Coordenação de Aperfeicoamento de Pessoal de Nível Superior
CEBRAP	Centro Brasileiro de Análise e Planejamento
CEPAL	Comisión Económica para América Latina y el Caribe
CIM	Inter-regional Mapuche Council
CLACSO	Consejo Latinoamericano de Ciencias Sociales
CNPq	Conselho Nacional de Pesquisa
CONADEP	Comisión Nacional para los Desaparecidos
CONADI	Corporación de Desarollo Indígena
DESAL	Centro de Desarrollo Social de América Latina
ECLAC	Economic Commission for Latin America and the Caribbean
EMBRAER	A Brazilian aircraft manufacturing firm
ESMA	Escuela Superior de Mecánica de la Armada (Navy School of Mechanics)
FAO	Food and Agriculture Organization of the United Nations
FAPESP	Fundação de Amparo à Pesquisa do Estado de São Paulo
FINEP	Financiadora de Estudos e Projetos
FUNDAP	Fundo de Defesa e Assistência Profissional
GDP	gross domestic product
GNP	gross national product
ICPD	International Conference on Population and Development
ICT	Instituto de Crédito Territorial
IDB	Inter-American Development Bank
IDES	Instituto de Desarollo Económico y Social
IMF	International Monetary Fund
INV	Instituto Nacional de Vivienda
IPEA	Instituto de Pesquisa Econômica Aplicada
ISI	import-substitution industrialization
MDS	managerial developmental state
MIR	Movement of the Revolutionary Left (Chile)
MITI	Ministry of Industry and Trade (Japan)
MST	Landless Workers' Movement

NAFTA	North American Free Trade Agreement
NEPP	Núcleo de Estudos Psicoanalíticos e Pedagógicos
NGO	nongovernmental organization
NUMP	New Urban Management Program
OBM	original brand name manufacturing
OECD	Organization for Economic Co-operation and Development
OEM	original equipment manufacturing
OIT	Organización Internacional del Trabajo
PIBS	Planning-Infrastructure-Building-Settlement
PME	Pesquisa Mensal do Emprego
PNAD	Pesquisa Nacional por Amostra de Domicílios
PNUMA	Programa de las Naciones Unidas para el Medio Ambiente
PREALC	Programa Regional del Empleo para América y el Caribe
PROCERA	Special Credit Program for Agrarian Reform
PROGRESA	Programa de Educación, Salud y Alimentación
PRONASOL	Programa Nacional de Solidaridad
PRONEX	Programa de Apoio a Centros de Excelência
PSDB	Partido da Social Democracia Brasileira
PT	Partido dos Trabalhadores
SERNAM	Servicio Nacional de la Mujer
SMO	social movement organization
SSRC	Social Science Research Council, New York
UNCHS	United Nations Center for Human Settlements
UNDP	United Nations Development Programme
UNESCO	United Nations Educational, Scientific and Cultural Organization
UNICAMP	Universidade Estadual de Campinas
UNICEF	United Nations Children's Fund
UNRISD	United Nations Research Institute for Social Development

Figures and Tables

Figures

Tables

Preface

The theme that marshals the diverse ideas set forth in this volume is inspired by an elemental disquiet shared by many of us who have long been engaged in the study of development in Latin America. The unease can be partly traced to our tentative understanding of the structural changes currently under way in the region, and to the novel challenges such changes pose for the conduct of research.

In response to the latest turns in Latin American history, but influenced also by scholarly debates within disciplinary specializations, many analysts have adopted theories and methods that differ qualitatively from those that once were staples of the trade. Scholars who endorse a clean break with the past contend that the new face of poverty in Latin America; the unprecedented mobilization for citizenship rights, the partial consolidation of new democracies, and the mounting imperatives of the global economy are among the events that demand new conceptual visions and analytical tools. More obstinate scholars convincingly counter that some of the discarded topics and perspectives may actually be more relevant today than when they were first formulated.

The continuities and breaks between past and present research traditions raise three critical questions: What factors explain the erosion or demise of once-dominant paradigms and the emergence of new assumptions, theories, and methods? What has been gained and what has been lost as a result of these changes? And, in the end, can we conclude with conviction that we are better positioned than before to understand today's realities?

These three questions prompted us to organize the conference "Latin American Sociology and the Sociology of Latin America," held in April 2001 and hosted by the Center for Latin American Studies at the University of Florida, Gainesville. The event brought together leading analysts in development studies from the United States and Latin America to assess the present state of development research. The agenda was limited to a small number of accomplished researchers drawn from a variety of disciplines, including sociology, economics, political science, geography, and demography. Rather than report results of specific research projects, participants were invited to present broadly conceived "reflective essays." As the term implies, the goal was to engage in thoughtful reflection about the concepts, theories, and methods analysts have invoked at different historical moments, and to distinguish transitory intellectual fashions from genuine advances in understanding.

Despite the range of topics addressed, and the diversity of disciplines represented by the authors, a striking number of themes repeatedly surface in the pages that follow. It is our fervent hope that, taken together, the essays presented here offer a panorama of insights that provide the basis for rethinking development in Latin America.

We owe sincere thanks to Amanda Wolfe and to the staff at the Center for Latin American Studies at the University of Florida for making the conference a success. At the University of Texas at Austin, our appreciation extends to Paloma Diaz, program coordinator at the Center for Latin American Social Policy, and Shannon Halley, assistant editor of the *Latin American Research Review*. Both Paloma and Shannon generously provided invaluable assistance in the preparation of this manuscript.

Finally, it is with heartfelt reverence that we dedicate this volume to the memory of Vilmar Faria, who passed away about a year after the conference in Gainesville. While Vilmar's scholarly and public careers were celebrated in Brazil, he was also recognized the world over as one of the most provocative and imaginative social scientists of his generation. If the death of a young man is always untimely, his loss is keenly felt today when the world seems to be in particular need of the very kind of insight, warmth, and intelligence that Vilmar so graciously imparted to everyone he knew.

CHARLES H. WOOD
BRYAN R. ROBERTS

Introduction:
Rethinking Development in Latin America

BRYAN R. BOBERTS AND CHARLES H. WOOD

Recent decades have witnessed profound change in Latin America. The imperatives of a globalized world economy have interacted with local economic, political, and cultural landscapes to produce an array of largely unforeseen consequences across the region. Confronted by new and increasingly complex realities, the perspectives that once dominated the social sciences during the "golden age" of development studies in the 1960s and 1970s have fallen from grace as new concepts, theories, and methods strive to make sense of the latest turns in contemporary Latin American history.

The material and conceptual transitions under way call for a timely assessment of the present and future state of development studies. The task can be organized in terms of a few basic questions: What historical events accounted for the demise of once-dominant paradigms? What new thematic directions and research priorities have come to define the field? And what implications do the answers to such questions have for the character of the social sciences, and their relationships to Latin America, in the twenty-first century?

Rather than report on specific research findings, the chapters in this volume are thoughtful reflections that, taken collectively, sketch the elements of the new conceptual and social agendas for Latin America. The issues and theories that informed our understanding of the region from the 1960s through the end of the 1980s serve as a reference point for critical analyses of current directions in the field. The challenge is to distinguish those frameworks and approaches which were overly embedded in the particular history of the time (and are therefore no longer applicable) from those which may have been discarded too hastily and could stand to be revived. The chapters take an equally measured view of newly proposed concepts and theories, distinguishing those which mainly reflect transitory fashions from those which represent genuine advances. The contributions pay particular attention to the relationship between research and policy, noting the new roles and responsibilities of the social sciences in a context that, today, is defined less by outright authoritarian governments than by weak democracies in which people struggle for political representation and citizenship rights. In the process of carrying out such assessments, the chapters provide an extensive and comprehensive bibliography on past and present publications and identify the research priorities that will define Latin American development studies in the decades to come.

The Golden Age of Latin American Development

Our benchmark is the period of Latin American development from approximately 1950 to 1980, when the region experienced industrialization and a rapid urbanization. Between 1950 and 1973, the region's gross domestic product (GDP) grew at an average annually compounded rate of 5.2 percent, compared with 2.6 percent in the period 1913–50 and 3.9 percent between 1973 and 1990 (Ffrench-Davis, Muñoz, and Palma 1994, 166). The 1950–73 period was also when the region had its highest percentage (30 percent) of the labor force working in industry. Thereafter, industrial employment declined as that in services and commerce grew.

The pace and extent of change differed by country. The southern cone countries—Argentina, Uruguay, and to a lesser extent, Chile—urbanized and industrialized earlier than other countries, with some 70 percent of their population living in towns and cities of twenty-thousand and over by 1980. Brazil and Mexico urbanized and industrialized later, but by 1980, just over half their populations were living in cities of twenty-thousand and over. In contrast, the Central American countries had just a quarter of their populations in such urban places by 1980. Urbanization and industrialization, along with high rates of natural increase in the countryside, produced substantial changes in the agrarian structures of the region. Urbanization and industrialization meant not only large-scale rural-urban migration but also increasing commercial pressures on subsistence agriculture. The highly uneven distribution of land in many Latin American countries and demographic pressures made peasant farming increasingly unviable, resulting not only in urban migration but in migration to other rural areas and to areas of colonization like the Amazonian frontier.

From 1960 to 1980, urbanization was closely linked to the direct and indirect effects of industrialization. Those countries which industrialized faster also urbanized at a quicker pace. The industrialization of the period was promoted by policies of import-substitution industrialization (ISI), which were widely adopted in the region. The United Nations Regional Economic Commission for Latin America and the Caribbean (ECLAC), under its arose in response to urbanization and industrialization, such as the peasant movements of the 1960s and 1970s and the "new" urban social movements. Yet their analysis also tended to deemphasize the capacity of social actors to produce significant change in the power relations that kept most of the population poor and bereft of rights. Touraine (1987) in his review of the literature was to conclude that Latin American urban movements were not true social movements in the sense of being able to transform the structures of power. As Foweraker points out in his chapter in this volume, the sights were set too high. A way of seeing became a way of not seeing the beginnings of significant changes in the structure and exercise of power in Latin America.

A key piece in this intellectual puzzle is the political economy of the Cold War. Particularly after the Cuban Revolution of 1959, democratic politics in Latin America took a back seat in the eyes of the United States to the imperative of preventing the spread of communism in the region. The United States was to play an important role in destabilizing regimes, such as that of Allende in Chile, that were seeking alternatives to dependent development, but that seemed to threaten U.S. political and economic interests. Military governments in the region were supported in their suppression of left-wing political movements and independently minded trade unions in countryside and city. It is thus not surprising that for many social scientists of the time, capitalist development in Latin America was linked to authoritarian government. The leading role that the state in Latin America took in economic development added a further element to this link. In his concept of the bureaucratic-authoritarian state, O'Donnell (1988) emphasizes the capacity of the rationally organized authoritarian state to create the conditions for economic growth because it is impermeable to the demands for a greater share of resources by politically organized groups such as the middle classes or organized working classes.

These studies of the structures of power and inequality in Latin America in the 1970s and 1980s captured some of the most salient trends of the time, but they also, we argue, overestimated the importance of these structures. During ISI, the formal, capitalist firms were mostly content to control the high- and middle-income sectors of the economy over which they had a monopoly. These firms were often not rationally organized in terms of economic efficiency. Workers and management were recruited clientelistically rather than in terms of their qualifications. They left considerable market scope to the small-scale informal enterprises, which catered, innovatively, to the lower-income end of the market. Likewise, the authoritarian state was neither bureaucratic nor efficient in practice. As Davis (1999) has pointed out, it had a limited and uneven governing reach. Its offices dealt with a small fraction of the population, mostly concentrated in the major urban centers. Even its police forces rarely reached into low-income neighborhoods. The authoritarian state had a considerable repressive capacity, but it was more effective in preventing protest than in mobilizing support, other than through the clientelistic political parties on which, at times, it leaned.

The New Challenges

At the beginning of the new millennium, the social and economic situation of Latin America contrasts sharply with that of the "Golden Age" of development. The urbanization process is almost over in most countries. The region is now 73 percent urban, and most of the urban populations live in very large cities. Rural-urban migration is replaced as the dominant pattern of migration by urban-to-urban migration and, in some countries, by international migration. Declining fertility means that population growth is substantially lower throughout the region, resulting in slower growth of the cities. The urban systems of most Latin American countries have diversified with the lessening of primacy and of the dominance of one major city over all others. Intermediate-sized cities have grown in importance, often as the locations of export-oriented manufacturing as in Mexico and Costa Rica. Many of the fast-growing intermediate cities, such as the industrial satellites of São Paulo and Rio de Janeiro, are, however, located close to the major metropolitan areas.

The maturing of urbanization has brought new issues to the social agenda. Housing self-construction and land invasion are less of a problem and a solution than are the issues of what to do with the consolidated, but dilapidated slums, which abound in Latin American cities, one of the themes in Peter Ward's chapter in this volume. Urban households increase and diversify as nontraditional household structures proliferate—single-person households, two-person households, often of the elderly, and single parent-, usually female, headed households, as Ariza and Oliveira note in this volume. The size of the nuclear family of two parents and children has dropped sharply throughout the region. These changes in household structure combine with changes in labor markets to alter the pattern of household coping strategies that was documented in the earlier period. The caring capacity of the household and, by extension, of the community, is potentially weakened in the current situation when there are fewer children to look after the elderly or to bring in an income to supplement that of the household heads and when women, including married women with children, increasingly work outside the home.

Industrialization continues, but the growth of employment is increasingly in the service and commercial sectors of the economy. There is now a more evident gulf than was the case in the earlier period between sectors of high productivity and high wages and the rest of the economy that pays low wages and provides insecure conditions of work. These economic changes are a direct result of the new, more export-oriented, free market policies that have replaced ISI. These policies have reduced tariffs to promote free trade and have deregulated capital and labor markets. A wave of privatization throughout the region has reduced the state's direct role in the economy. These changes have been promoted by the bilateral and multilateral institutions, such as the International Monetary Fund (IMF), as a means of incorporating Latin American countries competitively into the global economy. IMF arrangements with Latin American countries also emphasize fiscal restraint and the reduction in the size of the state.

The new policies brought an end to the inward-looking economic and political nationalism of the ISI period in most countries of the region. Mexico set aside its previous political and economic suspicions of the United States and joined the North American Free Trade Agreement (NAFTA), an agreement that was anathema to Mexican politicians as late as the early 1980s. Several countries either made the dollar their national currency or toyed with the possibility. Foreign capital entered Latin America with few restrictions on its direct investment. The consequences are clear in the trade statistics of the region. Imports and exports went from approximately 10 percent of the region's GDP in 1990 to 20 percent in 2000 (ECLAC 2001, 6). Foreign direct investment concentrated in the 1990s in the modern service sectors, such as telecommunications, finance, and supermarkets, followed by investment in high technology industry. By 1998 to 2000, some 42 percent of the five hundred largest Latin American firms by sales were under foreign ownership (ECLAC 2002, 50), and most of these were service or manufacturing enterprises. By 2002, foreign banks controlled most of the banking business of the region.

As significant a change is that in the political climate of the region, which was, in part, related to the ending of the Cold War, but also reflected, we would argue, longer-term changes in political awareness. By 2000, every country in the region was, formally, a democracy. Moreover, genuinely contested elections were more frequent throughout the region, as in the case of Mexico, which, for the first time since the Mexican Revolution, elected a member of an opposition party to the presidency in 2000. Despite the severest economic and social crisis of its history, Argentina continued with a civilian government, and its military remained in its barracks. The other, noneconomic face of international policies toward Latin America fostered this democratic climate. The United States, the European powers, and the multilateral lending institutions actively sponsored democratic practices alongside their policies of fiscal restraint and adjustment. These policies feature a greater emphasis on local government and on citizen participation at the local level. International nongovernmental organizations (NGOs) allied with local counterparts in the 1980s and 1990s to promote the rights of women, children, and minorities and to foster greater political participation.

As Faria emphasizes in his chapter, a major difference with the earlier period is the greater availability of empirical data. Micro samples of censuses and large-scale social surveys are publicly available, and in many countries of the region, census information can be mapped digitally. Development agencies in Brazil, Mexico, and Peru use detailed maps of poverty as a means of implementing targeted social policies. Household surveys are available for most countries of the region, providing representative information on intercensal trends in labor markets, incomes, and family structures. These data are often representative for major cities, as in the case of Mexico's quarterly Urban Employment Survey, which covers more than forty cities. International and national pressures for greater transparency in government mean that it is increasingly common for census bureaus and government ministries to make available data through the Internet. The more democratic environment of the contemporary period also encourages empirical research, as do the new social policies that seek to target beneficiaries and to encourage community participation. Fiscal restraints mean, however, that universities and research institutes cannot easily take advantage of this more favorable research environment. Public budgets for independent social science research are small in most countries, and researchers must often do their research through contracts with government or international agencies.

The Emerging Perspectives

The implications of this new social and economic situation are the subjects of the chapters that follow. Their aim will be both to evaluate the trends and assess the theories and concepts that are emerging to analyze them. How much in the present represents continuity with the past in Latin America and how much represents a real break? Is the contemporary situation in Latin America giving rise to new paradigms of explanation, and if so, how do these differ from those of the earlier period? One indication of the change in thinking about Latin America is the shift in the most frequent concepts that appear in the titles of social science books on Latin America. A key-word search in the extensive Benson Latin American Collection of the University of Texas showed that between 1966 and 1973, "dependencia" was the most popular concept, with the word appearing in eighty-eight titles. By 1993–2000, "dependencia" appeared in just seventeen titles. Five of these were revisits to the earlier theories of dependency. "Globalización/globalização" was the term that had replaced "dependencia." In 1966–73, the term appeared in only three titles, whereas by 1993–2000, it appeared in 276 titles.

What new perspectives and issues do we, as editors, see as emerging from this volume? In the next few pages, we will outline four areas where new theoretical and empirical agendas are being constructed. The first two are substantive areas of research. The first of these is the changing nature of the state in Latin America and of its relations with its citizens. This is the focus of the chapters by Davis, Foweraker, Jelin, Roberts, and less directly, of the chapters by Faria and Sunkel. The second is the meaning of poverty and disadvantage under the conditions of open economies and highly urbanized countries. These issues are taken up in the chapters by Ariza and Oliveira, Ward, and Wood.

The next two areas are conceptual and methodological. One of these reflects the new methodological challenges for social science research, resulting from the greater availability of census and survey data and from the need to integrate quantitative and qualitative data, issues that are the focus of the chapters by Faria and by Potter and Tuirán. Lastly, are what Faria calls the new paradigms of explanation that are emerging to replace the macrostructural explanations, whether of Marxism or modernization theory, that dominated social science understanding of Latin America in the past. These are middle-range in nature, and attuned to the variety and specificity of social and political processes in Latin America. This will be the prime focus of the chapter by Portes. All four areas are necessarily interconnected. Concepts and data identify the new realities, but these, in turn, demand greater refinement in concepts and greater accuracy in data collection.

In the period of economic and political nationalism associated with ISI, the state in Latin America was a key actor in promoting or subverting the welfare of its citizens. In contrast to this situation, contemporary neoliberal economic policies appear to create an "absent" state that is smaller in size and has less responsibility for the economy and for the universal provision of social welfare. Economic globalization would also appear to undermine the power of the national state. In Latin America, as elsewhere, it has eroded the significance of national boundaries for the movements of goods, capital, and even people, thereby reducing the national state's control over its territory.

The chapters that follow make clear that the presumed demise of the state is premature. The nature of the state is changing in Latin America, but, if anything, it has become a more pervasive part of the lives of its citizens than it was in the past. To appreciate the contemporary importance of the state in Latin America we need to focus on the changes in the practices of government, rather than on the supposed downsizing in the bureaucratic institutions of the state. The practices of government are the essence of state institutions as Gordon (1991), following Foucault, points out. In the past, the practices of government in Latin America have tended to follow the governmental ideologies dominant in the region, such as populism or bureaucratic authoritarianism. Currently, we argue, the dominant ideology of government throughout Latin America, though to different degrees, is liberalism in its economic, political, and social manifestations. Liberalism may have an "unbearable lightness" as Sunkel argues in this volume, but it is percolating into most spheres of Latin American society. Stillborn as a governing rationality in the nineteenth century in Latin America, it is now having a slow and halting triumph in the region, aided by the favorable international conjuncture resulting from the ending of the Cold War and the march of economic globalization. This slow triumph is resulting in radical changes in the practices of government. As Davis makes clear in her chapter, however, the characteristics and organization of existing state institutions must also receive attention. These can be quite resistant to the change in practices demanded by new governing rationalities.

Liberalism, as a long tradition in political thought argues, entails the individualization of rights and responsibilities, whether in the market, or in social and political conduct. This process is exactly what central governments in many Latin American countries are espousing when they decentralize responsibilities to lower-order jurisdictions, replace universal social programs with targeted ones, subcontract functions to the private sector or NGOs, and establish programs to train individual citizens for the challenges of the job market or to make the best of low budgets by altering their consumption practices. To what extent are these new ways of governing bringing new forms of central control based on efficient regulation and compliance ensured

PART I

Sociology in the Hemisphere:
Old Issues and New Directions

keep it in place. More consistently than the Catholic Church, which coined the term, Latin American sociology has exercised an "option for the poor," documenting the vast social injustices in the region and advocating models of development that would reduce them.

Though North American sociology has been less single-minded in this pursuit, there is also a strong egalitarian current within it, accompanied by a large research component focused on the analysis of inequality and its consequences. This field is usually labeled *stratification research*. Given the characteristics of a wealthy nation, U.S. sociology has not focused on documenting generalized poverty, but those persistent inequalities—defined by gender, ethnicity, and above all, race—that segregate certain groups at the bottom of society and relegate them to a caste-like status.[1] For this reason, race rather than class has been the dominant *motif* in sociological research on inequality in North America.

Despite the differences, a common focus on the fate of the downtrodden by sociologists everywhere did not emerge by chance. Like the impertinence and marginality of the discipline, this orientation traces its origins back to the nineteenth century. Here a comparison with economics is useful. As Heilbronner has observed, classical economics did not emerge as a scientific theory, but as a polemic in defense of the trading classes. Smith and especially Malthus and Ricardo acted as intellectual spokesmen for the interests of the rising industrial bourgeoisie. Theirs was a discourse from power, and from that perspective, the poor were essentially a problem: raise their wages and the wretches would proliferate, putting pressure on the land and threatening profits; provide "excessive" welfare and they would not work, discouraging new capital investments (Heilbronner 2000).

Modern economics has abandoned these assumptions, but retained their general orientation. Its theoretical framework has difficulty accommodating a concern for the poor or the implementation of inequality-reducing policies, since the latter can easily become a fetter to market competition. A theory that enshrines the competitive market and is critical of any attempt to bail out inefficient producers is necessarily inclined to look with suspicion at welfare programs or any other attempts to rescue "losers."

On the contrary, sociology's concern for inequality and the condition of the downtrodden dates back to the empirical studies of Quetelet and the theoretical focus of Marx and Weber on the dynamics of class, status, and

---

1. See David B. Grusky's *Social Stratification: Class, Race, and Gender in Sociological Perspective*, arguably the most complete collection on social stratification in U.S. sociology to date.

power (Collins 1994; Bendix 1962; Heilbronner 2000). How Marx turned the tables on neoclassical economics, standing Ricardo on his head, needs no further comment. It is worth remembering, however, that Weber's sociology also pivoted around two fundamental issues: how different market resources condition class differences in society and how the power of dominant classes becomes legitimized. The forces that kept the victims of the market in their place and led them to acquiesce to their own exploitation lies at the core of Weber's political sociology and, in particular, his analysis of the sources of authority (Weber [1925] 1947; Bendix 1962).

This orientation traveled the Atlantic and informed the first empirical studies in North American sociology. After leaving Spencerian evolutionism behind, the Chicago school, led by Robert Park and Ernest Burgess, embarked upon a series of field studies of the industrial metropolis and of the immigrant and ethnic minorities in it. This school produced a series of studies, which, like *Street Corner Society* and the *Social Order of the Slum,* have had a lasting influence on the discipline (Whyte 1943; Suttles 1968).

In Latin America, sociology at the turn of the twentieth century started under heavy French influence, particularly that of Comte and Durkheim. It was taught primarily in law schools and had no empirical referent. As soon, however, as Latin American sociology left the protected confines of the university to study its surrounding reality, the issue of social injustice became paramount. Briceño-León and Sonntag summarize poignantly this vocation of the discipline in the region: "Sociology experiences an important metamorphosis among us; its focus is not social equilibrium but change . . . sociology presents itself as an expression of disbelief toward so much poverty and inequality, but it does so with a commitment to express the ire, the rebellion, and the unconformity provoked by such great inequities and such pain" (Briceño-León and Sonntag 1998, 11–26).

Openness

A third common trait deserving attention is sociology's openness to external influences and indeed its disposition to incorporate them. This is reflected in the popularity and acceptance of the notion of "interdisciplinariness" by sociologists everywhere, indicating their willingness to establish cooperative relations across fields. In many countries, it is often difficult to tell the difference between a sociologist and a political scientist or a social anthropologist. This blurring of disciplinary lines is not only accepted as a fact of life but often welcomed as a sign of a common scientific enterprise.

Social/Cultural Capital

Introduced by the French sociologist Pierre Bourdieu, the twin concepts of social and cultural capital bring into focus the resources available to individuals and communities by virtue of their social ties and the fungibility of such resources with money capital. Actors possessing extensive and diversified social networks and having learned the "proper" manners can mobilize economic resources far more easily than others in the same circles. Communities endowed with dense ties of solidarity and reciprocity can pool resources for launching viable entrepreneurial ventures, leading to sustained growth (Bourdieu 1980, 241–58).

The heuristic value of these concepts led to their popularization by scholars less careful than Bourdieu and their conversion into a facile explanation for the most diverse affairs. Thus, the political scientist Robert Putnam acquired notoriety by attributing to the absence of social capital outcomes as varied as the failure of democracy in East European countries, the poverty and violence of U.S. urban ghettos, and the economic stagnation of southern Italian cities. Such explanations tend to be tautological because they infer the presence or absence of social capital from the very outcomes attributed to it. Thus if a city or nation is prosperous and well governed, it is because it has social capital; if the opposite is the case, then it obviously lacks this resource (Putnam 1993b, 35–42).

At this level of abstraction, social capital is synonymous with "civicness" and is not a very useful concept. More useful are applications of the concept to bounded communities—rural villages or urban neighborhoods. This is because, at this level of abstraction, the relative density of social networks within target communities can be measured and the historical origins of their internal solidarity and the presence or absence of trust can be traced.

Social capital at the level of specific communities can be defined as the collective resources available to them by virtue of the existence of social networks and larger social structures of which their members are part. Community social capital has two principal and observable manifestations: *bounded solidarity* and *enforceable trust*. Bounded solidarity is the level of loyalty displayed by members toward each other; a "we-feeling" leading to mutually supportive behavior in relations with the outside world. Enforceable trust is the confidence that individual obligations will be observed because of the sanctioning power of the community. In communities with high levels of social capital, there is little need for formal contracts or lawyers, since the threat of ostracism or other social sanctions acts as the best guarantor of normative behavior (Portes and Sensenbrenner 1993, 1320–50).

Cultural capital can be defined as the repertoire of knowledge available to specific communities to adapt to their physical and social environment and achieve their goals. It grows out of a shared history and is transmitted through the process of socialization. Cultural capital comprises formal education as well as a wide array of informal practical and social skills passed across generations (Bourdieu 1985, 241–58). Though less theorized than social capital and less used so far in research, cultural capital is also measurable and amenable to inclusion in hypotheses concerning receptivity to innovations and the viability of developmental initiatives at the community level.

Since their origins in the writings of Bourdieu, social and cultural capital have been conceived as bringing benefits to their possessors, be they individuals or communities. More recent studies have inquired about the "downside" of these phenomena. For example, high levels of social capital in a particular group can facilitate its access to privileged resources, to the exclusion of others. The existence of enforceable trust in a community necessitates high levels of mutual supervision, which can stifle individual initiative and freedom. The cultural orientations and intergenerationally transmitted "ways of doing things" of a particular group may become useless in the face of technological innovations and create barriers to successful adaptation to them (Portes and Landolt 1996, 18–22). Thus, like other social processes, the presence of social and cultural capital can yield both benefits and costs and produce diverging consequences for differently situated actors. Figure 1.1 summarizes these dynamics.

These twin concepts offer a useful entry point for the analysis of social change at the grassroots level and create the basis for a diversified research agenda concerning their origins and effects. In Central America, Pérez Sáinz has pioneered in the theoretical introduction and empirical application of social capital. His studies of the phenomenon and its effects in various towns and communities of Costa Rica and Guatemala represent a promising initiative worth pursuing (Pérez Sáinz 1994; Portes and Dore 1996, 133–62). Though even less used so far, cultural capital also holds promise for the study of as yet unexplored differences between social classes, institutions, and local communities.

Global Commodity Chains

A commodity chain is the range of human activities required for the design, production, and marketing of a product. Increasingly, commodity chains have become global, not only in the marketing of the final product, but in its design and production as well. Commodity chains are important because they represent the "inner workings" of economic development. While grand theorists and policy pundits may wax eloquent about the relative merits of different development models, it is actually how a country's productive apparatus is organized and becomes inserted in the circles of global trade that determine its changes for economic growth and labor absorption (see Gereffi and Korzeniewicz 1994).

Gary Gereffi and his collaborators have been carrying out an extensive research program based on this middle-range concept, linking it to both import-substitution and export-oriented policies in Asia and Latin America. Their investigations have led to several important conclusions. According to them, Asian and Latin American industrializing countries did not differ much in the adoption of import-substitution policies designed to protect domestic producers, followed by a shift to export promotion. While the

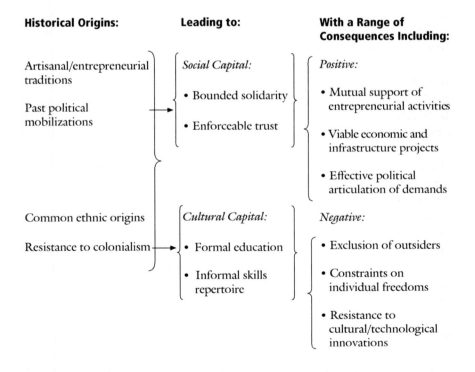

Fig 1.1   Social capital, cultural capital, and community development

timing may have been different, the evolution of policy models was the same. The true significant difference was in the character of the commodity chains implanted in each region (Gereffi 1989, 503–33).

Gereffi makes a key distinction between "producer-driven" and "buyer-driven chains." As portrayed in Figure 1.2, producer-driven chains are those in which large multinational corporations seek to control all aspects of production—from the procurement of raw materials to the final marketing of the product. This "internalizing" of different phases of production and sale is characteristic of large conglomerates in automobiles, aircraft, and semiconductors. Such firms not only control the final product but also employ multiple layers of subcontractors arranged in successive "tiers" of size and complexity. Buyer-driven commodity chains, on the other hand, are those industries in which large retailers and name brand firms play a key role subcontracting production of the entire commodity to plants in the Third World. As portrayed in Figure 1.2, these are "firms without factories" whose role lies in the initial phases of design and the final phases of marketing, but which do not actually produce anything (Gereffi 1999, 37–70).

This pattern of buyer-driven industrialization has become common in labor-intensive consumer goods such as apparel, footwear, toys, and consumer electronics. The key difference between both types of chains lies in the locus of control and profit appropriation. In producer-driven chains, it lies with the central industrial firm—Ford, GM, Toyota, or Boeing. In buyer-driven chains, it lies with the marketers—be they large department stores such as Sears or Wal-Mart or brand names such as The Gap or Nike. The fact that these firms do not produce anything does not prevent them from appropriating the lion's share of the profits. Their formula is simply "buying cheap" from dispersed Third World contractors and "selling dear" to customers in First World markets (Gereffi 1999, 37–70).

The emergence of buyer-driven commodity chains gives rise to the paradox, emphasized by Arrighi, that nowadays a country can become fully industrialized while remaining poor because the bulk of the value-added it produces is siphoned abroad (Arrighi 1994). This new form of unequal exchange confronts governments of industrializing nations with a paradox: to foster growth and employment they must become involved in the circles of global trade using whatever resources makes them competitive; if that resource is only cheap and abundant labor, this insertion can perpetuate their countries' poverty: from producers of low-cost foodstuffs and raw materials, they would simply shift to become producers of low-cost industrial goods, with the bulk of the profits going elsewhere.

At this point, Gereffi makes a second key distinction between export assembly production, original equipment manufacturing (OEM), and original brand name manufacturing (OBM). Assembly manufacturing is the simplest, "entry point" stage in global chains where Third World plants merely put together consumer products such as clothing items, footwear, and toys from parts and designs brought from abroad. OEM reflects a more advanced stage of subcontracting where industrial firms are able to outsource parts locally and produce the entire good to international quality standards. This stage commonly involves a qualitative shift from simple goods, such as apparel, to more value-added ones such as consumer electronics. Lastly, OBM firms represent an advanced stage of export manufacturing in which producer firms

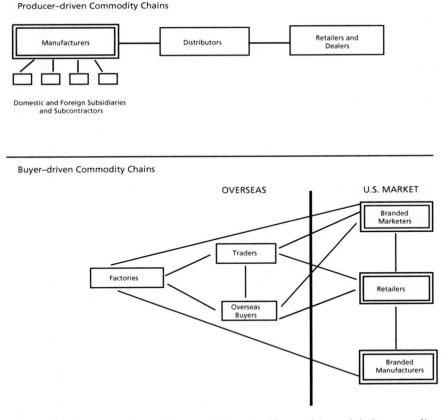

Fig 1.2   The organization of producer-driven and buyer-driven global commodity chains (adapted from Gereffi, 2001)

are mature enough to design their own goods and market them under their own labels. The shift of large Japanese industrial firms to this stage marked the transformation of the country into a major player in the world economy (Gereffi 1989; 1999). So far, only Japan and to a lesser extent South Korea have managed to break into this stage, which entails, in essence, the development of their own producer-driven chains.

This middle-range typology proves useful in understanding the differences between Latin American and Asian countries and in providing a framework for analyzing results of different developmental models. So far, Latin American export manufacturing has been confined to a subordinate role in producer-driven chains controlled by foreign multinationals, such as in autos and durable household goods, or to export assembly. There are few if any OEM producers subcontracting full production of consumer electronics or apparel for First World retailers. Latin American "brand names" in the world market are limited to goods closely tied to agriculture, such as wines, coffee, and cigars. Even in these lines, the appropriation of value is skewed toward the final wholesalers and retailers. Perhaps the single successful instance of OBM production in the region is the Brazilian firm EMBRAER, a state-initiated manufacturer of commercial aircraft. The entry of EMBRAER into global competition has been accompanied by numerous challenges by First World competitors that seek, in essence, to return Brazil to the status of a subordinate industrial exporter (Prebisch 2001, 65).

In synthesis, a commodity chains framework offers a point of departure for the understanding of Latin American economic prospects that goes considerably beyond analysis couched in a classic "models of development" perspective. It also opens up a series of important questions concerning the future of Latin American countries in an increasingly globalized economy. As Gereffi puts it, these include "the mechanisms by which organization learning occurs in trade networks; typical trajectories among export roles; and the organizational conditions that facilitate industrial upgrading moves such as the shift from assembly to full-package networks" (Gereffi 1999, 37).

Transnationalism

Though used in different contexts and with different meanings, the concept of transnationalism has increasingly come to mean the social fields created by immigrants to the advanced countries spanning the gap between their present communities and their nations of origin. Because of its economic subordination in the global system, Latin America has become an exporter not only of raw materials, foodstuffs, and assembled goods but of people as well. The increasingly internationalized character of these economies means not only their growing dependence on exports, but also greater access and information of their populations to living conditions abroad (Portes 1999, 253–70).

The relentless drive of multinational corporations to expand their market share leads to their growing presence in less-developed countries, exposing their citizens to the attractions of consumerism, lowering prices and extending credit, and facilitating access to the advanced world either through electronic communication or low-cost air travel. It should come as no surprise that approximately one-tenth of the population of countries like Mexico, El Salvador, the Dominican Republic, and Haiti lives abroad. Several Latin American countries have their "second city" in terms of population size in the United States—mainly in New York, Los Angeles, and Miami (Guarnizo and Smith 1998, 3–34; Landolt, Autler, and Baires 1999, 290–315).

While emigration from South American countries has not reached the levels of that from Mexico and the Caribbean, it is also growing rapidly. Colombian immigration to the United States has become massive, fueled by violence and political instability at home. Recent studies have uncovered a number of South American cities and regions that have become thoroughly transformed by mass emigration. This is the case of Governador Valladares in Brazil and of Otavalo and Cuenca in Ecuador (Levitt 2000; Kyle 1999, 422–26).

In the past, emigration has not figured prominently in sociological or economic analyses of Latin American development. From the public and official points of view, earlier emigrants were regarded as little more than defectors. Where the flow included substantial numbers of professionals and technicians, it was deplored as part of a "brain drain" depriving poor countries of their talents for the benefit of the developed world (Glaser and Habers 1974, 227–44; Oteiza 1971, 429–54). These perspectives did not take into account the possibility that emigrants would return and that they would establish ever-stronger networks between places of origin and destination. The same communications and transportation technologies that facilitated their departure allowed migrants to develop a continuous back-and-forth flow of information and resources transforming the character of both their communities of origin and their places of settlement abroad.

Transnationalism is the concept coined in sociological theory to refer to this phenomenon, and "transnational community" is the term under which its most visible consequences have been studied (Portes, Guarnizo, and Landolt 1999). Unlike the "multinational" activities of global corporations and the "international" relations conducted by states, "transnationalism" encompasses the unofficial cross-border contacts initiated and sustained by immigrants and their home country counterparts. The social fields thus created include economic enterprises seeking to capitalize on opportunities in sending and receiving areas as well as political mobilizations, cultural events, and religious exchanges. Indigenous communities may find a powerful voice to express their grievances by having them publicized by emigrants to the First World. Impoverished towns may find a way to bypass governmental inertia by having needed public works funded by their diasporas. Churches, Catholic and Protestant alike, enter the transnational field by providing guidance and protection for their parishioners abroad and, in exchange, channeling their remittances and gifts toward religious projects at home (R. Smith 1998, 19–24; Popkin 1999, 267–84).

Recent sociological research on transnationalism has established the growth and scope of the phenomenon and explored its principal causes. Table 1.1 presents the range of observed types and consequences in both areas of migrant settlement in the First World and countries and communities of origin. Studies of determinants of transnationalism have established that contexts of exit and reception of particular immigrant flows decisively affect the types of activities in which they become involved. The same studies indicate that it is the better educated and more legally secure migrants, rather than those in more marginal situations, who are most likely to involve themselves in transnational activities, be they economic or political (Landolt 2000; Itzigsohn et al. 1999, 316–39; Guarnizo and Portes 2001).

The concept of transnationalism is well positioned to guide a useful program of research—sufficiently abstract to encompass a vast array of empirical phenomena and still concrete enough to be modified and refined by studies of the same events. As governments of sending countries become involved in the transnational field by granting dual citizenship and voting rights to their nationals abroad and otherwise seeking to influence their loyalties, studies of this phenomenon acquire an importance seldom noted by prior theories of development (R. Smith 1998; Levitt 2000; Landolt 2000). Sending-country governments have been prompted to act by the size of migrant remittances, which in some cases approach or exceed the value of traditional exports, and by the growing political and cultural clout of their expatriates. In turn, governmental attempts to co-opt and rechannel these essentially grassroots initiatives give rise to a complex dynamic leading to several unexpected outcomes.

Roberts and his collaborators have made a promising incursion into these processes by applying a modified version of Hirschman's famous triplet of

Table 1.1 Types and consequences of immigrant transnationalism

Geographic setting	Type			
	Economic	Political	Religious	Cultural
Abroad	Transnational entrepreneurship as an alternative to low wage work	Mobilizations in behalf of home country causes Establishment of "foreign" branches of political parties	Local churches reorganize to respond to migrant concerns	Music and arts festivals organized in migrant communities
Home Community	Migrant investments in real estate, construction, and commerce	Civic committees plan and fund public works Local authorities elected with migrant support	Local parishes strengthened by migrant donations Local churchmen travel abroad to minister to their expatriates	Musical and theater groups are created to perform in migrant communities
Home Country	Migrant remittances become key source of foreign exchange	Laws granting dual citizenship and voting rights are passed to strengthen migrant loyalties	Churches organize binational exchanges of priests and pastors	Music industry is is reorganized binationally Government initiatives taken to support the diffusion of national culture abroad

exit, voice, and loyalty (Roberts, Frank, and Lozano-Ascencio 1999). As these authors point out, the interactions between governments and migrant communities are novel and paradoxical: migrants acquire new "voice" in national politics precisely by "exiting" their native countries; while their "loyalty" may remain firmly attached to their home communities, this sentiment does not necessarily extend to the government or ruling party. Governments empower their diasporas as an enticement to preserve their loyalties and financial contributions, but by so doing, open themselves up to migrant-led grassroots mobilizations aimed at changing, subverting, or even toppling them (Roberts, Frank, and Lozano-Ascencio 1999). These dynamics require additional investigation and theoretical reflection, especially on the part of researchers in the sending nations.

The Embedded/Weberian State

Past studies of economic development in Latin America have consistently emphasized the role of the state, either as a motor for growth or as an impediment to it. The positive view of the state in development is closely associated with the work of Raul Prebisch and the early ECLAC advocacy of import-substitution industrialization (Prebisch 2001, 65; Cardoso and Faletto 1979; Sunkel 2001). The negative view that has come to dominate policy circles closely reflects the resurgence of neoclassical theory and a "Smithian" distrust for state intervention in the markets (Portes 1997; Evans 1989, 561–87). In either version, the state is commonly portrayed as uniform and monolithic—an undifferentiated institutional black box expected to behave in similar ways across countries.

Case studies of the role of state agencies in development have shown consistently how wrong these views are. There is a great deal of contingency and inconsistency in the character and consequences of state action so that the same developmental "model" can yield successful results in certain countries and fail in others. Seeking to make sense of these differences, Evans focused on the character of the state apparatus itself, that is, the recruitment and functioning of core governmental bureaucracies. Initially, Evans developed a typology ranging from "predatory" states, which "plunder without any more regard to the welfare of the citizenry than a predator has for the welfare of its prey" (Evans 1989, 561–87), to "developmental" states capable of launching and implementing long-term entrepreneurial initiatives. Zaire under Mobutu Sese-Seko was used as an archetypical example of the first type, and Singapore and Japan as illustrations of the second.

This typology did not go far enough in identifying just what features of the state played a key role in leading their countries to stagnation or sustained growth. In subsequent work, Evans developed two concepts that played this critical differentiating role: "Weberianness," or the extent to which a state apparatus approaches Max Weber's ideal-type of bureaucracy as a meritocratic, internally cohesive, and rule-bound organization; and "embeddedness," or the extent to which such bureaucracy is capable of nurturing, guiding, and coordinating private entrepreneurial initiatives.

To the extent that governmental apparatuses approach the Weberian ideal-type they acquire a higher esprit de corps and become resistant to corruption. By freeing themselves from private "rent-seeking" interests, official agencies are able to implement long-term initiatives requiring sustained guidance and investment. This state autonomy is purchased, however, at the cost of the state's becoming progressively removed from its own society, losing contact with its most dynamic elements. It is at this point that "embeddedness" enters the picture by having powerful state agencies sponsor and nurture the development of competitive private firms. The story of MITI, the Japanese Ministry of Industry and Trade, painstakingly researched by Chalmers Johnson, is used by Evans as the archetypical example of a state's "embedded autonomy" (Evans 1995).

Figure 1.3 summarizes Evans's argument as a series of answers to successive dilemmas faced in the process of national development. There are logical problems with the "embeddedness" part of the theory because Evans has been unable to provide empirical indicators other than those of successful developmental instances, making the argument partially circular. The "Weberianness" part of the argument rests on more solid grounds, since it is possible, in principle, to create independent measures of the quality of state bureaucracies. This is indeed what Evans's research program subsequently did, developing a "Weberianness" scale for some forty less-developed countries on the basis of such criteria as recruitment through civil service examinations, career ladders rewarding long-term tenure, and competitive salaries (Evans and Rauch 1999).

Evans and Rauch were able to show that their "Weberianness" scale not only correlated highly with GNP per capita growth in their sample, but that it maintained a significant positive effect after controlling for standard predictors of GNP growth, such as initial GNP, average education of the adult population, and capital investment rates. Figure 1.4 presents the point location of individual countries in this scale indicating the poor quality of most Latin American states.

Embedded autonomy offers a valuable conceptual point of entry for the analysis of a paradox that has bedeviled grand narratives of development, regardless of the ideological quarters from which they came. This is the fact that, despite a common position of subordination and initial lack of resources, some countries have been able to move ahead much faster than others. Although external economic conditions and constraints are undoubtedly important, it is increasingly evident that endogenous institutional factors also play a key role. Of these, none is more important than the character of

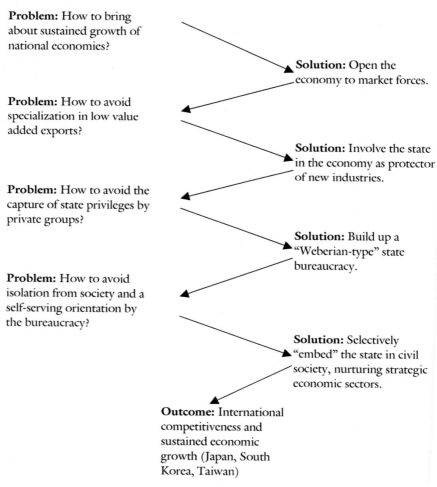

Problem: How to bring about sustained growth of national economies?

Solution: Open the economy to market forces.

Problem: How to avoid specialization in low value added exports?

Solution: Involve the state in the economy as protector of new industries.

Problem: How to avoid the capture of state privileges by private groups?

Solution: Build up a "Weberian-type" state bureaucracy.

Problem: How to avoid isolation from society and a self-serving orientation by the bureaucracy?

Solution: Selectively "embed" the state in civil society, nurturing strategic economic sectors.

Outcome: International competitiveness and sustained economic growth (Japan, South Korea, Taiwan)

Fig 1.3   Evans's theory of embedded autonomy

state bureaucracies and their ability to reorganize and lead society, rather than be captured by rent-seeking interests. Evans's "Weberianness" is a good term not only because it does honor to one of the founders of the discipline but also because it contains the promise of a solid sociological contribution to the analysis of economic change.

Conclusion

The concepts just reviewed form part of a proposal for a new theoretical and research agenda. Although presented in no particular order, they have two characteristics in common. First, as already noted, they provide an analytic handle for approaching vast amounts of empirical material and are simultaneously modifiable by the results of inquiry. Unlike grand narratives, a key characteristic of middle-range concepts is that they guide investigation by calling attention to certain aspects of the phenomenon under study, but do not anticipate the outcome. They thus leave room for inductive findings that were all but crowded out by past deductive reasoning.

Second, this set of concepts is future-oriented. In other words, they do not aim primarily at the historical roots of underdevelopment, but toward

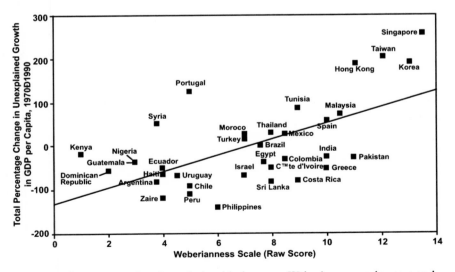

Fig 1.4   Scattergram showing relationship between Weberianness scale score and unexplained growth in GDP per capita, 1970 to 1990 (from Evans and Rauch 1999, 756)

exploring means to overcome it at the community or national levels. The dependency perspective gave us sweeping insights into the origins of Latin America's poverty and subordination. In contrast, the family of concepts just reviewed points toward concrete avenues of action for bypassing the constraints of economic and political backwardness.

Under certain conditions, communities can mobilize their social and cultural capital to overcome material scarcities in efforts to improve collective consumption and develop viable economic enterprises. Entry into global commodity chains represents the first step of a learning process that, when properly guided, can lead to technological innovation, greater value-added exports, and competitiveness in world trade. A state bureaucracy that approaches the Weberian ideal-type is in a much better position to implement long-term developmental strategies than the typically corrupt and personalistic state institutions found in the Third World. The general point is that, in a world where the wealth of nations and the well-being of their populations depend on intelligent insertion in a globalized economy, sociology's task cannot be limited to diagnosis of what went wrong in the past, but must also include the identification and mobilization of concrete mechanisms to bypass these ills.

In conclusion, little has changed since Weber published "Objectivity in Social Science" a century ago. As he presciently observed, the achievements of the discipline have consisted not in the accumulation of broad invariant laws, but in the interpretation of historically bound phenomena guided by ideal-types. At midcentury, Merton reminded us of the same point. Somehow, we forgot these rules along the way and lapsed into the disparate accumulation of historical or statistical facts or the equally fruitless search for the philosopher's stone. As we round a new century, sociology in the north and south of this hemisphere would do well in recalling and reenacting the methodological principles that are part of its own heritage. The discipline's chances for advancement and its very justification as an intellectual enterprise may depend on it.

PART II
Globalization, Neoliberalism, and Social Policy

2 The Unbearable Lightness of Neoliberalism

OSVALDO SUNKEL

The overwhelming priority given to state-led, long-term economic development and industrialization policies that prevailed in Latin America after the Second World War disappeared from the public agenda under the short-term pressures of the social, political, and economic upheavals of the 1970s, which culminated with the development and debt crises of the early 1980s (Griffith-Jones and Sunkel 1986). Afterward, the unlimited confidence regarding the ability to overcome these crises through the application of neoliberal adjustment and restructuring policies—the so-called Washington consensus (Williamson 1997)—prevented any further debate over long-term social and economic development. Among the goals of these policies were opening up the economy to international trade, financing, and investments; privatizing public enterprises and services; eliminating government interventions and regulations; and liberalizing the markets for goods, services, and factors of production. In brief, it was believed that minimizing the role of government and maximizing that of markets and private business (both national and international) would guarantee freedom, democracy, and economic development. The only alternative to this simplistic and naive recipe was neostructuralism, which acknowledged the need for fundamental changes in development policy but retained the state and civil society, although in new and different roles (ECLAC 1990; Sunkel 1993b; Sunkel and Zuleta 1990). Unfortunately, neostructuralism had little influence in the midst of neoliberal triumphalism, with the partial exception of some economic policy reforms adopted in Chile with the return of democracy.

The outcomes of the neoliberal policies adopted in the region have been disappointing. At the global level, the economic growth rate is half of what it was in the 1950s and 1960s, the new global economy is highly unstable (having undergone several severe financial and economic crises in the last two decades), and income distribution within and among both developed and underdeveloped countries has worsened (UNDP 1999; Cornia 1999). In

I am most grateful to Bryan Roberts for his help in transforming a very long and unwieldy manuscript into a publishable paper; but all responsibility for it rests with the author.

Latin America, important yet insufficient and exceedingly fragile progress has been made at the macroeconomic level—price stability has been achieved in many countries—but production, employment, and incomes are highly unstable. These reverses have been associated with serious adverse social trends in poverty and income distribution, damage to the environment, and an increasingly worrisome political panorama. As a consequence the subject of development has once again taken center stage (Stiglitz 1998; Emmerij 1997; World Bank 1999; ECLAC 2000; CEPAL 2001; Ffrench-Davis 1999).

The dominant monodisciplinary, neoliberal discourse (Hirschman 1981) prevalent in Latin America during the last decades of the twentieth century was propagated with missionary zeal by the socioeconomic and technocratic elites associated with the public international institutions and the private international corporations that support them and with which they are identified. They claimed that the current unprecedented processes of profound technological, economic, social, political, and cultural transformations, as well as the collapse of the socialist world and the globalization of the international system, were superseding traditional ideologies. Liberal democracy had imposed itself at the political level, and the market system, in its neoliberal form, at the economic level. Globalization and neoliberalism would insure appropriate economic policies and optimize the growth potential of the economy. According to this view, the end of the road had been reached in the process of historical evolution, the final stage of capitalist development.

This argument collapses under scrutiny. Far from experiencing a process of consolidation and deepening, democracy is in peril. Although in many countries democratic systems are formally in effect, their quality is poor, and deteriorating under renewed populist threats. Economic growth, with few exceptions, has been so modest that income per capita has hardly increased. Moreover, growth depends more than ever on international financing and, as a result, is highly unstable. This has once again been demonstrated by the repercussions of the recent financial crisis in Asia and the aftershocks reverberating through financial markets with the latest difficulties in Turkey, Argentina, Japan, and the United States. In many countries, social conditions are worse than in the 1970s and are becoming intolerable. The increasing number of the poor and the worsening of a historically appalling distribution of income are now the norm. Periodically, violent social protests erupt along with antisocial individual and collective behavior, such as drug trafficking, violence, and corruption. Insurgency is spreading, presenting serious governability problems.

In the international context, there are four principal characteristics to the current situation: a mediocre overall economic growth performance, a high and uncontrollable degree of financial volatility, an extreme weakness of international public institutions, and a sustained deterioration in income distribution on a global level (Ocampo 2000, 2001; Soros 1998). Small islands of extreme wealth in OECD countries, with about 15 percent of the world population, are now surrounded by the remaining 85 percent living in relative and absolute poverty (Sunkel 1995). It is no coincidence that the only policy definitively excluded from the neoliberal program of liberalization and deregulation is immigration.

Bearing in mind these and other, similar issues (such as the increasing threat to the planet's environmental equilibrium presented by global warming), there is a clear contradiction between the triumphalistic ideology of global-ization and neoliberalism and the objective reality of our current situation. We have been subjected to an overwhelming and fundamentally self-serving and dishonest discourse on the part of the power elites that has prevented us from properly distinguishing between reality and wishful thinking. We en-counter a similar situation regarding globalization. We are supposedly faced with a new and inalterable reality, without viable options or alternatives. This idea is supported by the international mass media (particularly the specialized business and economic press). It is also a view promoted by the overwhelm-ing majority of the economics profession and the technocratic elites. In such circumstances, it is absolutely imperative to develop a critical view of the dis-torted intellectual climate in which we are living (Helleiner 2000; Rodrik 1997; Mander and Goldsmith 1996). To do this we need to confront the mainstream ideas on the present historical process head-on and in a rational manner. We must make it clear that despite their triumphalistic tone, neolib-eralism and globalization are riddled with formidable contradictions, which are conveniently and systematically omitted from the popular discourse.

In contrast to the mechanical and linear vision of Fukuyama's (1992) *The End of History and the Last Man,* I consider it more fruitful to explore a somewhat similar hypothesis but using a dialectic approach, acknowledging the new contemporary realities, but in a nondeterministic way. According to this alternative hypothesis, the world is passing through a historical phase in which, for a multitude of powerful national and international reasons, the supremacy in both theory and practice of liberal democracy in the political field and the market system in the economic field has been widely recognized and accepted. This way of conceptualizing the present situation attributes a historical temporality of a cyclical and dialectic character to the current real-ity and makes a distinction between the central and peripheral countries.

This has at least two important implications. First, the future is in no sense predetermined, and consequently alternatives continue to exist. As a result, the conceptualization of ideal alternatives is not only possible and useful, but absolutely essential. Second, the individualistic Anglo-Saxon version of liberal democracy and the market economy is only one among several possibilities. In the contemporary world there are a variety of cases at variance with the Anglo-Saxon model of capitalism. This is certainly true of the countries that have adopted some kind of "managed capitalism," either in the form of institutionalized social negotiation and cooperation (Germany, France, Austria, Italy, and Sweden), or in its corporative form (Japan, Taiwan, Korea, and Singapore). Despite being subject to the same pressures and necessary adjustments derived from globalization, these countries constitute alternative models and demonstrate the diversity of political solutions in the economic as well as in the social and cultural spheres. There are also ex-socialist and other countries with a more state-centered tradition, like the Latin American countries, that currently find themselves at different stages of a difficult, diverse, and complex transition process.

The principal challenge is to recover the central role of politics and to recognize the new reality and demands of civil society as a means for promoting innovative interventions in the public sphere designed to establish a new equilibrium whereby the state, society, and the market complement each other in a context of globalization. This means recovering something of the experiences with mixed economies and developmental and welfare states of the postwar period. These experiences were characterized by the search for a complementary synergy between the market and the state—something that was in stark contrast to the socialist alternative on the one hand (which tried to supplant the market with the state) and the neoliberal alternative on the other (which strives to substitute the market for the state). A review of the current situation in Latin America is impossible without comparing and contrasting it to previous stages in Latin American development. It must also be placed within the context of the evolution of the international economic system—in other words, within the well-known conceptual center-periphery framework of Raul Prebisch.

Globalization and Neoliberalism: Ideology and Reality

I will begin by examining the concepts of globalization and neoliberalism more closely. The ideology surrounding globalization presents it as a totally new and historically unprecedented process, being fundamentally rooted in the contemporary technological revolution, which in turn is seen as an inherent part of the modernization process. To embark on a critical analysis of this version of globalization, I shall explore five of its principal characteristics: its historical dynamics, its cyclical nature, its extensive and intensive nature, its dialectic, and the imbalance between the symbolic integration that it promotes and the social disintegration it fosters.

The Historical Dynamics of Globalization

With regard to the alleged novelty of the globalization process, an extensive literature already exists on the process of the expansion of mercantile capitalism into foreign markets, a process that has been breaking up precapitalist societies since the beginning of the Middle Ages. Later, when the new entrepreneurial spirit coincided with the burst of technological innovation of the Industrial Revolution, the tendency of capitalism toward expansion worldwide became firmly established, especially when distance, time, and international transportation and communication costs fell dramatically. What we are currently witnessing is a new and extremely intense phase in this process (Ferrer 1996; Bairoch and Kozul-Wright 1998; Nayyar 2002).

At least since the era of the great discoveries beginning in the fifteenth century until the colonial empires of the nineteenth century and the evolution of the international system during this century, there has been a persistent and cumulative long-term tendency toward the growing integration of the diverse regions of the world. Nevertheless, this tendency is characterized by periods of intensification or acceleration followed by phases of disintegration or deceleration, particularly during transitions from one international order to another. It is interesting and suggestive to note the different terminology, concepts, and metaphors used to describe the periods of greater worldwide integration (Ianni 1996): colonialism from the sixteenth to eighteenth centuries, imperialism in the nineteenth and twentieth centuries, later internationalization, and more recently transnationalization (Sunkel 1973). It seems clear that these concepts correspond to specific stages in the worldwide historical process of globalization.

The Cyclical Nature of Globalization

The long-term analysis of the trend toward growing economic integration of the different regions of the world coincides with and is part of the historical process of the development of capitalism. But it must be noted that the expansion of the capitalist mode of production and the incorporation of new geographic areas into trading and investment relations, transport and communications networks, migratory flows, and transfer of institutional and judicial norms and culture occurred as a cyclical process (Maddison 1991). There were periods of expansion and periods of contraction. There were also changes in the nature of the links between the different territorial components.

The periods of acceleration evidently have had much to do with the process of technological innovation, which, as is well known, also occurs in periodic waves (Landes 1969). The discoveries of the fifteenth century are associated with notable technological innovations in navigational instruments. The great international economic expansion of the second half of the nineteenth century is associated with the extraordinary development of transport technology: the steam engine, the railway, iron-hulled ships, as well as advances in communications and the development of electricity. Likewise, the contemporary phenomenon of globalization is profoundly linked with the development of air transport, transnational corporations, the revolution in communications and computer technology, and the synergies between these key components of the process.

In an interesting study which attributes the essence of globalization to technological innovation (Birou 1997), Alain Birou equates the nature of globalization with pure technological progress. On this, he is simply incorrect. There are and have been periods of disintegration and setbacks in the globalization process without corresponding reversals in technological development, which can and has continued without interruption. As during previous periods of globalization, the contemporary technological revolution is but one of the fundamental mechanisms through which globalization occurs.

The periods of disintegration or setback correspond exactly with epochs of crisis and changeover in the dominant power structure and the subsequent reorganization of the existing international system and its institutions. In fact, in relative terms, the pre-1914 situation was comparable to the present day with respect to trade, finance, transportation, communication, migration, and institutional and cultural integration. A few years after the end of the First World War, Keynes remembered this period with nostalgia:

> What an extraordinary episode in the economic progress of man that age was which came to an end in August 1914. . . . The inhabitant of

> London could order by telephone, sipping his morning tea in bed,
> the various products of the whole earth, in such quantity as he might
> see fit, and reasonably expect their early delivery upon his doorstep;
> he could at the same moment and by the same means adventure his
> wealth in the natural resources and new enterprises of any quarter
> of the world, and share, without exertion or even trouble, in their
> prospective fruits and advantages; or he could decide to couple the
> security of his fortunes with the good faith of the townspeople of
> any substantial municipality in any continent that fancy or informa-
> tion might recommend. (Keynes 1920, 6)

Despite the continual appearance of a remarkable succession of technological
innovations, during the interwar period this wonderfully integrated world
Keynes recalled fell to pieces. Two world wars and the Great Depression
led to the displacement of the British Empire by the United States as the
dominant world power; the pound sterling by the dollar as the hegemonic
currency; the private financial, commercial, and international investment
markets by the system of international public institutions of Bretton Woods;
the first phase of the Industrial Revolution (coal, steam engines, railways) by
the second (oil, electrical, petrochemical industries, and the automobile).

   After the Second World War, the world unfolded into two antagonistic
systems. Within the capitalist area, there was an unprecedented advance in
the role of government with the formation of diverse types of mixed economies aimed at guaranteeing economic growth, full employment, and social
protection. The great majority of the mixed economies, as well as the socialist ones, enjoyed an exceptionally successful period of economic growth
and social improvement, without historical precedent, from the end of the
Second World War to the 1970s, the so-called Golden Age (Maddison 1991;
Sunkel 1993a). At the end of an extraordinary quarter-century, the stage of
state-led development completed its cycle. Colin Clark (1940) was one of the
first to predict that this was bound to happen. He was already arguing
in 1940 that a capitalist economy could not support very high tax rates.
But although his claims were vastly exaggerated, Clark was essentially
right. The tax "burden" reached levels that began to threaten the profitabil-
ity and therefore the workings of the private sector. As a consequence, economic and political pressure began to build up in favor of rolling back
and dismantling the state, and in support of policies that paved the way for
neoliberalism.

Some countries then entered a period of decadence, and others even collapsed. It was in this context that the new era of international integration that we now call globalization emerged and strengthened. It has also been characterized as a new technological, institutional, financial, and ideological revolution: neoliberalism (Hobsbawm 1994). The large-scale public sector, which emerged as a consequence of the establishment of the welfare state, has now been challenged.

Extensive and Intensive Globalization

Globalization has two dimensions—the extensive and the intensive. The extensive dimension is territorial and is marked by the incorporation of new geographic spaces into the market economy. The collapse of socialism has meant that areas where the market economy was prohibited for more than half a century are now rapidly, although not without great difficulty and uncertainty, incorporating themselves into the capitalist system. There has also been an expansion of the capitalist "frontier" in the large geographic areas within the underdeveloped capitalist nation states, areas that in the past were marginalized by the market. This has been the case, for example, in the Amazon Basin of South America and in many other "hinterlands" on all continents. One of its consequences has been the devastation of forests, soil, water, biodiversity, and ecosystems.

The intensification of the capitalist process is especially marked by the transfer to the private sector of traditionally public enterprises and productive activities. This has been accompanied by the profound penetration of mercantile and individualistic forms of conduct and values into social life, within families, social classes, public and private institutions, and the state itself. This is perhaps the most remarkable phenomenon of all. Anyone who is touched by this process changes his or her form of behavior, becoming a profit or utility maximizer, subordinating traditional conduct to cost-benefit analysis and rational choice, in the full capitalist sense of rationality, at the expense of social cohesion, altruism, solidarity, and identity.

The Dialectic Process

Another characteristic of globalization is that its dynamic trajectory is not linear or mechanical but rather dialectic, which implies that each step in the process generates reactions. Indeed, this is how Marxists conceive the historical development of the capitalist mode of production, viewing it as in conflict with the preexisting modes of production, leading to their eventual dismemberment and replacement. Joseph Schumpeter's (1939) conception of the economic cycle is similar. He considered that the economic cycle is a result of the process of technological innovation, whereby waves of innovation lead to the creation of new productive activities with destructive effects on those which are displaced. This is also the view of Karl Polanyi, whose conceptualization appears to me to be particularly insightful (Polanyi 1957). He analyzes the great expansion of capitalism in the nineteenth and the beginning of the twentieth century, and the far-reaching destructive effects it had on preexisting societies, as well as the emerging social and political movements aimed at protecting the social order. Polanyi calls this "the double movement," and I believe that his approach is very relevant to our current situation (Etzioni 1988).

Strangely enough, Marx, Schumpeter, and Polanyi find themselves in the company of none other than Michel Camdessus, the former managing director of the International Monetary Fund. In a recent article, he writes that we should not forget that the process of capitalist development, together with its great expansive efficiency, is also socially destructive and dislocating. As a consequence, governments have an essential role to play, a role that to some extent has been lost and needs to be recovered (Camdessus 1997).

Material Versus Symbolic Integration

The dialectical dynamics of the process of globalization effectively incorporate some into the modern transnational socioeconomic activities while others are totally or partially displaced, marginalized, and excluded. The globalization process is therefore an unequal, unbalanced, heterogeneous process. On the other hand, the intensive and extensive penetration of capitalist culture tends to be generalized to all, both the integrated and the excluded, as a consequence of global saturation by communications and audiovisual media. This process of globalization generates a widespread virtual or symbolic integration that most people, given their precarious socioeconomic reality, cannot realize materially (Hopenhayn 1998; Roncagliolo 1998). The much-trumpeted images of the "global village" and the "global citizen" communicated through the Internet are unattainable for the immense majority of the world population. They are still far from having access to electricity and the telephone, although it has been in existence for over a century. Nor do they have the educational and income levels necessary for achieving material integration.

The Medium- and Long-term Challenges

There are a number of crucial tasks to be faced at all levels in order to consolidate democracy and development. I will restrict myself to three that I consider of strategic importance.

The Challenge of International Integration

Our countries are increasingly integrated in the global system in terms of culture, environment, technology, economics, and politics. This situation presents opportunities from which to profit and dangers that need to be avoided. It cannot be accepted passively but requires proactive efforts. The success achieved in international markets in recent years by many countries of the region was based principally on the acknowledgement of the necessity to move from an inward-looking to an export-based development strategy. This required the establishment of the appropriate framework in terms of macro- and microeconomic conditions, greater self-confidence, and an extension of the role of the market and support for private economic agents. A greater innovative and entrepreneurial effort is likewise required on the part of the business community. Carrying out these urgently needed changes has been the priority for the democratic governments after the debt crisis. They have had to transform these objectives explicitly into government policy. Incidentally, this is why presidential candidates that run on progressive tickets have frequently had to change to neoliberal policies when in office.

It is only fair to point out that in order to achieve these objectives we have been able to count on a considerable patrimony or "stock" of existing productive potential that is the positive inheritance of the policies of previous decades. This includes the accumulation of knowledge; the availability of natural resources, transport, and energy infrastructure; the capacity for industrial production; and the availability of experienced and well-qualified human capital. In other words, initial conditions are now far more favorable than in the past.

On the other hand, as we shall see in the next section, this dramatic shift in economic policies has had serious social consequences: high and persistent unemployment and underdevelopment, lower wages, worsening income distribution, and poverty. To a large degree, the principal institutional changes and shifts in the orientation of the economic policy that were required have already been undertaken, and have been quite successful in terms of export growth. But the exceptional profit rates at the beginning of the period are tending to level out because of the pressures for a lower real exchange rate and the increase in national and foreign competition. The most accessible foreign markets are showing signs of saturation, and it is increasingly difficult to gain access to these markets. New competitors are appearing from countries in the process of adopting similar export strategies. The existing infrastructure and productive capacity are reaching their limits. Renewable resources are being depreciated by overexploitation, and the nonrenewable resources are running out or becoming increasingly costly. The entrepreneurial dynamism and innovative capacity, linked above all (although not exclusively) to the large enterprises, has to confront the challenge of interacting with medium, small, and even micro-firms.

Within the context of the new export-based model that has been adopted, the potential for economic and social development depends to a large extent on the successful promotion of export growth. This implies a whole new set of objectives and policies: an intensification of the processes of capital accumulation, innovation, and adaptation of scientific and technological knowledge; the penetration of new markets and the consolidation of the existing ones; the revitalization and modernization of domestic production in the less-competitive business sectors; and the promotion of linkages between the export sector and international markets. It also implies the incorporation of the informal productive sector into the modern sector; the exploitation of renewable natural resources through sustainable management practices that preserve the ecosystems upon which they depend for their survival; the replacement of nonrenewable resources that are being depleted by new investments in alternative technologies; a shift toward the export of goods with higher value-added; and singling out products in the most dynamic segments of international trade in goods and services (Sunkel and Mortimore 2001).

One particularly important characteristic of the most successful export-based economies has been the transformation in the organization of inter- and intra-firm relationships, as well as changes in the relationship with both the state and employees. The workforce must be awarded a greater degree of stability, dignity, and professional training. Its participation and collaboration in the management of the firm must be actively encouraged in order to increase productivity and contribute in a decisive way to flexibility, efficiency, discipline, and cooperation in the workplace.

To sum up, the challenge is to promote an "industrializing" export-led developmental model, in the sense of increasingly incorporating technology and knowledge and making better use of economies of scale through the deepening of the process of domestic integration between productive sectors, both horizontally and vertically. All this should be directed toward improving competitiveness and raising the share of technologically advanced, high value-added exports. There is also a need to link up the rest of the economy to the dynamism of the export sector.

This set of structural and institutional policies should be specified in detail in a development strategy over the medium and long term for each country. It represents the way of the future with regard to industrial, science and technology, human resource, and educational policies.

Some important initiatives already exist and have been put into practice, both in the private and public sectors. But a lack of a general awareness in the countries of the region about the need for a renewed collective effort of sufficient scope, tenacity, and coherence, especially with respect to regional integration, is disconcerting. All social and economic actors should be involved in an informed and systematic process of discussion regarding possible and probable scenarios.

It is also necessary to acknowledge that it is impossible to respond simultaneously and instantaneously to all social demands. We need to define medium- and long-term priorities and search for compromises that distinguish between what is feasible immediately and what can only be achieved gradually. This requires the elaboration of a fairly clear vision of the future, a vision in which all the different sectors can reach agreement, and in which even the most marginalized members can find a place in society and feel that they have something worth struggling for.

We have learned that it is not possible to supplant the market—it constitutes an irreplaceable system of signals by which economic transactions are ordered. Nevertheless, it is also necessary to recognize that the market is incapable of resolving the kind of questions raised in the previous paragraphs, all of which require important strategic decisions and public policies. These should be elaborated collectively by means of medium- and long-term strategies, articulated through all the actors involved (private, public, and foreign). These strategies should stimulate and bring forth proposals and initiatives that are complementary to those which emerge from the market process.

No organization, institution, or modern enterprise can dispense with a strategic vision. In the past, exemplary planning and developmental organizations were created in our countries, institutions which in their heyday were extraordinarily important: Corporación de Fomento de la Producción in Chile, Nacional Financiera in Mexico, Banco Nacional do Desenvolvimento Económico in Brazil, and so on. Perhaps it is worth remembering that many of the most successful enterprises today, and a considerable number of their owners and managers, owe their apprenticeship and development to these institutions. For the era in which we now live, we need to invent new institutions designed to deal with the medium- and long-term according to the realities and necessities of the present and with the objective of anticipating those of the future. In collaboration with the state, all the different social actors have a fundamental contribution to make in this respect.

The Threat of Social Polarization

Even during its most stable and successful periods, the different stages in the evolution of Latin America have been characterized by the persistence of an enormous disparity among its different economic and social sectors and geographic areas (Thorpe 1998). These imbalances are profoundly rooted in history. As a consequence, islands of modernity, progress, and wealth comparable to those in the developed world coexist in a dialectic interaction with oceans of backwardness and poverty similar to those of the most underdeveloped regions in the world.

In order to ensure that they remain economically competitive and financially trustworthy in a highly integrated global market, governments see themselves as forced to reduce or maintain their levels of taxation. However, to reduce their fiscal deficits, they have had to cut the expenditures that the maintenance of the welfare or developmental state required, forcing the adoption of conservative and restrictive monetary, fiscal, and incomes policies. This global constraint is the real reason why it has become extremely difficult to maintain independent and autonomous national policies at the macroeconomic level. It has also become the principal reason for attempts to reduce through privatization the state's role in the provision of welfare. To borrow the terminology used by Rosa Luxemburg at the beginning of the century, nowadays the interests of financial capital prevail totally over those of productive (and social and human) capital.

Much of the growth of the middle and organized working classes in Latin America was achieved during the previous period precisely through the expansion of government services and public corporations. The extension of public health, the educational system, housing and social security, as well as the growth of public enterprises, meant that the government had to expand considerably. As a consequence, the number of doctors, nurses, teachers, architects, administrators, engineers, economists, and other employees and workers grew enormously. Public employment, as Pérez Sáinz points out in this volume, became the pillar of formal employment.

Neoliberalism creates so many adverse reactions, from active hostility to feelings of despondency and insecurity, because it is not simply an economic policy. It is in fact a social and cultural policy that tries to supplant the type of society formed in the postwar period, which strived to achieve a difficult balance between economic efficiency and social solidarity. It tries to replace it with another kind of society that stimulates efficiency, competitiveness, and individualism. As a consequence the boundaries of the private and individualistic sphere are extended at the expense of the public sphere. This is accompanied by a great concentration of wealth, income, and power. Anything that stands in the way of these goals is swept aside. Everything becomes marketable. The public interest itself is privatized, disappears, or is severely weakened. In the academic and intellectual arena researchers are co-opted by the private sector or are scattered among precarious institutions or poorly financed public universities. There is little or no capacity to carry out research and teaching in the social sciences and culture. Research no longer receives adequate funding when it deals with the public sphere, social conditions, and long-term perspectives. The neoliberal society has no interest for this kind of activity.

Under what conditions have we entered the twenty-first century? I would argue that we are entering an era that will be characterized by a new kind of apartheid or social exclusion. The new economy, where everyone competes with everyone else, and which is extraordinarily intensive in the use of technology and capital, requires only a very few but highly qualified individuals, and consequently creates very little employment. This is true not only in Latin America, but also in the industrialized world, where social exclusion has become a major concern (Castells 1996).

There are violent social and demographic contrasts in levels of income and the quality of life in the large urban metropolis, within as well as between these urban centers and rural areas. The widespread and prolonged reduction in investment, employment, income, and consumption over the last decades is cause for great concern, and has led to an overwhelming expansion in the numbers of "new poor," in addition to those who are already living in poverty. One of the most significant elements of this phenomenon in most countries has been the lack of adequate public social expenditures. This has manifested in numerous ways: in the serious deterioration in educational and public health institutions and infrastructure; in the striking reduction in the salaries of professionals and others who work in these sectors; in a sharp decline in the middle and organized working classes; in serious shortages, and sometimes complete lack, of essential supplies and equipment; in the overcrowding of classrooms and hospital wards; in an alarming school dropout rate; in a lack of emergency services and a rise in the number of prolonged waiting lists at hospitals; in a precipitous fall in morale; and in a partial or total exodus of the most able staff. In general, there has been a serious deterioration in these public services. One especially shocking example is the neglect of preventative health-care facilities.

Another of the policies that has had serious repercussions in the social sector has been the privatization of health, educational, and social services. The quality of the services offered is generally good, but they can only cover the part of the population that enjoys a sufficient level of income to make the corresponding payments. Despite the diverse practices these firms have adopted to exclude high-risk groups (which represent higher costs for them and thus lower profits), and despite the hidden subsidies from the public sector that these firms enjoy, the highly unequal distribution of income in our countries leads to a situation where coverage reaches just between a quarter and a third of the population. Undoubtedly, such systems of private social services will have a hard time prospering in countries where the levels of per capita incomes are low. It will also be difficult to provide coverage in smaller cities and rural areas. For all these reasons, the feasibility of this policy is severely restricted to higher-income people and areas.

Seen in isolation, the privatization of social services could be considered successful. But the policy is flawed in the sense that these firms require constant and intensive regulatory supervision, especially in view of their tendency to excessive increases in costs. In addition, from a more general point of view, it cannot be stressed enough that this policy has been accompanied by the dismantling of essential public social services, further accentuating the lack of social protection for the great majority of the population. It is thus clear that a form of polarization is occurring that represents a new kind of apartheid. Whereas a select minority enjoys social services of a quality that is similar to that in the industrialized countries (even to the extent of having access to the most reputable hospitals of the United States), the great majority of the poorer members of society only have access to minimal services, usually of poor quality. This conclusion is all the more perplexing if we take into account the enormous concentration of property, wealth, and income in the hands of a minority, and the precarious state in which the great majority live.

If the problems are serious with respect to health care, they are equally critical with regard to education. As with health care, there is a growing disparity between the coverage and quality of the (mainly private) education for the minority and the public education available to the great majority of children and young adults. This situation becomes particularly disturbing when we bear in mind that education is fundamental for social access and mobility in the knowledge-based society of the future, and that the health care and education received during infancy and childhood mark a person for life.

Another issue intimately linked to the subject of poverty and social inequality is the widespread and profound change that has occurred in the employment structure during the past decade in Latin America. Together with attempts to dismantle the public sector, this phenomenon is of transcendental importance. This is particularly relevant in those sectors of the economy where public enterprises with the greatest innovative capacity are privatized and restructured in order to compete on the domestic and international markets. This signifies the creation of highly productive and well-paid employment for some, but also considerable job losses in the newly privatized, restructured enterprises and in the firms that do not resist the intensification of competition. Thus, divergent tendencies are in evidence between the workers who form part of the modern sector (characterized by high productivity and a considerable and growing degree of internationalization) and the rest, who either join the ranks of the unemployed, or are forced into low-productivity activities, or become self- or underemployed. Unfortunately, left to the spontaneous interaction of market forces, the latter group is usually far more numerous than the former, and together they make up what we could term "the new poor."

These problems become more or less serious depending on the following factors: the rate of growth of the population and the workforce; the severity of the need for restructuring arising from the liberalization policy; the scale of privatization of public enterprises and services; the intensity of international competition; the speed with which new capital intensive technology and highly qualified human resources are being incorporated; overall educational requirements, especially with respect to the youngest members of the workforce; the existence of institutional barriers which impede access to foreign markets; and finally, the extent to which the labor market is segmented. From an employment perspective, in practically every country in the region, it is well recognized that present tendencies do not bode well for the future (see Pérez Sáinz in this volume). Faced with such a situation, it is vital to seriously reconsider current strategies and employment policies.

The social challenge that Latin America faces is staggering in scope. There is a pressing need to tackle both the "old poverty" inherited from previous socioeconomic models and the "new poverty" generated by the present transition, crisis, adjustment, and restructuring. Moreover, the current social and demographic trends, which arise from the aforementioned inequalities, need to be halted and put into reverse. In this context, social policies represent no more than palliatives, since they constitute merely an attempt to ameliorate the current thrust of economic policy. To make social policy truly efficient, substantial modifications are required in economic policy, as well as changes in social policy itself (Sunkel 1994).

To achieve this objective, there is a need to distinguish between the initial income distribution and the degree of redistribution achieved after state intervention. Nowadays redistribution as a policy is very much constrained. As a consequence, it is necessary to alter the initial distribution of income by structural reforms, which promote better access to productive factors such as land, education, and knowledge, as well as facilitating the creation of new business ventures

The Challenge of Sustainable Development

The concern for the medium and long term also derives from the need to make fundamental adjustments in our development strategy, taking into account a new requirement, namely, the environmental sustainability of growth and the improvement of the quality of life (Sunkel and Gligo 1981). It is now widely accepted that on local, national, regional, and global levels, the biosphere is being subjected to unsustainable environmental pressures that threaten not just the process of development but human life itself. There is a growing acknowledgement of the fundamental importance of this issue in Latin America (PNUMA 2000). We need to move toward a developmental strategy that is environmentally sustainable, such as that proposed at the U.N. Conference on the Environment (1992 Rio Summit), if our countries are to participate in the increasingly globalized world economy. It is a subject that the ruling classes of our region will not be able to ignore any longer, except at the risk of serious domestic and international political difficulties.

The concept of sustainability, which has acquired so much coverage in recent years, links the themes of economic development and the environment. Development is in essence a process of a gradually increasing specialization of labor, together with the corresponding technological innovations and an increasingly intensive use of nonhuman energy. Labor productivity continues to rise, permitting a growing economic surplus, and so on. In this process of specialization of labor, technological change, and rising energy inputs, productivity is not the only thing to have increased—the volume of production and the size of the population have also risen, as well as the standard of living, even though this improvement has been achieved in a very uneven manner, with great differences among countries, classes, and social groups.

The increasingly intensive extraction of those natural products which are useful to human beings is also achieved via a process of specialization and increasing productivity of nature and the gradual replacement of nature's natural produce. Instead of leaving the ecosystems to produce naturally an infinite variety of plants and animal life, humankind eliminates those which it regards of no use and replaces them with the crops that are in demand. Apart from the perishable food required for the sustenance of the population, the other products have undergone a historical process of accumulation and at present constitute the built-up environment which surrounds us; housing, domestic artifacts; networks of sewers; drinkable water; electricity and gas; roads, railways, bridges, tunnels, and vehicles; ports, canals, boats; housing; commercial, governmental, and financial buildings; office equipment, the networks of communication, and so on. The majority of these elements, which make up the built-up environment, are increasingly concentrated (along with most of the population) in large cities, and at the end of networks and communication hubs that interconnect with smaller cities.

This new artificial environment is the tangible product of an enormous process of demographic, socioeconomic, cultural, and technological development and transformation that has taken place in the last half-century in Latin America. It represents the result of a very intensive, prolonged, and sustained period of extraction, use, and abuse of natural resources. From this perspective, economic development can be defined as a process of taking over and transforming natural environments and ecosystems relatively untouched and replacing them with ecosystems that are increasingly inhabited, constructed, and transformed by human beings. In fact, because most of the population interacts principally with this artificial environment, it has acted as a barrier between humanity and nature and creates the illusion that we depend less and less on nature. In the terminology of development theory, the primary sectors (agriculture, forestry, fishing, and mining) are losing importance, while the secondary sectors (industry) and the tertiary sectors (services) expand more than proportionally and become increasingly important.

The opposite is the case from an environmental perspective. In order for everything to work (for factories to produce, for transport to run, for buildings to be inhabitable, for the supply of food and water to be adequate, and so on, in other words, for the artificial environment to be habitable and productive) an energy supply is required, and for this we depend on nature. Moreover, energy is required to repair the deterioration that these artificially created elements normally suffer. For that purpose it is necessary to continue to extract materials from the biosphere. As the goods and services provided by the ecosystem are free, or at least enormously undervalued by the market, economic actors systematically tend to overexploit them.

This excessive interference with nature can be tolerated up to a point by the ecosystems, thanks to their heterogeneous and complex composition, which endows them with a relatively large capacity for the absorption and "digestion" of these changes, as well as for regeneration and self-reproduction. But if the intensity and persistence of these abuses exceed certain limits, the regenerative and reproductive cycles of the ecosystems can be damaged to the point of environmental collapse. Of course, each system's limit can vary enormously. Some, like the tropical rainforest, are very fragile, and others, such as wet grasslands, are more resilient.

To the extent that ecosystems suffer from deterioration in their capacity to produce and support clean air, fresh water, fertile earth, healthy flora and fauna, and so on, significant costs are generated. As a result, it becomes necessary to pay for the products the ecosystem once delivered free of charge, through new investments and technologies that purify the water and the air, that recycle wastes, that sustain fertility. Indeed, if the deterioration of the ecosystem becomes even more pronounced, it will reach a point where it will be on the brink of a catastrophe. When this occurs, the ecosystem enters into a process of collapse and ceases to function altogether (as happens, for example, when erosion causes the disappearance of topsoil). The regeneration of ecosystems in these cases is generally a very costly, if not impossible, long-term task. Avoiding such situations is what sustainable development is all about. Diagnosing the different problems each country in Latin America suffers is essential to the design of policies, programs, and projects that incorporate an environmental dimension and contribute to the improvement of the environment and sustainability.

Three types of active policies need to be adopted urgently: first, the reduction, control, and prevention of environmental degradation through the construction of sewage treatment plants, the adoption of decontaminating technologies, methods of clean production, recycling of residuals and wastes, improvements in materials and energy efficiency, and so on; second, the partial or total regeneration of damaged ecosystems via reforestation, the management of rivers and hydraulic resources, soil management techniques, urban and coastal area planning, the preservation of marine ecosystems and genetic diversity, and whatever else might be needed; and third, the adoption of strict guidelines and measures regarding land use, or in other words, physical and territorial planning.

Most "environmental" policies and projects are in reality not specifically "environmental" at all. Rather, they are activities that are habitually carried out in all the productive sectors (social, public, and private)—industry, mining, public works, construction, agriculture, health, housing, recreation. Policies must be redesigned, reformulated, and modified to incorporate an environmental approach. Explicit environmental policies and management must be introduced in areas where they are currently carried out only implicitly and where, as a result, they are also carried out very ineffectively, principally because of ignorance, shortsightedness, or ill-founded economic analysis.

Reducing and repairing environmental damage and pollution, and avoiding as much as possible the exhaustion and degradation of natural resources and ecosystems, requires human, institutional, and financial resources. This requires a change of priorities in the allocation of economic resources in favor of the environment. This requirement contrasts dramatically with contemporary financial priorities in the public sector. Due to a combination of ideology, foreign exchange constraints, fiscal imbalances, and the need to restructure the export sector, the national and international trend is to reduce public expenditure to protect the environment, despite the fact that the pressures on the environment are increasing. In these circumstances, the possibility of effective environmental policies has to be linked to the workings of the international economy. In particular, environmental conditionality cannot be accepted without the supply of additional financial resources. It will not be easy for our governments to carry out negotiation on this subject, because to a great extent our own survival depends on yielding to international policies. Nevertheless, the international economic, social, and environmental situation has deteriorated in such a way that the South now has some grounds on which it can negotiate with the North.

Over the last few decades, inequality between the South and the North has increased dramatically. The marginalized and excluded peoples in the South are increasingly pressuring the North through immigration. The devastation of forestry resources, desertification, the destruction of biological diversity, and so on in the South causes ecological problems in the North. The environmental, social-political, and international economic equilibrium is more and more closely linked, and this linkage cannot now be broken. If we intend to avoid worldwide environmental damage, the destruction of the tropical rainforests cannot be stopped while the Southern populations and economies are forced to colonize and exploit the tropical regions in order to generate employment and foreign exchange.

This reciprocal linkage between the environmental theme and the developmental one has to be a central element in the negotiations between North and South, but so that our case is correctly framed, it is vital that Latin American governments understand the true nature of the environmental problem and give it the priority it deserves. Governments must recognize that national and international environmental policy is already, and will increasingly become more of, an essential element in development policy and international relations.

The State, Economic Policy, and Political Economy

An essential and inevitable component of any policy proposal has to do with the role of the state. New goals must be identified where public intervention is needed through public policies. For example, greater supervision and regulation of activities that have passed to the private sector is required in order to protect the public interest. The state must also respond with social policies addressing the problems of poverty, inequality, and the improvement of public social services (education, health, housing, social security, environmental quality). It must also develop economic policies aimed at improving infrastructure, technology, productivity, innovation, creativity, competitiveness, and diversification of production and employment, particularly for the medium- and small-scale enterprises.

Moreover, it is absolutely imperative that governments contribute to the elaboration, with ample social participation, of a strategic vision of the long-term objectives of development. It is essential to provide a framework for the right incentives and regulatory structure coherent with this vision, as well as to provide the necessary consensus, through dialogue, between all the social and political sectors in support of this strategy. A state that is efficiently organized along these lines would contribute to a new era in Latin American development, characterized by the objectives of deepening democracy and overcoming poverty and inequality. In which direction should we look to put such orientations into practice, if they are indeed the correct ones? Three levels may be distinguished: the level of nation-state, the subnational level, and the international level.

At the level of the nation-state, for example, the reconstruction of the old welfare state to tackle the social problems seems inconceivable under present conditions. The public sector's total expenditure level has been compressed, but the proportion of government expenditure accounted for by social expenditure is growing. This implies the possibility of using state expenditure far more efficiently to improve the quality of the social services and coordinate and integrate them with the private sector. However, to achieve this effectively it might be necessary to create an institutional structure similar to that which exists in the economic sphere. Just as there is a central bank, a ministry of finance, and a budgetary authority to insure macroeconomic balances, within the context of a radical reform of the state, a parallel organization could be created in the social sector: a single social ministry, a budgetary authority, and a supervisory body to coordinate and oversee the "macro-sociopolitical equilibriums" (Sunkel 1992).

At the subnational level, there are enormous tasks ahead. There is one particular deficiency in Latin America that needs to be addressed. Unlike in the United States and Europe, where, historically speaking, villages grew into cities and regions grew into states, Latin American nation-states are societies organized from the state downward, with a centralist and authoritarian legacy inherited from the colonial administration and its continuity after independence up to the present. This is also, to a large extent, the case in countries organized along federal lines.

Consequently, there is need for a fundamental institutional reform framework regarding decentralization, regionalization, the promotion of local initiatives, grassroots organizations, a whole variety of associations, cooperative groups, municipalities, neighborhood committees, and social-developmental and philanthropic organizations. In other words, a network of grassroots institutions needs to be created where it does not exist and strengthened where it has emerged. This is perhaps the most challenging task that we have before us.

The third level is international. The same shift from public to private power has happened here as at the national level, leaving a large public void in the international system (Kaul, Grunberg, and Stern 1999). The multilateral public economic institutions—the World Bank, the International Monetary Fund, and the Inter-American Development Bank—have less and less power compared to the international private financial institutions. The rest of the multilateral institutions—such as UNICEF, UNESCO, FAO, and the UN World Conferences on Population, Women, and the Environment, or the Social Summit—constitute immense international institutional paraphernalia that have little or no power. The question is how to achieve something as well intentioned and well prepared for as, for example, the Social Summit, acquiring a true influence and able to oblige participants to undertake the required tasks, particularly since there is no public institution expressly dedicated to social issues at the international level.

In sum, the prevalent economic model has to be critically reviewed in light of these and other considerations and made more flexible through creative economic and political proposals concerning foreign debt, state reform, social and employment policies, dynamic insertion in the international economy, restructuring of the economy, and technical progress. These measures are necessary to make both the economic reorganization and the democratization process sustainable, something which is at the moment very much under threat.

Economic reform became inevitable and necessary. What is not inevitable or necessary is an ultra-neoliberal reform, with its enormous associated economic, social, environmental, and political costs. More moderate and less costly alternatives exist for applying the economic policy measures required to carry the reform through. The possibility for using them depends fundamentally on the capacity of the political sector to recognize its own crisis of ideas and methods, to renovate itself radically, and to realize that economic reform is a contemporary historical necessity. From then on, the political class will have to design, structure, and maintain a wide social and political consensus, with the primary objective of distributing more equitably the inevitable social cost of adjustment and restructuring, and with a more equitable subsequent distribution of benefits.

The sectors of the center-left of the political spectrum have been confused by the sharp shift toward neoliberalism that economic policy has taken. There are objective reasons for this shift: the collapse of "real" socialism; the developmental and foreign debt crises; the experience of overly bureaucratic and state-centered governments in Latin America; the problems of the welfare state in the industrial countries; and the globalization of the economy and society as a whole, all of which reduces room for maneuvering in economic policy. Nevertheless, there is also a powerful ideological reason for this shift: a significant proportion of the national and international academic and technocratic community have transformed the neoclassical approach, which economists developed as a means of analyzing the workings of the capitalist system, toward a normative end—that of transforming previously more or less state-run economies into market economies with as little government intervention as possible. We cannot, however, ignore the many cases of market failure and other weaknesses inherent in neoclassical theory regarding long-term growth, social conditions, and environmental problems. A systematic, critical, and more objective review of the experience of economic reform in the region is taking place with the goal of drawing positive lessons to guide future economic and developmental policy in Latin America (Stallings and Peres 2000; Weller 2000a and 2000b; Moguillansky and Bielschowsky 2000; Katz 2000). Using a pragmatic approach and the lessons drawn from experience, it should be possible to overcome the polarization of the debate and synthesize the less ideologically driven neoclassical position with the Latin American structuralist approach, reformulated in its neostructuralist version. This synthesis is now more possible as a result of a series of factors: the disappointing experiences of both camps when their ideas have been put into practice, the prolonged period of recurrent crisis and the less intense ideological atmosphere, and greater pragmatism that is beginning to permeate the debate in these post–Cold War years.

One way of interpreting the current historical period of transition would be to recognize that development has been sacrificed for growth, and to juxtapose the irrationality of capitalism with the nonviability of socialism. How can we infuse capitalism with the public and social concerns of socialism without scaring capitalist entrepreneurs away? At the same time, how can we avoid the militarized bureaucratic authoritarianism of the Right and Left, and fight for greater social and individual liberties and freedom? How can we achieve a synthesis between the mechanism of capitalist growth and the socialist concern for improving the lot of the victims of oppression, exploitation, marginalization, and discrimination? How can we avoid the process of international integration and the pressure for ever greater competitiveness that deteriorates into national disintegration on the economic, social, and cultural levels? How can we protect public goods from coming under attack from private, bureaucratic, and technocratic interests in areas such as the environment, human rights, and the judicial system?

Perhaps the common thread that unites these concerns and proposals is the search for a more radical conception of democracy, that is to say, a conception of democracy that entails a wider and more structured participation on the part of a strengthened civil society and a closer social control over bureaucratic statism and business—a control exercised by a more densely organized network of citizens' organizations to fulfill public functions and represent, in particular, the weakest groups and sectors of society.

3 Social Science and Academic Sociology in Brazil

VILMAR E. FARIA

The Center for Latin American Studies at the University of Florida invited me to write a "reflective essay" exploring the historical events that led to the erosion of once-dominant paradigms and to the emergence of new concepts, theories, topics, and methods in the field of social policy in Brazil. I hesitated to accept this invitation for one simple reason: in my present position—senior adviser to President Cardoso, working full-time for the federal government since late 1994—I have been distant from academic research and do not have sufficient time to carry out the careful analysis that such a complex and difficult question demands. However, this very dilemma made me accept the challenge, believing that my experience as a policymaker and former academic researcher could bring a different perspective to this issue.

An interesting essay on contemporary Mexico by the historian Hector Aguilar Camin (2000), titled "Mexico: la ceniza y la semilla," has been widely discussed in ministerial circles in Brasília, which nowadays include a reasonably large number of former academics. Three of the most important academics now occupying some of the highest positions in the political and administrative arena in the country are reputed to have made the following comments on the book: "It is a pity that we cannot find in Brazil, nowadays, an essay of such importance and quality." In cultural meetings in Brasília where former academics gather who are now responsible for agencies that contract evaluations from the Academy, it is common to hear the statement that this work has been increasingly dominated by economists, and that the quality of social policy analysis in the classical social sciences (anthropology, political science, and sociology) is, with some well-known exceptions, below expectation.

And last but not least, the debate in the Brazilian media about social policy is, almost without exception, neither profound nor innovative. The discussion is limited, in most cases, to acknowledging a widespread immorality and complex social ills. It contains the insatiable complaint—fair or unfair—about the lack of state resources to combat poverty, promote equality and citizenship, and create a broad system of high-quality basic social services.

Editors' note: Vilmar Faria died, in office, in November 2002.

From the supply side, however, the transformations that have taken place during the last fifteen or twenty years, both in the institutional arena and in the field of financial support for scientific research, indicate a significant expansion in the social sciences. This expansion occurred simultaneously in graduate studies and in scientific research. Presently, Brazil has one of the largest and most dynamic graduate studies systems in the developing world. There has been a significant increase in academic production in the social sciences. Paradoxically, the social sciences in Brazil have lost their excellence in the field where they were most in touch with the humanities—the arena, par excellence, for intellectual essays and critical reflection—without, on the other hand, gaining expertise in the fields of social sciences connected with the "hard" sciences.

Before analyzing this paradox, I need to define what is meant by social policy research. Broadly understood, social policy research in sociology—or in the classical social sciences—should include all research relevant for social policy, including identification of relevant social problems, analysis of social processes that generate social policy issues and needs, assessment and measurement of these needs, analysis of the policymaking and policy-delivering processes and institutions, and evaluation of their effects. Therefore, in order to answer the questions posed by the conference organizers, a broad analysis of sociological production and its transformations in recent decades is required. I accept this challenge, taking, however, a narrower understanding of the question to be addressed. We should study the emergence in Brazil, in the recent past, of a field of specialization, named public policy analysis, and on the contribution of sociology, political science, and anthropology to this emerging specialization.

With this definition, a manageable set of questions can be formulated as follows: Which factors affected the dominant paradigms making the emergence of this subfield possible? What concepts, theories, topics, methods, and research strategies characterize this subfield? What are its weaknesses and strengths? How do they affect social policy implementation and social policy institutions? The starting point for answering this set of questions must be identifying the more influential studies published in Brazil in the last decade in public policy analysis, particularly those relying on the contributions of anthropology, political science, and sociology.

To obtain a more objective idea of the most influential recent social science publications in the field of social policy, I conducted a small, nonsystematic e-mail inquiry. I sent a questionnaire to thirty-two persons, asking them to list at least three recent publications by scholars working in Brazil on

collective works and papers in journals and readers. Major comprehensive works by one or two authors are also mentioned, but do not predominate, in contrast to the earlier pattern of publication in the Brazilian social sciences. This reflects, in part, the volatility and competitiveness of fin de siècle intellectual production, but also, perhaps, the newness of the field.

A second point to stress is the growing role of economists in social policy areas such as the identification and diagnosis of social issues, and in the subfields of policy analysis and policy evaluation. Given the disciplinary bias of mainstream economists, the result is that the institutional, political, sociological, and symbolic aspects of social policy have been underemphasized.

And last—but not least—I think that it is important to mention another major influence on Brazilian social sciences, which is particularly relevant to the field of social policy. I am referring to the influence of the research sponsored by large bureaucratic organizations such as the Inter-American Development Bank (IDB), the World Bank, and other United Nations organizations, such as the United Nations Development Programme (UNDP). These large and powerful organizations are able to generate a mass of empirical information, to have a large, permanent and well-paid body of experts, mainly economists, and to control financial resources and social networks that make it easy for them to hire consultants and intellectuals all over the world. Furthermore, some of these international and multinational organizations have the clout to enhance their influence beyond the intellectual merits of their production, which is clearly present. The consequences of this influence for Brazilian social sciences need further and more careful analysis. It does not appear in the e-mail survey because the externally sponsored research is done (or seen as done) outside Brazil, even when Brazilian researchers contribute as consultants.

Within Brazil, large public and private bureaucracies, such as the Banco Nacional de Desenvolvimento Econômico e Social, are also becoming influential in social policy research, even if they do not command the same resources as the international organizations. This scenario sharply contrasts with that of the Brazilian academic world of twenty years ago.

What, then, are the historical processes, the ideological and paradigmatic transformations and institutional changes that could be associated with the emergence of social policy as a specialized field? And what are the contrasts with the previous way Brazilian social science dealt with social policy questions? What follows is the main thrust of my argument.

During the 1960s and 1970s, the expansion of social science research in Latin America and in Brazil took place in an epistemological situation characterized by a polarized consensus: social science developed under the tension of a permanent conflict between the positivistic-oriented modernization theory (in part associated with structural-functionalist social science), on the one hand, and so-called scientific Marxism, on the other. For a complex set of structural, scientific, and ideological reasons, including the erosion of authoritarianism in the region, this polarized consensus imploded during the 1980s, opening the way for a more flexible, pluri-paradigmatic epistemological space. This new situation allowed, if not encouraged, specialization and policy-oriented social science.

At the same time, in the last twenty years, there was a significant quantitative expansion of graduate studies and research in the social sciences in Brazil, leading to a growing institutional differentiation, increased competition, and density. Together with paradigmatic flexibility, this also led to a growing specialization.

Finally, an increase in the demand for innovative social policy can be attributed to the redemocratization that occurred during the exhaustion of state-led import-substitution industrialization, and by deep social crisis associated with these political and economic changes. Indeed, in large measure, the fight against authoritarianism was based on the worsening of the social situation and the collapse of welfare institutions. As a result of redemocratization, new political coalitions—which included significant numbers of social scientists of the critical school—gained access to government at the municipal, state, and federal levels, unleashing a growing demand for more policy-oriented social science research. Taken together, these are the main processes that triggered the development of the new field of social policy research. I will discuss each one of these aspects in more detail.

Technological Revolution and Globalization: An Epistemological Earthquake?

Teaching and research initiatives in the area of public policy analysis started in the late 1970s and early 1980s in Brazil. To my knowledge, the first institutional initiatives in this direction, in which I participated, took place in São Paulo. One, at the Fundo de Defesa e Assistência Profissional (FUNDAP), under the leadership of Vânia Santanna and Regina Barbosa Faria, and the other at UNICAMP, under the leadership of a group of scholars from the Political Science Department and from the Institute of Economics. At FUNDAP, the initiative centered on teaching, and was motivated by the need to improve the technical—and ideological—skills of career officials in the public bureaucracy of the state of São Paulo. The French École Nationale d'Administration Publique served as a model, but increasingly, the teaching material would be based on North American social science. At UNICAMP, the effort centered on social policy research and had a rather theoretically pluralistic composition. With time NEPP (Núcleo de Estudos Psicoanalíticos e Pedagógicos), the research center created at UNICAMP, became one of the leading research institutions in this field.

These developments reflected a paradigmatic change in the intellectual framework of Brazilian social science. During the late 1960s, and particularly in the 1970s, the intellectual debate revolved around the *insurmountable* conflict between the two prevailing intellectual frameworks: the so-called empirically oriented modernization theory inspired by positivistic social science (and also identified with a functionalist theoretical frame of reference in some sectors of the academy) and the critically oriented kind of intellectual framework identified, in one way or another, with scientific Marxism. Both fields were, of course, internally differentiated, and influenced each other to some extent.

In academic seminars titled "Theory and Methodology of the Social Sciences," held at the graduate course at UNICAMP during the 1980s, I referred to this intellectual situation as the "polarized consensus" of the 1970s and its growing "paralyzing embrace," using an expression I took from Professor Cândido Mendes de Almeida. This Brazilian intellectual paralysis had parallels elsewhere, as is clear from Jeffrey Alexander's (1995, 6) analysis of the debates between modernization theorists and world systems theorists at the American Sociological Association in the mid-1970s.

The best of social science production in Brazil during the 1970s were attempts to escape from this "paralyzing embrace," as in the case of Cardoso and Faletto's (1970) *Dependency and Development,* W. dos Santos's (1979) *Citizenship and Justice,* on social policy, and the vast literature on authoritarianism. Despite these exceptions, the two major frameworks performed functions similar to those attributed to paradigms by Kuhn (1970). These frameworks are clear in the mainly European academic literature of the 1970s and early 1980s on the functions of welfare institutions and the welfare state that was influential in Brazil (Mishra 1981; Gough 1979; O'Connor 1973; Offe 1984).

In the context of this "polarized consensus," most of the discussions centered on the functions of the welfare state: the functionalist literature stressed the integrative functions, and the Marxist literature emphasized the political legitimization, labor force domination, and labor force reproduction functions of welfare state institutions. The Marxist literature also emphasized the coming crisis of the welfare state, as a result, part and parcel, of the coming crisis of capitalism. There was also an increasingly influential literature based on more conservative ideological positions, stressing the deleterious effects of welfare institutions on poor families. This literature contributed to the ideological debate that undermined the legitimacy of the postwar welfare state, particularly in its European versions. (See, among others, Murray 1984, Lasch 1978, and Bell 1978.)

In Brazil, the Marxist literature was, by far, the most influential during this period. Who can forget Marta Haenecker's manuals? Associated with the version of Marxism based on the work of Althusser and Poulantzas, studies of the so-called ideological state apparatus examined education and health-care policy from this perspective, exploring the connections existing between authoritarianism and social policy institutions. This overall perspective even influenced academic professionals in charge of welfare institutions, the *assistentes sociais*.

Slowly but surely, this "polarized consensus" came to an end by the late 1980s under the pressure of a set of technological, demographic, economic, sociological, political, scientific, and ideological transformations. The net results of these processes for the prevailing frameworks were devastating.

To better understand this "paradigmatic" earthquake, we need to go beyond Kuhn. Using the tools of methodological analysis, I claim that in the 1980s the convergence of these transformations generated a set of methodological factors that eroded the dominant frames of reference, as well as their "paralyzing embrace." In addition to the reasons and mechanisms accounting for paradigm erosion and paradigm substitution analyzed by Kuhn, three others accumulated and converged to produce the implosion (from the inside) and the explosion (from the outside) of the "polarized consensus" in Brazil.

First, throughout the years of their hegemony, research results accumulated that falsified central hypotheses of both frameworks, in the manner of Popper's (1959) falsification criteria for verifying hypotheses. It was not empirically true, for instance, either that industrial modernization was leading to democracy, or that the industrial working class, with the growth of capitalism, was becoming increasingly impoverished and developing a revolutionary consciousness. However, because of the ideological grip of these "paradigms," these results were kept "under the carpet." Each side of the polarized consensus dismissed as ideological and nonscientific the production of empirical evidence and arguments that ran counter to their position.

The "Popperian" falsification mechanism did not work but the unexplainable evidence was accumulating at the periphery of both frameworks.

Second, at a deeper level, the transformations under way progressively affected what Imre Lakatos, in his *Methodology of Scientific Research Programmes*, called "the hard core of the program" (Lakatos 1978, 8–101), the inner "protection belt" of these broad intellectual orientations. This included, among other components, their strategic units of analysis (social classes and functional realms, for instance), the basically analogical models and metaphors used to build their objects of analysis (the conflict-producing infra- and superstructure metaphor, social systems in equilibrium), and their antireductionist epistemological assumptions, based on notions such as "the whole is greater than the parts," "systems," "mode of production," and "totality." As a result, "Lakatosian" erosion set in. Alexander (1995, 19) points out that "reality problems" began to intrude in modernization theory in a major way in the postwar period, therefore creating a "Popperian" mechanism of paradigm erosion. He goes on: "Factual problems, however, are not enough to create scientific revolutions. Broad theories . . . *such as modernization theory and scientific Marxism* . . . can defend themselves by defining and protecting a set of core propositions . . . *against these 'reality problems.'* . . . The decisive fact in modernization theory's defeat . . . *and in scientific Marxism, as well* . . . , rather, was the destruction of its ideological, discursive, 'mythological core,' a typical 'Lakatosian' mechanism" (Alexander 1995, 19–21; my emphasis).

Once historical conditions changed, including the end of the Cold War and the demise of the experience of "real socialism," the paradigms' "protection belts" lost their capacity to deflect and to leave "under the carpet" the existing falsifying evidence. The ideas that gave legitimacy to the elements forming the protection belt lost ground.

Last but not least, the same transformations generated changes at an even deeper level, affecting the epistemological foundations of classical social science and bringing to the surface the so-called crisis of modern reason. Following Foucault, the epistemic basis of both classical Marxism and classical positivistic modernization theory were under stress. The "Foucaultian" analytic mechanisms were, in large measure, crystallized in the major historical propositions of postmodernism and postmodern social theory: "the decline of the grand narrative and the return to the local, . . . the rise of the empty symbol or simulacrum . . . the end of socialism . . . the emphasis on plurality and difference . . . [as] responses to the decline of 'progressive' ideologies and their utopian beliefs" (Alexander 1995, 25–26). This mechanism multiplied the effects of the previous ones and opened room for paradigm fragmentation. As a result, the paradigms and their embrace collapsed.

In Brazil, as elsewhere, the sudden erosion of the polarized consensus through the methodological approaches that I have just described was provoked by the technological transformations that produced significant changes in capitalist production; by the demographic changes under way—in fertility, life expectancy, female labor force participation, and family structure; by the progressive shrinkage and transformations of the working class; by the rapid processes of economic globalization and restructuring; by the dramatic end of the experiment with "real socialism"; by the end of authoritarianism and redemocratization; and by the ideological offensive of the conservatives (or of neoliberals, to use the Latin American terminology).

At the same time, the transformations that generated this sudden erosion of the old paradigms also facilitated the emergence and/or strengthening of at least two other broad intellectual frames of reference in reaction to the postmodern critique. In the first instance, research programs built upon strongly reductionist epistemological assumptions became relegitimized. This is a complex change in the fin de siècle epistemic bases, resulting in part from the new ideological climate, but also associated with developments in other areas of science—such as molecular biology and computer science. In the social sciences, this has meant the growing influence of mainstream, neoclassical economics and the projection of this influence into political science (rational choice theory) and even into Marxism (Analytical Marxism).

In the second instance, the crisis of modern, progressive thought led to the strengthening of different types of postmodern approaches stressing "calls for social science to give up its one-dimensional quest for cognitive truth . . . and offering . . . social science as praxis or moral inquiry . . . or as hermeneutics of the concrete as alternatives" (Alexander 1995, 90). In Brazilian social sciences, this meant positively revaluing anthropology as a discipline. The "linguistic turn" associated with this same trend also contributed to the increasing use of qualitative research methodology as well as to the growing influence of hermeneutics and literary criticism.

These paradigmatic changes have at least two far-reaching consequences. First and foremost, there is a new and powerful dividing line within the academic social science community: those pushing for a strengthening in the direction of the hard sciences, and those defending a close identification with the humanities. Second, together with other factors that I discuss below, the ongoing paradigmatic changes are generating what could be called a "fragmented specialization" in the field of social policy research, emphasizing the abandonment of the "grand narrative and the return to the local." The first consequence is to facilitate the hegemony of economists in the area. The second consequence is the lack of a powerful, coherent social science research program in social policy studies resulting in the high degree of dispersion and fragmentation of the field. In the conclusion, I return to these points and make some recommendations.

Graduate Social Sciences in Brazil: Institutional Growth and Differentiation

In the last twenty years, social science institutions in Brazil have expanded significantly and have differentiated institutionally. The main engine of these changes has been the expansion of enrollment in higher education. Although Brazil is still a laggard in education at all levels, even when compared to other developing economies, clear advances have been made, particularly in the last five or six years. As the data in Table 3.1 shows, from 1.37 million students enrolled in universities in 1980, Brazil reached 2.37 million undergraduate students in the year 1999. Enrollment in the area of the social sciences increased, but declined proportionately, accounting for less than 1 percent (0.7 percent) of total enrollment.

The growth in the enrollment rate in higher education has been particularly sharp since 1994, when almost seven hundred thousand (700,000) new places were generated. The Brazilian federal universities, after their enrollment stagnated in the 1980s, increased their role during the 1990s. However, the market-oriented, private sector, took the lead after 1994, with 567,339 new places created, or 80 percent of the total.

These trends are summarized in Figure 3.1, which also shows the expansion in enrollment of social science graduate students. Even if slightly below the overall expansion of enrollment in higher education, this expansion is significant for the development of social science research in Brazil. It is the area of graduate studies, particularly in the public universities, that is responsible, not only for feeding the research system qualified professionals, but also for most of the research conducted in the field. A few government research institutes and nonprofit private research centers play a complementary role.

Twenty years ago, ANPOCS (Associação Nacional de Pesquisa e Pós-Graduação em Ciências Sociais), a scientific association whose membership is based on graduate programs and research centers of a high standard, had

Table 3.1 Enrollment at Brazilian universities, 1980–1999

Year	Total	Public					Private	Social Sciences
		Total	%	Federal	State	Municipal		
1980	137,7286	492,232	36	316,715	109,252	66,265	885,054	12,230 (0.9)
1990	154,0080	578,625	38	308,867	194,417	75,341	961,455	13,441 (0.9)
1994	166,1034	690,450	42	363,543	231,936	94,971	970,584	13,538 (0.8)
1999	236,9945	832,022	35	442,562	302,380	87,080	1,537,923	16,984 (0.7)

SOURCE: INEP, Ministry of Education, 2001.

forty-three members, including twenty-six graduate programs, mainly master's degree courses. In the year 2001, ANPOCS membership reached sixty-three, a growth of approximately fifty percent. There are now forty-two graduate programs, many of them offering Ph.D. programs.

The only long-term (going back to 1980) data series on graduate studies that I could obtain refers to fellowships granted to students by the government funding agencies, CAPES (Coordenação de Aperfeicoamento de Pessoal de Nivel Superior) and CNPq (Conselho Nacional de Pesquisa). The following two figures summarize this evolution. The first, Figure 3.2, shows that 523 fellowships were granted in 1980 by these two institutions. Throughout the two decades, the number of fellowships granted increased regularly, at least until 1996. One thousand five hundred-three (1,503) fellowships were granted by the year 2000, or a tripling of grants during this period. These figures refer to different types of fellowships, however, including those granted to undergraduate students (Bolsas de Iniciação Científica). Figure 3.3 provides the relevant information on graduate studies and research development by showing the evolution of fellowships granted to Ph.D. students and research fellowships granted to senior researchers. The graph shows that

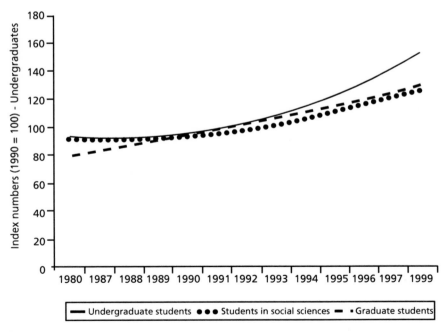

Fig 3.1   Enrollment in higher education and in the social sciences

around one hundred (100) fellowships were granted in 1980; in the year 2000 we reached almost seven hundred (700) fellowships and research grants, an almost sevenfold linear growth! Everyone familiar with the Brazilian graduate system knows that at least one other agency plays a crucial role in supporting graduate studies and scientific research in Brazil, namely FAPESP (Fundação de Amparo à Pesquisa do Estado de São Paulo). If the data from

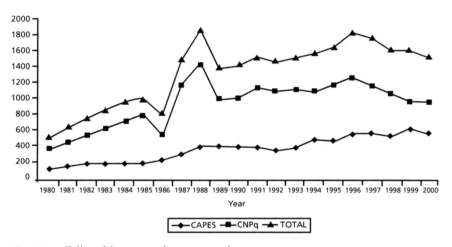

Fig 3.2   Fellowships granted—CNPq and CAPES

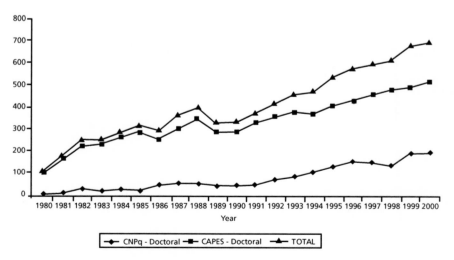

Fig 3.3   Graduate fellowships granted

this source had been included, the numbers showing the expansion of the system would be even better.

From 1987 on, annual data on the Brazilian graduate system are available. The expansion of the system, even in this short period of time, is unequivocal. Student enrollment in graduate courses (both Master's and Ph.D.) steadily increased until 1990, reaching around two thousand students (from 1,650 in 1987) and remaining at this number until 1993. Since 1993, a new linear expansion began, and by 1999 Brazil had 2,643 graduate students enrolled in social science programs (anthropology, sociology, political science, and social science) as Figure 3.4 shows.

The growth in the number of graduate students receiving a degree annually is even more impressive: from around 150 in the early 1980s, this number grew to 624 by 1999, a fourfold increase in around ten years (Fig. 3.5).

Figure 3.5 presents additional information on the scale of graduate studies in the social sciences: by 1999, the system had about five hundred Ph.D. professors, or one Ph.D. professor per five students enrolled. According to CAPES, the downturn after 1995 is a result of a change in data collection

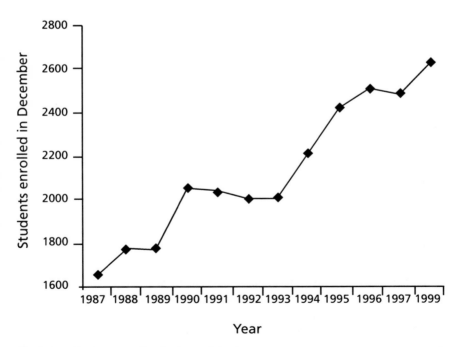

Fig 3.4   Graduate studies in the social sciences

techniques toward greater accuracy, making it impossible to double count (the same person teaching in two or three institutions).

Detailed information on the evolution of financial support for research in the social sciences in the last two decades is much more difficult to obtain. Qualitative information collected in the main agencies, including FAPESP, indicates a similar trend: resources for social science research increased markedly. In addition to the growth in the financial support provided by the responsible agencies (mainly CNPq, CAPES, FINEP, and FAPESP), other state agencies such as the Education, Health, Family Agriculture and Agrarian Reform, Labor, Welfare, and Planning ministries increased the amount of resources given for research contracts in the social sciences.

There is also some indirect evidence of growth. At least three new institutional arrangements to support financially scientific research have been created in Brazil recently. The grants provided show that the social sciences have benefited from these arrangements. In 1995–96 a new program was created at the federal level for providing financial support to high-quality research groups, named PRONEX (Programa de Apoio a Centros de Excelência). At present, around ten research groups in the social sciences (anthropology, political science, sociology, and interdisciplinary groups involving the three

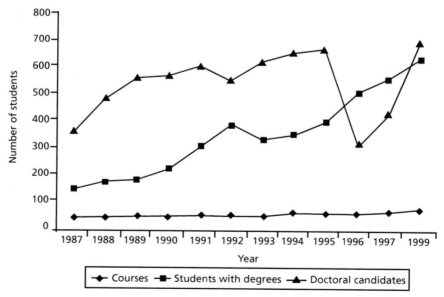

Fig 3.5   Data on social science graduate studies

disciplines) qualified for this support. In the broader field of the so-called human and social sciences (including economics, administration, psychology, demography, history, and philosophy), twenty-five such groups have received support.

At the state level, in São Paulo, two such initiatives took place in the 1990s. FAPESP began providing financial support on a more stable basis for research groups organized around issues that were considered strategic. These projects, (*projetos temáticos*) became very important as a source of stable, longer-term, financial support. More recently, FAPESP used an open competition judged by an international jury to finance more complex, inter-institutional research groups for a period of eleven years, subject to periodic evaluations of the progress of the group. Ten such research groups were chosen, in all scientific fields. Two social sciences research networks were selected, and both have a strong policy-oriented component. One, organized around CEBRAP (Centro Brasileiro de Análise e Planejamento), deals with the metropolitan area of São Paulo. The other, organized around the Núcleo de Estudos sobre Violência, from the Universidade de São Paulo, will study violence, perhaps the most critical social problem in contemporary Brazil.

The CNPq (Conselho Nacional de Pesquisa), the leading institution in basic scientific research support in Brazil, organized a directory of research groups in all academic areas. According to their latest data, in the year 2000 there were 325 research groups in anthropology, political science, and sociology (113, 72, and 187, respectively), involving almost two thousand Ph.D.s and working on 1,447 research topics. Publications by Brazilian scholars in foreign journals and presses have reached almost four hundred (394) articles and books—a sevenfold increase from the figures ten years earlier (57).

There is another dimension to the organizational and institutional changes taking place in recent decades that are relevant to the growth of the social science literature on social policy analysis. This is the material infrastructure underlying academic research and publication in the social sciences. Two aspects of this material basis deserve mention. One is the growth in computing facilities that results from the revolution that occurred in information technology, particularly the availability of the personal computer. Besides the access to global information that this revolution is promoting, there is an increase in the availability of means—including sophisticated and easy-to-use software—to quickly process large amounts of information. Today this is available at the desks of most social scientists, together with advanced mathematical, statistical, and econometric analytical tools, adapted to the characteristics of social information data.

Second, but also related to the material infrastructure, is the availability of large sets of data relevant to social processes, public opinion, and social policy. These data bases are becoming larger, more up-to-date, and increasingly available in Brazilian universities, and even among the larger public. This includes governmental data of all sorts. The joint effect of the pressures for an increase in governmental transparency and the spread of the so-called e-government, are and will continue to guarantee the continued growth in the production of this kind of data. Effective policy analysis can benefit from both material conditions.

All these trends lead to at least one conclusion: during the last twenty years, the social sciences expanded and their institutional space became denser. As a result, competition is increasing, and some differentiation is taking place. Together with the change in paradigms and the differentiation in the demand for social science inputs, this institutional transformation partially explains the emergence of a specialized field of inquiry dedicated to the study of public policies.

The last strategic component of this process that I intend to highlight is related to the political and governmental spheres. It is to the discussion of this last aspect that I now turn.

Redemocratization and "the Government of the Professors"

The last social process associated with the emergence of public policy analysis as an academic field of inquiry in the Brazilian social sciences is the end of authoritarianism and the consolidation of democracy. The end of authoritarianism and the consequent progressive strengthening of democratic institutions in Brazil was the result of a long process. It can be attributed to factors internal to the military regime, to factors associated with the exhaustion of the growth regime associated with state-led import-substitution industrialization, to factors linked to the third wave of democratization, and to the technological revolution and its impact on the reorganization of capitalism worldwide.

For the purpose of studying social policy analysis, a specific component of this process is also relevant, namely the deterioration in state policies of social protection. After a set of initiatives taken by the authoritarian regime in the early 1970s, the capacity of the Brazilian state to provide adequate institutions and policies of social protection grew progressively worse. In a context of immoral inequality, rampant poverty, extremely high inflation rates, very high internal and external debt, growing fiscal crisis, and slow economic growth, the highly centralized, fragmented, corporatist, and expensive social protection policies almost collapsed in the period from the 1970s onward (Draibe 1985; Faria 1992; Camargo 1974). In fact, the mobilization against this social crisis was one of the points around which the democratic opposition could rally. Social scientists and intellectuals played a preeminent role in this mobilization (Faria 1995). After democratization, the renewal of Brazilian social policy became a central concern of democratic, progressive forces.

In the first phase of democratic consolidation, which took place between 1978 and 1990, this concern was expressed through the administrations of the mayors elected democratically in this period, and through democratically elected governors chosen in 1981, particularly Governor Franco Montoro, in the state of São Paulo (1982–86), through the administration of President Sarney (1985–90), and particularly through the Constitutional Reform (1988). In this phase, the concern with social policy appeared in the emphasis on the extension of social rights and on the expansion of social expenditures, together with a strong emphasis on decentralization and popular participation. The constitutional reform of 1985, by incorporating these demands into the Constitution, in detail and extensively, culminated this stage.

However, at this stage, there was limited reform of the social protection policies inherited from the past, and scant attention was given to the worsening fiscal situation. The economic and social crises deepened in a situation of "controlled hyperinflation." The election and the disastrous administration of President Collor de Mello (1991–92) ended this phase by introducing the need for structural reforms into the policy agenda to face the challenges resulting from the collapse of state-led import-substitution industrialization. Social investment and expenditures shrank, and social services deteriorated further.

A new stage of economic and social reforms followed the impeachment of President Collor, particularly with the onset of the Plano Real, designed by the then finance minister of President Itamar Franco, the sociologist Fernando Henrique Cardoso. Elected president in 1994, Fernando Henrique Cardoso organized a center-right political coalition under the hegemony of the Partido da Social Democracia Brasileira (PSDB), committed to a program of economic adjustment (fiscal austerity, opening the economy, macroeconomic stabilization, and privatization) and social policy reform (universal social services, fiscal equilibrium, decentralization, participation and public control to end clientelism, and restructuring of benefits to increase their redistributive impact).

Throughout these years, social scientists and intellectuals, who had previously been critical of social policy and politically active in opposition
to government, became increasingly involved in policymaking and policy
implementation in municipal and state administrations, culminating in their
performing a key role in implementing Cardoso's reforms. Their presence
as central actors in these processes became so salient that Cardoso's government was sometimes referred to, somewhat critically, as the government
of the "professors." Though the government of President Cardoso was based
on a large and heterogeneous center-right party coalition, the majority of its
ministers, particularly in the strategic economic and social sectors, were former university professors, including economists, sociologists, and political
scientists. These "cadres" occupied, among others, the Ministries of Finance,
the Central Bank, Planning, Foreign Relations, Education, Health, Labor,
and Culture, and had a preeminent role at the President's Office, and at the
Ministry of Agrarian Reform.

The growing demand for social protection policies resulting from the
strengthening of democracy, the need for and the commitment to reforming welfare institutions, and the need to maintain, and even increase, social
investment and expenditures in a context of fiscal austerity all combined to
increase the demand for a more rational design, implementation, and evaluation of public policy. Also, the renewal of democratic institutions implied
a growing role for the Congress and other institutions of representative
democracy. It also promoted the further development of new and diversified mechanisms of public control and popular participation. The increase
in democratic electoral competition between parties, freedom of the press,
and strengthening of public debate entailed the growth of deliberative
democracy. All these processes converged to increase the demand for social
policy analysis and evaluation. Economists have been playing a central role
in meeting this demand, but the same is unclear with respect to the social
sciences. What is unquestionable, however, is the growing demand for their
contribution.

Social Science and Social Policy:
Some Conclusions and Two Recommendations

Carol H. Weiss (1993) has called attention to the different ways in which
the public agenda and sociology (or more broadly, the social sciences) are
or could be related. She summarizes this relationship in terms of four basic

scenarios: government influences the sociological agenda; sociology affects government policies; sociology and government have little mutual influence; and sociology and policy both respond to the zeitgeist of the times. She also mentions the possibility of two-step flows: for instance, sociologists influence economists and the latter influence government, or sociologists influence the media, and the media influence the policy process (Weiss 1993)

In this short paper I cannot explore these alternatives rigorously. But I suggest that, in Brazil, scenarios one and four are the more plausible, as well as the importance of two-step flows, particularly those involving economists. In the same book, John W. Kingdom asks an interesting question: "Why should politicians and other policymakers pay attention to social scientists? . . . what special claim might they be able to make?" (Kingdom 1993, 47). Kingdom's answer is as follows:

> If public policy needs to deal with [a host of] problems, then perhaps social scientists who have studied these things would be a useful resource. But the claim turns critically on the existence of a solid foundation of basic research in which the methodology is sound, the findings are firmly established, and the interpretations of data are not subject to dispute. It turns furthermore on the relevance of that research for practical public policy problems. Social scientists need to ask themselves realistically how often their expertise really is a reliable guide to public policy, how sure they really are of their findings and interpretations, and how much the purposes of public policy really can be served by the research. Without solid claims to expertise, social scientists are just another interest group in the political process [and not a very powerful one, one should add], no more and no less important. (Kingdom 1993, 47–48)

My conclusion is that in Brazil we are a long way from meeting these exigencies. Let me give two examples dealing with how the technical literature covers two central concerns of social policy: the measurement of poverty and policy recommendations to fight inequality. In a recent paper, Székely and others (2000) examine the literature on poverty estimation in Latin America, including Brazil. They explore the consequences of adopting different poverty lines, different methods of international comparison, and different parameters that depend on the assumptions and choices made by the analyst (economists and social scientists). The latter include adopting an adult equivalence scale, varying assumptions concerning economies of scale in consumption, treating missing and zero incomes in different ways, and adopting a range of adjustment for misreporting or underreporting. They reach the conclusion that "if it were believed that poverty should be measured by following [a selected] benchmark method, the conclusion would be that there are 243.5 million poor individuals in Latin America and the Caribbean, equivalent to 50.7 percent of the population. However, if some underlying assumptions *vary within reasonable boundaries,* the proportion of poor could be said to be either 60.96 or 315.8 million, which is 12.7 percent or 65.8 percent of the total population" (Székely et al. 2000, 29). For Brazil, the figures could vary between 16.4 percent and 66.7 percent! Which of these varying estimates are based on solid research, sound methodology, firmly established, and not subject to dispute?

A final illustration comes from studies of policy recommendations for fighting income inequality in Brazil. After careful and sophisticated econometric and statistical analysis, some researchers reached the conclusion that a redistribution of income of about 3 percent of the Brazilian national income would be sufficient to eliminate poverty. The implication implicit in some of these studies is that only "political will" would be necessary to develop such a policy. Would a social scientist with an average knowledge of the politics of social policy sponsor such a candid view?

To conclude, let me offer two simple and straightforward recommendations for enhancing the influence of social science research on social policy. First, social science in Brazil should considerably increase its expertise in and its commitment to comparative studies. By doing so, public policy analysis would benefit from the quality of research conducted in other places and also learn from the experiences of policy implementation in different contexts. Comparative studies, hopefully, would call attention to the role played by institutions and would help to illuminate opportunities and restrictions stemming from different institutional frameworks. Comparative research would also help Brazilian social scientists exercise what Guerreiro Ramos, long ago, called *redução sociológica,* that is, the ability to take seriously the sociological limits to the transfer and adoption of abstract policy recommendations.

Second, a cursory examination of graduate curricula shows that Brazilian social science graduate students lack adequate training in disciplines that are basic to high-quality social science, both in the hard sciences (mathematics and statistics, for example) and in the humanities (philosophy and sophisticated, up-to-date, social theory). Without improved training, the social sciences in Brazil, particularly in the field of policy analysis, will continue to lose influence despite its numerical expansion in recent years.

Appendix

1. Persons interviewed by e-mail: Sergio Abranches, Alice Paiva Abreu, Maria Lygia Barbosa, Pedro Luiz Barros Filho, Luiz Carlos Bresser Pereira, Fernando Henrique Cardoso, Antonio Octávio Cintra, Amaury De Souza, Sonia Draibe, Gelson Fonseca, José Arthur Gianotti, Maria Helena Guimarães Castro, Ricardo Henriques, Celso Lafer, George Lamaziere, Bolivar Lamounier, Roque Laraia, Fernando Limongi, Pedro Malan, Marcus Melo, Eduardo Rios Neto, José Américo Pacheco, Fábio Wanderley Reis, Maria Celi Scalon, Simon Schwartzmann, José Serra, Alexandrina Sobreira, Lourdes Sola, Maria Hermínia Tavares De Almeida, Gilberto Velho, and Francisco Weffort.

2. Publications mentioned by the persons interviewed:
   a. Most frequently cited works:
      (1) Those conducted under the supervision of IPEA:
         Barros, Ricardo Paes, ed. 1997. *Bem-estar, pobreza e desigualdade de renda: uma avaliação histórica das disparidades regionais.* Rio de Janeiro: IPEA.
         Barros, Ricardo Paes de, Ricardo Henriques, and Rosane Mendonça. 1993. "A Evolução do Bem-Estar e da Desigualdade no Brasil desde 1960." In *Desenvolvimento Econômico, Investimento, Mercado de Trabalho e Distribuição de Renda,* ed. Ricardo Paes de Barros, Rosane Silva Pinto de Mendonça, et al. Rio de Janeiro: Banco Nacional de Desenvolvimento Econômico e Social (BNDES).
         ———. 2000. "A estabilidade inaceitável: desigualdade e pobreza no Brasil." In *Desigualdade e Pobreza no Brasil,* ed. R. Henriques. Rio de Janeiro: IPEA.
         ———. 2000. "Pelo fim das décadas perdidas: educação e desenvolvimento sustentado no Brasil." In *Desigualdade e Pobreza no Brasil,* ed. R. Henriques. Rio de Janeiro: IPEA.
         Henriques, Ricardo, ed. 2000. *Desigualdade e Pobreza no Brasil.* Rio de Janeiro: IPEA.
      (2) Those conducted by NEPP (UNICAMP):
         Draibe, Sonia. 1998. *O Sistema Brasileiro de Proteção Social: o Legado Desenvolvimentista e a Agenda Recente de Reformas.* Campinas: Editora da UNICAMP, NEPP.
         ———, ed. Various years (1985, 1986, 1987, 1988). *Brasil 19 . . .—*

Relatório sobre a Situação Social do País. Campinas: Editora da UNICAMP, NEPP / UNICAMP.

Draibe, S. M., and M. Arretche, eds. 1995. "Políticas y Programas de Combate a la Pobreza en Brasil." In *Estratégias para Combatir la Pobreza en America Latina: Programas, Instituciones y Recursos,* ed. Dagmar Raczynski. Santiago: CIEPLAN / BID.

Faria, Vilmar. 1991. "A montanha e a pedra: os limites da política social brasileira e os problemas da infância e da juventude." In *O Trabalho e a Rua—Crianças e Adolescentes no Brasil urbano dos anos 80,* ed. Ayrton Fausto and Ruben Cervini. São Paulo: Cortez.

———. 1992. *A conjuntura social brasileira: dilemas e perspectivas.* Novos Estudos CEBRAP no. 33. São Paulo: CEBRAP.

Faria, Vilmar, and Maria Helena G. Castro. 1990. "Social Policy and Democratic Consolidation in Brazil." In *The Political Economy of Brazil: Public Policies in an Era of Transition,* ed. Robert Wilson. Austin: University of Texas Press.

Faria, Vilmar, and Guillermo O'Donnel. 1995. *Social Policies for the Urban Poor in Southern Latin America.* New York: Kellogg University.

Silva, Pedro Luiz Barros. 1998. *Reforma do Estado e Política Social no Brasil. Êxitos, Problemas e Desafios da Coordenação Intergovernamental.* Campinas: NEPP.

(3) The following books:

Coutinho, Luciano G., and João C. e Ferraz, ed. 1994. *Estudo da Competitividade da Indústria Brasileira.* Campinas: Papirus.

Pastore, José, and Nelson do Valle e Silva. 2000. *Mobilidade Social no Brasil.* Rio de Janeiro: Makron Books.

b. Bibliography (Anthologies, Articles, and Books)

(1) Anthologies (*Coletâneas*)

Abreu, Alice, ed. 2000. *Produção Flexível e novas institucionalidades na América Latina.* Rio de Janeiro: Editora da UFRJ.

Affonso, R., and P.L.B. Silva, eds. 1996/7. *Série Federalismo no Brasil.* 6 volumes. São Paulo: Editora UNESP / FUNDAP.

Barros, Ricardo Paes, ed. 1997. *Bem-estar, pobreza e desigualdade de renda: uma avaliação histórica das disparidades regionais.* Rio de Janeiro: IPEA.

Baumann, Renato, ed. 1996. *Brasil e a Economia Global.* Rio de Janeiro: Campus.

Bolívar, Lamounier, and Steven Friedman, ed. 1997. *Brasil e África do Sul—Uma Comparação.* São Paulo: Editora Sumaré.

Castro, Antonio B., Mario Possas, and Adriano Proença, eds. 1996. *Estratégias Empresariais no Brasil- Discutindo o Desenvolvimento.* Rio de Janeiro: Forense.

Coutinho, Luciano G., and João C. Ferraz, eds. 1994. *Estudo da Competitividade da Indústria Brasileira.* Campinas: Papirus.

Draibe, Sonia M., ed. 1988. *Brasil 1987. Relatório sobre a Situação Social do País.* Campinas: Editora da UNICAMP, NEPP / IE-UNICAMP.

Fiori, J. L., ed. 1999. *Estados e Moedas no Desenvolvimento das Nações.* Rio de Janeiro: Editora Vozes.

Henriques, Ricardo, ed. 2000. *Desigualdade e Pobreza no Brasil.* Rio de Janeiro: IPEA.

Micelli, Sérgio, ed. 1999. *O que ler na Ciência Social Brasileira (1970–1995).* São Paulo: Editora Sumaré / ANPOCS.

Pinheiro, Armando Castelar, ed. 2000. *Judiciário e Economia no Brasil.* São Paulo: Editora Sumaré.

Sadek, Maria Tereza, ed. 1999. *Justiça e Cidadania no Brasil.* São Paulo: Editora Sumaré.

Schwartzman, Simon, ed. 1995. *Science and Technology in Brazil: A New Policy for a Global World.* Rio de Janeiro: Editora Fundação Getúlio Vargas.

Tavares, M. Conceição, and J. L. Fiori, eds. 1997. *Poder e Dinheiro.* São Paulo: Editora Vozes.

Veiga, Pedro da Motta, ed. 2000. *O Brasil e os Desafios da Globalização.* Rio de Janeiro: Relume Dumará.

Velloso, João Paulo dos Reis, and Roberto Cavalcanti de Albuquerque, eds. 1994. *Modernidade e Pobreza.* São Paulo: Nobel.

———. 2000. *Pobreza, Cidadania e Segurança.* Rio de Janeiro: José Olímpio.

(2) Articles

Amaury de Souza. 1999. "Cardoso and the Struggle for Reform in Brazil." *Journal of Democracy* 10:49–63.

Barros, Ricardo Paes de, and Rosane Silva Pinto Mendonça. 1993. "A Evolução do Bem-Estar e da Desigualdade no Brasil desde 1960." In *Desenvolvimento Econômico, Investimento, Mercado de Trabalho e Distribuição de Renda,* ed. Ricardo Paes de Barros, Rosane Silva Pinto de Mendonça, et al. Rio de Janeiro:

Banco Nacional de Desenvolvimento Econômico e Social (BNDES).

——. 2000. "A estabilidade inaceitável: desigualdade e pobreza no Brasil." In *Desigualdade e Pobreza no Brasil,* ed. R. Henriques. Rio de Janeiro: IPEA.

——. 2000. "Pelo fim das décadas perdidas: educação e desenvolvimento sustentado no Brasil." In *Desigualdade e Pobreza no Brasil,* ed. R. Henriques. Rio de Janeiro: IPEA.

Barros, R. P., and F. Ferreira. 1999. "The Slippery Slope: Explaining the Increase in Extreme Poverty in Urban Brazil, 1976–1996." World Bank Working Paper no. 2210, World Bank, Washington, D.C.

Bolivar, Lamounier, and Edmar Bacha. 1995. "Democracy and Economic Reform in Brazil." In *Democracy and Economic Reform in Latin America and East Europe,* ed. Joan Nelson. Washington, D.C.: Overseas Development Council.

Bresser Pereira, Luiz Carlos. 1999. "From Bureaucratic to Managerial Public Administration in Brazil." In *Reforming the State: Managerial Public Administration in Latin America,* ed. Luiz Carlos Bresser Pereira and Peter Spink. Boulder, Colo.: Lynne Rienner.

Cardoso de Melo, J. M., and F. A. Novaes. 1998. "Capitalismo Tardio e Sociabilidade Moderna." In *História da Vida Privada no Brasil,* vol. 4, ed. F. Novaes. São Paulo: Cia das Letras.

Castro, Antonio Barros de. 2000. "Blockage versus Continuity in Brazil." In *Institutions and the Role of the State,* ed. Leonardo Burlamaqui, Ana Celia Castro, and Há Joon Chang. London: Elgar.

Castro, Nádia de. 1995. "Modernização e trabalho no complexo automotivo brasileiro. In *A Máquina e o Equilibrista. Inovações na indústria Automobilística brasileira.* São Paulo: Paz e Terra.

Diniz, Eli. 1995. "Governabilidade, Democracia e Reforma do Estado. Os desafios da construção de uma nova ordem no Brasil dos Anos 90." *DADOS* 38.

Draibe, Sonia M. 1997. "Repensando a política social: dos anos 80 aos anos 90." In *Lições da década de 80,* ed. L. Sola and L. Paulani. São Paulo: Edusp.

Draibe, S. M., and M. Arretche. 1995. "Políticas y Programas de Combate a la Pobreza en Brasil." In *Estratégias para Combatir la Pobreza en America Latina: Programas, Instituciones y Recursos,* ed. Dagmar Raczynski. Santiago: CIEPLAN / BID.

Faria, Vilmar. 1991. "Os limites da política social brasileira e os problemas da infância e da juventude." In *O Trabalho e a Rua—Crianças e Adolescentes no Brasil urbano dos anos 80,* ed. Ayrton Fausto and Ruben Cervini. São Paulo: Cortez.

———. 1992. *A conjuntura social brasileira: dilemas e perspectivas. Novos Estudos CEBRAP,* no. 33.

Faria, Vilmar, and Maria Helena G. Castro. 1990. "Social Policy and Democratic Consolidation in Brazil." In *The Political Economy of Brazil: Public Policies in an Era of Transition,* ed. Robert Wilson. Austin: University of Texas Press.

———.1989. "Política Social e Consolidação Democrática no Brasil." In *O Estado e as políticas públicas na transição democrática,* ed. Alexandrina Sobreira de Moura. São Paulo: Vértice.

Fry, P. 2000. "Politics, Nationality and the Meanings of Race in Brazil." *Daedalus* 129, no. 2:83–118.

Galvão, Marcus. 1998. "Globalização: arautos, céticos e críticos." Pts. 1 and 2. *Revista Política Externa* 6, no. 4 (March 1998); 7, no. 1 (June 1998).

Hoffmann, R. 1992. "Vinte anos de desigualdade e pobreza na agricultura brasileira." *Revista de Economia e Sociologia Rural* 30, no. 2:97–113.

Lafer, Celso. 2000. "Brazilian International Identity and Foreign Policy: Past, Present and Future." *Daedalus: Journal of the American Academy of Arts and Sciences* 129, no. 2 (spring).

Lamounier, Bolivar. 1992. "A democracia brasileira dos anos 80 e 90: a syndrome da paralisia hiperativa." In *Governabilidade, Sistema Político e Violência Urbana,* ed. João Paulo dos Reis. Rio de Janeiro: José Olímpio.

———. 1997. "Inequalities Against Democracy." In *Democracy in Developing Countries,* ed. Larry Diamond. Boulder, Colo.: Lynne Rienner.

Limongi, Fernando, Argelina Figueiredo, and Ana Luiza Valente. 1999. "Governabilidade e concentração de poder institucional? Governo FHC." *Tempo Social—Revista de Sociologia* 11, no. 2:59–62.

Mesquita, M., and S. Najberg. 2000. "Trade Liberalization in

Brazil: Creating or Exporting Jobs." *Journal of Development Studies* 36, no. 3.

Moura Castro, C. 2000. "Education: Way Behind, But Trying to Catch Up." *Daedalus* 129, no. 2:291–314.

Nakano, Yoshiaki. 1994. "Globalização, Competitividade e Novas Regras do Comércio Mundial." *Revista de Economia Política* 14, no. 4 (October).

Proença, Adriano, and Heitor M. Caulliraux. 1997. "Estratégias de Produção na Indústria Brasileira: Evolução Recente." In *Brasil: Desafios de um País em Transformação,* ed. João Paulo dos Reis Velloso. Rio de Janeiro: José Olímpio.

Reis, Elisa P. 2000. "Percepções da elite sobre pobreza e desigualdade." In *Desigualdade e Pobreza no Brasil,* ed. R. Henriques. Rio de Janeiro: IPEA.

Reis, Fábio. 2000. "Cidadania, Corporativismo e Política Social no Brasil." Republished in *Mercado e Utopia: Teoria Política e Sociedade Brasileira,* ed. Vilmar Faria. São Paulo: Edusp.

Rocha, Sônia. 1992. "Pobreza no Brasil: Parâmetros Básicos e Resultados Empíricos." *Pesquisa e Planejamento Econômico* 22, no. 3 (December).

———. 1996. "Renda e pobreza: os impactos do Plano Real." *Revista Brasileira de Estudos Populacionais* (Campinas) 13, no. 2 (July-December).

Sola, Lourdes. 1994. "Estado, Transformação Econômica e Democratização no Brasil." In *Estado, Mercado, Democracia,* ed. Sola Lourdes. São Paulo: Paz e Terra.

Souza, Amaury de. 1997. "Redressing Inequalities: Brazil´s Social Agenda at Century´s End." In *Brazil Under Cardoso,* ed. Susan Kaufman Purcell and Riordan Roett. Boulder, Colo.: Lynne Rienner.

Veloso, João Paulo dos Reis. 2000. *Brasil 500 anos—Futuro, Presente, Passado.* Rio de Janeiro: José Olímpio.

(3) Books

Abramo, Laís. 1990. *Novas tecnologias, difusão setorial, emprego e trabalho no Brasil.* Washington, D.C.: BID.

Almeida, Maria Hermínia Tavares de. 1995. *Federalismo e políticas sociais. Revista de Ciencias Sociais* 10, no. 28:88–108.

Arantes, Rogério Bastos. 1999. *Judiciário e Política no Brasil.* São Paulo: Editora Sumaré.

Barros, Ricardo Paes de, and Fábio Giambiagi. 1999. *A Economia Brasileira nos Anos 90*. Rio de Janeiro: Banco Nacional de Desenvolvimento Econômico e Social—BNDES.

Becker, Bertha, and Cláudio Egler. 1993. *Brasil: Uma Nova Potência Regional na Economia-Mundo*. Rio de Janeiro: Bertrand Brasil.

Bresser Pereira, Luiz Carlos. 1998. *Reforma do Estado para a Cidadania*. São Paulo: Editora 34.

Cardoso, Adalberto M. 2000. *Trabalhar, verbo intransitivo*. Rio de Janeiro: Fundação Getúlio Vargas.

Carvalho, José Murilo de. 1990. *A Formação das Almas—O Imaginário da República*. São Paulo: Companhia das Letras.

———. 1998. *Pontos e Bordados—Escritos de História e Política*. Belo Horizonte, Brazil: Editora UFMG.

Castro, Cláudio de Moura. 1994. *Educação brasileira consertos e remendos*. Rio de Janeiro: Rocco.

———. 1999. *Estratégias de reforma do ensino superior na América Latina*. Washington, D.C.: BID.

Castro, Nádia de. 1995. *A Máquina e o Equilibrista*. São Paulo: Paz e Terra.

Cohn, Amélia. 1991. *A Saúde como direito e como serviço*. São Paulo: Cortez / cedec.

Diniz, Eli. 1997. *Crise, Reforma do Estado e Governabilidade*. Rio de Janeiro: Fundação Getúlio Vargas.

Diniz, E., and S. Azevedo. 1997. *Reforma do Estado e Democracia no Brasil*. Brasília: Universidade de Brasília.

Draibe, Sonia. 1998. *O Sistema Brasileiro de Proteção Social: o Legado Desenvolvimentista e a Agenda Recente de Reformas*. Caderno de Pesquisa, no. 32. São Paulo: unicamp.

Dupas, Gilberto. 2003. *Economia Global e Exclusão Social*. São Paulo: Paz e Terra.

Faria, Vilmar, and Guillermo O'Donnel. 1995. *Social Policies for the Urban Poor in Southern Latin America*. New York: Kellogg University.

Figueiredo, A., and F. Limongi. 1999. *Executivo e Legislativo na nova ordem constitucional*. Rio de Janeiro: Fundação Getúlio Vargas.

Fonseca Jr., Gélson. 1998. *A Legitimidade e Outras Questões Internacionais*. São Paulo: Paz e Terra.

Franco, Gustavo. 1995. *O Plano Real e Outros Ensaios.* Rio de Janeiro: F. Alves.

Furtado, Celso. 1992. *Brasil: A Construção Interrompida.* Rio de Janeiro: Paz e Terra.

Gouvêa, Gilda Portugal. 1994. *Burocracia e Elites Dominantes do País.* São Paulo: Editora Paulicéia.

Hasenbalg, Carlos A., and Nelson do Valle Silva. 1998. *Estrutura social, mobilidade e raça.* São Paulo: Vértice.

Lafer, Celso. 1998. *A OMC e a Regulamentação do Comércio Internacional: Uma Visão Brasileira.* Porto Alegre: Livraria do Advogado.

Lamounier, Bolivar. 1996. *A democracia brasileira no limiar do século 21.* São Paulo: Konrad-Adenauer-Stiftung / Centro de Estudos.

Lavareda, Antonio. 1999. *A Democracia nas Urnas. O Processo Partidário Eleitoral Brasileiro, 1945–1964.* Rio de Janeiro: Iuperj / Editora Revan.

Martins, C. E. 1997. *Da globalização da economia à falência da democracia. Economia e Sociedade.* Campinas: Instituto de Economia, unicamp.

Mello, Guiomar Namo de. 1991. *Política Educacional do Governo Collor.* São Paulo: FUNDAP.

Pastore, José, Nelson do Valle e Silva. 2000. *Mobilidade Social no Brasil.* São Paulo: Makron Books.

Ramos, Alcida. 1998. *Indigenism. Ethnic Politic in Brazil.* Madison: University of Wisconsin Press.

Ribeiro, Gustavo Lins. 1991. *Empresas transnacionais. Um grande projeto por dentro.* São Paulo: ANPOCS / Editora MarcoZero.

Rodrigues, Leôncio Martins. 1998. *Destino do Sindicalismo: crisis o declinio.* São Paulo: Editora USP.

Santos, Wanderley Guilhermo dos. 1993. *Razões da Desordem.* Rio de Janeiro: Rocco.

Scalon, Maria Celi. 1999. *Mobilidade social no Brasil: padrões e tendências.* Rio de Janeiro: Editora Revan.

Schwartzman, Simon, Carlos Osmar Bertero, and Eduardo Krieger. 1995. *Science and Technology in Brazil: A New Policy for a Global World.* Rio de Janeiro: Fundação Getúlio Vargas.

Salles-Filho, Sérgio. 2000. *Ciência, Tecnologia e Inovação—A reorganização da pesquisa pública no Brasil.* Campinas: Editora Komedi.

Silva, Pedro Luiz Barros. 1998. *Reforma do Estado e Política Social no Brasil. Êxitos, Problemas e Desafios da Coordenação Intergovernamental.* Campinas: NEPP.

Vianna, Maria Lucia Werneck. 1998. *A americanização (perversa) da seguridade social no Brasil.* Rio de Janeiro: Editora Revan.

Zaluar, Alba. 1996. *Da revolta ao crime S. A.* São Paulo: Editora Moderna.

(4) Theses and Dissertations

Sola, Lourdes. 1994. *Qual Estado? Ajustamento Estrutural como Política e como História: o Brasil em Perspectiva Comparada.* Thesis for the Department of Social Sciences of the University of São Paulo, March.

(5) Some interviewees also cited the following individual authors, without specifying any books or articles: Roberto Da Matta, Lena Lavinas, Yvonne Maggie, Laura Mello e Souza, Marcus Mello, Renato Ortiz, and Vanilda Paiva.

PART III

Citizenship, Politics, and the State

4 Toward a Political Sociology of Social Mobilization in Latin America

JOE FOWERAKER

The Big Picture

This chapter will address the changing trajectory of social mobilization in Latin America through the transitions from authoritarian rule to democratic governance. It will focus on the relations between grassroots organizations and democratic governments in a period of neoliberal ascendancy and assess their influence on the making and implementation of social policy. In doing so it will seek to question the prevalent interpretations of first, social movements, and subsequently, NGOs. There is no disputing the enormous investment of political energy and imagination in social mobilization. But what political difference does it make?

In this way the chapter sets out to respond to the challenge of presenting a coherent view of the political sociology of social mobilization in Latin America in a spirit of positive inquiry. Necessarily, the inquiry will encompass some rather grand themes, including social movements and citizenship rights, democratic transitions and the decline of social movements, the transformation of grassroots organizing and the rise of the NGOs, and the possibilities of social development in the continent. The aim is to move beyond the particular histories of mobilization and look at the big picture.

This picture shows that much has changed in Latin America in recent years. The general elections in Chile and Brazil in 1989 marked "the first time that all the Ibero-American nations, excepting Cuba, enjoyed the benefits of elected constitutional governments at the same time" (Valenzuela 1993, 3). This occurrence was not as dramatic or visible as the collapse of Communism and the transitions to democracy in Eastern and Central Europe, which began in the same year, but it did mark a historical watershed. After almost two centuries as independent states, the countries of Latin America now comprised a new democratic universe.

At the same time, most of the new democracies in Latin America embarked upon the kind of economic stabilization and structural adjustment policies that are known collectively as the Washington consensus. The conventional list of policy initiatives in the Washington consensus includes stabilization by orthodox fiscal and monetary constraints, an increase in international competition, and a reduced role for the state in the economy (Bresser Pereira 1993). The consensus has been grudgingly accepted even in countries where the state had traditionally played a salient economic role, such as Brazil, as a result of the debt crisis of the 1980s and the ensuing economic recession.

Consequently, it is important to ask how social mobilization has adapted (or not) to this new context of democratic rule and neoliberal policy prescriptions. It will be seen that social movements have often declined or been transformed (or both), leading to an emphasis on negotiation rather than mobilization, and an increasing interaction with state agencies. NGOs, in contrast, have both multiplied and become more visible, but where they interact with the state they may become subordinated to state policy, and where they fail to interact they may be ineffective.

Not only the organization but also the focus of grassroots mobilization has changed over the period of military or oligarchic rule, democratic transition, and neoliberal democracy. The early efforts of the 1960s focused on popular organization and education. The grassroots groups of the 1970s were more fully engaged in the struggle against poverty and the fight for citizenship rights. Those of the 1980s were more concerned with gender issues, survival strategies, and human rights. In very recent years the priority agenda has become the environment and "micro-financing" such as communal banks, rural cooperatives, and credit unions (ALOP 1999), as well as local development projects and technical assistance programs (Valderrama 1998, 11). These diverse initiatives have accumulated over the years and are all present in greater or lesser degrees in Latin American civil societies today, so that the panorama of grassroots organizations has become ever more plural (Patrón 1998, 194). This does not mean that social movements and NGOs cannot achieve some positive impact on social policy or institutional reform, but it does mean that their impact is unlikely to be fundamental.

The Analysis of Social Movements

It must be said that the mainstream analysis of Latin American social movements is ill equipped to address the big questions. This is because its dominant perspective is typically parochial in at least two respects. On the one hand, its obsessive focus on the particular and often local identities implicit in social movement organization tends to preclude proper attention to social movements as regional and national political actors (Calderón 1986; Escobar and Alvarez 1992). On the other, it does not encompass the study of social movements in other places outside Latin America at other historical times, and so may simply mistake the true political meaning of social movement activity—a point I shall return to. Alain Touraine is a significant exception to this tendency. But Touraine sets his analytical threshold too high for most Latin American social movements to qualify as such. According to Touraine, reflection and action on the foundations of social life (reflexivity) become possible for the first time in postindustrial society. The action of social movements will always challenge the fundamental rules of the political system. In this view, there are no social, but only ephemeral popular movements in Latin America (Touraine 1988a, 1989).

Two separate but related points need to be made about the notion of social movement identity and the difficulties it has created for the sociology of social movements. First, there is nothing essential about this identity, since it depends, at least in part, on prior organization, leadership, and strategic decision-making (Foweraker and Landman 1997, 38). What really matters, in other words, is the (political) activity of social movements. Second, the search for identity entails a focus on the microrelationships of community and civil society where political change is imagined as a unique result of changing identities and personal empowerment. Important though these processes may be, this focus tends to ignore the central question of the political and institutional impact of social mobilization. A corollary of the focus on identity is an almost exclusive preoccupation with so-called new social movements and the demotion of older social movements like the labor movement that have a proven capacity to impel political change.

The evidence assembled in Foweraker and Landman (1997) demonstrates the primacy of the labor movement in the popular and democratic struggles of recent decades in Latin America and makes a clear case for "bringing labor back in" (Foweraker and Landman 1997, 231–33). Analogously, it is interesting to note how the mainstream readings of the *zapatista* movement in Chiapas see it as typically "new" in this sense, emphasizing its emblematic presence on the Internet. Yet it could equally well be interpreted as a classic peasant uprising (N. Harvey 1998).

To a variable degree, this parochial perspective constrains the scope of the methods used to study social movements. These tend to be descriptive and reliant on anecdotal evidence of different kinds. There is virtually no

systematic record of social mobilization that counts the incidence of protest, the number of people protesting, the kinds of people protesting, and the
reasons for the protests. Equally, there is remarkably little rigorous ethnography that documents and analyzes the political process of a modern social
movement.[1] Above all, there is a dearth of comparative studies, and no
study at all that can emulate the comparative elegance of Timothy Wickham-
Crowley's (1992) investigation into Latin American guerrilla movements.[2]

   In some instances the scant regard for evidence in the social science
account of social movements appears to seek compensation in a surfeit of
theory. Indeed, the self-conscious search for theoretical innovation of a postmodern stripe is characteristic of much of the literature. Typical in this regard
is the attempt to view Latin American social movements through the lens
of a "cultural politics" that "resignifies" much of the political landscape
(Alvarez, Dagnino, and Escobar 1998, 1–29). In fact there is little that is new
here, once the conceptual inflation has been discounted. These accounts
serve to project the wishes and aspirations of the sociologist onto the social
movements, and latterly the NGOs, under study. They may even project
the sociologist—"scholars, intellectuals and intellectual activists" (Alvarez,
Dagnino, and Escobar 1998, 23)—into the heart of the political drama. The
theory is simply a vehicle for wishful thinking. Such wishful thinking remains unconstrained by evidence. The self-conscious intention and recurrent
claim is to investigate the "less measurable and less visible or submerged
dimensions of contemporary collective action" (Alvarez et al. 1998, 12). Conveniently, investigations of this sort require little in the way of empirical
research.

The Political Meaning of Social Movements

By definition, a parochial perspective does not encompass the big picture
and can miss important analytical opportunities as a consequence. But considering the political meaning of social movements can create an alternative
perspective. Charles Tilly's original definition of a social movement focused
on political activity in the form of pressing political demands through mobilization, on the one hand, and the formal exercise of power on the other. A
social movement is "a sustained series of interactions between power holders

---

1. Among the honorable exceptions are Rubin 1997 and Schneider 1995.
2. Leigh Payne's recent book, *Uncivil Movements: The Armed Right-Wing and Democracy in
Latin America,* combines serious ethnography with an effective use of comparative method.

and persons successfully claiming to speak on behalf of a constituency lacking formal representation, in the course of which those persons make publicly visible demands for changes in the distribution or exercise of power, and back those demands with public demonstrations of support" (Tilly 1984, 306). In the modern era the formal exercise of power is mainly vested in the state, and social movement demands are expressed as claims to rights, or have a potential impact on the extension or exercise of rights. Social movements, therefore, act to mediate the relationship between the individual and the state (Hegel), and to protect individuals from state oppression by defending their rights (Durkheim). In other words, the effective enjoyment of individual rights requires active associations, not just legal guarantees. This is why for modern theorists like Robert Dahl a full sense of citizenship combines the two dimensions of *participation* and (sufficient organizational resources and rights to achieve) *public contestation* (Dahl 1971). Much of the modern history of social movements can be interpreted as the political struggles required to vindicate individual rights in more or less adverse political circumstances.

The rise of modern social movements coincided with the formation of the national and "nationalizing state" in the late eighteenth and early nineteenth centuries (Tilly 1990). The state became a "target for claims" as the movements took advantage of the political spaces created by the state to press for political rights. At the same time the movements developed a new "repertoire of contention" (Tilly 1978) that sharpened their strategic responses to the new political context and prepared them for sustained campaigns of collective action. Local, communal, and reactive struggles became national, thematic, and proactive as many social groups combined to fight for the rights to vote, hold office, and make policy. This does not mean that no social movement has a communal identity any longer (many do) or that reactive claims are not typical of many modern movements, including the labor movement (they are). It is rather that most movements came to recognize a "modular" repertoire of action that could be used by very distinct groups for a wide variety of purposes and goals (Tarrow 1994). The repertoire includes protest meetings, electoral rallies, demonstrations, strikes, and barricades. For its part the state developed standardized procedures for dealing with its citizens, so providing a framework for political action and contributing to shape the trajectory of social movement activity. Long waves of protest firmed up the conventions governing the interaction of social movement and state and prepared the ground for the fully national social movements of the twentieth century.

At the same time the specific demands of particular movements found common expression in a language of rights that underpinned political alliances between the now modular movements. This language is the set of tools used to assemble the components of social struggle and has served the strategic purposes of different movements in widely different cultures, since strategic economy favors the adoption and adaptation of a language that appears universally effective. In fact, it is a perfect example of the kind of "master frame" that promotes effective social mobilization. Thus, the modern social movement is characterized by the historical encounter between modular forms of mobilization and a common language of rights. Just as the new forms of mobilization diffused rights demands, so the language of rights raised the tempo of citizenship struggles (Foweraker and Landman 1997, 34–38). To illustrate, the core notion of "equality of opportunity" sustained the civil rights movement in the U.S. South by binding the Southern black middle class to the white liberal "constituency of conscience," whose external support was essential to the movement's success. A traditional rhetoric of rights was adapted to a new "repertoire of action" that included sit-ins and staged media events (Tarrow 1994).

Social Movements and Citizenship Rights in Latin America

As suggested above, most studies of social movements in Latin America explain them in terms of civil society and confine them to civil society (Foweraker 1995, 24–35). In fact, these social movements have developed in continual and intimate interaction with the state. José Alvaro Moisés (1981), for instance, has argued that the very identity of social movements in Latin America is not formed through social relations so much as forged in close interaction with the state.

Since the state is the main source of scarce resources, social movements have had to approach the state to secure resources. Since the state tends to monopolize power and decision making, it becomes a prime focus of protest and "demand making." The growth of public administration and the multiplication of productive and regulatory agencies that have expanded state involvement in economic and social life have meant that even class struggles typically pit the poor against the state (Davis 1989, 227). Hence, in Latin America as much as in Europe, modern social movements arose at the same time that "institution building took place in the political system as a whole" (Boschi 1987, 201).

The recent history of this relationship between social movements and the state in Latin America is marked, first, by the shift to a predominantly urban society that changed the nature of grassroots mobilization, and second, by the emergence of modern authoritarian and military regimes. The rise of urban social movements was then seen as a response to the precarious conditions of urban life, on the one hand, and the repressive policies of the state, on the other—including the suppression of more traditional forms of political organization like political parties and trade unions. Depending on time, place, and circumstances, urban movements might include new forms of the labor movement, women's movements, teachers' movements, student movements, and movements on behalf of the "disappeared" and exiled. None of this is meant to suggest that labor and agrarian movements suddenly ceased to exist. On the contrary, the labor movement sometimes took on a new salience in opposition to the military regimes.

Since this seemed to be an authentically popular response, the movements were soon seen as a political panacea (Davis 1992, 401)—in much the same way as NGOs in more recent years. Despite this romantic overstatement of their political potential, the movements did express the presence of new social actors, especially women, of new forms of organization, and of new demands stated in a language of *rights* that became widespread throughout Latin America from the 1970s on.

Most of the movements were initially motivated by immediate, concrete, and material demands that were frequently transformed into claims for civil and political rights (Foweraker 1989). Since the material demands were often restricted, repressed, reversed, or delayed, the rights demands tended to focus on the civil and political conditions for pressing demands and making claims. In this way, mobilization driven by the material demands of peasants, workers, women, and poor urban residents could promote struggles for universal rights. If the material demands represented claims for social inclusion and greater participation in the "republic," the demands for legal and political rights (habeas corpus, equality before the law, land rights, labor rights, voting rights) together represented a claim to citizenship and an implicit challenge to the authoritarian regimes of the time.

Some pioneering studies argued cogently that the accumulation of rights claims constituted a popular assertion of democratic citizenship (Jelin 1987, 1990). Yet the peculiar potency of rights demands tended to be attributed to the discovery of international languages of human rights and feminism during an epoch of authoritarian control. In the Latin American context, however, the rights demands were not necessarily separate from the material demands either in space or time, but were integral to the same sui generis and more or less continuous process of demand making.

This process of demand making and the popular assertion of citizenship rights subsume the usual questions of theoretical inquiry such as the distinction between "old" and "new" movements, or the relationship between identity and strategy. These questions are taken as primary, but are in fact subsidiary to the political meaning of social mobilization in the continent. For example, the labor movement often fought first for "economic-corporate" privileges, so tending to trade civil and political rights for social rights. But the restricted form of regulated citizenship achieved through the struggle for social rights provided a political platform for subsequent demands for civil and political rights and eventually made the labor movement into the vanguard of the citizenship struggle.

But the political content of demand making certainly increased during periods of military rule in at least some countries of the continent (Foweraker and Landman 1997). For example, political demands became more important during the latter years of the military regime in Brazil, expanding rapidly during the *diretas já* campaign of 1984, and peaking during the transition to civilian rule of 1985. In Chile, these demands outstripped all others from the early 1980s on, peaking at the height of the national days of protest in 1984. Yet the political effects of the rising tempo of rights demands were very different in the two countries. Social movement activity in Brazil was accompanied by a gradual liberalization of citizenship rights, but in Chile these same rights remained restricted and static until the 1988 plebiscite, despite the social movement struggles of the 1980s (Foweraker and Landman 1997, 143–50, chap. 4).

The rising content of rights demands confirms the close interaction of social movements with the state, since it alone is capable of delivering the rights in question (Caldeira 1990, 48). The "inevitable institutionalism" (Foweraker 1993) of the movements applies a fortiori to grassroots political activity following the democratic transitions in Latin America. Some areas of the state apparatus may become gradually more receptive to popular participation, especially in the urban context (R. Cardoso 1992), while some movements might become "valid interlocutors," in the vernacular, and begin to play significant roles in negotiating policy decisions and political outcomes. But, on the evidence, the movements did not achieve general policy change or innovation. Rather, they pressed the state to fulfill some specific obligations, such as guaranteeing individual security, protecting the property of the poor from fraud and violence, and enforcing its own regulations and price controls. Contrary to the heady utopianism of the early commentaries on social movements, scholars were eventually exhorted to "acknowledge just how limited their short-term impact really is" (Boschi 1987, 184).

It might be expected that the grand exception to the rule might be the long-term legacy of social mobilization for citizenship rights in Latin America. Yet such a conclusion would sit uneasily with the growing body of work on the "low-intensity citizenship" (O'Donnell 1999) and imperfect legal protections (Diamond 1999) of the illiberal (Merkel 1999) or defective (Zakaria 1997) democracies of the continent. This work, and that of Guillermo O'Donnell in particular, is imaginative and important. But the analysis does remain rather static. It is true that civil, political, and minority rights must be guaranteed by the state, and that their presence requires an effective rule of law. But historically these rights have nearly always had to be won by social and political struggles against the state, or against powerful actors in civil society. What is missing is a sense of popular political agency, and the failure of the analysis of social movements to engage with this assessment of the quality of democracy in Latin America represents a missed opportunity.

Democratic Transitions and the Decline of Social Movements

Most studies of democratic transitions still focus on elite actors and derive their typologies of transition from the ex post modeling of elite decision making. Some consider the choices made by different attitudinal groups of elite actors (liberalizers and hard-liners). Others examine the elite pacts and settlements made at the moment of transition. In short, it is the short-term maneuvering of elites that remains central to the analysis, with little or no consideration of the links to mass publics or popular organizations. Despite O'Donnell's (1999, xii) claims to the contrary, his "process-oriented" approach to democratic transitions suffers from a similar weakness. By ignoring the question of popular agency, and the role of social movements in particular, these studies miss an important dimension of democratic transitions, and so may misunderstand the making of democracy. Yet the social science literature has missed another opportunity by failing to complement the accounts that concentrate exclusively on elite and state actors with a social movement perspective.

Democratic transitions tend to be seen as discrete moments in historical time. But in his seminal article Dankwart Rustow (1970, 352) argued that most transitions are "set off by a prolonged and inconclusive political struggle" and suggested that one generation is usually the minimum period required to achieve such transitions. It is, therefore, helpful to distinguish between democratic *transition* per se and the period of democratic *transformation* that precedes and creates the political conditions for it (Foweraker 1989). In this perspective, democratic transition refers to the change of political regime and the legal-constitutional norms governing the new regime, while democratic transformation encompasses the social movement activity within civil society that prepares the political ground for these changes. The labor movement in particular may play a key role in the latter process both by asserting a sense of rights and by forging a tradition of free collective bargaining that can underpin the new democratic arrangements.

The failure of social science literature to engage systematically with democratic transition is again a matter of perspective. The preoccupation with identity tends to exclude a more strategic orientation, and in particular, the literature has ignored the strategic implications of "resource mobilization theory" (Foweraker 1995, 16ff.). Consequently, despite the importance of interaction with the state, there is little appreciation of political constraints, or what the current theory calls the "political opportunity structure" (Kitschelt 1986). Equally, the insensitivity to strategy ignores the complexities of projecting social movement activity into political society, and the contingent nature of the political outcomes that ensue (Foweraker 1989). Insofar as politics becomes more open and competitive, and parties and interest groups begin to move to center stage, the targets of mobilization become blurred and the rules of engagement are no longer clear. For social movements, or more especially their leaders, political society becomes a *jôgo surdo,* or dance of the deaf. They would need no convincing that "the process of establishing a democracy is a process of institutionalizing uncertainty" (Przeworski 1986, 58).

Despite this lack of interest in the political process of social mobilization, the literature has been quick to embrace the thesis of social movement decline, contrasting the clarity of the principles of mobilization and struggle under authoritarian regimes with its loss of direction with the transition to democracy. Since mobilization had not led to any formal representation within the state at the time of the democratic transitions, it was relatively easy to sideline social movements from power and policymaking. By a process of "transition through transaction" (Share and Mainwaring 1986) the traditional elites retained inside influence in the state, and such political and institutional continuities meant that the movements had no realistic hope of defining the political agenda. At the same time, the state restored the universal promise of individual rights, as the question of citizenship moved to the constitutional sphere, and so answered the rights demands of many of the movements. Without recourse to the language of rights, their objectives lost focus, and their political energy began to dissipate. "Successful social movements inevitably lose their reason for being" (Jaquette 1989, 194).

Social movements lost ground for reasons of economics too. Most transitions took place in conditions of economic crisis. The austerity programs promoted by the IMF and the foreign banks reinforced its adverse effects. The movements' ability to survive as organizations, and the legitimacy of their leaderships, often depends on their success in extracting material concessions or benefits from the state. With the state's capacity for material distribution severely curtailed, the movements may wither and die. This neoliberal policy was founded on a conception of civil society as a market economy of atomized individuals, and not as a social arena of collective interests. This policy's prescription for the economic ills was expressed politically as a clear predominance of "elite" over "popular" democracy. In sum, it was soon all too apparent that the neoliberal approach precluded popular aspirations to the achievement of greater social justice through social development. If that was so, what role remained for social movement activity in the new democracies of the 1990s?

The Transformation of Social Movements

The most visible and significant change in the form of grassroots political activity across the continent was the rise of the NGOs. Some of the first took the form of research institutes staffed by social scientists expelled from the universities by military governments.[3] Initially, international agencies or foreign governments funded them, and some actively sought funding for consultation and advisory work. Such income-generating activities became their most salient feature following the debt and fiscal crises of the early 1980s, as they began to connect grassroots organizations to the international funding community and broker financial support for ground-level development projects. It was the funding by foundations, foreign aid programs, and international NGOs in the United States and Europe that fueled the massive expansion of Latin American NGOs from some 250 in the early seventies to some 25,000 today (Vetter n.d., 2).[4]

---

3. In 1971–72 I myself was a visiting researcher at one of the first such NGOS, CEBRAP in São Paulo.

4. It is notoriously difficult to estimate the number of NGOS across the continent because the counting criteria vary from country to country. Numbers can be inflated if the count includes all

Social movements, on the other hand, do not simply decline, as the mainstream thesis suggests; they also adapt and change. The changes involve both objectives and organization. On the one hand, with the rights demands defused, economic and fiscal crisis makes material demands primary once again. Simply surviving in the city becomes the main focus of their demands. On the other, their organization has to become more agile to survive in political society and negotiate with state agencies. As Paul Oberschall (1973) points out, social movements seek to overcome the problems of collective action through increasing organization and try to increase their resources by adopting lower-risk and more "institutional" forms of action. They will develop their own so-called social movement organizations (SMOS) to assume the executive functions previously exercised by informal groups, and to carry out "the crucial task of mediating between the larger macro environment and the set of micro dynamics on which the movement depends" (McAdam, McCarthy, and Zald 1988). New SMOS have emerged in Latin America and connect with NGOS at home and abroad. As the foregoing analysis makes clear, these changes do not represent a sudden switch from civil to political society. Social movement organizations were generated in and shaped by their interaction with the state. But there is a significant change in emphasis in social movement activity that is epitomized in the change from social *movement* to nongovernmental *organization*. This should not be taken to imply that all social movements are becoming more organized, still less that they are all becoming organized within NGOS. Many social movements have declined or disappeared, and many others have turned toward self-help activity and local survival or development projects. But it is safe to assume that some social movements somewhere are always experimenting with new forms of organization (Joseph 1999).

The sociology of social movements has recognized both the decline of social movements and the rise of NGOS, but has not explored the possible connections between the two processes. Consequently, it may be difficult to discern the political significance of the changes. The process of institutionalizing social movements is not new, but it accelerates. And increasing institutionalization and diminishing autonomy may be two sides of the same coin. Tensions between leaders and base, elite and mass, professionals and

---

"third sector" organizations, such as philanthropic, welfare, cultural, and sporting organizations. A recent estimate based on survey evidence from different countries talks of 50,000 NGOS (ALOP 1999), but reckons that only 5,000 to 10,000 are "genuine development NGOS" (Valderrama 1998, 8), while another source puts the figure at 14,000 (Reilly 1998, 413). Vetter's current figure of 25,000 therefore seems plausible, if perhaps somewhat optimistic.

volunteers, tend to be resolved by more organizing and less mobilizing. The changes are driven both by the need for politically agile actors to prosper in a more complex political environment and by the need for financial survival. But "who says organization, says oligarchy" (Michels), and social movements may be uprooted from the people they grew up to serve. The results may include increasing clientelism and the co-optation of leaderships.

The Clientization of Democratic Citizens

As social movement activity becomes more organized, and as the balance shifts to SMOS and NGOS, the question of financial survival becomes primary. The NGOS emerged within and often responded to a new funding context that included international linkages among movements and NGOS, the emergence of international agencies like Amnesty International and the World Council of Churches, and the global presence of donors from wealthy countries. During the democratic transitions, the NGOS were protagonists of the development drama, participating in meetings and forums sponsored by multilateral institutions such as the World Bank and the Inter-American Development Bank. But the foreign agencies proved fickle as in the case of Chile or highly selective in their agendas as in Brazil, with their funding of NGOS dropping vertiginously—by as much as 50 percent in some regions (Vetter n.d., 1). Chile had an "intense romance" with the international donor community under authoritarian rule, but "was jilted after the transition" (Diamond 1999, 256). The annual U.S.$100 million in international NGO income at the end of the 1980s, comprising about 70 percent of total income, subsequently suffered drastic cuts, with major international NGOS like Christian Aid and Oxfam withdrawing from Chile completely. Brazil's massive social needs found emotive but exclusive expression in street children and the destruction of the rainforest.

Since Latin America has no tradition of large-scale private philanthropy that might substitute for the decline or fastidiousness of international funding, both SMOS and especially NGOS had to turn toward the state to survive. Some newly democratic states, for their part, were seeking to restore a developmental role, partly for reasons of legitimacy, and to deploy and involve NGOS in an array of community and social welfare projects. In Chile, once again, the switch to state funding was facilitated by technocratic elites who favored NGO-style management methods, and by 1993 the state was funneling some U.S.$35 million into the NGO sector (Kirby 1996, 21).

The development NGOs were especially receptive to state initiatives as a solution to their chronic financial deficits. Competing for start-up capital was easier than generating income to maintain their projects and pay the staffing costs of educational courses, health centers, and rural extension programs. At the same time their budgets were absorbed by public relations as they strained to make a plausible case for renewed funding.

In principle some convergence can be envisaged between the antistate philosophy of neoliberal policymakers and the traditional hostility to bureaucratic interference of social movements. But in practice state funding meant that SMOS and NGOs began to act as "transmission belts" for government social policy and as clients of the government bureaucracy. The funding, credit, training, and technical assistance came at the cost of an autonomous vision and voice. The consequence was less social mobilization and less capacity to criticize government policy or pursue alternative solutions, a problem recognized in the Alternative Declaration of NGOs at the UN's Social Summit in Copenhagen in March 1995. International agencies like the UN and USAID are sensitive to these constraints and have begun to advocate agency-to-people programs in addition to traditional agency-to-government aid. But the practical possibility of "alternative development" in the new democracies will continue to depend on the capacity of NGOs and social movements to influence social policy. This influence is certainly reduced by co-optation and the process of "clientization."

The Contemporary Profile of Social Mobilization

The main changes in the profile of social mobilization are not a matter of dispute. As NGOs have multiplied, so social movements have lost impetus and changed trajectory. As NGOs have come to monopolize the funding agendas of both international agencies and state development agencies, so social movements have had to develop their own NGOs, or adopt NGO styles and strategies in pursuing their goals. Yet whatever the strength of these tendencies, it would be incorrect to conclude that all "popular sector" organizations are now the same. On the contrary, they vary both by their (potential) social base and capacity for mobilization and by their relationship to the state, and in particular, their client status as a vehicle for state services or more proactive capacity for shaping policy and its implementation.

Take the traditional demand for land rights that historically has sustained some of Latin America's most radical social movements. In Chile the most visible struggle for land is led by the Interregional Mapuche Council (CIM), which seeks to defend the territorial integrity of the Mapuche peoples against dam and highway construction, and the extractive activities of large, often multinational companies. Potentially, the Mapuche comprise a massive social base, since by the estimate of the 1992 Chilean Census the Mapuche nation comprises about one million people, or 10 percent of the population of Chile, with some 400,000 Mapuche now living in Santiago (CIM 1998). However, the Council is simply an umbrella NGO that attempts to coordinate a disparate collection of regional NGOs, community organizations, and local chiefs. In Brazil, in contrast, the same struggle is led by the Landless Workers' Movement (MST) — now the largest social movement in Latin America. The MST has moved from pure mobilization to production and marketing, and a strategy that seeks to influence state agencies from the inside, while building an international network of NGO and agency support. Yet although the movement now conforms to the image of a developmental NGO (or the coordinating committee for different NGO-style development projects), the operational core of the movement remains the frequently illegal process of land occupation. The MST claims that some 57,000 families are currently occupying formerly uncultivated land across twenty-three states of the union, and that some 150,000 families have been settled since its beginnings in 1984, most through mass mobilization and direct action.

These distinctions do affect outcomes in some degree. The Mapuche complain that the violations of their land rights and the usurpation of their lands continue unabated. In classic NGO style the CIM combines media campaigns with educational outreach to advertise these violations, but lacks any capacity to press its claims through social mobilization. The limitations of this approach mean little practical success, as the Mapuche are the first to recognize (CIM 1998). In Brazil, on the other hand, the government responded to MST pressure by creating PROCERA, the Special Credit Program for Agrarian Reform, to invest in social and economic projects on MST "encampments." There are also piecemeal attempts to assuage the most violent land conflicts by titling the landless. Yet, despite its mobilization and its broad-based political alliances, the MST has failed to move land reform to the top of the political agenda.

The distinctions are sharpened by state organization, as illustrated by the same two cases. Chile is an example of a highly centralized and relatively cohesive state that has pursued the reform of its social sector through delegating policy implementation to autonomous agencies and NGOs. This was a self-conscious strategy of bypassing the line ministries by recruiting NGOs to disburse social funds and provide safety nets and basic services to the poor. At the same time, new state agencies were set up to target social spending to priority projects, and extra taxes were raised to fund the antipoverty programs in health and education in the pursuit of a political economy of "neoliberalism with a human face" (Kay and Silva 1992, 293; Paley 2001; Schild 2000). The main examples are the Servicio Nacional de la Mujer (SERNAM), the Instituto Nacional de la Juventud (INJ), and the Corporación Nacional de Desarrollo Indígena (CONADI).

The Brazilian state, on the other hand, continues to provide extensive pension, health, and welfare services—however inefficiently—through a complex and sprawling bureaucracy of ministries and executive agencies. Most Brazilian NGOs attempt to remain independent of government and actively resist co-optation, even if this leads to less practical and effective activity.

In Chile, although the antipoverty drive did extend benefits to the disadvantaged and deprived (Angell and Graham 1995, 194), the democratic government anticipated popular demands rather than responding to them, since it was government, not parties, movements, or NGOs that initiated the reforms (Oxhorn 1994, 752). It is clear that the client status of many NGOs is both cause and consequence of this process, with most popular sector organizations too weak or passive to campaign for their concerns or shape the outcome of social policies. In Brazil, in contrast, there were instances of proactive social mobilization for social reform in health (Weyland 1995, 1996), environment (Mello Lemos 1998), and rural development (Tendler and Freedheim 1994; Ostrom 1996). But all too frequently these reform efforts foundered as they became embroiled in bureaucratic infighting.

The counsel of despair might suggest that these are all distinctions without a difference. In the end, all NGOs and movements with a more critical or more radical stance are sidelined, and the poor and dispossessed condemned to a kind of political silence (Kirby 1996, 42). Social movements blend into an amorphous "third sector" and lose their edge as defenders of the excluded. Indeed, surveys of NGOs reflect a certain disorientation and lack of clear purpose among NGOs across the continent (Valderrama 1998, 42). The traditional Left, for its part, has lost its relevance and its appeal (Castañeda 1993). It is, therefore, nigh impossible to mobilize and press for effective rights of citizenship, or strive to hold newly democratic governments to account. This is the price to be paid for the pragmatic politics of the neoliberal era. This conclusion would certainly conform to a vision of Brazil and Chile, among others, as "dual democratic" regimes that support an elite project comprising political pacts between the state, business, and organized labor, but excluding the great majority of the poor and uneducated (Smith and Acuña 1994, 19).

State Reform and Social Mobilization

This summary inquiry into the conditions of social mobilization in Latin America has moved from the conceptual inflation of wishful thinking to a pessimistic statement of the practical constraints. The evidence of recent survey research[5] confirms the financial pressures acting on popular organizations everywhere in Latin America. Latin America is no longer a high priority for private foundations, with not only Chile but also Venezuela and Uruguay suffering complete defections; and the multilateral organizations send funds to the state (90 percent in the case of Peru, for example), not to the grassroots. Moreover, support for NGOs comes increasingly in the form of contracts for specific projects, accompanied by demands for quantifiable results. The primary consequence has been an increasing reliance on state support. Not just in Chile and Brazil, but across the continent the state is now subcontracting the delivery of social services in education, health, and welfare to NGOs. Approximately a third of all NGO funding in Colombia and Argentina flows from the state, and some 70 percent of Brazilian NGOs and nearly all Peruvian NGOs work more or less closely with the state. State funding in Brazil is often conditional on conformity to state policy (ALOP 1999, 48), and in Peru the state is known to create its own NGOs to ensure such conformity (Patrón 1998, 185).

This support entails the privatization and outsourcing of services in education, health, welfare, and environmental protection (Reilly 1998, 425; J. Navarro 1998, 95). But it may reflect a deeper process of state reform, especially decentralization, and a devolution of real resources to municipal governments (Gerstenfeld 2002). The income of municipal governments increased by over a third both in Chile in the early 1990s and in Argentina in more recent years (ALOP 1999). Such reform, it is argued, can promote new mechanisms of social mobilization and popular participation. This was the osten-

5. The research was conducted by the *Asociación Latinoamericana de Organizaciones de Promoción* (ALOP) and the *Programa de Fortalecimiento Institucional a las ONG* (FICONG), and was designed to evaluate the current condition of grassroots organizations in the continent (ALOP 1999; Valderrama 1998). ALOP encompasses some fifty of the major development NGOs and conducted its research in Mexico, Guatemala, El Salvador, Nicaragua, Colombia, Ecuador, Peru, Bolivia, Argentina, and Uruguay—with information on Brazil provided by FASE, the *Federação de Órgãos para Assistência Social e Educacional.*

sible objective of Colombia's transfer of resources to the municipalities after 1993, Bolivia's Law of Popular Participation of 1994 (Valderrama 1998, 34), Brazil's numerous municipal councils (Bresser Pereira and Cunill Grau 1998, 36), and the new links between development NGOs and the metropolitan governments of Mexico City and Lima (Joseph 1999). State reform is often linked to the implementation or monitoring of welfare policies, or to the protection of specific groups such as children. In this way it may enable greater "social control" of the state administration and stimulate a nonstate public sphere (Bresser Pereira and Cunill Grau 1998; Roberts in this volume).

The most salient example of the new style of social mobilization is the experiment in participatory budgeting conducted by the Partido dos Trabalhadores (PT) administration in Porto Alegre from 1989 to the present. Its result was a dramatic reversal of expenditure patterns from high-profile projects to small-scale urbanization and infrastructure works of benefit to every neighborhood. Neighborhood meetings took on new life, and hundreds of new activists emerged as neighborhood councils multiplied to monitor policy and the implementation of projects (Z. Navarro 1998, 320). Each year some fourteen thousand people participated in the budget debates with over 8 percent of the adult population participating in the budget assemblies at some moment during first five years (Abers 1998, 40–49). But the increased participation did not wrest final control from the municipal authorities, who both set the agenda and drew up the budget, while direct democracy only advanced at the cost of representative democracy, with opposition party delegates losing voice and influence. As Abers (1998, 53) points out, direct democracy can itself increase rather than diminish inequalities if the poorest inhabitants are too involved in surviving to press their claims. Despite the fashion for analogous policies in municipal governments across Brazil (Reilly 1998, 422), the new participation may have been idealized in some degree and its benefits overestimated.

The political effects of such mobilization can be ambiguous (Z. Navarro 1998, 100). Just as NGOs may seek to deliver state services for the sole purpose of financial survival, so increased mobilization may create new interest groups that seek to win resources or capture state rents rather than serve the broader public. Group lobbying of local government may dilute demands and lead to eventual co-optation (Nassuno 1998, 352). Clientelist relationships can then reassert themselves at the expense of community interests, especially at election times (Reilly 1998, 422). In this way the promise of popular participation and local democracy may eventually reproduce traditional structures of poverty and exclusion (ALOP 1999, 29), with government now creating or inducing the creation of "user groups" that are subject to tight legal and political controls as in the case of the legal restrictions on the "participatory" provisions of the Colombian constitution, the Bolivian Law of Popular Participation (Lander 1998, 465–66), and the Brazilian project for increasing "social control" of social services (Barreto 1998). A controlled participation of this kind is redolent of classic corporatism and is unlikely to make any impact on the "public agenda" in the form of public policymaking (Lander 1998, 465).

Back to the Future?

At least some aspects of social mobilization—or its lack—in Latin America can be described with some confidence. Much else remains entirely speculative. But nothing in this analysis should be taken to suggest that this mobilization has come to a full stop. What is described is a specific historical conjuncture that mainly discourages such mobilization. Economically, a strong adherence to neoliberal policies precludes a political emphasis on social development. Politically, the governments of the new democracies remain "unconnected with the lived experience of the mass of the population" (Whitehead 1992, 154). But a historical perspective shows that social mobilization, whether in Latin America or elsewhere, always occurs in waves. Any informed speculation about the prospects for social mobilization in the continent must therefore look beyond the present conjuncture and consider the longue durée.

The major works of political sociology have argued that the present conjuncture represents a sea change in the politics of the continent, and hence in social mobilization. Touraine (1989, 185–92) interprets the half-century from 1930 to 1980 in Latin America in terms of the dominance of the "national popular model," where the state is not clearly differentiated from the political system, and where social mobilization is mainly subordinated to political power. In analogous fashion the Colliers define the same period in terms of the political incorporation of the labor movement, with social agency mainly expressed through the choices of national political elites (Collier and Collier 1991). In both works the recent change is a consequence of attempts to achieve a more autonomous expression of "interests" by the labor movements and other popular actors. In this inquiry, in contrast, the current conjuncture is characterized not by the social mobilization of *interests* but by the historical encounter between social mobilization and the language of *rights*. In this perspective the wave of mobilization around democratic transition may have subsided, but the full effects of the encounter are unknown.

It is at least plausible that the rights agenda has yet to realize the rudiments of its political potential.

The historical clock cannot be turned back. Civil society, however defined, is now more diverse and "resourceful." Despite the many constraints, NGOs can and do create new resources for social mobilization, including education, leadership, know-how, and information. Even without a social base, NGOs may promote social mobilization, as the democratic transition in Chile demonstrated. This may not eventually be the *same* social mobilization as before, but it will continue to express the impetus and invention of "society getting organized" (Monsiváis 1987). The last century of modern Mexican history, for example, has been marked by successive waves of social mobilization. Is it plausible that this history has come to a halt? The experience of Chiapas suggests not. On the contrary, today as in the past, new forms of social mobilization continue to emerge and enrich the panorama of grassroots political activity.

One telling example is the recent politicization of ethnic cleavages across the continent and the emergence of indigenous movements around an agenda of minority rights (N. Harvey 2001) and political representation (Dandler 1999; Yashar 1999). Remarkably, and in stark contrast to the postcolonial history of Africa, indigenous peoples were not a significant presence in the national politics of Latin America until the 1990s. But recent years have seen major mobilizations around demands for collective rights in the areas of land tenure, education, and self-government (Van Cott 2000). This indigenous mobilization has frequently been linked to political parties, labor unions, churches, and guerrilla movements (Rubin 1997; N. Harvey 1998). In some cases, this struggle for collective rights has even brought about constitutional changes, especially in Nicaragua (González Pérez 1997), Colombia (Van Cott 2000), and Ecuador (Beck and Mijeski 2001)—though the implementation of newly acquired rights remains a lot less certain.

In some degree the indigenous movements have been successful insofar as they found support in international networks of indigenous rights activists and bolstered their demands by reference to international conventions like Convention 169 of the International Labour Organisation.[6] In this respect

6. The United Nations' ILO Convention 169 of 1989 is supportive of the collective rights of indigenous peoples and, in particular, their right to participate in political decisions affecting their social, cultural, and economic development. It also defends their right to practice customary law within their own jurisdictions. The profile of the international networks was enhanced by the United Nations' declaration of 1993 as the "Year of Indigenous Peoples" and of 1994–2004 as the "Decade of Indigenous Peoples."

the indigenous movements are illustrative of a growing tendency toward local linkage with international nongovernmental organizations (INGOs) and the subsequent formation of "transnational advocacy networks" that mobilize populations and opinions around a range of policy areas like the environment and trade, or political issues like women's rights and human rights (Keck and Sikkink 1998a; Risse, Ropp, and Sikkink 1999). With the advantage of new forms of electronic communication these networks are able to project local concerns and regional struggles across the globe and so bring international pressure to bear on national governments to recognize legitimate popular demands.

This may well become typical of the activity and objectives of most social mobilization in the future. The initial focus of the historical encounter between social mobilization and rights in Latin America was democratic transition. In the future, social mobilization for rights may mainly seek to improve the quality and consistency of democratic government in the continent. This perspective differs from the view of democracy as the historical result of good behavior in the form of the civic community (Putnam 1993a). This latter view takes "civicness" as a functional prerequisite for democracy rather than exploring the popular agency that may achieve or improve it. To the dismay of those peoples still aspiring to achieve or improve democracy, Putnam's "civicness" may take centuries to accumulate—it took nine centuries in Northern Italy, the focus of his study. "Civicness," therefore, includes neither popular political struggle nor individual rights. An emphasis on social mobilization, in contrast, suggests that it is "bad behavior" in the form of the fight for rights that can do most to improve the quality of democracy and deliver its substance to the citizenry at large.

For Putnam, more "civicness" will lead inexorably to better democracy. In fact, the historical relationship between the associational capacity of civil society and the quality of democracy is indeterminate, since it will depend in large degree on the variable success of social mobilization in achieving and exercising citizenship rights. Such success is usually partial and always reversible. But it does mean that democracy can be improved generation on generation, and without waiting for the slow historical sedimentation of civic virtue. In the near future it is not likely to be a democracy made in the image of a perfectly civic society. But social mobilization may achieve the political conditions for piecemeal social development and greater efficacy in the rule of law.

5 Citizenship, Rights, and Social Policy

BRYAN R. ROBERTS

This chapter traces the evolution of research on Latin American development and its relationship to citizenship and human rights. Although citizenship and human rights have long been intellectual and policy concerns, they have only recently become a major focus in Latin American studies. The trend is evident in the dramatic increase in the number of publications devoted to the topic of citizenship. An inventory of library holdings in the Benson Collection at the University of Texas at Austin found that, between 1966 and 1973, only three titles in Spanish or Portuguese used the keywords *ciudadanía* or *cidadania,* two of which were manuals about citizenship. Between 1993 and 2000, the number rose to 139 titles, with the majority of references (91 titles) appearing in analyses of Brazil. The current attention given to the concept of citizenship appears to have replaced the priority once accorded such venerable concepts as dependency, marginality, and even social class. But what is it about citizenship that accounts for its striking ascendancy among social scientists? Perhaps its popularity is simply a reflection of an ephemeral intellectual fashion. Or perhaps the current attention given to citizenship is a meaningful response to fundamental changes in the objective reality of Latin American development.

Before delving into these issues, we should recognize at the outset that the concept of citizenship, at least as it was initially elaborated in the British context, is not directly applicable to Latin American countries, where poverty is endemic, political representation is circumscribed, and human rights are routinely violated. The analysis of citizenship in the developing world is therefore as much about its contradictions and limitations as it is about an ideal goal, which nonetheless serves as a benchmark against which to measure contemporary reality. Citizenship thus serves both as an organizing concept in empirical critiques of existing sociopolitical structure as well as the focus of normative social policy promulgated by international agencies, Latin American governments, community groups, and a wide range of nongovernmental organizations (NGOs). The task of sorting out and sizing up these empirical and policy issues requires a review and assessment of the "citizenship perspective."

The Citizenship Perspective

Citizenship is formally defined as a relationship between an individual and a state. It involves the individual's full and equal political membership in the state, with its attendant civil, political, and social rights. This basic definition has spawned a vast and well-established literature in political philosophy, as well as in political science and sociology. My focus is on the substance of citizenship in Latin America rather than on the formal rights and responsibilities of citizenship, and in particular, on the social relations among and between citizens, the state, and its agents. As such, the concept encompasses what Evans (1996, 1130) sees as the necessary basis for the synergy between state and civil society involving the interaction between social identities (such as class, ethnicity, age, and gender), the informal norms and networks that constitute an individual or a group's "social capital," and the operation of state organizations.

The sociological analysis of citizenship can, with some simplification, be categorized into two overlapping perspectives. The first perspective is concerned with the content of citizenship, particularly with the different kinds of rights that make for a full and equal citizenship. T. H. Marshall was the first to formulate the sociological distinction among civil, political, and social citizenship while, at the same time, arguing for the necessary interdependence of all three types (T. H. Marshall [1949] 1964, 78–79). Marshall hypothesized that citizenship, as an ideal, would constantly be undermined by the social inequality resulting from differences in power, and from the operation of a market economy. For Marshall, however, the relation between citizenship and the market was both interdependent and contradictory. The market depends upon and strengthens individual rights, such as property rights and the right to work, thus supporting the extension of a civil citizenship that equalizes people's rights before the law irrespective of their statuses. In this way, Marshall explicitly linked the mixed economy to democracy (T. H. Marshall 1981, 135).

At the same time, Marshall (1981) stressed the dangers that the market posed for social citizenship. The market generates inequality in individual wealth, destroys the traditional community-based solidarity that once mitigated hardship, and increases individual economic insecurity. There is a tension between individual rights, particularly rights to property, and collective rights to welfare (Reis 1996). It is especially manifest in a fourth type of rights, those which Bresser Pereira (1997) identifies with republican rights—

environmental rights, rights to the historical/cultural patrimony, and rights to the public economic legacy.

Such tensions are an important part of the substance and analysis of citizenship. Citizen rights are unlike human rights because the former can be given or taken away by law. The exercise of citizenship is thus limited and shaped by class differences (Barbalet 1988). The state is unlikely to act neutrally in the interests of all citizens, even in a democracy, since it will bend to its own corporate interests and those of elites. The rights of citizenship can also be shaped by struggles from below, as Bryan Turner (1990) points out in the case of France. The "from below" perspective on citizenship has been the chief focus of the literature on social movements in both Latin America and elsewhere (Melucci 1989; Touraine 1987, 1988a; Jelin 1987, 1996b).

The second and complementary perspective focuses on how the relation of the individual to the state is organized and institutionalized. This relation changes as the evolution of citizenship redefines what is private and what is public. Individual property rights, for instance, can contribute to a strong civil society, but they also create a private sphere of the household, where the home is the castle against both the state and the community. This raises the issues of the political, social, or economic processes, among others, that make the rights of children or women a public concern, nationally and globally. As these rights become a public concern and thus a matter of social policy, then the relationship of state and citizen is transformed. The outcomes of this transformation raise further research issues. Will legislation over women's and children's rights follow a universal model, or will it be specific to particular national and local cultures (Gledhill 2002)? What are the implications for state organization and the orientations of state personnel when states become involved in enforcing individual rights even in the privacy of the home?

The conflicts over the content of citizenship rights are sharp in the modern state because, as Scott (1998, 32) points out, the extension of citizenship rights has been an integral part of the process by which the modern national state creates a uniformity of customs, perceptions, and statuses. The spread of citizenship is thus an integral part of the modernization process. Citizenship rights and responsibilities enhance the central control of the state over its members. They become part of the rationalization process in law, administration, and economic life, which Weber saw as increasing the control of the modern state over the lives of its subjects. This focus on the link between rationalization and citizenship is used by Habermas (1998, 76–81) to examine how state-mandated social rights and responsibilities limit diversity and choice.

Countering the omnipotence of the state and strengthening the individual citizen in face of that power are the formal and informal associations of civil society. From De Toqueville to Robert Putnam, this analytic tradition views active civic associations as a vital component of a healthy democracy and focuses on the conditions that promote and limit civism. This focus ties into the analysis of social networks. Associations and networks are the social capital that individuals and communities can draw upon to enhance their own capacities and, by extension, make more effective use of the resources that the state makes available (Coleman 1988; Durston 1999a). However, social capital may also isolate individuals and communities from the external relationships and information that they need in order to cope with the demands of the modern economy (Portes and Landolt 1996; Portes 1998b). This dark side of social capital is further manifest when it is used to enforce authoritarian control of communities, as in the case of the Mafia or drug gangs.

The relation of the individual to the state is thus a mediated one in which, in practice, the individual citizen does not deal directly with "the state," but with various different agencies of the state through community organizations, NGOs, or networks of friends and family. These encounters or interfaces bring together actors who are part of separate social and organizational worlds. Consequently, the encounters are likely to be confused by the differences in perspectives and interests that arise from the internal norms, systems of stratification, and priorities of each of these worlds. An important research tradition in rural sociology has emphasized, for example, that the interface between state agencies and local communities can be a barrier to community development initiatives (Long 2001). Studies of rural communities show the multiple channels for miscommunication and mutual exploitation that arise from the interface between officials who are bounded by career preoccupations and bureaucratic rationality, as well as by citizens who are locked into their own local relationships.

I shall argue that the research issues deriving from the citizenship perspectives I have outlined are made salient by significant changes in Latin America both in the role of the state and in individuals' social and economic situations. The next section begins with a brief review of the changes in the context of citizenship between the period of import-substitution industrialization (ISI) and the contemporary one of free markets and export-oriented industrialization.

The Changing Historical Context of Citizenship in Latin America

I begin with the ISI period and Gino Germani's (1973) use of the concept of marginality to analyze the limits of social and political modernization in this period. For Germani, marginality was coterminous with the lack of citizenship and thus emphasized the responsibility of the state and of political parties to extend social rights to the marginal population. For Germani, marginality is the condition of not having access to possibilities to which people are normatively entitled (Germani 1973, 34–39). In a text reference to T. H. Marshall, Germani defines marginality in terms of the substantial sections of the Latin American population who have not benefited from the progressive extension of civil, political, and social rights in modern society.

Germani uses Marshall's concept of citizenship as a benchmark for evaluating the Latin American situation and to emphasize the multidimensionality of marginality. Marginality is exclusion from the range of civil, political, and social rights. The most marginal are those excluded in all dimensions—from a decent job, from the protection of the law, from an adequate income, from education, from political participation, and from the dominant urban culture.

For Germani, as for other marginality theorists, the solution for these inequities lay in resolving politically the macrostructural limitations on development. Faria (1976, 273) pointed out that, under the undemocratic conditions of the 1960s and 1970s, policy-relevant research on how best to combat poverty had less priority than working politically to achieve democracy. The struggle for equal citizenship rights in the courts or through politics was limited by authoritarian governments, both military and civilian, and by populist politics. In most countries, democratic politics based on competition between class-based political parties did not exist. The state was, by and large, an enemy that curtailed rights and restricted opportunities.

How the Latin American cities were settled also deemphasized the rights or entitlements that citizens had vis-à-vis the state. The studies of urban sociologists and anthropologists in the 1960s and 1970s demonstrated the capacity of the poor to fend for themselves and to cope with urban life (Roberts 1995, 157–83). These studies showed that migrants, along with other poor urban inhabitants, were skilled in organizing themselves and in using community organization and social relationships to survive in the city. The poor built the Latin American city and, to an extent, created their own job opportunities through the informal sector (Bromley 1979; Portes, Castells, and Benton 1989). Much of this was achieved without state involvement. Indeed, individual and community successes and failures usually had little relation to the formal legal, administrative, and political institutions of the state. In these struggles, then, citizenship rights were neither gained nor lost.

There were exceptions, such as those reported by Degregori, Blondet, and Lynch (1986) in their account of the "conquest" of Lima by provincial migrants in which land invasions resulted in a sense of citizenship and some official recognition of the new communities. However, even when land titles were regularized, these favors from above did little to generalize a right to shelter. Nor did governments need to modify labor codes in order to give employers more flexibility. The prevalence of informal employment provided effective labor market deregulation. The lack of connection between struggles for existence, whether individual or collective, and the institutions of the state was one reason why Touraine (1987) dismissed the urban social movements of Latin America as not being true social movements. Their fragmentation, episodic nature, and the nature of their demands posed no fundamental challenge to the existing power structure.

The dynamism of the Latin American urban labor markets also deemphasized the contest over labor rights. Analyses of the urban labor markets in Latin America in the 1960s and 1970s indicated their capacity to absorb the rapid growth of the urban labor force that resulted from migration and high birthrates (Balan, Browning, and Jelin 1973; Faria 1976; Oliveira and Roberts 1994). Self-employment declined steadily between 1950 and 1980, and rural migrants as well as urban natives were absorbed into the manufacturing industry (Muñoz, Oliveira, and Stern 1983). The period up to 1980 was also one of a high degree of urban intergenerational social mobility, not just from farm jobs to nonfarm work, but also from manual to nonmanual occupations. The expansion of government and social services and the increase in white collar and technical jobs in manufacturing brought a structural shift in the urban occupational structure that accounted for most of the intergenerational mobility (Oliveira and Roberts 1994, table 4, 269). Along with rising educational levels, the shifts in the occupational structure meant better urban prospects for the next generation. And in an expanding labor market, attaining them did not depend on fighting for rights.

During this period social rights were gradually extended in most countries of Latin America. Though the extension of social rights did respond to the demands of the middle and formal working classes, this extension was state-directed. Mesa Lago (1978) shows, for example, how the extension of social security rights began with key sectors of the employed population, such as government workers, transport workers, workers in key extractive industries, and so on. The principle of universal coverage was, however, tacitly accepted and had been achieved in the Southern Cone countries by the 1970s. The extension of pension rights to all rural workers in Brazil in the 1990s is a recent expression of the universal principle. This "universal" right was not, however, based on being a citizen of the state, but on having formal employment.

In this context of top-down government, citizenship as a legitimate and universal basis for the general population to make claims on the state had little importance for advancing or defending rights. The characteristics of states also contributed to the invisibility of this aspect of citizenship. During the period of ISI, commentators inevitably focused on the role of the state in economic development rather than on the contribution of the market or civil society groups. Because of tariff protection and restrictions on foreign investment, states became prime actors in promoting economic development through building infrastructure and the ownership of major enterprises. Key issues were the efficiency of the state and its capacity to act with relative autonomy from rent-seeking interests (Evans 1992). The Latin American state was a problem because it did not have an efficient bureaucracy, and both decisions and appointments depended not on set procedures but on the personal whims of those in charge.

There were few civil organizations that had a strong independent base. ISI in Latin America created a middle class that was highly dependent on state employment. Data from the 1970s and 1980s show that as much as half of white-collar employment in urban Latin America was state employment (Oliveira and Roberts 1994). In Mexico, there were few professional or even business associations that were independent of the state (Escobar and Roberts 1991). Also, the nation as the imagined community of shared interests and identities was appropriated for the near exclusive use of the state in most of Latin America. The state during ISI was both economically and politically nationalistic. It led the push to economic development against external interests and often saw itself as forcing a national project on recalcitrant regional interests.

The ending of ISI in the 1980s, and the opening of most Latin American economies to the free movement of trade and capital, created the conditions for the conceptual breaks that led to the increasing use of citizenship perspectives in analyses of development issues in Latin America. Globalization is, indeed, a major reason for the contemporary focus on citizenship. The global triumph of Western capitalism has, for the time being, taken

alternative economic models off the social science agenda in Europe and
Latin America, as Sunkel points out in this volume. If capitalism and representative democracy are the only games in town, then, as Marshall suggested,
citizenship becomes the major defense against inequality. This line of analysis, along with Marshall's stress on the importance of the market in democracy, underpins the contemporary rethinking of citizenship by advocates of
the "Third Way" in Latin America and elsewhere (Cardoso 1999; Bresser
Pereira 1999; Giddens 2000).

Globalization has also directly promoted the relevance of citizenship
through giving human rights an increasing importance internationally.
Though poor relatives in the mainly economic feast of globalization, NGOs
and United Nations agencies have vigorously pursued a human rights agenda,
which seeks to universalize certain basic rights—for children, for women, for
minorities, and so on (Keck and Sikkink 1998a). The international financial
agencies, such as the World Bank and Inter-American Development Bank,
have also promoted key elements of the contemporary citizenship perspectives: decentralization, local citizen organization and participation. In this
context, decentralization policies are urged upon governments as a more
cost-effective way to administer social services.

Neither the suddenness of this shift nor the role of external agencies in
promoting citizenship should be overemphasized. As Foweraker and Jelin
argue in this volume, the social movements that struggled against military
dictatorships were the basis for the revival of interest in human and citizen
rights issues (Jelin 1985; Calderón and Jelin 1986). They created a citizenship
agenda for the democratic governments that followed the dictatorships.

A further factor in the increasing saliency of citizenship concerns and
particularly those of social citizenship were the social and economic changes
of the 1980s and 1990s, associated with the maturing of urbanization
throughout Latin America (Roberts 1996). By 2000, 75 percent of the Latin
American population was urban, and most of the urban population lived in
cities of over 100,000 people. The urban environment began to consolidate
spatially and demographically as rural-urban migration declined (Roberts
2002). These urban populations are no longer "making the city," but are settled populations whose welfare depends increasingly on the quality of public services. This is clear in the labor market, where the major transformations
in the occupational structure from farm to nonfarm work, from manual to
nonmanual work, are now over. For those with higher levels of education, the
growth in the numbers and proportions of white-collar service jobs provides
good job opportunities. For those with low levels of education, the situation

is more difficult as technologically advanced industry, supermarkets, and cheap foreign imports displace labor from a hitherto thriving small-scale sector in industry, commerce, and the services, making them truly marginal, as Cimillo (1999) argues for Buenos Aires. High youth unemployment rates in many cities of Latin America attest to the ending of the expansive employment opportunities of the cities of ISI (Kaztman and Wormald 2002).

In the following sections, I outline research and discussion on three major areas in which the relation of the state to the individual citizen altered in the 1990s. My aim is to integrate the discussion of citizenship with that of changes in the nature of the state, in the focus on community development, and in social policy. Each issue has a key research topic. The first is the reform of the state in Latin America and the rationalization of citizenship. The second is decentralization and the development of "local" citizenship. The third is the formalization of urban life and the impact of social policy on social stratification.

The Interface of State and Civil Society

We can begin with the caveat that despite being exposed to similar external forces, each Latin American state has its own institutional and historical peculiarities with consequent variation in the extent of the state's relation to its citizens. For example, the ratio of public social expenditure to the GNP varies among Latin American countries from 5 to 23 percent (Gerstenfeld 2002). Consequently, understanding the nature of the interface between state and civil society in Latin America would be best achieved by comparing states according to their level of economic and social development, contrasting those which developed earliest and most bureaucratically with those which developed later and with less complexity. For the purposes of this chapter, however, I shall confine my analysis to the general tendencies in the evolution of the state in the region.

Administrative decentralization has proceeded apace in most countries of Latin America. Typically, this takes the form of delegating more administrative autonomy to lower levels of government. This decentralization occurred most radically in Brazil with the constitution of 1988, which assigned a percentage of national taxes to municipal governments and placed primary health care and primary and secondary education under municipal control. Accompanying decentralization is a privatization of state services and of state productive enterprises. An example of this is the creation of privately managed pension schemes in Chile, though other Latin American countries, such as Argentina, Mexico, and Peru are now experimenting with the full or partial privatization of pension schemes (Madrid 2003). Private health schemes have also been encouraged in various countries—Chile and Colombia being among the earliest. Grindle (2002, 84–85) lists thirty-four major reforms in the three social sectors (health, education, and pensions) that were enacted in Latin America in the 1990s. Only three countries (Dominican Republic, Ecuador, and Paraguay) had no reforms, whereas eight countries had reforms in all three sectors (Argentina, Bolivia, Brazil, Chile, Colombia, Costa Rica, Mexico, and Nicaragua).

An integral part of decentralization is transferring responsibilities to the public nonstate sector, which ranges from NGOs to state-financed or state regulated, but autonomous corporations that administer public health, pensions, higher education, scientific research, cultural activities, and environmental protection (Bresser Pereira and Cunill Grau 1998). In addition, Latin American governments are making extensive use of contracted personnel to administer national welfare programs. These personnel work as employees of the state, but are not permanent and do not have security of tenure. An indication of this transfer of responsibilities is the growth of employment in the not-for-profit sector, which in Brazil added 344,149 jobs between 1991 and 1995 to employ 1,119,533 people (Landim and Beres 1999). In contrast, Landim and Beres show that state employment in the social areas grew less rapidly, adding some 293,000 jobs for a total of 3,297,706 employees.

Despite decentralization, there has been relatively little loss of central control over revenue and its allocation. Thus administrative decentralization has not been accompanied by fiscal decentralization. In Brazil, the central government has re-exerted control over the budgets of states and municipalities through legislation that imposes a tighter specification of the legitimate uses of mandated revenue transfers (Melo 1996). In other countries, such as Chile or Mexico, the control of revenue allocation by the central state remains strong despite decentralization. In Argentina, the central government is also seeking energetically to rein in the debts of the provinces.

These changes in the organization of the state are based on a new way of conceptualizing the role of the state—as managerial public administration and not as bureaucratic public administration (Bresser Pereira and Cunill Grau 1998). In Brazil, the reform of the state involved four key elements: (a) a reduction in size as a result of a transference of responsibilities; (b) a reduction in bureaucratic regulation, particularly of the market; (c) an increase in managerial capacity to make the implementation of government policies more effective and increase the fiscal independence of the state; and (d) an increase in governability through making the state more accessible to civil society (Barreto 1998).

The new state emerging in the 1990s is a developmental state like its predecessor, the nationalist state of the ISI period in Latin America. It should not be confused analytically with the "absent" state that neoliberal economic policies attempt to foster (Gerstenfeld 2002). Borrowing from Bresser Pereira and Cunill Grau (1998), I shall label this new state a *managerial developmental state* (MDS). Remember, however, that the MDS is an ideal type, and the states of Latin America vary considerably in their approximation to the ideal type. Key components of the MDS, as compared to the bureaucratic state, are decentralization, control through evaluation of results rather than bureaucratic procedures, and thus, an emphasis on technical efficiency and information gathering. Madrid (2003) points to the increasing importance of technically competent people in the highest reaches of government, who are usually economists and often trained in the United States.

The social and developmental functions of the managerial state are exercised through fiscal and administrative regulation rather than direct administration. Many of the features of the managerial state borrow from the innovations in the business firm associated with total quality control management that emphasize organizational and employee flexibility, customizing of products and services, just-in-time inventories, and openness to clients. The MDS, however, is biased toward the individual rights of citizenship and against collective rights.

The managerial state is a modernizing state, intent on rationalizing government to provide more efficient and cost-effective services. Part of this process is the formalization of Latin American citizenship. Civil rights are being codified and extended through judicial reform movements. These reforms reach down into low-income neighborhoods, not only through experiments such as neighborhood policing or women's police stations, but also through semiformal dispute resolution courts, staffed often on a voluntary basis by lawyers, city officials, and NGO personnel. Independent electoral commissions and the issuing of voting credentials are safeguarding political rights. Social rights are promoted through training courses in leadership, job skills, and gender awareness as well as through courses targeting the young and old. These are positive trends for the deepening and consolidation of citizenship rights. I want, however, to emphasize some problematic aspects of these developments.

One of these is the degree and nature of external involvement in local communities. There are probably few low-income communities in Latin American cities that do not have some development program sponsored by either an NGO or local, regional, or national government. These external actors also, at times, compete with one another for local clients. Thus, an NGO and the local municipality may offer similar care facilities for the elderly, and the regional government facility may compete with both.

The increased involvement of state and nonstate public agencies in local communities in Latin America is likely to emphasize the instrumental and calculable content of citizenship rather than the content of its rights. External donors demand that the programs that they finance follow certain guidelines in terms of participation by beneficiaries. These normally include prescriptions for calling consultative meetings with the community over priorities, such as publicizing meetings widely in advance, as well as guidelines for conducting surveys to determine the objective characteristics of target populations. Guidelines set out the number and sequence of evaluations to check the number of beneficiaries and ascertain whether they are representative of the targeted population. Within state agencies, these practices are increasingly seen as being equivalent to good government. Spink (2000) describes the "audit" culture, in which the inability to measure performance precisely is taken to mean that a program cannot have merit.

There is an inherent contradiction between the formal promotion of citizenship and the substantive development of citizenship. The latter is essentially conflictive, depending on citizens getting together to advance rights and consolidate threatened identities, as workers, as women, as environmentalists, as consumers, as ethnic groups, and so on. Organizing citizenship from above can easily result in limiting demand making by channeling demands through set procedures, as Foweraker argues in this volume in respect to the co-optation of social movements and NGOs. The state co-opts the issues and replaces conflict by committee work. Thus, SERNAM, the women's ministry in Chile, has many programs aimed at advancing women's rights, but their impact is limited by the agency's insistence that the way forward is to work on the means necessary to institutionalize gender equality rather than to encourage gender-based demands from below. Basing her observations on interviews with Mapuche women and with SERNAM officials and on a review of the proceedings of official meetings, Richards (2004) shows how difficult it is for the agency to respond to differences between women based on class and ethnicity. Mapuche women make their demands on all three fronts, emphasizing the special nature of Mapuche culture and of the class and gender relations within it. The tendency of SERNAM officials is to reduce

this complexity to general issues of women's inequality and avoid the ethni-
cally specific demands that are made by Mapuche women's organizations.

Yet in face of widespread poverty and severe regional, class, and ethnic
inequalities in Latin America, the state has an evident responsibility for promoting equality of citizenship. In this context, identifying the appropriate
role of the state in attending to both the felt and the objective needs of
citizens becomes a research priority. What, then, is the proper field of state
action and what is the proper field of citizen action? This is the issue in
Tendler's (1997) account of good government in the state of Ceara in Brazil,
where she identifies the ingredients of successful state-civil society cooperation. One is that the highest government authority—in this case the state
government—retains overall control of the development program. It does
not delegate choice of local promoters to municipal authorities, which may
be too embedded in particularistic local relations and likely to act clientelistically. Another is that local promoters live locally and gain training that
enhances both their own and their communities' prospects. A structure of
incentives is created that rewards individuals as part of collective achievements. Also, state agents are more successful when they have flexibility in the
ways that they can implement state plans. This means adapting plans to local
circumstances and having a variety of skills that allow government agents to
give a broad spectrum of advice. Tendler's cases demonstrate that the state
has been a necessary part of successful community development in Ceara and
in promoting small-scale economic enterprises. In her cases, however, state
agents are careful to avoid the bureaucratic rationalization of programs and
of the way that citizens participate in these programs.

Evans (1996) emphasizes the developmental potential of synergistic relations between state and organized communities and examines some of the
conditions under which these can be constructed. He builds upon Tendler's
cases as well as ones drawn from Mexico, Russia, and Asia to specify what
makes for and what acts against good synergy. He stipulates two basic conditions for managing a development interface. One is a complementarity
between what the state agency does and what local citizens do. The state
provides, for instance, the basic infrastructure, and citizens provide the local
knowledge and the subsidiary infrastructure that maximizes use of state
resources. The other requirement is that there be trust between state officials
and community, which is most likely to occur when officials are sufficiently
stable to have a degree of embeddedness in the local community. Evans takes
up the issue of the constructability of good state-society synergy. He notes
the difficulty of constructing these synergies in highly stratified societies, such

as exist in most developing countries. He also emphasizes the importance of local identities and traditions of organization in permitting the "scaling-up" of local ties and solidarities as the basis for effective local and extralocal organization. This is the issue that we take up in the next section.

Local Citizenship

A second important contemporary characteristic of citizenship in Latin America is that locality not nation is emphasized as the basis of citizenship and of citizen rights and responsibilities. The significance of this emphasis can be brought out by comparison with Brubaker's (1992) analysis of the basis of citizenship in Germany and France. In both cases, citizenship is opposed to locality. In Germany, this opposition arises because ethnic Germans can live in localities that are not part of the German/Prussian state. In France, it arises because citizenship is used by the state to unify and impose uniformity on localities that are territorially within the French state but are diverse in law and custom. In both countries, citizenship is an instrument in state centralization and modernization. In Latin America, in contrast, citizenship has become an instrument in decentralization and local-level modernization, which may result in regional inequalities.

The emphasis on locality results from two distinct contemporary trends. One is the increase in decentralization and community-targeting policies in national and international development programs. The other is the growing importance of experiments in participative democracy, particularly in Brazil, but also elsewhere in Latin America. The question here is the extent to which local government is being replaced by a local state with its own particular configuration of relations with citizens. If so, does this lead to political fragmentation at the national level, greater or lesser dependence on central government, greater or lesser empowerment for citizens?

Social investment funds and many national developmental programs, such as Comunidade e Solidaria in Brasil or PRONASOL and PROGRESA in Mexico, target communities as a means of reaching individuals in need. Their aim is to enlist local-level participation in development programs for health, education, community infrastructure, and employment. The programs have a clear citizenship focus, seeking to develop, through training courses and incentives for participation, a more informed and active civil society at the local level. It is still too early to judge what the overall impacts of such programs will be, but certain limitations can be noted. First, only relatively few communities are targeted, even among those meeting the criteria for inclusion. At times, communities must compete for inclusion by submitting their own programs. Second, the programs are necessarily concerned with local solutions to developmental problems.

Under these programs, a community progresses by its own efforts rather than by alliance with other communities in a like situation. The community focus also tends to obscure social class divisions within a community and thus does not promote solutions that are class specific. Calderón and Lechner (1998, 18) argue that social actors become weaker as their numbers multiply. This proliferation and fragmentation generates demands for special treatments that cannot easily be subsumed under national party political platforms. Research topics here are the circumstances that allow community issues to be "scaled-up" to create regional, national, and even international bases for political parties and political alliances (Kearney 2000; Fox 1996).

Experiments in participative democracy have sought to counter the top-down organizing of citizen participation. Perhaps the best-known experiment is that of the municipality of Porto Alegre, a Brazilian city of approximately two million that is described by Foweraker in this volume. The municipal budget has favored the lower-income sectors of the city, but without alienating the middle classes or local business people. Participatory budgeting built upon and enhanced the active neighborhood movements that existed in Porto Alegre prior to the victory of the PT (Partido dos Trabalhadores) in 1989. About half the participation is by lower-income people, and a third of participants are women, whose activism has increased with participation (Biaocchi 2003). A similar increase in participation occurred in Belo Horizonte. There are, however, some potential downsides to participatory budgeting. A major role of elected representatives, to decide programs and budgets, is sharply curtailed. Also, local priorities in participatory budgetary programs remain those of basic infrastructure such as street paving and lighting. More complex social equity issues of improving health or education have not yet become a significant proportion of priority proposals.

In Porto Alegre, participation could build upon prior community organizations. These provided the "scaling-up" that made for the citywide success of the participative budgeting process. How general is this likely to be? Here, the relevant research is on social networks and social capital. The most prevalent use of the concept of social capital, particularly among international agencies, follows that of Robert Putnam. Social capital is the sum of the organizational resources available to a community in terms principally of civic associations, but including more informal, yet stable patterns of association, such as recreational activities. Communities that possess a dense and lively associational activity are able to mobilize effectively to capture external resources and put them to use in developing the community. One piece of Latin American research that has made convincing use of the concept of social capital is based on rural communities (Durston 1999b, 2000). Durston (1999b) shows, for example, how a set of impoverished *ladino* villages in the eastern highlands of Guatemala succeeded in joining together and developing the civic organizations to make effective use of an international development program. The success was partly due to the skill of the external promoters in flexibly managing the program. A considerable part of the success, however, was due to the community's embedded memories of cooperation based on extended kinship and ritual.

Building social capital is not, however, likely to be a generally applicable solution for community development. Some of its limitations are related to the negative sides of social capital (Portes and Landolt 1996). Social capital can restrict both individuals and communities to an overly narrow a set of relationships, which inhibit their capacity to make use of external opportunities. Also, the historical sense of community that can be present in rural areas is much less likely to be present in cities. Social capital depends on a context that engenders trust. This can be found in urban communities through the mechanisms of common values, reciprocity, bounded solidarity, and enforceable trust, created, for instance, by religious or ethnic solidarities (Portes 1995a, 1998b).

In Latin American urban communities, a preexisting tradition of civicism or ethnic and religious bases for trust are often not present or have been weakened by intra-urban population mobility. Espinoza's (1998) careful analysis of networking among the urban poor in Santiago shows the importance of these networks to the survival of the poor. Based mainly on small groups of neighbors, they have, however, a limited capacity to negotiate for state services or to generate collective action.

In documenting the lack of civicism and community fragmentation in Chile, Lechner (2000) underlines the weakness of the social capital approach and suggests a more focused alternative. Referring to Granovetter's (1973) argument, he points out that certain types of "weak" ties may be most effective in enabling individuals and communities to participate effectively in the modern Latin American city. Access to information about jobs, education, and health is increasingly important in ensuring equality of opportunity. It is no longer the presence of a school or a health clinic that guarantees some equality of citizenship, but having people who are well informed about relative standards and relative possibilities. In order to make effective demands for improving facilities and equalizing opportunities, information is vital. "Weak" relationships that bridge neighborhoods and social classes are essential for obtaining information. Civic associations and NGOs can foster these bridging activities. They also require the active support of state agencies, which can provide comparative information and help institutionalize channels of discussion and debate.

Social Policy and Citizenship

Citizens in Latin America are now more dependent on state services than they were in the 1960s and 1970s. An important reason for this increasing dependence is the formalization of the living environment, particularly in the cities of Latin America. Though there are some contrary trends, such as the increase in informal employment in some countries, the overall trend is toward formalization as land tenure is regularized, streets are paved, and water, electricity, and sewage services are extended to the great majority of urban dwellings. Formalization brings benefits, but it also imposes costs as when regularizing land titles leads to taxes, city ordinances, and building standards. Educational services cover a much larger part of the population at the end of the 1990s than they did in the earlier period, and cover them for more years of a child's life. Improvements in public health also increase people's contacts with state services through immunization campaigns, care during pregnancy, and the monitoring of children's health. Formalization does not necessarily mean an improvement in services and effective coverage, but it does mean a deepening of citizen-state relations.

Also, Latin American cities now appear to be more dangerous places than they were in the 1960s and 1970s, making security both a public and private concern. Declining legitimate opportunities, combined with the spread of drugs, make the issue of urban crime and violence a serious community preoccupation in most of the large cities of Latin America. It is one factor in the spread of gated communities and of a spatial segregation that isolates the poor and encloses the rich (Sabatini, Cáceres, and Cerda 2001). They also involve the police more directly in low-income settlements than would have been the case in the 1960s. The police may be ineffective and neighbors deeply divided over their presence, but the issue of adequate policing is a major preoccupation of citizens of all classes.

The involvement of various external actors in the lives of low-income communities is now extensive. In addition to police, health, and educational workers, it has become relatively normal for community welfare and development workers to be present. These may work for the local or provincial government, or for the central state, either as direct or contracted employees, or for an NGO. Protestant and Catholic churches were a strong presence in low-income communities in the 1960s (Roberts 1968). They remain so in the 1990s, but their role in articulating local populations with external actors has, I suggest, become a more prominent one.

The increasing impact of public policy on local populations is occurring in the context of an increase in individualization brought about partly by changes in family structure and partly by market-based consumption. Family size is declining throughout Latin America as a result of the sharp fertility declines since the 1970s. Also, households are becoming smaller as a result of the decline in extended families and a rise in single person, single parent, and two-person families (Roberts 2002). It is an important research issue to explore whether these demographic trends undermine household survival strategies based on pooling resources, on family caring for the elderly or infirm, and on collective consumption. Also, as the market in consumer goods has diversified with free trade and economic growth, patterns of consumption within families are likely to have become more individualized, with males and females, young and old, having distinctive patterns. Consumerism is part of the development of citizenship, as Sorj (2000) points out. In Brazil, for instance, consumers' rights movements are among the most powerful social movements in the country and have one of the largest memberships.

One of the most important issues in the institutionalization of the relation between the individual and the state is the gendered nature of citizenship and social policy (Jelin 1996c). Maxine Molyneux (2000a), in her review of studies of how women have been represented in social policy in Latin America, shows how the policy focus has evolved over time. Its focus changed from an exclusive concern with promoting and protecting motherhood and instilling in men a sense of responsibility as the breadwinner. In the 1990s, social policy addressed issues of women's public roles, such as their equitable representation in public office and their rights in the labor market, without, however, abandoning concern for women's traditional roles and upholding the principle of gender difference (ibid.). The legal involvement of the state in gender relations has intensified and diversified as a result. Molyneux also points out that there was considerable legal activity on gender relations in the 1990s. The greater sensitivity of the state to women's demands brings a variety of dilemmas between the relative advantages of co-optation and continuing opposition and between pursuing the politics of difference and the politics of equality. Rights of difference imply demanding rights that safeguard the unique identity and practices of the group to which the individual belongs, which in the case of ethnicity, can extend to demanding autonomy from the state (Escobar 1999; Gledhill 1997). Equality, in contrast, means demanding rights that guarantee that individuals, irrespective of their identities as women or members of ethnic groups, are treated as other citizens are, whether in the workplace, in politics, or in the home.

Exploring the extent and range of social policy impacts on gender relations are key issues for research. Does social policy present an undifferentiated image of the citizen that clashes with the way gender roles are socially defined in a given time and place (Molyneux 2000b)? And what is the changing reality of gender roles? A woman may be socially defined as dependent on her husband and viewed as an available unpaid caregiver, whereas in reality her employment contributes a substantial part of the household income and gives her less time for unpaid activities.

These various trends mean that the citizen's relation with the state in Latin America is now more based on individual identities, more multi-stranded, and a more necessary part of everyday life than it was in the 1960s and 1970s. Contemporary social policy is a mix of state and private systems of service provision. The state system in health, pensions, and education becomes increasingly a system for lower-income populations. In this context, the impact of social policy on social stratification is complex and potentially far-reaching.

Current research approaches to understanding poverty in Latin American cities that use the concept of vulnerability illuminate this complexity (Kaztman et al. 1999). Changes in the economy and in family structure bring risks to the contemporary Latin American city that can no longer be as easily handled as in the past through self-help and extended kin-based networks. Examples of groups made vulnerable by changes in economy and society are family businesses, the young in face of unemployment, workers on temporary contracts, female-headed single-parent households, and the elderly. Neighborhood can also be a factor in vulnerability. Thus there is evidence that the poor are doubly disadvantaged when they live in homogeneously poor neighborhoods—from being poor and by the lack of local facilities or sources of aid and information (Kaztman 1999; Filgueira 2002).

Social policy in several Latin American countries has adopted a vulnerability perspective. Programs in Argentina and Chile, for example, target "vulnerable" groups, usually on a community basis providing special programs for single mothers, the elderly, the young, and the handicapped. An issue with this approach is that it does not take an integrated view of the family and community context of vulnerability. As Kaztman and others (1999) point out, the disadvantage of the vulnerability perspective is that it can focus attention exclusively on the situation of the poor and neglect the responsibilities of other actors, such as state or private agencies. Absolute poverty and state neglect may be less of an issue than is the state's uniform handling of poverty situations that need more flexible and individualized approaches (Rosanvallon 2000). Uniform treatment makes the poor dependent on state services and less able to manage individually and strategically the range of institutional resources in education, information, or health required for survival in modern society. The poor are socially excluded not by neglect, but by the way more powerful actors in society channel the access of the poor to resources. Inequality of opportunity, rather than poverty, becomes the major research issue from the social exclusion perspective. And inequality is a more persistent feature of Latin American urban economies than is poverty.

In the 1960s and 1970s, the spread of education among low-income populations was a net benefit that enabled the young to take on the increasing numbers of jobs that demanded literacy and numeracy. The end of the 1990s may reveal education to have been less of a net benefit to low-income populations because the fit between education, income, and occupation has become a closer one. Low relative levels of education are more likely to disadvantage job seekers than they did in the past. It is no longer simply a question of getting some education, but of getting the right kind of education. Thus, the disadvantages of low-income populations now rest on questions of the quality of education that they receive in the schools they attend compared with the quality of education in private schools or schools in middle-class areas. These are the familiar issues concerning equality of educational opportunity in Europe and the United States. They are now important issues for Latin America (Roberts 2002).

Citizenship and the New Bases of Inequality

The changes in Latin America's political economy brought about by the ending of the Cold War and by economic and cultural globalization have made citizenship a key analytic perspective, as have the socioeconomic and demographic changes within the region. International pressures for electoral democracy and free markets have given a new salience to the individual rights of citizens. The decline in fertility and in family size, the gradual aging of the population, the closing of opportunities in urban labor markets, the increasing insecurity of even formal employment, and the increasing spatial consolidation of cities make family-based coping strategies less effective than in the past. Meeting people's needs for shelter and subsistence increasingly requires government and public nongovernment intervention as populations differentiate into groupings with special needs, such as the young, the elderly, single-parent mothers and mothers who work outside the home, and the unemployed. The affected populations emphasize the rights aspects of these needs. In contrast, governments tend to emphasize the duties involved, such as learning appropriate skills to compete in the market place, adopting practices that safeguard health, and helping maintain public security.

The increasing salience of citizenship issues occurs in a regional context in which there is little tradition of civic organization or of democratic government, and in which there are sharp inequalities between city and countryside, between regions, and between classes. This context poses the three particular challenges to the development of citizenship that are the focus of this chapter. First are the opportunities and dangers present in the new and individual relationship that is emerging between the state and the citizen, in which the state intervenes more deeply in the lives of citizens and expects more of them in terms of individual responsibilities. This relationship is often indirect as when the state delegates responsibilities to the private sector or to NGOs. When handled flexibly and with attention to local context, it can result in more effective government by targeting those with special needs. The downside, however, is that the new, more managerial state undermines civic organization and demand making as in the case of weakening trade unions through labor market deregulation or the cooptation of NGOs that previously had worked as advocates of community demands.

Second, citizenship is being increasingly experienced as a local, not a national, practice. There are many potential advantages to central government and local populations alike in fostering greater local participation in both administering services and in deciding priorities. There are also clear disadvantages, particularly in face of severe regional and local inequalities in resource distribution. The challenge is one of localities overcoming internal divisions and allying politically with other localities in like situations to remedy inequalities in resource distribution.

The third challenge is that of social policy. Though welfare is now more dependent on state provision than in the past, this trend runs the very real risk of promoting social differentiation and inequality. In the 1960s and 1970s, Latin American populations were considered marginal because they did not have access to state services. Contemporary marginality, as Wood argues in this volume, is more akin to an active process of exclusion in which social policy often plays a key role by tolerating differences between public and private services that condemn those dependent on public services to an inferior quality of life and constant insecurity.

One aspect of this is the increasing segregation of social classes in schools, medical facilities, consumer outlets, and neighborhoods. If this segregation is taking place, then as Kaztman (2001) argues, there are dire consequences for civic social capital—citizens with a common identity and interest in promoting the collective good. The pressing issue facing Latin America is sharp inequality in income and in quality of life, and that is a question of both class and citizenship. The emphasis on individual citizenship and participation has limited utility when citizens have inequality of access to needed services and where the potentially integrating institutions of citizenship—the health and educational services—segregate citizens by their social class.

6

The State of the State in Latin American Sociology

DIANE E. DAVIS

Seeking a Pulse

What is the state of the Latin American state these days, in both theory and practice? It may be hard to arrive at a ready answer to this question, because the attention paid to state theory and research seems to be dissipating. As the new millennium unfolds, other issues are slowly but surely crowding this topic off the sociological agenda. From social movements to civil society to globalization, the analytic focus for most sociologists interested in Latin America—including those who previously studied the state—seems to be shifting. Most of the current work on the Latin American state today is being advanced by political scientists, not sociologists, and for that reason its focus tends to be state policy outcomes or states as institutions governed by their own complex organizational dynamics. As such, the predominant analytic points of entry as well as the larger theoretical and practical questions about power, inequality, and development that sociologists used to pose with respect to the state are disappearing. Why is this the case, and what, if anything, should be done about it?

My objective in this paper is twofold: to track the "health" of the state as a vibrant conceptual subject and popular focus of scholarly research in the field of Latin American sociology; and to offer an analytic interpretation for its vicissitudes as a preferred topic of critical sociological inquiry. I begin with some preliminary remarks about epistemology and the framing devices that originally sustained sociological interest in the Latin American state.

The research for this paper was drawn with a close review of articles published in the following journals over the last fifteen years: *American Sociological Review, American Journal of Sociology, Latin American Research Review, Latin American Perspectives, Journal of Latin American Studies, Bulletin of Latin American Research, Revista Mexicana de Sociología, Tiempos Gerais: Revista de Ciencias Sociais e Historia, Revista Brasileira de Ciencias Sociais*. For the bibliographic review, I used the New School for Social Research and New York University's on-line searching index for books and periodicals as well as JSTOR and electronic databases available at Colombia University and the University of Washington. I thank Sun-Hee Yoon for research assistance with this bibliographic material.

Then I turn to conditions in Latin America and how (and why) they bolstered this sociological preoccupation. I start with a focus on the early 1970s
and 1980s, when the state was a bullying if not vigorous conceptual force to
be reckoned with, and follow the field through the 1990s up to the present,
when this inescapable thug appears to become a feeble ninety-pound weak-
ling relegated to the sidelines of scholarly contention. After examining the
historical and scholarly developments that account for these shifts, I present
some of the common prescriptions scholars now employ with the aim of
restoring the state's conceptual well-being and its centrality in contemporary studies of Latin America. I close with my own alternative remedies for
nursing the subject back to health, that is to say, for bringing a concern for
the state's relation to society back into the center of contemporary inquiry on
Latin America.

My focus is on the state as an independent variable in social change and
in economic development. This Weberian tradition of analysis has, until recently, been more common among sociologists based or trained in the
United States. I have tracked the trends in the analysis of the state on the
basis of my own primary and secondary research in this field over the last
several decades as well as through a bibliographic search and review of
recent books and articles produced by Latin Americanists both here and
abroad.

The Latin American Sociological Imagination and the Initial Framing of Research on the State

Historical shifts in interest in the state cannot be well understood without first surveying the ideals, scholarly aims, and larger professional ethos
of Latin American sociology and of the sociologists studying Latin America.
Over the decades, most sociologists of Latin America have carried with them
a telos, or an identifiable set of normative, theoretical, conceptual, and analytical frameworks drawn from their training or political commitments. As
such, the varying degrees of concern with the state among Latin American
sociologists were due not merely to the "facts" at hand but also to the political objectives and interpretive frameworks employed as scholars defined
their research aims and the field at large. Among the three most defining
features were a commitment to normative theorizing, a bias toward issues
of justice and radical social critique, and an analytic preoccupation with
power more than with the institutional or organizational configurations of

states. As society changed, these frameworks were transformed in ways that continued to affect whether, why, and how the state captured scholarly imagination among Latin American sociologists.

Normativity and Latin American Sociology

One of the most stable and defining characteristics of sociological research in Latin America, and one that still drives study among many sociologists, is its normative orientation. I define normativity as a primordial concern with effecting social change and a commitment to prescribing socially desirable practices and just political outcomes. Of course, in some sense sociologists all over the world have been preoccupied with what makes societies more fair, equitable, and harmonious, to a greater or lesser degree, such that this orientation could be said to define, to a great extent, the entire profession. But in some places, including the United States, a scientific orientation has tended to prevail over the normative one. In this context, the rules of "objectivity" and scientific method have been valued much more than the activist orientation and social implications of the work, almost to the point of assuming that these divergent approaches were mutually exclusive.

Among Latin Americanists, however, conditions have been quite different, at least until recently. Many leading sociologists born in the region have been social or political activists who were expected to—and frequently did—take public positions on society's most pressing problems. During periods of authoritarian rule a considerable number even went to jail or worked underground to achieve their larger political, social, or ethical aims. The strong normative orientation of Latin American sociology stems not merely from a principled position on the (in)appropriateness of the scientific method, but also from the larger philosophical tradition in which it is historically embedded. Until recently at least, Latin American sociologists were most influenced by the European tradition of social science not the North American. European social science itself developed through a direct engagement with European philosophy and the quest for normative propositions (especially as compared to the American schools of philosophy, where pragmatism reigned), Latin American sociologists were, by intellectual inheritance, inspired to pursue an openly normative orientation in their own work; and this did not easily translate into a focus on the state.

The social, class, and developmental dynamics of the times also factored into this orientation. As a profession, sociology in Latin America came into its own during the 1960s, at a critical juncture in the post–World War II history of the region when conditions were in rapid flux and when the challenges of political, social, and economic modernization were squarely on the table. Not only did this mean that social change, rather than stability, was a watchword of the discipline; it also meant that there existed a sense that many of the newfound transformations in Latin American societies could be still guided, and positively at that—an optimism that became increasingly rarer among scholars and citizens alike as the same old conflicts and problems relentlessly persisted or reemerged throughout the decades. For many years, the hope of turning traditional Latin American societies into "modern" and ostensibly "better" places inspired scholars to join the profession of sociology. And many chose this field rather than the more traditional specialties of law, political science, and economics, precisely because they were motivated to resist long-standing structures of power and offer different social alternatives for building the new world that conceivably lay just over the horizon.

The state's fate, however, was not only linked to the normative concerns of creating a better society that predominated in the field of sociology between the 1950s and the 1990s. The pervasiveness and character of state research was also directly affected by what was occurring in Latin America itself. Indeed, much of the failure to focus on the state during the 1950s and early 1960s stemmed not just from the prevailing currents in the field of European and North American sociology (where the state also failed to rate as a prime subject of study), but also from the fact that many in Latin America in the immediate postwar era were still working under the normative assumption that the region was primarily democratic and that its national states were doing the best they could to develop their nations economically in the face of new opportunities provided by the reigning political economy. One of the most popular and frequently cited Latin American sociological studies of this period, in fact, was Pablo González Casanova's *Democracy in Mexico* (1965), in which Mexico's system of one-party rule was still understood to be relatively democratic.

By the early 1960s and into the 1970s, there was growing sociological treatment of the hybrid styles of governance that were materializing in Latin America, especially but not exclusively the emergence of populism and populist regimes. However, these regimes were not usually analyzed in statist terms, that is, as forms of *state* rule. Di Tella's classic *Latin American Politics* (1985 Spanish version; 1990 English version) does not have a single chapter reserved for discussion of the state (he focuses instead on authority, power, and the military). The tradition of looking for the cultural—as much as economic or even bureaucratic—underpinnings of both power and politics, as exemplified in the work of one of Argentina's leading sociologists/historians, Juan Carlos Portantiero (1981), continued for decades. Rather, the starting point for most treatments of Latin American governments from among this early generation of sociologists was political ideology (namely, fascism, democracy, or populism), not state form or structure. This is well evidenced in the key works of leading Latin American sociologists of the time, such as Gino Germani's (1962) *Política y sociedad en una época de transición*. And for all these reasons, until the 1970s sociologists were not that prone to study the state, or even the government or political system for that matter, leaving these topics to political scientists and focusing instead on questions of modernization, the shift from rural to urban society, migration, industrialization, and demographic transition (see Germani 1955).

A Subject Is Born

During the 1960s and early 1970s, the concept and character of Latin American sociology also ebbed and flowed in response to the popularity of Marxist theorizing. At first, this meant that the grammar of regime type—a conceptual notion that lent credence to the idea that the form of the state could make a difference—still held little conceptual appeal for sociologists, who instead saw both democratic and authoritarian regimes as equally capable of sustaining capitalist development. To the extent that all capitalist regimes were frequently seen as equal—of a piece as it were—few Latin American sociologists found a need to pay attention to particular regime types, let alone different government administrations and their policy actions. This also meant that until the 1970s, more or less, most sociologists conceived of the state as an institution with a more universal function than that of specific regimes, and it was usually treated as if it existed as an entity independent of the ideology and political character of any particular regime. It was an "idea" as much as an identifiable actor.

However, starting in the mid-1970s, the rise of highly repressive state regimes acting with force against their own populations brought a new round of inquiries into the nature and power of states in their own right. Military rulers did not come to dominate all Latin American governments during this period. But because the major industrialized countries of Chile, Argentina, and Brazil were central in the practical and scholarly imaginations of social scientists at the time, the rise of authoritarian politics in these countries set the tone for the field as a whole. That the conventional sociological understanding of politics was shifting from a preoccupation with populism and democracy to that of states as bureaucratic institutions (a long-standing concern of the eminent sociologist Max Weber) was evident in several important works of this period, each of which preserved the sociological preoccupation with modernization of the capitalist variety but attempted to link it to the study of state forms and structures. Guillermo O'Donnell's seminal book, *Modernization and Bureaucratic-Authoritarianism: Studies in South American Politics* (1973), was highly influential in shifting the intellectual emphasis to states. Although a political scientist by training, O'Donnell's study appealed to sociologists not just because, like Weber, he focused on bureaucracy, but because he argued that the bureaucratic-authoritarian state form—in which democratic legislatures became irrelevant as ever more powerful administrative structures of the national state made all key decisions—was central to the aims of economic modernization and class power.

Biography of a Field: From Healthy Subject to Ninety-Pound Weakling

Among sociologists who subsequently turned their attention to these repressive and highly bureaucratized states, three key directions prevailed. One focused more on the class projects embedded in state structures and practices. For example, Ian Roxborough (1984a) examined national populism in terms of the institutional connections between working classes and state structures. To the extent that this meant recasting populist regimes in state-centric as much as cultural or ideological terms, a concern with the state was introduced to those who cared about political systems and ideologies more generally (Roxborough 1984b). The second focused more on the state's relative autonomy (a condition still understood as related to class power in Nora Hamilton's (1982) *The Limits to State Autonomy*). The third was a hybrid of the first two: a preference for integrating a concern with class power and capitalist development into studies of state power and structure, be it military rule or bureaucratic-authoritarianism. This third approach was particularly evident in the work of another group of sociologists, many of whom were preoccupied with normative questions of how to understand and reverse economic dependency and underdevelopment. Building on the path-breaking work of Fernando Henrique Cardoso and Enzo Faletto (1967), who analyzed the relations between class politics, the states that embodied them, and the resulting differences in dependent economic development, a growing number of sociologists began to study the state from the vantage point of its role in economic processes. In the United States, Peter Evans's *Dependent Development: The Alliances of Multinational, State, and Local Capital in Brazil* (1979) further set the terms for subsequent studies on the state's role in economic development by offering a masterful synthesis of both the global and domestic class dimensions of underdevelopment. In his analysis, the Latin American state had a special role in forging a "triple alliance" between state, class, and multinational forces in such a way as to generate prospects for development even in the context of economic dependency. By identifying the state as a key actor in developmental class alliances, Evans's writings also opened a new window for social activism and a sustained normative critique of the political and economic status quo. And combined with the continued interest in the authoritarian and repressive features of these (same) governments, studies of the state began to loom large among sociologists working on Latin America.

To be sure, diverse approaches were employed in this burgeoning collection of political and economic writings on the state. Some preferred to focus on historical studies of state formation, while others examined the state's policy actions, and still others concentrated on the pacts between the state, labor, and capital. Among the most interesting of these studies were Susan Eckstein's *The Poverty of Revolution: The State and the Urban Poor in Mexico* (1977), Maurice Zeitlin's *The Civil Wars in Chile: or, the Bourgeois Revolutions That Never Were* (1984), and Viviane Brachet-Márquez's *The Dynamics of Domination: State, Class, and Social Reform in Mexico, 1910–1990* (1994). However, the so-called developmental state took the lion's share of attention; and among those scholars who examined the developmental state specifically, healthy debate about its origins and contours continued throughout the 1980s and into the 1990s.

One of the most contested theoretical issues was the notion of state autonomy. The growing preoccupation with state autonomy among sociologists working on Latin America may also have resulted from efforts in the discipline overall to "bring the state back in," a theme fueled by the Weberian-oriented writings of Theda Skocpol and Charles Tilly, among others. Skocpol's influence on the debate over state autonomy in Latin America was most keenly felt as a result of the book she co-edited with Peter Evans and Dietrich Rueschemeyer, titled *Bringing the State Back In,* which included several articles on the developing world. But no matter the angle, approach, or position on autonomy, the state reigned as a central point of reference for many sociologists working on Latin America in the 1980s and early 1990s, whether they were concerned with economic development, repressive states, or the interrelations between the two.

Maintaining Strength Despite Global Challenges

At first, scholars comparing development in different world regions began to place more emphasis on the world-systemic or global dimensions of development in late industrializers, arguing that East Asian countries were more successful than Latin American countries because the character of their articulation with the global economy and the nature of the world-system at the time they began industrialization were entirely different (Gereffi and Wyman 1990). This argument both followed from and reinforced the insignificance attributed to the state in world-system theory. Yet once world-system theory began to replace dependency theory as the paradigm of choice, the state threatened to drop out of the picture. The relative neglect of the state among world-system theorists, in fact, has only recently been overturned in the work on hegemonic transitions by Giovanni Arrighi and Beverly Silver (1999), in which they incorporate analysis of states and interstate relations into their world-system framework.

Many sociologists of Latin America, even if they did not study the region in direct contrast with East Asia, tended to reinforce this trend by turning their attention toward commodity chains and other global linkages and away from domestic dynamics, particularly the relations between states and classes that had been central in dependency theory and in the dependent development argument. Still, rather than undermine research on the state, the academic challenges of the "real world" ended up reinforcing an interest in this subject of study. This was first evident in arguments that it was the extent of state autonomy that was responsible for differences and similarities among East Asia and Latin America, not merely differences in the global contexts and networks of development. And this, in turn, led to another round of discussions of state autonomy—and its presence or absence—in Latin America.

Another positive outcome of the efforts to come to terms with the seemingly divergent developmental paths followed in Latin America and East Asia was that sociologists began to cultivate a more nuanced view of the similarities and differences among these regions and their states, as well as how to study them. And in these studies, where history and culture were as important as politics and economy, sociologists further buttressed the centrality of state research by extending their cross-disciplinary engagement to include anthropologists and historians. Accordingly, the overall implications of debates over state autonomy and comparative development for the vibrancy of state research were rather positive.

The steadfast character of research on the state is perhaps best exemplified in recent work by Peter Evans. His book *Embedded Autonomy* (1995) makes a renewed if not even stronger case for the importance of studying states and classes in the global context almost twenty years after many of these ideas first hit pay dirt, while a most recent article (Evans and Rauch 1999) on development actually posits the causal importance of state autonomy. For Evans and others, then, the world-recognized successes of the East Asian tigers did not completely bump studies of the developmental state (in Latin America and elsewhere) or state autonomy off the sociological map. Rather, they provided a basis for continually reformulating central claims about the state and how to study it, thereby saving this subject from complete extinction (Davis 2004).

The paradox, however, was that arguments that kept the state ascendant if not central in sociological research for so many years, especially the concept of state autonomy, also ended up laying the conditions for its subsequent decline in popularity. This occurred mainly because the notion of autonomy, no matter the theoretical frame in which it was cast, emphasized the state's analytical disconnection from society. And as the state became increasingly considered as distinct from society, sociologists slowly began to lose their theoretical, normative, conceptual, and analytic interest in the topic, while political scientists and economists stepped in to fill the void.

From Robust to Poor Health: Social Movements as First Antidote to State-Centrism

The declining normative and theoretical interest in the state as an agent of change was first evident in the late 1980s and early 1990s. One of the key intellectual challenges leveled at scholars committed to state-centered research in the late 1980s and early 1990s was the upswing in citizen-led social movements, coupled with the rise of a new round of struggles over democracy (Eckstein 1989; Foweraker in this volume). These mobilizations not only shifted the normative sentiments of activists and scholars away from the developmental state and toward civil society; they also turned a considerable number of sociologists away from the long-standing concern with political economy that had been central to the sociological quest. Notably and in contrast, sociologists examining other regions of the world were still working hard to integrate studies of state formation and social movements, rather than dropping the former for the latter (Barkey and Parikh 1991).

As social movements began to be studied more and more on their own terms, a strong but minority holdout of sociologists still insisted that it was impossible to understand the successes of social movements without a closer understanding of the state (Davis 1994). But with the growing popularity of social movement studies among sociologists working on Latin America, the state was increasingly ignored; and without conscientious or careful nurturing, it receded to the sidelines of study, only to languish in the darkness of inattention. The renewed interest in civil society, culture, and identity became so pronounced among Latin American sociologists that even studies of the most quintessential form of "old" statist politics—namely, those of populism—were by the late 1990s being analyzed once again as cultural practices and networks as much as state-centered institutional allegiances that linked citizens (or classes) to a governing state apparatus. One of the most innovative studies to take this approach was Javier Auyero's study of populism in Argentina, *Poor People's Politics* (2001). But despite the gains made in this scholarship, the overall shift in emphasis did not bode well for the state, which faced continual discrediting as the institutional location or intellectual focus for understanding or even "doing politics" of the social justice variety.

A Near-Death Experience? The Combined Weight of Poststructuralism, Liberalization, and Globalization

If the activation of civil society could not kill the state as both subject of theoretical inquiry and object of normative struggle, the rise of poststructuralism as an academic movement, the triumph of liberalization as a political and economic movement, and the advent of globalization as the signature postmodern movement of the contemporary world all conspired to send it directly to the steps of the morgue.

In sociological studies of Latin America, the poststructuralist influence of scholars like Michel Foucault and Jacques Derrida was evident in the critique of Marxism and an expanding understanding of power and domination to include its social constructivist dimensions. Together, these epistemological "correctives" meant that seizing state power was no longer considered a legitimate aim, and that domination and repression were no longer confined to the coercive arms of the state apparatus. These assumptions further pushed activists and sociologists to seek normative redress for their problems in civil society and the market as much as the state. By the late 1990s, in fact, the state's power was likely to be understood as "de-centered," or resting outside of the formal bounds of government agencies as much as within them. In this reading, articulated in books like Jeffrey Rubin's *Decentering the Regime: Ethnicity, Radicalism, and Democracy in Juchitán, Mexico* (1997), a national state's power was socially constructed in "de-centered" regional practices and among citizens whose actions either supplanted or undermined national state projects (Rubin 2002).

As if that were not enough, during the 1990s the extensive reach and growing popularity of political and economic liberalization, as both an ideal and a World Bank–imposed practice, gave a solid rationale for more conventional scholars to jump on the global bandwagon and further bypass the state as a serious subject of study. Not only did economic liberalization generally entail downsizing of state budgets and capacities and a commitment to decentralization, thereby limiting the national state's policy capacity to make a difference in citizens lives. Political liberalization generally exposed the corrupt and rent-seeking practices of state actors and institutions in such a way as to delegitimize efforts to recast them as suitable forces in the liberal reconstitution of society. As a result, the tasks of democratization, political reconstruction, and social ordering were left to citizens, or at least that was the normative argument being advanced from domestic and international corners of NGOs, multilateral lending agencies, and international financial institutions. If any government agency was to be involved, it was most likely the municipality, owing to the increasing commitment to decentralization that accompanied political and economic critiques of strong, rent-seeking national states.

Clearly, there may have been a chicken-egg dynamic occurring here. With political and economic liberalization ascendant, a steady demise of protectionist-oriented ISI programs, and the triumph of market ideals and practices, states and national political parties were already banishing sociologists from their inner circle of advisers. In those conditions, it was not surprising that the bulk of normatively oriented and left-leaning sociologists, who in the past might have devoted their energies to supplying states with research justifying protectionism and other social policy gains, would now shun the state too, and ally themselves with citizen movements as both an offensive and defensive posture. Whatever the origins, the state's failure to embrace the normative and theoretical ideals of sociologists tended to match their own intellectual disenfranchisement with the leviathan, turning them into enemies much more than collaborators. There were only a few exceptions, such as Fernando Enrique Cardoso and his chief policy adviser, Vilmar Faria.

Decentralization Fuels an Eleventh-Hour Recovery

Paradoxically, the wave of academic and policymaking interest in political and economic decentralization did offer a temporary antidote to the decline in state studies. Decentralization as political ideal and institutional practice captured the attention of a growing number of Latin American scholars in the late 1990s, and with these studies the state as a key institution slipped back into view (Ward, Rodriquez, and Mendoza 1999; Rodriguez 1997; Willis, Garman, and Haggard 1999). Many of these new studies posed questions about the actual logistics of state reform, selecting for further scrutiny certain state programs (poverty, health, education, and so on) that were being decentralized and transformed by liberalization requisites (Kay 1999; Lloyd-Sherlock 1997; Pastor and Wise 1997; Angell and Graham 1995).

As such, discursive reference to the state experienced a mini-revival, as did a newfound commitment to studying its intra-institutional dynamics and internal logic, since reforming government structures both locally and nationally was considered to be among the principal tasks at hand. It was in the context of this new round of literature on state reform and decentralization that questions about the welfare state entered the Latin American scholarly lexicon, further reviving an interest in state research, if only by offering a possible point for cross-national comparison in ways surprisingly absent in the past. Examples are Nicholas Spulber's (1997) *Redefining the State in Latin America: Privatization and Welfare Reform in Industrializing and Transitional Economies,* Evelyne Huber and John Stephens's (2000) *The Political Economy of Pension Reform: Latin America in Contemporary Perspective,* and the edited collection of Evelyne Huber (2002), *Models of Capitalism: Experiences from Latin America.*

But somehow the promise of full renewal—or better said, any hoped for resurgence of serious interest in the state—has remained surprisingly unmet, at least in the field of sociology. If anything, it is political scientists who are most likely to be taking up the mantle, by turning en masse to studies of the welfare state, decentralization, and state reform (Kaufman 1999; Mares 1993; E. Silva 1996). In itself, handing over the baton is nothing to be criticized. But it is important to acknowledge, not only because it speaks to the fate of the state in the discipline of sociology in particular, but also because it explains why so many current studies of the state in Latin America fail to pose eminently sociological questions about relations between state and society, or between states and social or political justice, or even between states and economic development. Such relational questions are not high on the agenda for most political scientists, many of whom, in addition to accepting state agencies as relatively discrete institutional entities, also tend to lean toward a rational-choice framing for their research (or at least that is so among North American political scientists studying Latin American states). It is for this reason, in fact, that so many of the current studies examining decentralization or state reform in Latin America conceptualize the state as a relatively autonomous set of bureaucratic actors, governed by rational procedures and efficiency-producing practices, who are almost completely unconnected to the social and political forces or conditions around them.

Accordingly, when the state was understood as a neutral and rational institutional subject rather than an embodiment of unjust force, most sociologists with experience on the topic turned to other issues that could provide a better point of entry for their normative concerns. Some of the first defections came from among well-known state scholars who now turned their attention to domestic and international social movements or to newer versions of the national development question that transcended the nation-state, such as the study of regional paths of change (Gereffi and Fonda 1992). Peter Evans's (2002) interest in labor and municipal-level struggles in the context of globalization also is exemplary in these regards. Still, in a slight departure from the past, many of these concerns began to be studied in the context of globalization rather than with a direct view to the state and its actions. Evans, Rueschemeyer, and Huber Stephens's *States Versus Markets in the World-System* (1985) was one of the first to stake out this territory. Since its publication more than fifteen years ago, the volume of writing on globalization and its impact on the state has multiplied dramatically (Sassen 2000; Robinson 2004; Sklair 2002).

Sociologists working on Latin America still continued to study the state, but turned their attention to how it operated in an ever more liberalized, decentralized, and globalized political and economic context. One of the best initial studies in these regards was Miguel Angel Centeno's *Democracy Within Reason* (1994). More recently, Teivo Teivaninen's *Enter Economism, Exit Politics: Experts, Economic Policy, and the Damage to Democracy* (2002) continued the tradition, but comes in much more highly critical of the political impact of globalization than does Centeno. Even so, the concern with democracy and national politics evident in both these books is now being eclipsed as the state is increasingly held conceptual hostage to discourses of globalization. If politics or national development trajectories are being studied, they are just as likely to be seen as in direct articulation with globalization in ways that bypass the state altogether, as evidenced by both Marcus Schulz's (1998) article on transnational social movements in Latin America and Smith, Chatfield, and Pagnucco's *Transnational Social Movements and Global Politics: Solidarity Beyond the State,* as well as by Mauro Guillén's study of firms' organizational adaptation, *The Limits of Convergence: Globalization and Organizational Change in Argentina, South Korea, and Spain* (2001). Accordingly, there is growing recognition that globalization has transformed Latin American societies and economies in such a way as to push domestic dynamics out of the picture, with the state being one of the first casualties. Discourses of globalization seem to have almost entirely trumped consideration of the determinative role played by the national state, even among those Latin Americanists who used to examine national and global interconnections. Robinson has gone so far as to argue that "globalisation represents a shift from the nation-state to a new transnational phase of capitalism" (1998b, 111).

Just What the Doctor Ordered? Common Prescriptions and Alternative Remedies

So is there any hope for resuscitating the state as a compelling subject of study for sociologists? I would hope so. Both in theory and in practice, there appear to be at least three areas of study in which scholars are working earnestly to revive the moribund patient. The first and most common approach is to recast old questions about the conditions under which Latin American states have been able to maintain some independent institutional autonomy or political capacity, despite the onward march of globalization. Methodologically speaking, this is old wine in new bottles of course, since this task has long engaged Latin American sociologists, especially in the context of academic tensions between world-system and class-centered theorists of the region. But scholars taking this approach today are making efforts to pop the cork in a slightly different fashion. In the past much of the focus was placed on the ways that domestic politics and social movements gave national states the wherewithal to direct foreign investors or global capital flows. In the present we see much more analysis of the selective institutional and territorial mediations within nation-states and between them and certain global markets. Thus the conclusion among some scholars today is that, far from destroying the role and significance of the national state, globalization may actually increase its importance, but only with respect to some of its institutions and policies; or perhaps even just with respect to certain subnational state agencies, like provinces, large cities, and even regions that have more political or economic leeway to negotiate investment packages and trading relations with global firms than do national states.

Among the most intriguing lines of analysis in these regards are those which focus on exchange rate and banking policy (Maxfield 1997; Sassen 2001), as well as those which ask questions about the politics of macroeconomic policymaking in the context of a renewed commitment to federalism. Some conclusions drawn from these studies suggest a rethinking of the increasingly dominant view that international institutions like the World Bank, or a global network of capitalists, will, by nature, overdetermine the domestic economic policymaking capacity of states. They also suggest that in future studies we should pay more attention to the articulation of domestic financial institutions and practices with the state, or more specifically, to the state's fiscal and monetary policy, rather than just to the state's industrial and employment policies or to politics and the social movements that affect them—themes that preoccupied sociologists in the past. We also should be prepared to understand the different territorial components of the state, as well as the ways that national states connect to municipalities and regional authorities or other "local states," through federalism or other nationally and locally agreed-upon power-sharing relations.

To do so, sociologists will have to continue reaching out to their old disciplinary partners in political science and learn from them, by introducing more intra-institutional nuance into their work while avoiding a fall into the rational choice trap of conceptualizing the state as an inherent "thing" with agency. The nation-state is not the only state bureaucracy that matters; there are also internal divisions in the national state and subnational state agencies. Sociologists also must be prepared to draw equally from economists, whose expertise in financial and monetary matters have helped push forward this effective deconstruction of states, if you will, by analyzing the source and dynamics of multiple domains in which decisions are made about flows of money and commodities. Both insights will lead sociologists to study and make sense of intrastate conflicts or countervailing tendencies within the same states. That is, rather than see the state as a single conglomerate of institutions, organized as a nationally coherent apparatus sitting on top of civil society and working hand-in-hand with domestic or global capital, sociologists must be prepared to conceptualize states as both embedded in and cross-cut by competing territorial, social, economic, and institutional dynamics.

A closer examination of the ways that fiscal and monetary policies mediate globalization helps make this point. Many of the financial agencies in charge of facilitating globalization, among them central banks, have been historically isolated from the more "politicized" institutional arms of government. This means that these institutions are less apt to be affected by domestic social and political conditions. But it does not necessarily follow that their organizational dynamics do not conceal certain class or political interests, or that they are completely unconnected to the state and its governance aims. Sarah Babb's (2001) study of economists in Mexico, *Managing Mexico: Economists from Nationalism to Neoliberalism,* which chronicles the political and social ties of central bank personnel to both national and internationally situated academic and institutional elites, makes this absolutely clear. The better lesson to draw, then, is that organizational and policymaking dynamics of state-run organizations might be different in a more global context, as will the social and political (and personal) networks governing flows of capital; but both will still be situated in domestic institutional and political conditions. At minimum, such knowledge must be integrated into the understanding of a state's overall profile to produce such new questions as *which* of its component parts hold autonomy or are embedded, vis-à-vis whom and with what larger political, social, and global significance?

Once these questions are raised, we might be well advised to return to "older" topics like power, party structures, and the extent of organization of civil society. Yet rather than pose these with respect to states as a whole, democratic or nondemocratic, we should pose them in the context of certain agencies or components of the state and how they employ conflict or harmony to produce certain outcomes, global and otherwise. Would Latin American countries with certain party systems, certain regional histories, certain economic legacies (e.g., exporting vs. importing), or certain democratic transitions use different structures, decision-making processes, or procedures to staff their central banks or finance ministries than other dependencies? Under these and other conditions, would different ministries find themselves more or less estranged from the requisites of electoral politics, or more or less limited by internal administrative infighting between separate arms of the government (such as secretaries of industry, labor, environment, and so on)? It is only by answering these questions that we will know about the contemporary dynamics of Latin American states and their impact on political and economic development in particular countries or the region as a whole.

From Generic Prescriptions to Alternative Medicine

A second area of study that holds the potential to renew interest in the Latin American state is citizenship. As Bryan Roberts (in this volume) shows, the study of citizenship is a growing topic of research that is already moving beyond its infancy. Until recently, however, it was developed primarily in the context of questions about democratization and social movements, not necessarily the state. So in what ways would the direct study of the relations between citizens and the state provide points of continuity as well as discontinuity within this larger body of literature?

In some ways, it depends on the angle. There is the regime-type angle, which links citizenship to the emergence of democratic structures and procedures, making it possible for individuals to participate in politics and make claims on the government in return for their acceptance as electorally enfranchised members of a larger political body. Although commonly related to questions of formal democratization and pursued primarily by political scientists, this is a topic that goes far beyond an understanding of the presence or absence of a democratic political system. If anything, it presupposes some deeper understanding of the changing institutional structures of the state and how they articulate with socially constructed concerns about inclusion, identity, and a political or social commitment to liberalism as a modern state project.

To truly understand citizenship, then, it is necessary to cultivate a deeper understanding of the political and social histories of certain countries. It also requires a better knowledge of the institutional histories of states and their governing institutions, including the extent of centralization/decentralization and the role that parties play (or not) in mediating the participation of citizens and these new structures of the state (Negretto and Aguilar-Rivera 2000). It is along these lines—already established by Huber (2002) and her Latin American collaborators, such as Fernando Filgueira—that scholars could work harder to link the study of citizenship to more eminently sociological topics like the welfare states. By linking citizenship to this theme, scholars of Latin America would consider some of the central questions about structures of claim-making and participation noted above, yet they also would raise them in the context of questions about the state's social policy obligations to citizens. This move could take studies of the Latin American state in a new direction by forcing them to think about what states "owe" their citizens, thereby putting the state back into civil society rather than just pursuing long-standing questions about how to get the state *out* of citizens' lives (as has been customary as of late).

To pay more attention to the conditions under which national states do or don't have legitimate cause to be involved in social policymaking for their citizens will also provide a unique opportunity to link long-standing sociological questions about rebellion, guerrilla movements, cultural pluralism, and even nationalism to the emergence or legitimacy of the Latin American state. This means connecting standard old issues to entirely new concerns, and posing questions about them within an alternative analytical and theoretical packaging that itself can be the source of debate. Probably the best if not most provocative example that comes to mind here is the Zapatista movement of Chiapas. One principle organizing issue carried forward by this social movement is its claim that the people of the Lancandon region of Mexico should have their own political, cultural, and social institutions and structures, and specifically, that they should be able to exist alongside—but not subordinated to—the Mexican national state. What makes this movement so significant for state theorists, then, is not its composition and character, or even its potential for building alliances and achieving successes, but the larger implications of its existence for long-standing projects of national states, especially those states that define themselves as offering services and institutions of national integration in exchange for loyalty and monetary tribute.

Movements such as the Zapatistas could be studied not merely in collective action or civil society terms but also as challenges to conventional forms, practices, and routine expectations associated with welfare states and the conventional views of citizenship, offering in their place new ideologies and practices of governing and citizen participation in an alternative "imagined community," as Benedict Anderson would call it. In short, such movements raise new questions about who is to determine the scope and membership of the national state, and possibly even whether competing "welfare states" within the same national territory can still be considered part of the same nation. Notice that these questions hold some elective affinity with those raised in the context of the literature on decentralization, municipalization, and even local political participation. But they are posed in the context of a highly mobilized citizenry that offers a very different understanding of what legitimately constitutes the state as a larger political, social, and national ideal, not merely how it is structured as an interrelated set of local and national institutions.

Toward a Healthy (New) Subject:
Beyond States as Institutions

I close by discussing one last area of inquiry that promises to offer a particularly innovative means for bringing research on the state back into the center of Latin American studies, namely, the rule of law, a topic that is just beginning to capture scholarly imagination. I see this topic as comprised of three subareas of inquiry, although obviously there may be more. One is the study of constitutions and constitutionalism; the second is the study of the judicial system and how it functions; and the third involves the examination of the police, violence, and criminality. All three of these themes are capturing attention from a variety of corners in Latin America, ranging from citizens, politicians, and international agencies to a small but growing number of academics; and they each reflect or speak to some of the most pressing political and social challenges facing Latin America today. Juan Méndez, Guillermo O'Donnell, and Paolo Sergio Pinheiro in *The (un)Rule of Law and the Underprivileged in Latin America* (1999) argue that the democratic transition and the demise of authoritarian rule have placed questions about constitution-building directly in the center of public debate and active political contention—either because old constitutions were in disarray, because they were formulated under old political, social, and economic arrangements that no longer hold in the newly liberalized and democratic societies, or because they were ignored or violated in ways that sustained the repressive actions of states against their peoples. Now that democracy has materialized across the hemisphere, however, at least in a formal sense, many Latin American politicians and activists are turning to the rule of law as embodied in constitutions or constitutional constraints on state action in order to insure that such practices will not continue or to establish alternative legal foundations for a new, hopefully more just, and deeply democratic, society (Ensalaco 1994; French 1998).

Although formal democracy is in place, many of the problems associated with arbitrary power remain, and in some instances they have intensified, producing what Guillermo O'Donnell and his colleagues have called the "unrule" of law. Indeed, political and economic liberalization is partially responsible for this lawlessness (Davis and Alvarado 1999). It cannot be a complete coincidence that in three of the main "transitional" countries of Latin America—Mexico, Brazil, and Argentina—police and military impunity and violence have skyrocketed out of control even while new democratic institutions and practices have taken root. Granted, the perpetrators of the violence are not always acting on behalf of the (authoritarian) state as in the past, as Martha Huggins (1991) shows in her work on vigilantism; nor are state-employed actors the only ones to participate in illegal and violent practices. But much of the problem as perceived in Latin America today owes to actions of those who are now, or were in the immediate past, directly employed by the state, as is obvious in the cases of military and police impunity (Zaverucha 1993; Pereira and Davis 2000). Anthony Pereira's book on this subject, *Political (In)justice: National Security Legality in Brazil and the Southern Cone,* as well as Martha Huggins's body of work on military and police torturers (Huggins, Haritos-Fatouros, and Zimbardo 2002) and her study *Political Policing* (1998), make this distressingly clear.

Knowing the formal institutional structures and legislative actions of a governing state apparatus is not sufficient if one seeks to understand the political and social conditions that govern civil society and everyday life. The secret, rather, lies in closer examination of the character and viability of the rule of law more generally. For this reason, perhaps, we are starting to see studies of the rule of law and constitutions, not just in terms of their relationship to democracy, but also as related to economic development, as seen in the recent study by Yves Dezalay and Bryant G. Garth, *The Internationalization of Palace Wars: Lawyers, Economists, and the Contest to Transform Latin American States* (2002).

The study of constitutions or other legal practices, and how they sustain rule of law, takes sociological work in new directions by offering alternative analytical ways of thinking about the best types of institutional arrangements that must be guaranteed in order to protect individual freedoms. It allows sociologists to pose those questions not through examination of the particular regimes or state structures that uphold legal or illegal practices, so much as through an examination of the "contractual" arrangements or social and political franchises agreed upon (or not) between state and society and embodied in constitutions in ways that give life and continuity to these practices. Again, this analytic aim is not so different than that embodied in some of the initial sociological work on Latin American states in the 1970s and 1980s, particularly corporatist ones. But rather than see labor movements or political parties as the socially or politically significant "integrative" forces in the state-society nexus, in today's Latin America it appears to be constitutions that are being conceptualized as one of the key mediating or integrative institutions linking citizens to the state and establishing the programmatic and legitimate contours of the social and political contract.

To be sure, one could argue that studying constitutions—or offering normatively oriented scholarship for constructing new ones—does very little good in settings where the constitution is continually ignored or routinely violated, as Dezalay and Garth (2002) point out. But what makes this topic theoretically compelling is precisely the fact that there may not necessarily be any direct correlation between regime type, state strength, constitutionalism, and rule of law generally speaking. For this reason, scholars are consequently turning to a second issue as well, the judicial system, and linking studies of constitutions to studies of a nation's legal structures and practices in their entirety. Some of the most interesting work in these regards is offered by those who are examining how Latin American states, under pressure from civil society, are playing an active role in restructuring their judicial systems in an effort to put an end to judicial corruption, streamline the administration of justice, modernize the legal apparatus, and create new arenas of arbitration for marginal populations. For example, Mark Ungar's *Elusive Reform: Democracy and the Rule of Law in Latin America* (2002) examines how public officials' efforts in democratic Argentina and Venezuela have, in the end, given police more (and not less) power, in no small part because the main strategies used to reform police by democratic governments usually entail embedding them in the state, where they are affected by budget crises and a weak judiciary, both of which contribute to further abuses of power. One implication of Ungar's findings is that police reform cannot be effective unless it simultaneously entails a full overhaul of the judiciary, which, in a democracy, is bound to be a long and drawn-out affair. And this in turn suggests that democracy and police reform (which, again, must be accompanied by a reform of the judiciary) can make slightly uneasy bedfellows. The study of judicial systems, like constitutions, involves a deeper understanding of the state-society nexus and how it is both implicated in and transformed by recent social and political developments.

A third and final subtheme of study that both speaks to questions of the rule of law and serves as a principal means of bringing the state back into the Latin American sociological research agenda is that involving crime and violence, be it military and police-related or not. For too long, this topic was effectively absent in Latin America, with the exception perhaps of a series of country-specific studies (mainly Colombia and more recently, Brazil). Now, as crime and violence dramatically continue on the upswing across the region more generally, it is time for sociologists across the region to start making some theoretical and analytical headway, perhaps by linking these questions to an understanding of state formation, liberalization, and regime change.

As just noted, some of the first work linking violence and impunity to the state was produced more than two decades ago by Paul Oquist, in his *Violence, Conflict, and Politics in Colombia* (1980), in which endemic violence was attributed to incomplete processes of state formation. His writings still serve as inspiration for contemporary scholars of Colombia, who continue to examine the role of regional elites and paramilitaries in conflict with the national state and the ways this reinforces citizen and state violence. More recently, Miguel Centeno has picked up where Oquist left off, providing an account of Latin American state formation with a more comprehensive and sociologically well-theorized framing. His *Blood and Debt: War and the Nation-State in Latin America* (2002) links a series of problems long identified with the Latin American state—institutional weakness, endemic corruption, and repressive violence wielded against its citizenry to name but a few—to the absence of external war-making. Books like *Blood and Debt* are especially important for those with an interest in contemporary Latin American states because they pose queries about violence and impunity in the context of both state de-formation as much as state formation, as well as with a view to the ethos and activities of agents of the state (police, paramilitaries, militaries) and how they determine conditions in civil society, independent of authoritarian or democratic regime-type (Davis and Pereira 2003).

In the past police, military, and even paramilitary violence tended to be seen as an artifact of military or authoritarian rule (Chevigny 1995; Huggins 1998, 1991). But the fact that these problems seem to persist even after democratic transition has spurred further examination of their origins and dynamics as well as how or why they may persist within formally democratic states. Some scholars now choose to focus on international markets for drugs and arms, either as a problem itself or as part and parcel of processes of liberalization and globalization. Others choose to look at the ways that economic liberalization produces growing income inequality and new market practices, both of which are seen as fueling criminal behavior and informal networks of gang and mafia organizations. But what most of these studies tend to share is the assumption that current and former agents of the state have somehow become involved in the violence and criminality, thereby sustaining a larger ethos of impunity and unrule of law. And with this framing, even those scholars who focus on more traditional explanatory factors like income inequality, poverty, and drugs also have directly engaged issues of state transformation as well as the new context of state-society relations.

Where to Now?

We close by offering two sets of sociological questions that build on these newer lines of research, in the hopes that they may lead the way in fueling a new round of innovative theoretical and empirical inquiry into the Latin American state and its relationship to society. One is the extent to which political and administrative changes in the agencies, institutions, and structures of the state are keeping up with changes in regimes, in this case the shift from authoritarian to democratic regimes. Insofar as structures and institutions of the police and military stay intact even with regime change, and insofar as efforts to purge old repressive elements of the coercive state apparatus, if it is done at all, can never be entirely comprehensive, new democratic regimes will have structures, networks, or individual elements of the authoritarian state embedded within them. The task at hand, then, is how to document, account for, and theorize these developments—the embeddedness of old regimes in new states, if you will—as well as chart their larger impact on and significance for the state's legitimacy and power as well as for public security and rule of law.

A second area of questioning would build on a much closer examination of the police, and how they have developed the corrupt ethos, coercive capacities, and rent-seeking structures that currently prevail across many of the countries in the region. Most previous work by Latin Americanists on the coercive state apparatus took the military as its main point of departure. But this meant that scholars in the past failed to cultivate a deeper theoretical and analytical engagement with the police, who have been and continue to be formidable agents of political repression, social control, and now more than ever, impunity vis-à-vis citizens and the state itself. Yet with the exception of several important historical studies focused on authoritarian regimes or criminality (Kalmanowiecki 2003, 2000; Aguirre and Buffington 2000), and new work by Huggins and Ungar noted earlier, Latin American sociologists still know very little about the police, how they see themselves, how they operate, and the extent to which they are structured as institutional forces standing between the state and society even as they overlap with or work against both. These questions are important, not just because of our general ignorance of these socially pressing topics, but also because now, in the heyday of transition, such mediating or "liminal" elements like the police seem to have held ever greater sway, in no small part because the transition leaves both state and society in the process of reorganization. Police hold inordinate power in transitional moments not just because they generally preserve their institutional continuity (it is very hard to fire police, especially those implicated in past governmental abuses), but also because state structures, regime profiles, and even economic practices are themselves in formation and not yet consolidated. In these conditions, police remain a central but potentially dangerous force.

If one were to identify a key normative research aim for sociologists in the new millennium, then, one that touches on questions of social justice, I would vote for a closer examination of policing, police impunity, and the attendant violence of everyday life sustained by police abuse of power. To the extent that much of the initial sociological research on the state owed to a concern with those institutions and actors holding unjust coercive capacity and repressive potential, who seemed unresponsive to citizen demands for social justice and a better quality of life, then this topic clearly holds considerable affinity with past state-centered research. Constitutions, legal systems, police: these are the pressing new subjects still waiting to be studied, and each can shed new light on age-old questions of security, freedom, rights, and justice as well as the formal and informal practices that link (or divide) state and society, or ruler and ruled, in the achievement of these grand normative aims.

7 Human Rights and the Memory of Political Violence and Repression: Constructing a New Field in Social Science

ELIZABETH JELIN

This article analyzes the growth of a new field within Latin American social sciences: human rights and the memories of repression and political violence. It also outlines the conceptual background and historical conditions that promoted the growth of this interdisciplinary field. Its history is a short one, spanning the last twenty years. We will need, however, to take account of the last forty years of sociopolitical changes in the region, which have constantly posed interpretative challenges and produced changes in the paradigms and frameworks adopted by the social sciences.

To a certain extent, this account of the development of the field covers my own intellectual biography, although I choose to present it in a more impersonal way, as a text that covers the development of ideas and paradigms rather than as autobiography. Alternative presentations could have focused on names and networks of colleagues, or on the personal encounters and heated debates that accompanied critical analytical and political choices of various sorts.

Changes in social processes and in analytical conceptualizations in the region were neither isolated from each other nor self-contained. They occurred within the framework of worldwide processes and in close relation to them. Even though the emphasis of this article is on Latin America, the world context will be part of the analysis. The following pages give special attention only to some landmarks and themes in the development of the social sciences, while less visible strands will receive less emphasis, remembering, though, that even the subplots prepared the ground for subsequent paradigmatic advances.

The 1960s

In the 1960s, Latin American social sciences consolidated their modern development. The basic approach was to study the challenge posed by the economic and social development of "peripheral capitalism." The influence of CEPAL (Comisión Economica para America Latina y el Caribe) was important in these years, first in the works of Raúl Prebisch, and then in the notion of "dependence" (Cardoso and Faletto 1967, among others). The issue of social modernization linked to the processes of industrialization and urbanization dominated social analysis. Two key issues emerged that identified the specificity of Latin America: populism and marginality. Situating himself within the modernization paradigm, Germani proposed a six-stage stylized scheme of the development of the political transition or evolution in the region (Germani 1962).[1] In the last stage of total participatory democracy, Germani proposes an alternative: national-popular revolutions, suggesting that on the way toward a "modern society," political participation in Latin America could take the form of "immediate" mass action, backing authoritarian forms of government. Scholars of populism (Weffort 1976; di Tella 1966) would deepen the analysis of the relationships between charismatic political leaders and their social base.

Scholars of urbanization and employment in the late 1960s became interested in the relation of these processes to marginality. The debate was between those who conceive of marginality as temporary and transitory, and others who saw marginality as a structural phenomenon and more permanent feature of Latin American economies (the dispute between Nun and Cardoso, reproduced in Nun 2001; see Wood in this volume). Marginality and populism acted as obstacles to the success of modernization processes.

Nevertheless, some events were taking place in the larger Latin American countries (Mexico, Brasil, and Argentina) that could not be understood in these terms. It was perhaps the "new" union movement and the large-scale student protests of 1968 (Tlaltelolco in Mexico, *passeata dos cem mil* in Rio de Janeiro, the autonomous union movement in Argentina) that first publicly demonstrated the importance of social forces that had not been incorporated analytically in the previously dominant model, which had emphasized economic and class structures. The dominant paradigms of the time, stemming from Marxism and modernization theories, analyzed involvement with the political system without taking account of the role of institutions, actors, and social movements.

---

1. The stages of this scheme are "(1) liberation wars and the formal declaration of independence; (2) civil wars, "caudillismo," anarchy; (3) unifying autocracies; (4) representative democracies with "limited" participation and "oligarchy"; (5) representative democracies with extended participation; (6) representative democracies with total participation; and as a possible alternative to the various forms of democracy, "national-popular revolutions" (Germani 1962, 147).

The Tragic 1970s

In the early 1970s, state repression of youthful revolutionary activism and fierce political confrontations resulted in a cycle of dictatorships in South America. Armed guerrilla movements were a major factor in these developments in various countries. First, Brazil, then Chile and Uruguay, and finally Argentina joined the more traditional dictatorships, such as the Stroessner regime in Paraguay, which had been in power since 1954. The domestic and international political panorama changed. The world turned its eyes toward the region because of the installation of state terrorism and illegal repression. In the process, the frameworks and models used to analyze the area were significantly altered.

It was as a result of the military coups in the Southern Cone in the mid-1970s that international networks of activists and human rights organizations became significant actors in the protests against repression and state terrorism (Keck and Sikkink 1998a). From the Latin American perspective, what happened in this period was the incorporation of the issue of human rights in the fight against dictatorship. Previously, domination or social and political struggles were interpreted in terms of class or national revolution. The incorporation of the notion of "violations of human rights" was a truly paradigmatic shift that meant conceiving of human beings as bearers of inalienable rights and assigning central responsibility to state institutions for respecting these rights.

Even when these principles were included in the liberal constitutions adopted in all the countries of the region during the nineteenth century, their actual presence in everyday life was almost nonexistent, especially for the popular classes and subordinate sectors. Now someone—initially from outside the region—was defining what was going on in human rights terms, and that definition came to be included in the antirepression demands. Significantly, the political parties, supposedly the "specialists" in working within the political system, played no central role in this movement. Instead, the main impetus came from the large network of victims' relatives, members of religious communities, activists, international organizations, intellectuals, and some politicians, mainly those who had gone into exile. An example is the antidictatorship movement in Uruguay that developed mainly through the exile of political leaders, who changed their revolutionary discourse toward one based on the new language of human rights (Markarian 2003). In Brazil and Argentina, new social movements made up of social actors that in the past had little presence led domestic opposition. Thus, the amnesty movement in Brazil in 1978 was organized and led by women, and women were also central to the human rights movement in Argentina (Jelin 1995). By rethinking violence in terms of human rights, the paradigm extended to other, more structural, forms of discrimination and violence: the rights of the native populations, the situation of women, and so on (Stavenhagen 1996; Jelin 1993; see Ariza and Oliveira in this volume)

The 1980s: Democracy, Citizenship, and Social Movements[2]

In 1978, the Consejo Latinoamericano de Ciencias Sociales (CLACSO) organized a seminar in Costa Rica entitled "Social Conditions for Democracy." The seminar challenged intellectuals of the region to begin thinking of ways of visualizing the conditions and strategies of exit from dictatorial regimes. This was a foundational moment for political science thinking on the very concept of democracy (Germani et al. 1985).

The idea of democracy emerged in opposition to authoritarianism and dictatorships. The emphasis on thinking about the political regime converged with an international context in which the human rights discourse was hegemonic. The ideal democracy incorporated the protection of the individual's basic rights as a central issue. By doing so, analysts privileged the political system, and the analysis of social and economic conditions fell into the background (Lesgart 2003, chap. 2). From then on, the development of political ideas was first centered on the "transition to democracy," and then on its "consolidation." The controversies revolved around oppositions between formal democracy and substantive democracy. For present purposes, however, it is important to note that with the emphasis on human rights and social participation, the issue of citizenship was emerging, even though political scientists gave it relatively little attention.

In the early 1980s another field of concern and analysis emerged alongside and, initially, separately from the preoccupations of political scientists with the transformations of state institutions and with democratic forms of participation and exercise of power: the forms of protest and of social expression that were not articulated by the political system or by preexisting institutional channels (see Foweraker in this volume). The "new" social

---

2. Lesgart (2003) makes a thorough systematic presentation of the development of political thought during the 1980s, including in her analysis the meeting, in Mexico, of political exiles from the Southern Cone.

movements and other forms of collective action that developed in this period attracted the attention of the region's social researchers. These developments occurred both in countries with dictatorial regimes where formal channels were cut off, and in countries in which existing democratic institutions were closed to popular influence, such as Mexico.

In the 1970s and 1980s, new social actors and collective practices with more localized and focused demands and goals appeared both in classic social movements, such as those of workers and peasants and in the new movements (women, youth, urban ethnic, human rights, and so on). In 1975 the First Intergovernmental Conference on Women in Mexico took place. The big surprise was the important role women played in forums and conferences parallel to the Intergovernmental Conference. Since then, the practice of having parallel activities, promoted by social movements and NGOs, has extended to most officially sponsored conferences (on population, environment, women, human rights, social development, and so on). Since the 1970s, social movements have maintained a permanent public presence in the region. There has been considerable research on this issue. The Program on Popular Participation of the United Nations Research Institute for Social Development (UNRISD) (Jelin 1987) and the CLACSO Program of Research (Calderón 1986) are good examples of such regional comparative efforts.

The transition to democracy and the institutionalization of democratic mechanisms in local governments during the 1980s resulted in many urban movements becoming incorporated as legitimate social actors recognized by local governments. At the same time, the demands of human rights and women's movements were incorporated in the social and political agendas of the transitions. In this way, the feminist social criticism entered societal organizations, unions, business organizations, the state, and even the church. The debates about discrimination against women, on the logic of equality, and on transformations in the legal structure generalized, including (at the margin) the social and political recognition of certain violations of women's rights, such as domestic violence (although not matrimonial rape). Also, the debate on reproductive rights (except for abortion) became part of the public agenda of the region (see Ariza and Oliveira in this volume).

As the discourse of human rights was appropriated by broad sectors of society and ceased to be restricted to groups of activists, the very definition of success and failure of a social movement was called into question. While the human rights organizations could be weakened, as they were in Argentina in the first half of the 1990s (Jelin 1995), their agenda and the issues raised extended to other actors in society. The defense of human rights, or on another level, the recognition of gender subordination, was incorporated into the broader democratic interpretative framework—an indication of success. The issues were adopted by society, even when the specific organizations were weakened and in conflict.

From a broader historical perspective, the profile of social demands represented in collective movements has been shifting. The working class and peasant movements were, in their heyday, projects of total social transformation (Calderón and Jelin 1987). At the end of the nineteenth century and the beginning of the twentieth, European trade union militants came to America to spread the notions of "workers' consciousness" and internationalism. They entered the new local industries as workers, spreading their ideas in face-to-face contacts and through the anarchist and socialist press. In those times, union organizations and press had a strong influence on immigrants both in Argentina and Brazil. Most of the militants were Italians, but there were also Spaniards, Portuguese, and French (Fausto 1976; Godio 1972; Oved 1978). What would come after was a stage of union struggles that mixed specific labor demands with projects of national transformation.

Since the 1970s, the situation of social movements and the view that social researchers have of them have shifted. The changes can be traced to the end of the import-substitution industrialization model and the spread of authoritarian regimes. The Latin American social sciences had previously focused mainly on power issues in analyzing political transformations. From this perspective, noninstitutional collective actions by the lower classes were interpreted either as prepolitical protests or as embryonic of popular participation waiting to be channeled through a political party. Now the emphasis was on the internal functioning of these movements, discovering in them "new ways of doing politics" (Lechner 1982). However, the main issue was still power, and everything was analyzed from that perspective.

The paradigm for the analysis of social movements changed when it became possible to see in them, not only a new way of doing politics, but also a new way of socializing and changing the patterns of social organization (Evers 1985). The heterogeneity and multiplicity of actors became more visible. One had to pay special attention to the microsocial processes that led to the construction of new collective actors. This implied a redefinition of the interface between public and private spheres. Social processes had to be observed, not only as large-scale political events or as the result of changes in economic structures, but also in their everyday manifestations as well as through the social relationships that took place on a day-to-day basis. Such studies showed that through the specific and concrete aspects of daily life, the main principles of social organization were being questioned (Calderón 1986; Escobar and Alvarez 1992). The movements were heterogeneous and diverse, and the logic of collective identity in the symbolic sphere emerged in combination with the interests and demands of specific groups (Jelin 1985).

The developments in the ways of thinking about social movements in Latin America paralleled those taking place in Europe. European thinking about "new" social movements had considerable influence in Latin America. What characterized Latin American research was its emphasis on the way that these new actors in the public sphere brought, at the same time, a "new way of doing politics" and new forms of sociability and subjectivity. It was a new way of relating political and social issues to the private and the public sphere in which daily social practices combined and interacted with ideological and political-institutional issues. The question raised was whether this was a "new reality," or a reality to which social sciences had hitherto been blind because of the dominant paradigms that emphasized economic processes and political systems.

The main new issues brought by the concern with social movements can be summarized in four points: first, the existence of a participatory structure linked to the content of the demands and the nature of the struggle, which participants felt to be their own; second, a specific temporality defined by the convergence of historical alternations between continuity and disruption, crisis and conflict; third, the heterogeneity and multiplicity of meanings that the same issue could have in different moments and contexts; and fourth, their connection with and impact on institutional systems and power relations in society (Calderón and Jelin 1987).

These years were marked by the partial liberalization of dictatorships and transitions to democracy in the Southern Cone. It was a period of heightened demands for the democratization of Mexico and pressure to end political violence in Central America. Political science was concerned with the performance of the political system and its institutions (parliaments, political parties, "generations" of reforms of the state and public policies). The space to examine the processes "from the grassroots" was free to be developed by anthropologists and sociologists, who focused on the diversity of social actors and on cultural and spatial heterogeneity.

From a grassroots perspective, a central concept was "citizenship." A way of understanding this concept, following the tradition of T. H. Marshall ([1949] 1964), was to explore the contents of citizen rights and their historic evolution. In Latin America during the twentieth century, the expansion of the welfare state and social rights did not always coincide with an expansion of civic and political rights (see Roberts in this volume) and still less by a subjective citizenship. The formal recognition of social and labor rights in the region was not always the consequence of the universality of social and political rights (Collier and Collier 1991). In the 1980s, the recovery of political rights in the transition to democracy was accompanied by extensive civil rights violations (Caldeira 1996). In general, until the structural adjustments and state reforms of the 1980s, socioeconomic rights were more generalized than political rights. At the same time, political rights were more widespread than civil rights, despite significant historic reversals.

Speaking about citizenship rights in this way—namely, by establishing the presence of concrete and specific rights—ran the risk of turning natural rights into positive ones (Habermas 1991). The danger was to reify and freeze the concept, identifying citizenship rights with a set of concrete practices: voting in elections, exercising freedom of speech, receiving public benefits (health, education), or any other concrete practice. From an analytic perspective, even when these practices constituted specific demands, the concept of citizenship (necessarily more abstract) refers to a conflictive struggle over *who* can say *what* in the process of defining the shared problems and how they should be addressed (Van Gunsteren 1978). This means that both citizenship and rights are always in construction and reformulation.

This perspective implies a premise: that the basic right is "the right to have rights" (Arendt 1973; Lefort 1987). Citizenship action is conceived in terms of its qualities of self-maintenance and expansion: "Citizen's rights are only those which tend to maintain, and if possible increase, the future exercise of citizenship" (Van Gunsteren 1978, 27; also Lechner 1986). This perspective has important consequences for the analysis of the struggles against discrimination and oppression: the content of the demands, the political priorities, and the contexts of struggle may change from place to place and time to time; yet within this diversity of demands, their consequences on the strengthening of citizenship are similar if what is at stake is the right to have rights and the right to public debate over the content of laws.

Central to this new paradigm is the notion of human rights, the concern with subjectivity and with the processes involved in constituting "bearers of rights" (individually but also collectively, especially among indigenous communities). Tensions and dilemmas between collective and individual rights, between universal rights and cultural pluralism, and between the state's public responsibility and the protection of privacy and intimacy are the central issues of the debate in the region (Jelin and Hershberg 1996; Jelin 1993). Empirical research in these matters emphasizes the distance between citizenship rights recognized by law and state and social practices that reflect bonds of dependency (*clientelismo, asistencialismo*) more than a consciousness of autonomy or a subjectivity grounded in citizenship (Jelin 1996a; Auyero 2001). In this vein, the development of the concept of "empowerment" (originally conceptualized in feminist thought as a process of overcoming inequalities and subordination) refers to greater collective and individual autonomy and the ability to mobilize and transform the structures of discrimination (León 1997).

The 1990s: Memory, Truth, and Justice in a Neoliberal Context

The central point to be stressed here is that the political concerns about democracy, together with the development of new social movements and their focus on everyday life, and the new thinking about citizenship and the constitution of citizenship as a subjective identity, involved a paradigm shift. A new interpretative framework for understanding the public sphere, the relationship between state and society, and how material conditions, institutions, subjectivity, and the cultural symbolic level related to each other, was in sight.

The first element of the new framework emphasizes the articulation between social actors and the state. I want to mention a very interesting thesis on this issue, which Dagnino (2003) developed for Brazil but that can be extended to other countries. Dagnino shows the "perverse" confluence between, on the one hand, the democratizing and participative impulses of the post-dictatorship period and, on the other, the imperatives of the minimal state imposed by the dominant neoliberal mandates of the 1990s. The confluence can be found in the fact that both proposals require an "active and purposeful civil society." The perversion resides in the fact that this confluence is only superficial, since the aim in neoliberalism is to shrink the state and to transfer the social issue and the concern for public goods to civil society. The terminology used by both political projects (democratization and neoliberalism) is the same: participation, civil society, citizenship, and democracy, yet their intentions and understandings are clearly different. "On the one hand, the constitution of public spaces represents the positive outcome of decades of struggle for democratization. . . . On the other hand, the process of making the state smaller and the progressive transference of its responsibility to civil society would give a perverse dimension to these novel experiences" (Dagnino 2003, 1; also Dagnino 2002).

It is also clear that the conditions that prevailed in the region in the 1990s, with the imposition (and crisis) of neoliberal policies, impoverishment, social polarization, and the increasing implementation of policies making for the exclusion of substantial parts of the population lead to revisiting the ideas about marginality of the 1960s (Nun 2001; Ward et al. 2004).

The concerns about issues such as inclusion and the individual or collective character of demands emerge in a historical moment of change. Social research increasingly emphasizes the temporality of social phenomena and seeks to introduce it as an analytical dimension. Temporal horizons of social phenomena include the present, past, and future. The issues raised focus on how to contribute to the construction of democracy and equity. This includes institutional processes, concerns with equality and distribution, and social empowering processes. Regarding the past, it implies looking for ways to settle accounts with a violent and repressive state. The dominant idea is that there is no way of constructing a future until past atrocities have been accounted for and punished. Here is where social memory enters the scene.

The human rights movement calls for the recovery of a system of fundamental values: life, truth, and justice, identified with a universal ethical standpoint. At first, the emphasis of the demands was on stopping illegal repression. In the post-dictatorship transition, the main ideas shifted first toward a claim for "truth and justice," and since then the movement diversified its goals and demands. On the one hand, it demands truth and justice with respect to the past. This has proven to be a key and enduring action, multiplying its strategies and international dynamics (Keck and Sikkink 1998a). On the other hand, the human rights movement redefines its demands in face of the new realities of inequality, social exclusion, and social polarization that have been a persistent feature of the 1990s. This strand has been recuperating and integrating the issues of economic, social, and cultural rights within the logic of human rights and citizenship participation. In between these two strands, there is a move toward incorporating issues of the past into social memory.

Memory and oblivion, commemoration and remembrance, are crucial when connected to traumatic political episodes, to situations of repression and annihilation, and when we are talking about deep social catastrophes and situations of collective suffering. At the individual level, the traumatic scars influence what the subject can remember, silence, forget, or elaborate. In a political sense, settling accounts with the past in terms of assigning responsibilities, recognitions, and institutional justice is combined with ethical priorities and moral demands. The tensions between remembering and commemorating painful facts and traumatic gaps in memory, and open psychological wounds are, at the same time, issues to be analyzed and one of the main obstacles to their study (LaCapra 2001; Jelin 2002a).

Political struggles that seek to settle accounts with the past have had different facets during the post-dictatorship era: the search for truth, the search for justice, and the search for meaning of a painful past. The initiatives have come from the human rights movement's advocacy of the need to recognize what has happened. This recognition involves both the state and societal expressions—in art and in other aspects of the cultural and symbolic world. The struggles over the memories and the meanings of the past thus became a new field of social action in the region. It also became a new field of social research, characterized by different but complementary approaches and disciplines needed for a perspective centered on issues that simultaneously involve institutional patterns, subjectivities, and symbolic manifestations.

The issue of memory refers to the temporality of social phenomena because it is placed at the crossroads of past, present, and future, at a point in which past experiences and the horizons of future expectations converge. Indeed, struggles to recover the meaning of the past are always developed in a subsequent moment, in a present, and their relation to desired ideals and futures gives them their significance. In contrast to a linear and chronological conception of time, in which the past, present, and future are ordered in a "natural" way, Koselleck (1993, 14) points out that "historic time, if we accept the fact that the concept has its own meaning, is closely related to political and social unities of action, to concrete men that act and suffer, to their institutions and organizations." Studying those concrete men (and women), the meanings of temporality are established in a special way, because the present contains past experience and future expectations. Experience is a "past present, whose facts have been incorporated and can be remembered" (Koselleck 1993, 338). Furthermore, one person's experience incorporates the experiences that have been conveyed to him or her by others. On the other hand, expectation is a "future made present, and aims at the not-yet, at the non-experienced, at what can only be discovered." In that complex point of intersection between that present in which the past is the space for experience and the future, with its horizon of expectations, is where human action happens, "in the living space of culture" (Ricoeur 1999, 22).

Locating memory temporally implies referring to the "space of experience" in a present time. The memory of the past is incorporated dynamically because experiences can be modified with time. "The facts of 1933 definitely happened, but the experiences based on them can be modified with time. Experiences overlap and nurture one another" (Koselleck 1993, 341). On the other hand, experiences are also molded by the "horizon of expectations" that refers to a future temporality: "New hopes or disillusions, new expectations open breaches and influence them." (341).

We are talking, then, about subjective processes of signifying and resignifying in which the subjects of action move and position themselves (or get lost and disoriented) among "past futures" (Koselleck 1993), "present pasts" (Huyssen 2003), "never ending pasts" (Conan and Rousso 1994). In terms of research, the complexity of multiple temporalities entails locating the contexts and events when memories (or silences) are activated in a frame shaped by transformation and historical change, that is to say, recognizing that research always has to focus on *historicized* memories.

The problematization and systematic study of the social processes involved in the construction of memories evolved in the academic field in the Southern Cone as a result of the encounter of academics with the reality of political practice. Analytical or disciplinary concerns played a secondary role. There was a moment (in the post-dictatorship era) in which a "mandate for memory" appeared among the human rights movements' demands. In Argentina, this happened during the transition (the mid-1980s) (Jelin 1995). Even the title of the CONADEP (Comisión Nacional para los Desaparecidos) report, *Nunca Mas* (Never Again), which was used by other reports of the region (Brazil, Guatemala, Uruguay, and so on), gives us an idea of the cultural context of the region and of the meaning given to the acts of memory. The fact that the experience should never be repeated started being identified with the "truth," with the recollection of all the information that existed about the atrocities. And to ensure that the atrocities not be repeated, memory needed to be kept alive. *To remember in order not to repeat* emerged as a message and as a cultural imperative. It was at this point that public initiatives and projects appeared whose aim was to register, to mark, and to commemorate: memorials, monuments and other territorial markers, commemoration of important dates, recovery and organization of documentary archives, literary and artistic productions, testimonial or documentary literature and films, etc. Changes were also introduced in school curricula, in judicial institutions, and in the military.

Once research on the issue begins, it becomes clear that there is no single version of the past. Different actors confront their differing interpretations and meanings in a context of struggles over finding the truth about what really happened, over the diverse meanings of that past, and of justice. At times, the human rights movement depicts the struggle as the fight between memory and oblivion or silence. This obscures what in fact is the opposition of different and rival memories, each with its own oblivions. They are in fact struggles of "memory" against "memory," and this can be seen repeatedly in the commemoration of dates and places in the region (Jelin 2002a, 2002b). Perhaps the best example is September 11 in Chile. Year after year on this date there are struggles in the streets of Santiago and other cities between progressive political forces and those who glorify Pinochet and his regime (Candina Palomer 2002). The human rights movement is not the only actor concerned with memory. The Pinochet Foundation has an interest in it as well. This shows that finding one true memory is impossible. There is an active political struggle over meaning—both the meaning of what happened and the meaning of the memory itself. Hence, the political struggle for memory is not a confrontation between memory and oblivion, but between co-existing and conflicting memories.

Furthermore, neither the democratic and progressive forces nor the human rights movements constitute a homogeneous and unified group. Struggles arise as different actors clash over the "appropriate" ways to commemorate, over the content of what should be commemorated, and over the legitimacy of the different actors who vie to be the keepers of memory (this is the issue of property rights in memory and "legitimate" voices) (Jelin 2002a).

There are controversies and political conflicts over monuments, museums, and memorials everywhere, from Berlin to Bariloche. They are affirmations and discourses, facts and gestures, a reality with a political meaning, collective and public. People struggle over public and collective signposts that affirm and convey their sense of belonging to a community based on sharing an identity built on a tragic and traumatic history. These signposts can also function as key attributes of the intergenerational transmission of historic continuity, although the "success" of the transmission and its meaning are not assured.

The urgency to study the memories of political violence and repression developed in the region as a result of the public events of the transition processes. Yet this was not an academically isolated development. International social science offered a significant amount of intellectual and academic production. The Nazi policy of genocide during World War II gave way to the creation of the field of research and cultural reflection on these issues. History and psychoanalysis, literary critique and anthropology, especially in Europe, took up the theme. The commitment also stemmed from the pressures of political and social actors: the world Jewish community, German and French societies, and other groups in Europe, the United States, and

Japan. As in the case of Latin America, intellectuals and social scientists were not absent from these debates. Moreover, this is a field of research in which the civic commitment and the researchers' own subjective feelings are permanently involved.

The accumulation of theoretical and empirical knowledge in the central countries influenced the analytical issues raised to understand the struggles over the memories of the recent dictatorships in Latin America. Yet the analytical and empirical field is not closed. It keeps growing and incorporating other historic periods (such as the conquest of the indigenous peoples and their genocide) and other actors that had previously been silenced and hidden by the "official stories" that the winners of the battles over history were constructing.

There are certain questions that reiterate classic social science issues. How and why does a certain issue (memory) become a public issue in a given time and place? Why does the interest in memory emerge now, at the moment in which we are moving from one century to the other? Issues related to the "culture of memory" (Huyssen 2003, chap. 1) can be significant, although making an issue a publicly important one requires time, energy, and perseverance. In the field of memories of a recent political past in a conflict-laden contemporary context, the human rights movement has been and still is a privileged actor, a "memory entrepreneur" (Jelin 2002a) that aims to obtain social recognition for and to politically legitimize a particular understanding of the past. It is a heterogeneous actor in which diverse experiences and multiple expectations coexist, although not without tensions and conflict. There are also economic and business interests that become involved in a mix of criteria and of logics: the lucrative and moral issues can be combined in diverse ways. Claudia Feld (2002) analyzes Argentinean television and the "spectacularization" of the memories of dictatorship. When in 1998, a major television channel broadcasted a special program on the Escuela de Mecánica de la Armada (the main center of clandestine detention during the military dictatorship) hosted by Magdalena Ruiz Guiñazu, a well-known journalist and ex-member of CONADEP, the newspapers announced the event as: "The trial (of the ex-commanders) has a high rating" (Feld 2002). There are also strategic and contextual political issues to consider.

There is no doubt that one special group has a privileged role, namely the direct victims and their relatives. In France they could be ex-deportees or ex-resistance fighters. They could be war veterans (from Vietnam or Malvinas), or survivors of massacres. They may be the children and grandchildren (as in contemporary Spain). Their demands and struggles differ from one another.

They can try to influence and change the meaning and the contents of the "official" or the dominant history of a period, in order to eliminate historic distortions or make public stories and reports that had been hidden, censured, and silenced public and legitimate. Based on their position as victims, they can look to repair and correct, demanding that the state assume and recognize responsibility for its past wrongdoings. They can search for communities of people in the same situation to which to belong and receive support for their injuries and sufferings. They can develop rituals, participate in commemorations, and claim symbolic marks of recognition in memorials, monuments, or museums. They can also translate their experiences into more generalized demands on the institutional system, converting their personal experiences and their group demands into test cases from which more general learning experiences can be gained (Todorov 1998). Here the issues of memory enter a new arena, that of political and judicial institutions.

An Institutional Intervention

Within the context of the post-dictatorships in the Southern Cone, in 1998 the Regional Advisory Panel for Latin America of the SSRC (Social Science Research Council, New York) decided to launch a program for comparative research and training of researchers on collective memory of repression.[3] The initiative of organizing a program of research and training on the social memories of repression in the Southern Cone emerged from a diagnosis of the gaps in social research in the region. In the first place, there was a thematic absence or void: the issue of memories (how societies deal with the recent past of dictatorships), the sources and the nature of memories, their role in the constitution of collective identities, and the consequences of the social struggles over memory for social and political practices in countries that have suffered political violence and dictatorships. A second gap was an institutional one: the effect of dictatorships on the formation of young social researchers and on social science networks in the region. Hence the need to help in the training of a new generation of academic researchers with strong methodological and theoretical tools that would enable them to develop new analytic and comparative perspectives on these issues. The program was aimed then at filling the gaps in training and in the dialogue between researchers in different countries.

3. The program was under the academic direction of Elizabeth Jelin and Carlos Iván Degregori (for Peru).

The focus of the program can be summarized in three premises. The first is to conceive of memories as subjective processes, but ones anchored in material and symbolic experiences and signs. This necessarily implies entering into the analysis of the dialectic between the individual and society, between subjectivity and the sense of belonging to a cultural group. The second is to work on struggles or conflicts over memories. This puts the emphasis on the "agency" of those who participate in those struggles. Power and hegemonic claims are always present. It is a struggle for "my truth," with its promoters, "entrepreneurs," and attempts to monopolize and appropriate. The third is to recognize the constructed and changing character of the meanings of the past, of the silences and historical oblivion, as well as the place which societies, ideologies, cultural climates, and political struggles assign to memory. Hence comes the need to "historicize memory."

The research projects focused on the Southern Cone countries (Argentina, Brazil, Chile, Paraguay, and Uruguay) and Peru. Its fellows came from various academic disciplines (anthropology, history, sociology, law, social communications, psychology, literary criticism, and so on). It was structured to facilitate comparisons and to analyze relationships between countries, as well as to make comparisons with experiences elsewhere, to emphasize both the similarities and the differences among the diverse geographic and historic contexts. The countries of the region experienced dictatorships of different types and durations, as well as multiple forms of state repression. Today, they all are on the road to democratization. In all of them, the problem of how to deal with the past is still open, both in the arena of state policies and in terms of the ongoing social and cultural debates. The first stage of this multidisciplinary project began in 1999. A second group of fellowship holders joined the project in 2000, and a third one in 2001.[4] The program is also publishing a series of books, "Memories of the Repression" (see appendix), and various articles have been published in academic journals of the region and abroad. A specialized library was developed in IDES (Instituto de Desarrollo Economic y Social), Buenos Aires.

Intellectual Developments and Political Challenges

This chapter discusses a potential paradigmatic change in the ways of understanding the contemporary reality of Latin America, in which multiple issues

---

4. More information and a list of the issues dealt can be found in www.ssrc.org.

and processes converge and merge, through incorporating new interpretative frameworks that break through specialized disciplinary traditions (law and psychoanalysis, sociology and political science, anthropology and history). What is new about this type of approach? In the first place, it facilitates the recognition of subjective processes and cultural frames of action. It is not that these were absent in the classics, but they had been forgotten—both by Marxism and structuralism as well as by more functionalist trends of thought. To relate the institutional level with cultural patterns of meanings and with the processes that constitute an actor's subjectivity transcends the normal framework of any single discipline of social research.

Second, the act of trying to face new issues (or new questions about old issues) brings the focus squarely on the *social agents* that develop their strategies in contexts of struggle, of confrontation, of negotiation, of alliances, and of attempts to gain power and to impose their practices on others. The implicit model of action in this kind of analysis returns to classic issues in political sociology, such as the construction of authority and of social legitimacy. It incorporates a temporality that is not just chronological—previous experiences and future expectation enter the scene—and an explicit consideration of feelings and subjectivities. Furthermore, it involves the constant presence and reference to "alterity," to the Others to whom we orient our actions. There is no social action without an Other. This statement may be as old as the Greeks, but it makes sense to reiterate it every once in a while in a world in which we are led to believe that there is only one solution to our problems and only one model that should be followed.

Third, it is an attempt to intervene actively in the intellectual field. Despite the tendencies to professional specialization in the region, we tried to take advantage in our project of the presence of spaces for intellectual criticism, of spaces for public commitments by participants in debates that ideally combine academic rigor with personal and political involvement in public life. Let us remember that it is at this point of convergence between personal concerns and public issues that C. Wright Mills found the "sociological imagination."

The urgency to work on memory is not an isolated concern; it is embedded in a specific political and cultural context. Our general analytical reflections come from a particular place and time: the preoccupation with the scars left by the dictatorships of the Southern Cone and by what was done in the 1990s, in the post-dictatorship period. Our research was not of the ivory tower type, but rooted in our own ethical and political commitments as active citizens. This implied redefining the criteria for "objectivity" present in positivist thought, while emphasizing rigorous research methods.

But there is something else, perhaps even more significant. Events linked to the political violence and repression of the past are multiplying in the region, in an international context in which "crimes against humanity" and the issue of national sovereignty in the handling of these crimes are in vogue. As of the latter part of 2003, as I was finishing this article, the list of events includes major developments that are worth mentioning:

The Comisión de la Verdad y Reconciliación of Peru delivered its final report on August 28, 2003. This report informs about 69,000 fatal victims during the period of political violence in Peru between 1980 and 2000 (75 percent of which were Quechua-speaking peasants). In the presentation ceremony, the president of the commission affirmed that Peru is, with this report, confronting a "time of shame," but also a time for justice and reconciliation.[5]

The Argentinean Congress declared the laws of *obediencia debida* (due obedience) and *punto final* (final point) null and void. This is done in a context where the Supreme Court has to pronounce itself vis-à-vis the constitutionality of these laws. Congressional action led to the reopening of several cases of human rights violations during the military dictatorship (1976–83), including the cases of the ESMA and the First Army Corps. These were added to the ongoing judicial cases, involving the legal actions to establish what had happened (*juicios por la verdad*) and the illegal appropriation of children.

In Chile, the commemoration of the thirtieth anniversary of the Pinochet military coup (September 11, 1973) was full of events. Simultaneously, the organizations of relatives and children of the victims of the repression are protesting against the new policies announced by the government of President Lagos for prosecuting crimes carried out under the repression and for his proposals for reparations.

In Mexico, social and political movements have been actively and successfully pressing the government to establish a commission to investigate the Tlaltelolco killings of 1968.

In Uruguay, the thirtieth anniversary of the military coup (June 2003) was commemorated with numerous public events. When the findings of the Commission for Peace were made public, numerous sectors of the population expressed their unhappiness with these results, reiterating their commitment to continue with the demands for truth. New demands stemming from the Gelman case are constantly being made.

In Brazil, the preparations to commemorate the fortieth anniversary of the military coup of March 1964 have already begun.

5. The report has nine volumes and annexes. For more information, see http://www.cverdad.org.pe/

In France and other European countries, a documentary film called *Escuadrones de la muerte: La escuela francesa* (Death Squads: The French School) was aired on television. This documentary clearly establishes the collaboration of the French army in the training of personnel to perform illegal repression in the Southern Cone. The testimonies in the film by Argentinean and Chileans trained by the French admitting the torture and killings perpetrated during the dictatorships caused a political furor.

In Paraguay, a Truth Commission to study the crimes of the Stroessner regime is being established.

This incomplete list shows the political importance of dealing with the past in the current political context of Latin America. This "memory surge" at this point in time is perhaps the clearest demonstration that remembering and forgetting are not linear processes in time (it is not the case that "as time goes by, memory fades") but dynamic processes, whose presence is linked to a complex social, cultural, and political web. In a sense, the research and reflection that the SSRC program produced allows a deeper and better understanding of what is now going on, how that past is recaptured, of the struggles for memory, and of the different actors that participate in it. The existence of a group of young researchers and analysts, with the capacity to study these phenomena and to participate in the political-intellectual debate is, without a doubt, an accomplishment of the intervention made by the program.

Appendix: Titles in the series Memories of the Repression

Elizabeth Jelin. 2002a. *Los trabajos de la memoria.*
Elizabeth Jelin, ed. 2002b. *Las conmemoraciones: Las disputas en las fechas "in-felices."*
Claudia Feld. 2002. *Del estrado a la pantalla: Las imágenes del juicio a los ex comandantes.*
Ludmila da Silva Catela and Elizabeth Jelin, eds. 2002. *Los archivos de la represión: Documentos, memoria y verdad.*
Elizabeth Jelin and Victoria Langland, eds. 2003. *Monumentos, memoriales y marcas territoriales.*
Ponciano del Pino and Elizabeth Jelin, eds. 2003. *Luchas locales, comunidades e identidades.*
Elizabeth Jelin and Federico Lorenz, eds. 2004. *Educación y memoria. La escuela elabora el pasado.*
María Angélica Cruz. 2004. *Iglesia, represión y memoria. El caso de Chile.*

PART IV
Work, Families, and Reproduction

8 Exclusion and Employability: The New Labor Dynamics in Latin America

JUAN PABLO PÉREZ SÁINZ

The labor market is a privileged vantage point from which to analyze fundamental social processes. It is one of the major channels between economy and society through which the sweet or bitter fruits of economic development are distributed among the population. The modernization of the last century brought the emergence of national labor markets in Latin America with two basic characteristics that revealed the prevailing mode of development in the region. First, these labor markets were not homogeneous in terms of the universality of wage employment. Instead, they were deeply segmented, reflecting the heterogeneous character of Latin American society. Second, this segmentation was based on occupation, which became the main channel of social integration.

Segmentation has dominated discussion about Latin American labor markets. Its most familiar expression is the dichotomy between formal and informal employment. Two perspectives have been particularly important. One is the structuralist perspective developed by the now extinct Programa Regional del Empleo para América y el Caribe (PREALC), which emphasized the break in the productive structure between the formal sector, consisting of large firms with higher levels of technological development, and the informal sector, consisting of small-scale establishments characterized by low productivity (Souza and Tokman 1976; Mezzera 1987). The other is the regulative perspective, which emphasized the distinction created by state intervention within the labor market between the formal sector of regulated labor relations and the informal sector of unregulated relations (Portes 1995b; Itzigsohn 2000). I shall argue that this distinction is losing importance as the modernizing state, which sought to construct the nation, gives way before a more global modernization in which the market predominates and in which the centrality of the nation-state is questioned.[1] Consequently, the explanatory power of the formal/informal distinction is diminished (Pérez Sáinz

1. This shift underlies the crisis of development theories, particularly those in sociology, which now must find a replacement for the nation-state as the prime unit of analysis (Robinson 1998). But see Davis, Roberts, and Sunkel in this volume for contrary perspectives.

1998). New dynamics are structuring labor markets in a different way and challenge us to provide new analytic perspectives.

The main aim of the present chapter is to begin the work of understanding these new processes. I begin with an analytic perspective that looks at labor markets both from the three structuring logics of wage employment, expulsion, and self-employment, and through the dialectic between their including and excluding processes. In this first section, the basic hypotheses are set out that guide this analysis. The following sections seek to specify the including/excluding dialectic for each of the logics.[2] The chapter concludes with a set of reflections on the challenges that the new labor dynamics pose to the redefinition of social citizenship.

Global Modernization and the New Labor Dynamics: Some Hypotheses

Every labor market can be analyzed in terms of the interplay between integrative and excluding processes. Thus, obtaining work implies integration and has a whole series of consequences for society. On the other hand, every labor market has a labor surplus, which is only partially shown through open unemployment. In the previous period of modernization to that of the present, this interplay occurred around the centrality of formal employment, which was synonymous with modern employment. This structured labor processes both in terms of the migration flows from rural areas and from small towns to metropolitan areas (the territory, par excellence, of national modernity) and in terms of occupational mobility that became defined as gaining formal sector employment. The emphasis was on integration, although integration was limited, since there existed a labor surplus that, in the face of the difficulties of surviving when unemployed, became self-employed in the urban informal sector.

Contemporary global modernization brings important transformations. The first hypothesis is that the trend is increasingly that of exclusion. Levels of unemployment, despite the dynamism of the economies of the 1990s, have not decreased, but on the contrary, have tended to increase. There is a crisis of formal employment resulting from the declining importance of public employment, the hard core of formal employment, and from the

2. These two sections bring together a considerable number of the ideas that I have been developing in recent works (see Pérez Sáinz 2003a and 2003b).

increasing insecurity of wage employment. Self-employment at below the subsistence level persists in urban areas and, above all, in rural areas. The following sections deal with each of these issues. The predominance of excluding tendencies does not mean that the possibilities of integration into the labor market have disappeared. However, integration proceeds in a different way than in the past. Integration shifts from the demand side (generation of jobs in the formal sector) to the supply side (generation of work opportunities as a result of workers' own initiatives). This will be our second hypothesis and introduces the notion of employability.

Employability can be defined, in the first instance, as the workers' own capacity to generate employment or to adapt their existing work practices and relations to the changes in the market. This capacity has historical antecedents in the region, both in terms of rural self-employment—the peasant economy—and in terms of urban self-employment, the informal economy. The opening of the economy with globalization has, however, redefined employability. Fundamentally, volatility has become a hallmark of contemporary markets, including the labor market, making risk a structural element of the new model of accumulation. Employability becomes synonymous with the capacity to manage labor market risks. Following Douglas and Wildavsky's (1983) definition, handling risk depends equally on knowledge of how to handle future uncertainties as well as on agreement over group aspirations.

Knowledge entails the development of human capital, but the cognitive dimension cannot be reduced to this aspect alone. Consensus over aspirations is challenged by the changes that have happened to the labor trajectories of the past that aimed at protected jobs and upward mobility within the internal labor markets of enterprises and organizations. The uncertainty that affects the world of work undermines these aspirations (Beck 2001; Sennett 2000). This questioning affects the formation of work identities crucial to which is the generation of a reflexive subjectivity that can appropriate effectively the lessons of the past (Dubar 2001). The emphasis on subjectivity can have opposing consequences for consensus. On the one hand, reflexivity can lead to a more strategic consensus. On the other hand, subjectivity can result in individualistic orientations opposed to collective action. The inclination to the collective or the individual is essential given that, in the first case, employability counters exclusion, while, in the second case, the employability of some can mean the exclusion of others (Pérez Sáinz 2003a).

From this perspective, employability would entail the generation of a work ethic and culture in which the workers show their capacity to confront the volatility and change inherent in increasingly globalized markets. These strategies of risk management need to be analyzed as social actions and thus as generating social actors. They can have diverse expressions depending on the work context. This brings us to the issue of the logics that structure labor markets.

Three logics can be identified: development of wage employment, expulsion, and self-employment. What matters is identifying the form that these logics take in different historical periods as well as their corresponding model of accumulation in order to avoid confusing both analytic levels and their reifications (Pérez Sáinz 2003a). The first of these logics, the development of wage labor, is based on the purchase and sale of labor power. In the period that I call national modernization in Latin America, formal employment was the paradigmatic expression of this logic. But the market does not always use the available labor supply, resulting in discouragement and withdrawal from the labor market. Clearly, the manifestation of this second logic is open unemployment. The labor force does not, however, find itself inextricably trapped between having to work for a wage or be expelled. There is a third possibility, the self-generation of employment. The phenomenon of informality in the previous modernizing period is the best example of this type of logic (Pérez Sáinz 1999).

Crossing these three structuring logics with inclusive and exclusive tendencies identifies the principal labor market dynamics that characterize contemporary global modernization. These are summarized in Table 8.1.

The Crisis in Formal Employment and New Forms of Employability

The Decline of Public Employment

The most inescapable sign of the crisis in formal employment in Latin America is the loss in importance of public employment, which had previously been the most developed form of formal employment and its mainstay. This loss calls into question the centrality of formal employment in the labor market.

This process began in 1983 when the rate of growth in public employment began to decline (PREALC 1991). This was the first sign of the effects of the structural adjustment programs and, concretely, of the reform of the state, the principal cause of the decline in public employment. This tendency

Table 8.1 Employment tendencies in Latin America during global modernization

Logics	Forms	Exclusion	Inclusion
Wage employment	Crisis of formal employment	Reduction in public employment. Deformalization resulting in job insecurity	Nonsolidary Individualism / Union neocorporativism
	Emerging proletarianization	Insecurity	Nonsolidary Individualism/ Union neocorporativism
Expulsion	Unemployment	Structural	Very limited unemployment insurance
	Migration	Territorial	Transnational
Self-employment	Individual entrepreneurship	Unsustainable	Autonomous upgrading
	Sub-contracting	Insecurity	Subordinated upgrading
	Territorial Clusters	Insecurity	Collective upgrading

increased during the 1990s. The proportion of public employment in the total nonagricultural economically active population (EAP) of the region declined from 15.5 percent in 1990 to 13.0 percent in 2000 (OIT 2001, table 6-A). There are, however, three distinct patterns in the region (see Table 8.2).

The large majority of countries in the region fall within a single pattern of public employment. Their weight was high at the beginning of the decade but, through the 1990s, the relative importance of this type of employment declined. Particularly striking are the declines in Costa Rica, Venezuela, and especially in Panama, where public employment was 32.0 percent of the non-agricultural EAP at the beginning of the period, but 21.8 percent at the end. Brazil and Chile are the atypical cases. Remember that Chile is the region's pioneer in neoliberal policies, which were first implemented by one of the most authoritarian regimes in Latin America. Thus, the cut in public employment had already taken place before 1990, and with the return to democracy the proportion of the labor force employed in public institutions increased.

These patterns derive from the different weight that political and institutional factors have had in each country. Adriana Marshall (1996) points to three that have been important in the impact of the first wave of state reforms on public employment. The first is the internal composition of public employment in terms of the difference between central and local governments, since the reform of the state includes the strengthening of local government with the possibility of an increase in jobs at this level. The second is the degree to which, in the democratic wave that characterizes the region,

Table 8.2 Evolution of public employment in Latin America, 1990–2000

Level of public employment in 1990	Increase 1990–2000	Decrease 1990–2000
High (> 15.5%)		Argentina (12.7%) Costa Rica (16.4%) Ecuador (17.6%) Mexico (14.5%) Panama (21.8%) Uruguay (17.1%) Venezuela (16.1%)
Low (≤ 15.5%)	Brazil (14.2%) Chile (10.8%)	Colombia (7.0%) Honduras (10.1%) Peru (7.0%)

SOURCE: OIT 2001, table 6-A.
NOTE: Percentages in parentheses are the percentage of public employment in 2000.

electoral clientelism has been able to neutralize fiscal discipline. And the third is the degree of resistance of public employees and their unions to neoliberal reforms.

The importance of this decline in public employment is its impact on the centrality that formal work had in the previous model. The impact is not only material—fewer jobs in the state—but also symbolic. The institutionalism of employment is diminished, and worse yet, state employment becomes stigmatized as unproductive and liable to corruption.

The Various Expressions of Job Insecurity

The crisis in formal employment is also one of the increasing insecurity in wage employment. This phenomenon affects not only existing work relations but also the more recent ones created by the new model of accumulation.

Job insecurity (*precarización*) is a term that has mainly been used empirically in Latin America and with little analytic precision. Mora (2000) points the way to conceptual precision by separating out three dimensions of the phenomenon: labor deregulation, the restructuring of production and labor flexibility, and the weakening of union power. We will take each of these dimensions in turn and see their manifestations in the region.

The deregulation of labor relations is one of the basic traits of the new economic model that dominates the region, inspired by the so-called Washington consensus (Bulmer-Thomas 1997; Lozano 1998). The World Bank, which has been the chief advocate of deregulation, evaluated its progress in the region up to the mid-1990s and concluded that the majority of countries still showed "labor rigidities."[3] There were two exceptions to this "rigidity." The first is Chile, where at the beginnings of the 1990s, a flexible labor market had already been achieved. The second is Peru, which in the 1990s was the other case of radical deregulation. Mexico and Nicaragua appear at the opposite extreme (Burki and Perry 1997). The International Labour Office (known in Latin America as the Organización Internacional del Trabajo, or OIT) offers a different perspective on the reach of labor reforms in Latin America (OIT 2000). It shows that the great majority of changes in the laws have affected individual labor relations, especially through new forms of contract and new dismissal procedures. In Peru and Argentina these reforms

---

3. It would be helpful if the Bank would include among its indicators the proportion of work inspectors in the total workforce in order to have an indication of the real possibilities of enforcing labor legislation.

have been drastic, while they have been more limited in Brazil, Colombia, and Panama. The winds of reform have even affected countries with a protectionist tradition, such as Venezuela and the Dominican Republic. In fact, in eleven of the sixteen countries studied, which include 70 percent of wage employment in the region, there have been labor reforms aimed at deregulating the labor market, questioning the prevalent assumption that the efforts in this direction have been insufficient. Chile is an exception, since the labor reform of 1994, under a democratic government, improved the existing legislation that had been drawn up under the previous authoritarian regime. This reform permitted the unionization of public employees and seasonal workers, protected union leaders from the threat of dismissal, and incorporated other labor benefits (Cortázar 1997).

The second dimension is productive restructuring and labor flexibility. In evaluating flexible practices in the region, La Garza (2000) reaches the following conclusions. First, instituting labor flexibility is more common in the more developed countries of the region. Second, when collective agreements have been broken or weakened, enterprises tend to impose flexibility unilaterally. Third, flexibility is still more common in the functional and numeric modalities than in the wage form, although it is gaining ground in the latter. Fourth, the state appears as a major promoter of flexibility, whether through legislation (Argentina or Colombia) or through neocorporativist agreements (Mexico). Using the different perspective of the organizational innovations in the region provides an illuminating diagnostic (Carrillo 1995). These innovations are not introduced systematically, but result from individual firm initiatives. They are imposed unilaterally on the workers without any negotiation. As a consequence, the involvement of the workforce is limited. But, it is also important to remember, as Mora (2000) himself points out, that not every process of reorganization brings with it increasing job insecurity.

The third dimension is the weakness of organized labor as an actor. Organized labor was one of the major losers in the crisis of the 1980s (Roxborough 1989). This weakness is related, in the first place, to the change in the model of accumulation. With global markets, wage costs become crucial and cannot so easily be passed on to consumers as happened under the protectionism of import-substitution industrialization (Murillo 2001). This change appears in a new relation between politics and the economy that brought into question the previous model of union action focused more in the state and political arena than in that of the enterprise (Touraine 1988b; Zapata 1993).

However, this tendency for unions to be weakened is conditioned by two factors that help explain national specificities. On the one hand are the democratization processes that have coincided with the change in the model. Unions were often important in bringing democracy, but democracy can also provide alternative political channels to that of union action (Koonings, Kruijt, and Wils 1995). Zapata (1993) has pointed to the break occurring between citizenship and class identity in working-class consciousness, which uncouples political citizenship (democratization) from solidarity. On the other hand, the very change in the model of accumulation needs to be considered. This change has occurred through the processes of structural adjustment, in which the unions are not always passive participants. Their historical alliances with populist parties, now converted to neoliberalism, have allowed unions to have some influence on structural adjustment (Murillo 2000). Background factors that are obviously also important in these processes are the changes in the occupational structure that are eroding the traditional basis of union recruitment (Zapata 1993; Koonings, Kruijt, and Wils 1995; Murillo 2001). The crisis in formal employment, analyzed above, explains this erosion.

At present, the Latin American labor union movement is marked by two tendencies: its weakness at the political level, expressed in the crisis of the so-called corporative unionism of populist orientation, and its greater presence at the firm level. The issue with this last tendency is that it is too recent to evaluate (Lucena 2000). Thus, it has been argued that there are two union tendencies (La Garza 2000). On the one hand, there is the neocorporativist, in which the union becomes the partner of the firm in improving productivity, and on the other hand, there is the autonomous tendency. This last tendency establishes new political and social alliances, with new parties and nonprotected workers respectively (Murillo 2001).

Job insecurity also affects the newly emergent wage relations. This is apparent in how the new model of accumulation affects wage inequality. Emerging export activities, where new processes of proletarianization are occurring, are one of the fundamental components of the new model of accumulation. Export activities mean a greater generation of jobs, since tradable activities use more labor-intensive techniques. Those benefited, in terms of type of jobs, would be the less-qualified labor force, given its relative abundance and, it is argued from a neoliberal perspective, would additionally raise levels of pay with unmistakable redistributive effects.

We can evaluate these predictions by analyzing the evolution of wages in the 1990s. The evidence shows three main tendencies. The first is the higher wages paid to those with higher levels of education. Thus, wage inequality, in terms of educational levels, has risen, not fallen. Only in a few countries have deliberate wage policies succeeded in offsetting this growing inequality. The second tendency is for wage differences between large and small enterprises to increase once again, after diminishing with the crisis of the 1980s. The causes of this increase are to be found in the large firms' strategies of reorganization: by reducing their job rolls they raised their productivity. This, in turn, made it possible to raise the wages of the workers that were kept on. The third tendency is a decrease in wage inequality by gender. The causes of this decrease are, on the one hand, higher levels of labor force participation by highly educated women relative to men and, on the other hand, the expansion of service activities, which are more feminized. Indeed this reduction in wage inequality between men and women is the only material gain for labor brought by the adjustment strategies in Latin America (Weller 2000b). This has served to offset the loss of the positive impact that public employment had previously on gender equity as public employment declined (Psacharapoulos and Tzannatos 1992).

The crisis in formal employment basically consists in the decline in public employment and in the growing insecurity of labor conditions. The new model of accumulation thus has its employment expression. Although this expression is often interpreted as increasing informalization, this interpretation is flawed because it basically ignores the change in the model of accumulation that is occurring. Remember that from the regulative perspective, the concept of informality is a relational one. The concept of informality depends on the existence of a formal sector that defines the nature of the relation. Consequently, if the concept of the formal sector is in question, then the formal/informal distinction becomes vague. For different reasons, the other definition of informality used in Latin America, that of PREALC/OIT, is also in question. With the new technological revolution based on microelectronics it is no longer possible to assume the Fordist association between size of establishment and its technological level.

Thus, the concept of informality in its two interpretive dimensions is losing its heuristic capacity (Pérez Sáinz 1998). It is more appropriate to talk of "deformalization," which should not be seen as synonymous with informalization. Deformalization better captures the processes whereby the world of work of the former period of modernization is disappearing in face of a new model of accumulation that brings with it different labor logics. "Deformalization," which is basically the increase in job insecurity, is the relevant phenomenon with which to analyze the new transformations occurring within wage relations.

Labor Flexibility and Employability

However, the increase of excluding tendencies does not mean that there are no possibilities of integration within the logic of wage relations. Examples are strategies of employability whose principal expressions are a nonsolidary individualism and neocorporative unionism as responses to labor flexibility. We can look at how both strategies are sustained on the basis of those elements of the management of risk which employability entails.

The new model of accumulation entails a redefinition of the type of wage relations that predominated in the previous period and which took formal employment as their paradigm. This results in two basic situations with all their possible variations. The first is the situation that occurs when the market opening imposed by structural adjustment exposes existing activities to new competition without the possibility of their absorbing increases in costs through state subsidies or by passing them on to consumers. This situation has led firms to move toward increases in productivity through technological and, above all socio-organizational innovations. These last have affected labor relations through the flexible labor practices just discussed. The second is the situation when occurs when new export-oriented activities, which are completely incorporated into the global market, come into existence. The experiences to date show that the activities that predominate take the "low road," where their competitive advantage is based on cheap labor. There are, however, examples of the "high road," in which competitive advantage is based more on human capital. Examples of this type are found in the electronic sector in Costa Rica or in the so-called third generation maquilas of Mexico (Carrillo and Hualde 1998).

Employability as the capacity to manage risk entails, in the first instance, knowledge relevant to a changing future. This requires, in the first place, the formation of human capital as a response to the demands of the technological and organizational changes that globalization brings. In this respect, the change in the model of accumulation requires a redefinition of the criteria for categorizing what is a suitable workforce and in different ways from that of the period of import-substitution industrialization. This process must also appear as a way of thinking about the labor process. The introduction of post-Taylorist models of organization requires that workers become more active participants in the labor process. Notions of polyvalence and involvement come into play. Employability becomes more and more a matter of having generally relevant competencies, and less and less a matter of having specialized skills (Mertens 1996; Hirata 1997; Leite 1999; Carrillo and Iranzo 2000; Hualde 2001).

The key question for the other factor in the management of risk, consensus, is how to implement effectively the socio-organizational innovations. Are these to be based on an authentic negotiation or not? We have already seen that in the past decade in Latin America innovations have not been introduced systematically, but by individual firms, and have been imposed unilaterally on the workers without negotiation. In general, the involvement of workers has been limited (Carrillo 1995). It remains to be seen if there have been advances in the degree of participation of the workers.

I suggest two hypotheses on the issue of social action. The first is that one of the possible expressions of employability within the logic of wage labor is that of individual actions with little cooperation or solidarity. This would be the concrete embodiment of what Castel (1997) has called "conquering individualism," distinguishing it from "collective individualism," which is institutionally framed, and from "negative individualism," which is marked by disaffiliation. In terms of the type of knowledge required, this implies a clear preference for human capital and the development of generalized abilities. Consensus is not achieved, but imposed unilaterally by the firm. The second hypothesis is that within this same logic of the new pattern of wage relations, another type of social action can emerge with a collective character and can be expressed in terms of union action, but of a neocorporativist type. Such unions become partners with firms to improve productivity (La Garza 2000). Although still important, knowledge is not the primary issue, as it is in the first situation. Here, the primary issue is consensus, which makes the creation of a collective actor (i.e., a union) possible (Pérez Sáinz 2003b).

I end this section by emphasizing that the types of social action in the context of the new forms of wage relations are not limited to the above two types and their possible variations. An autonomous union movement is emerging that is opposed to neocorporativism (La Garza 2000; Murillo 2001). Equally important are the development of transnational labor actions, as Quinteros (2000) shows in case studies of garment maquiladoras in Central America. These involve a variety of actors (union and nonunion, local and global) and whose results are given concrete form in labor regulations of global incidence (codes of conduct, social monitoring, and so on).

The Deepening of Labor Expulsion

High rates of unemployment have persisted throughout the 1990s despite economic recovery. Weighted regional averages show urban unemployment at 8.3 percent in 2000, which is identical to the average in 1985 when the region was in the midst of the debt crisis (OIT 2001, table 1-A). Table 8.3 shows the evolution of open urban unemployment in the region. The largest group of countries in Table 8.3 began with a high initial level of unemployment, which has increased with time. It is precisely this situation that suggests that with the new model of accumulation, unemployment is becoming structural and not merely cyclical. Note, however, the groups of countries that show high initial levels of unemployment, but whose levels of unemployment diminish during the 1990s. Several of these countries have been sources of important international migration flows, as in the cases of El Salvador, the Dominican Republic, and Peru. This suggests that international migration is serving as a mechanism of labor market adjustment in these countries.

Note also that by 2000, eight countries have alarmingly high rates of unemployment: Argentina (15.1 percent), Colombia (17.2 percent), Ecuador (14.1 percent), Panama (15.3 percent), Paraguay (10.0 percent), the Dominican Republic (13.9 percent), Uruguay (13.6 percent), and Venezuela (13.9 percent). As in the past, the most affected groups are women and, above all, young people. The female unemployment figures are the more significant because of the increasing feminization of the labor force in Latin American for some decades now (Tardanico and Menjívar Larín 1997; Stallings and Peres 2000). Of these eight countries, only in Argentina is the male rate of unemployment higher than the female rate.

Table 8.3 Evolution of open employment in Latin America, 1990–2000

Level of unemployment in 1990	Increase 1990–2000	Decrease 1990–2000
High (> 5.7%)	Argentina (15.1%)	El Salvador (6.6%)
	Bolivia (7.4%)	Honduras (5.2%)
	Chile (9.2%)	Panama (15.3%)
	Colombia (17.2%)	Peru (7.0%)
	Ecuador (14.1%)	Dominican Republic (13.9%)
	Nicaragua (9.8%)	
	Uruguay (13.6%)	
	Venezuela (13.9%)	
Low (≤ 5.7%)	Brazil (7.1%)	Costa Rica (5.3%)
	Paraguay (10.0%)	Mexico (2.2%)

SOURCE: OIT 2001, table 6-A.
NOTE: Percentages in parentheses are the percentage of public employment in 2000.

The importance of unemployment goes beyond that of market adjustment and raises four key issues. The first issue is the nature of the new economic model and its incapacity to generate sufficient employment (Tokman 1998). In fact, unemployment is the worst outcome of the labor market trends in the region during the 1990s (Stallings and Peres 2000). Two phenomena need emphasizing. First, labor deregulation is clearly under way, which means that such levels of unemployment cannot be attributed solely to the "rigidities" of the labor market. Second, self-employment is now becoming more limited and cannot play the same role in absorbing surplus labor that informal employment did in the previous decades. Worse still, the trade opening that is part of the programs of structural adjustment exposes a series of self-employment activities to international competition and makes them unfeasible. Thus, the informal sector's anticyclical function in adjusting labor supply and demand is limited, and some self-employment activities increasingly acquire a procyclical character (Cerrutti 2000).

The second issue concerns the erosion of social capital and, in particular, the networks that access the labor market. It is important to remember that the resources mobilized by poor households in confronting poverty are not immune from social change and that it is likely that the situation is changing from one of "resources of poverty" to one of "poverty of resources" (González de la Rocha 1999a).

The third issue is related to the theme of identity. It is a familiar claim that work identities are central in a society in which work is socially recognized through wages (Dubar 1991). Unemployment represents a severe challenge to those identities, particularly for new entrants to the labor market who have not had the time to form clear work identities and develop work aspirations. The result is the development of anomic patterns of behavior, a recurrent situation among the young, which is the group hardest hit by unemployment. These behavior patterns can take perverse paths of violence in face of the pressure of consumerism. They are no longer constrained by moral norms that ensure the material and symbolic reproduction that have historically underpinned social integration up to the present. Thus, there are processes of identity formation among the young that entail forms of community integration that are distinct from the classic models. Identity is based on consumption, and this latter can be attained by transgressing norms and by recourse to violence. Individualism dominates over collective action, competition over cooperation, and there is a distancing from the public sphere and an imprisonment in the private world (García Delgado 1998).

Finally, unemployment is strongly associated with poverty and vulnerability. Its positive correlation with impoverishment has been demonstrated in many studies. This process acquires a disturbing slant in the case of young people, since it can lead to an intergenerational transmission of poverty that calls into question the historical tendencies to reduce poverty (Tokman 1998). Less studied is the relation of unemployment to vulnerability. Vulnerability reminds us that in societies that are not highly polarized it is necessary to overcome dichotomous visions, such as poor and not-poor, and incorporate a third analytic and empirical category, that of vulnerability (Minujin 1998; Filgueira 1999). In this situation, the threat of unemployment implies a source of risk for a certain stratum of households that can fall into a poverty situation if the threat materializes. Pérez Sáinz and Mora (2001) have shown that in Costa Rica during the 1990s, despite the decrease in the percentage of homes in poverty, the number of households at risk of impoverishment has increased. It is the poverty risk line and not so much the poverty line that is the true barrier for upward social mobility.

Labor Migration and Transnational Employability

International migration is a paradoxical phenomenon that, on the one hand, implies an extreme form of exclusion that entails a territorial uprooting, but that, on the other hand, globalizes the labor force. In terms of this second dimension, migration can be interpreted as a strategy of employability.

There are two related issues that need mentioning. First is the emigration of the labor force as a labor market adjustment mechanism in some Latin American countries. Whereas in the past, the excess labor force was absorbed in informal activities, emigration is now another safety valve in the face of the ever-increasing limits on the expansion of viable self-employment. Furthermore, remittances can affect labor force participation rates, levels of unemployment, levels of wages, and consequently, labor market dynamics in the country of origin. The second issue is the redefinition of the territorialism of labor markets and, concretely, of their national character. The previous model of modernization had a clear referent that was both social and territorial. These were the urban areas, especially the metropolitan ones, fed demographically by rural-urban migration. This was the sense in which it was possible to talk of national labor markets. Nevertheless, globalization is changing this type of spatial configuration. International migration now calls into question national labor markets as the only sources of jobs (Pérez Sáinz 2003a).

The current international migrant flows entail three novel phenomena in terms of preceding patterns of migration. First, they are the product of global capitalism, since they respond to labor demand from the North. Second, they represent a social fact that is different from traditional patterns of migrant adaptation. Third, they create greater opportunities for popular initiatives (Portes, Guarnizo, and Landolt 1999). This experience not only affects those who migrate and their respective households but the totality of the community, which through participating in this transnational process, can acquire a particular global territorial and social identity.[4]

In migration, knowledge as an element in the management of risk acquires a particular characteristic because it represents a resource that is managed through networks. Networks constitute the spinal cords of migration processes. As has been frequently shown, the presence of a family member makes possible the subsequent displacement of other members of the household and helps people settle in the host country in terms of housing or employment (Massey et al. 1987). Two aspects of network analysis are relevant to the issues discussed here. The first is that knowledge, or knowing how to migrate, becomes converted into a nonmonetary resource. This does not eliminate the issue that the act of migration is something, depending on the destination, that not everyone can afford. Knowledge forms part of the reciprocity between the people involved: those who have already migrated and those who are about to do so. Second, the closeness of those involved, which is the basis of trust, is a social proximity that it is not limited to ties of kinship. A physical closeness also functions within the confines of the community of origin, but one radically redefined by the transnationalism that globalization facilitates through the revolution in communications.

Two basic situations that are usually found in combination affect consensus. The first and most frequent is that the decision to migrate is part of a family survival strategy to avoid impoverishment. As with every family survival strategy this develops in the context of a family's consensual agreements. Such a consensus is not always easy to reach. Age and gender-based tensions enter the arena. Indeed, migration itself can exacerbate these tensions by questioning established family hierarchies through the proactive role that women and young people can play in the migration process (Popkin and Andrade-Eekhoff 2000). The second situation is the construction of a collective actor in the country of immigration with the establishment of migrant

---

4. Pries (2000) distinguishes among immigration (integration into the receiving society), remigration (return to the place of origin), and transmigration. This last is based on family networks in a transnational social space.

associations. In this situation, consensus can develop through the function-ing of this type of organization, and in this process the possible hostility of the environment plays its part through expressions of xenophobia. Thus, bounded solidarity can be an important source of consensus in face of exter-nal harassment.

The first type of action focuses on the reproduction of the original house-hold through family remittances. The principal effect of these remittances is the struggle to overcome poverty. The most visible case, at the macro level, is El Salvador, where international migration contributed to the reduction in poverty in the 1990s. This type of action is individual, but constrained by family contexts. There is also, however, the possibility of developing actions that are not individual. These occur when collective remittances are sent by migrant organizations of the community of origin (Andrade-Eekhoff 1997). The destination of these remittances is for the development of infrastructure, which entails an unprecedented transnationalization of the local public sphere (Sojo and Pérez Sáinz 2002). These types of actions can become an important axis of local development in the communities involved (Pérez Sáinz 2003b).

The Diversity of Self-Employment

Surplus labor in Latin America has not appeared historically as open un-employment. In rural areas, its most significant manifestation has been self-employment in the peasant economy. In the urban areas, informality has fulfilled that role. Informality had considerable importance in the crisis of the 1980s, becoming the principal mechanism through which urban labor markets adjusted (PREALC 1991). Self-generated employment, including the wage employment attached to it, gained importance in the 1990s, with its share of total nonagricultural employment rising from 37.0 percent, in 1990, to 40.2 percent, ten years later (OIT, 2001, table 6-A).

Subsistence Self-employment

My first concern with self-employment is to identify that part of it charac-terized by a subsistence logic, which would place it among the excluding tendencies. The predominance of a subsistence logic implies that there is no clear separation between enterprise and household and that the priorities of the latter prevail. The pressures of poverty determine these priorities in the majority of cases. Thus, my hypothesis is that a considerable part of this type of self-employment corresponds to an economy of poverty: the poor producing for the poor. Consequently, the relation between this type of self-employment and poverty can provide an idea of its magnitude and evolution. Table 8.4 shows us this association both in urban and rural areas.

The majority of countries show a situation in which there has been a general reduction in poverty, and in which the self-employed in agriculture show greater reductions in poverty than the total rural labor force. El Salvador and Mexico show the opposite pattern in that there has been a general increase in poverty and this has been most pronounced among the self-employed. Although the table shows improvement in poverty levels, two important facts must be kept in mind. First, in all the countries, the levels of peasant poverty are greater than those of total rural employment. Second, in the majority of countries, the majority of the peasantry lives in poverty. These levels are particularly high in the cases of El Salvador (80 percent), Honduras (89 percent), and Nicaragua (87 percent).

The new economic model has had two important effects on rural labor markets. First, in those cases in which the peasants have communal land, policies directed at creating land markets have had a negative effect, leading to the proletarianization of the peasantry. Second is the introduction of new capital-intensive technologies, which have displaced labor and thus increased the seasonality of agricultural employment (Thomas 1997). This last effect reinforces a historical tendency present in the previous modernization (Gómez and Klein 1993).

Table 8.4 Poverty and the agricultural self-employed, Latin America, 1990–1999

Evolution of poverty among the total employed in rural areas, 1990–1999	Greater decrease/increase than among total of those employed in agriculture	Less decrease/increase than among total of those employed in agriculture
Decrease	Brazil (55%) Colombia (66%) Costa Rica (21%) Guatemala (69%) Panama (42%)	Chile (21%) Honduras (89%) Nicaragua (87%)
Increase	El Salvador (80%) Mexico (64%)	Venezuela (44%)

SOURCE: CEPAL 2001, table 18.
NOTE: Percentages in parentheses are the percentages of agricultural self-employed workers in poverty at the end of the 1990s.

We can carry out the same analysis of the relationship between poverty and self-employment for the urban self-employed using the available information to differentiate between those in productive and those in non productive activities (see Tables 8.5 and 8.6).

In Table 8.5, the majority of countries show a pattern where poverty in self-employment diminished more than among the total of those employed. However, there are cases in which this decrease was less (Brazil) and, worse still, countries where the poverty of the urban self-employed increased despite the overall decline in poverty among the total urban employed (Guatemala, Mexico, Nicaragua).

Nonproductive activities (commerce and services) show similar results (Table 8.6). Nevertheless, as with the peasantry, it is important to emphasize that with the exception of Chile, levels of poverty among both types of urban self-employed are higher than those of the urban employed. It is also important to emphasize those cases where the majority of these self-employed are living in poverty. This is the case among the self-employed in manufacturing and construction in Bolivia (66 percent), Colombia (60 percent), Ecuador (68 percent), Guatemala (51 percent), Honduras (80 percent), and Nicaragua (59 percent). It is the case among the self-employed in commerce and services in Colombia (54 percent), Ecuador (62 percent), Honduras (72 percent), and Nicaragua (52 percent). These countries of late modernization continue to show a generalized poverty economy in the urban areas.

In general, then, reduction in poverty during the 1990s has resulted in some diminution of subsistence self-employment, but there are still significant contingents of workers of this type that live in poverty, especially in rural areas.

The Upgrading of the Small Enterprise in the Global Market

Although subsistence self-employment persists, the current technological revolution, based on microelectronics, questions the Fordist association between size of establishment and technological level. Technological progress is no longer reserved for large firms. Entrepreneurs can create small firms that are able to enter the global market and compete there.

We can distinguish three principal ways in which small firms insert themselves into the global market (Pérez Sáinz 2002). The aim of this insertion is upgrading by which the small firm gains greater muscle in the global chain in which it locates through generating greater value-added (Bair and Gereffi 1999; Gereffi et al. 2001). The three ways can be labeled autonomous,

Table 8.5 Evolution of Latin American poverty among the self-employed in manufacturing and construction, 1990–1999

Evolution of poverty among the total employed in urban areas	Greater decrease/increase than among total employed in urban areas	Lower decrease/increase than among total employed in urban areas	Opposite direction[a]
Decrease	Chile (11%)	Brazil (33%)	Guatemala (51%)
	Colombia (60%)		Mexico (39%)
	Costa Rica (17%)		Nicaragua (59%)
	El Salvador (43%)		
	Panama (24%)		
	Uruguay (12%)		
Increase	Bolivia (66%)	Ecuador (68%)	
	Nicaragua (59%)	Venezuela (33%)	
		Honduras (80%)	

SOURCE: CEPAL 2001, table 17.

NOTE: Percentages in parentheses are the percentages in poverty by 1999.

[a] Opposite direction means that the evolution was the reverse of the overall tendency—an increase in poverty when the overall tendency was one of decline.

Table 8.6 Evolution of Latin American poverty among the urban self-employed in commerce and the services, 1990–1999

Evolution of poverty among the total employed in urban areas	Greater decrease/increase than among total employed in urban areas	Less decrease/increase than among total employed in urban areas	Opposite direction[a]
Decreased	Brazil (27%)	Colombia (54%)	Guatemala (46%)
	Chile (9%)	Uruguay (9%)	Mexico (30%)
	Costa Rica (16%)		
	El Salvador (35%)		
	Panama (26%)		
Increased	Bolivia (43%)	Ecuador (62%)	
	Nicaragua (52%)	Venezuela (34%)	
		Honduras (72%)	

SOURCE: CEPAL 2001, table 17.
NOTE: Percentages in parentheses are the percentages of self-employed workers in poverty by 1999.
[a] Opposite direction means that the evolution was the reverse of the overall tendency—an increase in poverty when the overall tendency was one of decline.

cooperative, and subordinated. Remember, however, that the empirical evidence suggests that there may be more than three modes, that the modes are not mutually exclusive, and that upgrading converts the small entrepreneurial business into a large firm. This last transformation implies that labor relations can no longer be analyzed in terms of the logic of self-employment, but in terms of that of wage relations. The alternative facing the firm is whether it opts for the "low road," which is based on cheap labor and precarious labor conditions, or the "high road," which is based on developing human capital and encouraging the employability of its labor force.

The autonomous way is the path followed in market niches that are still not controlled by the leading firms and that give small firms the space to transform themselves into global firms. The case of the "software" sector in Costa Rica is an example of this kind. This path is likely to be an increasingly difficult one to follow in the future, but it is also unlikely to disappear completely. The cooperative way corresponds to territorial clusters of small firms in localities constituted as neighborhood communities. The concept of cooperation suggests a certain collectivization of the upgrading process, with two intervening sets of factors. First are the different types of external economies: specialization, information, labor force, and symbolic forms of communication. The second consists in drawing upon the various forms of community capital. Small owners reinforcing entrepreneurial identities and avoiding opportunistic behavior can interject community values. Also, networks based on loans of different types (raw material, tools, labor, information, and so on) must be able to generate repeated exchanges that develop the trust that results in cooperation. The external threats that come from the competitive jungle of globalization must succeed in creating organizational responses among the owners. It is also important that the dominant norms promote an economic morality that favors innovation and not imitation (Pérez Sáinz and Andrade-Eekhoff 2003).

The subordinate way is one that seeks simply to adapt to the situation of global chains. The challenges of this type of relation are fundamental when small firms find themselves inescapably located in the lowest links. As Coriat (1993) points out for the Japanese firm, the spectrum can vary between situations that reproduce traditional relations, both vertical and hierarchical, and those where the relations are institutionalized and promote technological and organizational innovations in the supplier or subcontracted firms. Clearly, the possibilities of upgrading for small firms are greater in this latter type of situation than in the former. These different paths cannot be freely chosen. To a great extent, the options are determined by the strategies of the leading firms, which, as the major players, determine most of the rules of the game.

The knowledge required to insert and maintain the small firm in the global market has, at least, a double aspect. There is organizational learning in terms of the accumulation of know-how from running an enterprise (routines or operating procedures, organizational structure, handling of documents), rather than from research and development. Thus, the basis is knowledge accumulation—including small innovations, specializations, competencies, and implicit knowledge that improve efficiency. As Hershberg (1998) emphasizes, upgrading is above all a social and political challenge, which involves groups and institutions in terms of their capacities to learn and to act on the basis of what they have learned. It is also the capacity to monitor, which, in turn, implies two aspects. The first has to do with the vision of the global market taking as reference points global enterprises and their strategies. The second involves the capacity to translate specific know-how coming from the global market in concrete ways of acting that produce tacit knowledge.

Knowledge acquires particular characteristics depending on the path of globalization taken by the small enterprise. In the autonomous path, learning is a fundamentally individualized process of the enterprise with few previous experiences as points of reference. In the cooperative path, if external economies of information and communication are present, and also a community capital that underpins cooperation, knowledge tends to be spread within a group more easily, becoming something of a collective resource within the cluster. Finally, in the subordinate path, the possibility of knowledge comes through the global firm; and consequently, the type of relation with the global firm is fundamental to the acquiring of this knowledge. Relations of a horizontal type are more suited to such a transmission to the small enterprises, while the contrary happens when the relation is vertical.

The possibilities of reaching consensus on shared future aspirations also vary with the path of globalization. Autonomy represents the situation of greatest atomization, where the issue of agreement is of least importance. The contrary is the case of the cooperative path where agreement becomes embodied in much broader projects of local development. In the subordinate path, agreement is a relative term, since aspirations are, to a great extent, imposed from above by the strategy of the global firm.

Employability in this type of logic refers, as has already been pointed out, to the process of upgrading. The different paths show different types of action. The autonomous path leads to individual actions that can resemble

the nonsolidary individualism we found with respect the logic of wage relations. The cooperative way makes possible a collective action, which is
not inevitable, since it depends on the dynamics within the respective cluster
and on whether the external economies, and especially community capital,
become mobilized. This situation has considerable affinity with that pointed
out with respect to collective remittances. Finally, the subordinate path is
an action constrained within the hierarchy of the chain and, consequently,
entails delegated employability (Pérez Sáinz 2003b).

Social Citizenship, Labor Exclusion, and Employability

I conclude with some reflections on the impact of these new dynamics on
the type of social citizenship that is emerging with the new model of accumulation. To begin, we can remind ourselves about the type of citizenship
that appeared in the previous period of modernization.

For several decades, Latin America experienced a kind of harmonious
triangle that connected the labor market with social policy and with welfare.
This triangle implied the mutual interrelationship of three factors: formal
employment, state regulation, and social integration. Urbanization and social
mobility made possible the construction of a social citizenship that was
shaped in the formal segment of the urban labor market and which the state
consolidated particularly through social security coverage. Clearly, different
types of modernization (early, accelerated, and late) and their corresponding expressions at the national level resulted in different outcomes in each
country (Mesa-Lago 1994; Roberts 1995, 1996). However, this triangulation
of national modernization was called into question by the crisis of the 1980s.
Two separate relationships became redefined in terms of social integration.
On the one hand, state intervention became oriented to a construction of
social citizenship that does not necessarily depend on employment. Targeting, which has characterized social policies in Latin America for some years,
directly deals with social groups (preferably the extremely poor) in terms of
certain types of needs (education and housing, principally). On the other
hand, the substitution of the state by the market means that the latter is at the
heart of constructing society. In this context, the labor market emerges, with
more force than previously, as a factor in the dynamics of social (dis)integra-
tion. Nevertheless, its impact is now distinct because of major transformations in the structure of employment following the crisis and the structural
adjustments that followed.

At the heart of these transformations are the dual consequences of globalization for social integration. First, integration no longer entails the constitution of the nation as an integrated community. This implies that there may be social sectors that are not a necessary part of that community. Consequently, in the present, the term "exclusion" acquires an analytic importance when integration does not form part of the globalizing project. And second, insofar as the market has displaced the state, the crucial issue becomes access to opportunities. Among these, access to knowledge stands out as the key social issue in globalization (Sojo and Pérez Sáinz 2002).[5]

The labor sphere is seeing a change from the emphasis on rights (adequate work) to duties (self-generation of work opportunities). In the previous period of modernization, emphasis was on labor rights embodied in national labor codes that basically protected formal workers. The counterpart (the duties of the workers) was accepting a populist type contract (a type of pseudo-Fordist agreement) guaranteed by the state, which became the principal actor. This type of alliance entered into crisis in the 1970s with the development of authoritarian regimes that showed the historical limits of this contract. The crisis of the 1980s and the implementation of programs of structural adjustment generated a new context of hegemonic uncertainty that has converted poverty and exclusion into basic problems of governability (Lozano 1998).

These changes raise two fundamental questions. In the first place, the development of labor exclusion is synonymous with the erosion of existing labor rights. The current erosion of labor rights is basically that of insecurity in wage employment. The issue is that of differentiating between different types of rights. Portes (1994) has proposed the existence of four types of rights: basic (right against the use of child labor, against physical coercion, and against involuntary servitude); civic (right to free association, to collective representation, and to free expression); survival (right to a living wage, accident compensation, and a limited work week); and security (right against arbitrary dismissal, to retirement compensation, and to survivors' compensation). Portes argues that the first two rights constitute agreed international standards, while the others will be more flexibly applied depending on the context.

5. Filgueira (1999) has suggested that there is a certain historical parallelism between the disintegrative effects of market expansion on precapitalist peasant communities and the effects of the actual process of globalization on the nation-state and its role in providing social protection.

Maintaining basic rights entails that the regulatory function of the state continues and is effective in ensuring the legal observance of these rights. In the context of a general process of deregulation, such as characterized Latin America in the 1980s and 1990s, the protective intervention of the state remains important in shaping work conditions (Itzigsohn 2000).

The second major question is that of the diverse forms of employability that emerge as social actions to manage the risks that are peculiar to global modernization. I focus on the two extremes of the spectrum of this diversity, which have a clear effect on the configuration of social citizenship.

The first is what I have labeled as nonsolidary individualism that is present both in the new forms of wage relations and in the globalized self-employment activities. The concept nonsolidary applies to that situation in which for workers the process of acquiring human capital does not bring with it social responsibilities. The subjective reflexivity of this type of worker is a narcissistic one focused on their individual potentials and achievements, distancing them in this way from a collective action that appears unnecessary. The risk culture that develops in this situation entails tackling the volatility of the labor market and accepting the possibility of exclusion. This type of individualism sees exclusion as a "natural" result of the functioning of the labor market. The resultant type of employability is not only compatible with the labor exclusion that is currently tending to predominate but also reinforces it (Pérez Sáinz 2003a).

The other extreme of the spectrum are the examples of the sending of collective remittances to pay for public goods in the communities of origin and the cooperative path that can produce a collective upgrading of small firms belonging to the same cluster in neighborhood communities. Both cases represent collective actions, which also reinforce community cohesion. They are examples of local development strategies in which equity is an important component because participation in globalization is not limited to a few, the "winners," but available to the majority. Thus, employability in this situation does not necessarily lead to nonsolidary individualism, but to greater social equity. Whether employability becomes an integrative force with positive effects on equity depends basically on knowledge. The form that knowledge takes influences the other defining factor in risk: consensus (Pérez Sáinz 2003b).

This is the key resource in globalization that plays a similar role in terms of the structuring of society, as did the means of production in the previous phase of modernization. The key issue is access to knowledge, which has three components. The first is that this resource, in its multiple expressions, is a public good and one of global reach (Stiglitz 1999). Obtaining knowledge is thus a right and, consequently, entails a truly democratic access. Thus, knowledge becomes the keystone of a new social citizenship. The second component, a corollary of the first, is that the state must play a central role in the provision of this resource. This entails that the gulf in the quality of access to knowledge between public and private sector must disappear, given that this gulf is one of the main sources of future inequalities. Third, access to knowledge, as a public good, generates social responsibilities and obligations, even if that access is basically individual. These responsibilities and obligations guarantee that employability is not inevitably expressed as non-solidary individualism (Pérez Sáinz 2003a).

When knowledge is organized as a public good, with global reach and democratic access, the dimension of consensus becomes a collective one excluding the impositions of any one of the actors involved. As a result, the risk that is brought by the very process of globalization can be a source for promoting equity. Employability, consequently, does not necessarily have to entail atomization and the acceptance of social exclusion.

9 Families in Transition

MARINA ARIZA AND
ORLANDINA DE OLIVEIRA

Despite the apparent stability of family structure, and the predominance of ideological discourses that extol traditional domestic life as a social ideal, the Latin American family is beginning to show timid yet unequivocal signs of change, at least among some social groups. Detectable transformations in family organization, composition, and behavior can be traced to a host of demographic, cultural, and economic processes, each of which operates at its own pace and interacts with the others in complex ways.

Recurring economic crises and the contradictory tensions that emanate from the globalization of national economies have begun to undermine the cultural underpinnings of the patriarchal ethos and the rules and agreements that govern both intrafamily behavior and how families relate to their economic, political, and institutional environments. Faced with a shifting profile of opportunities and constraints, people have constructed new images of men and women and have devised novel forms of family organization and behavior. The symbolic and structural changes observed within the family thus reveal the close connection between family life and the social context in which families are embedded.

The transformations in the Latin American family in recent decades have called into question conventional analytical strategies and have stimulated the use of new conceptual approaches in the field of family sociology. This chapter addresses the linkages between family organization and macrostructural processes, noting how these relationships have prompted a reassessment of conventional research strategies. The analysis is divided into three sections. The first addresses the macrostructural changes taking place in Latin America. The second explores how the macrolevel analysis frames the emerging trends in family organization. The third section sets forth a critical assessment of conventional approaches to family studies and examines the conceptual reformulations that have come about as a result.

Macrostructural Trends and Family Change

A summary of the broad transformations that influence family organization serves to introduce the main theoretical assumptions that guide this chapter. The socioeconomic and demographic changes to which we refer have different implications for families and the individuals that comprise them. Although analytically separable, in reality the various processes occur simultaneously, enabling modifications in some aspects of family structure while constraining others.

In recent decades, most of the economies in the region have moved away from the postwar style of development that gave priority to import substitution and to domestic consumption. In contrast to the earlier period, current trends promote the insertion into global markets, the expansion of tourism, and the search for international investments as the main sources of capital accumulation. Globalization, which produces both fragmentation and homogenization, has reconfigured the basic aspects of social life, including the process of social identity, a trend that deeply affects the world of family affairs (Giddens 1991). Other consequences of globalization include the compression of time and space, the intrusion of new values, and the increasing exposure to foreign cultural realities.

The globalizing character of today's world economy accounts for the magnitude and intensity of international migration (Portes 1996b; Guarnizo 1998). In the face of persistent social exclusion (see Wood in this volume), international migrants have learned to take advantage of new forms of communication (Alexander and Smith 2000; Beck 2000) and have drawn on social capital in sending and receiving areas to create a system of transnational linkages that define an entirely new social terrain (Glick Schiller, Bash, and Blanc-Szanton 1992; Guarnizo and Smith 1998; Portes, Guarnizo, and Landolt 1999). Operating through various mechanisms, the transnational network of social relationships has transformed the way that families are structured, and the way family members interact. By fragmenting residential space, the international migration that occurs within a transnationalized setting has undermined the significance of coresidence as a defining characteristic of families and households (Guarnizo 1995; Ariza 2000; Popkin and Andrade-Eekhoff 2000).

The depth of the transformations induced by globalization is palpable in the "quiet revolution" that has taken place in the organization of work (*Le Monde Diplomatique* 1998). The change is associated with the gradual but systematic erosion of the structures and practices that once characterized the labor market in the decades immediately following World War II. The latter included the prevalence of full-time employment, the existence of predictable career ladders, the predominance of men in the workforce, the possibility of social mobility, and the existence of social security and various forms of social assistance. Current trends, under way in every country in the region, are defined by an increase in part-time employment, underemployment and unemployment, the loss of job security, the growing polarization in the labor market, the deregulation of labor, and lower income returns to labor skills (see Pérez Sáinz in this volume). All these factors characterize the growing job insecurity intrinsic to globalization (Beck 2000).

Increased employment in the tertiary (service) sector is another aspect of the restructuring of the economic system. The trend is plainly evident in many countries in the region, including Mexico, Argentina, and Uruguay. In some instances, the "tertiarization" of the economy has been accompanied by a polarization of the labor force characterized by the emergence of "protected" and "unprotected" domains within the service sector. Workers in financial services, for example, are far more protected than service workers employed by microenterprises that pay low wages and offer minimal job security (Oliveira, Ariza, and Eternod 2001).

Because the service sector typically generates jobs held by women—such as teachers, secretaries, receptionists, waitresses, and nurses, among others—the growing tertiarization of the economies has expanded employment opportunities for women, thereby contributing to the growing number of women in the labor force (Arriagada 1994; Infante and Klein 1991). The increase in female employment has been further stimulated by the growth of offshore assembly plants (*maquiladoras*) in some countries, especially Mexico. In keeping with the drive to decrease production costs, the *maquiladoras* found a ready source of relatively cheap labor in the female population, particularly in the industry's early years. Other factors that contributed to the "feminization" of the labor force included the proliferation of jobs in the informal sector of the economy and the expansion of subcontracting for tasks performed in the home (Oliveira and Ariza 1997; Standing 1999).

The long-term shifts in employment structure, together with the economic crises that plagued the region in the last few decades of the twentieth century, have led to a number of consequences, including a decline in family income. Financial hardship has forced household members (even nonresidents) to intensify their efforts to provide economic support and has compelled women to enter the labor market. In addition to contributing to the feminization of the labor force, these trends have had deep repercussions in terms of family structure and the organization of domestic life. A combination of sociodemographic factors has also had a decisive influence. The accelerated demographic transition, marked by a rapid fertility decline in recent decades (see Potter and Tuirán Gutiérrez in this volume), has lowered average household size throughout the region (CEPAL 1995). The trend toward smaller households has led to a decline in the number of multigenerational units and an increase in the proportion of single-person households (Jelin 1998). At the same time, other factors work against these trends. The increase in life expectancy and the aging of the population, for example, have unexpectedly prolonged the traditional functions of the family (López Barajas 1998). Similar outcomes are associated with the increase in schooling—an urban trend that has extended the period of adolescence and postponed the age at which sons and daughters leave the nuclear family.

The fertility decline was facilitated largely by the widespread adoption of contraceptives, which made it possible to separate reproduction from sexuality. In this way contraceptive use struck at the very core of family life by freeing women from the subjugation of natural fertility regimes and by allowing them to choose from a wider menu of social options. Advances in reproductive technology shortened the amount of time devoted to reproduction and child rearing and permitted such novelties as artificial insemination. The effect was to liberate procreation from the confines of the traditional family unit. Changes such as these modified many of the primary functions of the family as the site of control of reproduction and sexuality (Arriagada 1998).

The decline in fertility and mortality rates defined the initial "demographic transition." Although the family did not figure prominently in analyses of vital rates, the decline in fertility and mortality nonetheless had decisive consequences in the family domain. The changes in family life—still incipient in many Latin American countries, and limited to particular social groups within the region—evidence the beginning of the so-called second demographic transition (Lesthaeghe 1998).

The economic and demographic trends that took place in the last few decades of the twentieth century were accompanied by cultural changes that have begun to transform the image of women through new social constructions of femininity that are less centered on motherhood (Roussel 1987). For some analysts (e.g., Hobsbawm 1996), this change in women's identity is so significant that it represents a true "cultural revolution." The change was preceded by a number of processes, the more salient of which included an increase in the number of women achieving higher levels of education, the urbanization of the population, the expansion of telecommunications, the continual exposure to other cultures, the use of contraceptives to control reproduction, the growing proportion of women engaged in paid employment, and in particular, the questioning of women's traditional roles brought about by the mobilization of women.

Since the 1960s, feminist movements to enhance women's rights have steadily undermined the legitimacy of traditional family roles, giving way to a conceptualization of women as autonomous beings capable of forging their own destinies. As Castells (1996) contends, whatever may have defined their original objectives, the number and diversity of feminist movements have collectively deconstructed and reconstructed women's identity, demystifying traditional gender roles and beliefs. In the process, the domain of sociobiological reproduction has gradually shed its "natural" attributes to become the subject of theoretical questioning. The individualized image of women, based on their biological potential for reproduction, has given way to a more complex conceptualization of reproduction as a shared domain in which both men and women count on the possibility of choices and assume rights as well as responsibilities (Figueroa Perea 1994).

In the same way that new meanings have emerged with regard to women and childbearing, so too have the notions of masculinity and fatherhood been redefined. Among younger generations, paternal responsibilities are beginning to encompass a range of childrearing tasks that were once entirely delegated to women (Guttman 1993; Rojas 2002; García and Oliveira 2001).

It is worth pointing out, however, that the changes we have identified are indicative of incipient cultural trends that are not, as yet, accepted unconditionally by the majority of people. It is more accurate to think of the various tendencies as fraught with tensions and contradictions, displaying both continuity and breaks with the past, and characterized by temporal disparities in the pace of change within economic, demographic, and social spheres (Flores 1998; Salles and Tuirán 1998). The shifting configurations of these forces and counterforces have clear implications for family life.

Continuity and Change in Family Structure and Behavior

The goal of this section is to demonstrate how the changes we shall describe have left their imprint on various dimensions of family life. We will pay particular attention to the structure, formation, and dissolution of families, as well as the organization of domestic life and certain aspects pertaining to cohabitation.

Household Structure

When we examine the kinship composition of families in Latin America, the image that stands out is one of stability. Nuclear families, composed of a couple with or without children, continue to be the norm. Similarly, the large proportion of extended families and composite households (those which include unrelated individuals) has remained relatively constant in recent decades. The prevalence of extended families, especially among the poor, has been interpreted as a response to adverse economic circumstances to the extent that additional members make a valuable contribution to the household by performing domestic chores and bringing in additional income (Selby et al. 1990; Chant 1994).

Despite the observed stability in family composition, two changes under way merit attention. One is the small increase in the proportion of single-person households, particularly in those countries in which the demographic transition is most advanced and the population is significantly older. Another is an increase in the number of female-headed households. Taken together, these trends point to a greater diversity in family structure in the urban areas of Latin America at the turn of the twenty-first century (Arriagada 1997).

Female-headed households are of signal importance to the study of family change. Female headship is a heterogeneous category that encompasses diverse situations, including single mothers, elderly widows, and educated young women. It is precisely this category that has experienced the largest increase over the last few decades (Arriagada 1998). The rise in the number of female-headed households is the net result of a variety of demographic, economic, and social causes, the most significant of which involve sex differentials in life expectancy, male migration and emigration, childbearing among unmarried women, and the prevalence of domestic violence, associated with alcoholism, drug abuse, and poverty. The increase in educational attainment among women, their growing economic independence, and changing gender roles have further contributed to the increase in the number of female-headed households (Massiah 1983; Oliveira, Eternod, and López 1999; González de la Rocha 1999b).

Formation and Dissolution of Families

Even though changes in the processes by which families are formed and dissolved are only beginning to occur, modest shifts in family dynamics can be understood to represent emergent trends in Latin American family structure.

Modifications in the family life cycle are evident in the gradual change toward a later age of marriage, a decline in the number of married couples, an increase in consensual unions, and a rise in adolescent pregnancy. The increase in life expectancy has further contributed to family dissolution by simply prolonging the number of coresident years, thereby raising the probability of separation, divorce, and second marriages (CEPAL 1994; Quilodrán 2000). This ensemble of trends is particularly evident in European countries that have entered the so-called second demographic transition (see Van der Kaa 1987; Lesthaeghe 1998; Ariza and Oliveira 1999b; Quilodrán 2000; and García and Rojas 2003).

The striking social inequalities in Latin America make it difficult to delineate precisely the significance of the incipient trends in the formation and dissolution of families. It is likely that the increase in consensual unions and the postponement of marriage have different meanings for families in different social strata. Among middle- and upper-income groups, the trends may be associated with women's greater autonomy, whereas among poorer groups, the decline in living standards is a more plausible explanation. Among the latter group, the difficulty of finding a job and the decline in family income may cause young people to delay marriage and to enter into consensual unions, particularly when financial resources are scarce, and when the couple cannot reside in the man's household.

The Organization of Domestic Life

As in the case of other aspects of family life, the tasks routinely performed by household members show signs of both continuity and change. In addition to the consequences of long-term demographic and sociocultural trends, the deterioration in working conditions and the increase in poverty have begun to erode traditional models of domestic life that assume a male head of household with an income level sufficient to support his family. In contrast to the conventional model, there is an increase in the prevalence of families headed by a woman who is responsible for domestic chores, childrearing, and the care of sick and elderly relatives (see Arriagada 1997; Oliveira, Ariza, and Eternod 1996; and Oliveira 1999).

As a result of their participation in the labor force and their economic contribution to the family, women have managed to redefine their social roles, at least to some extent. However, when it comes to domestic chores and child care, very little has changed. Despite the greater flexibility evident among the younger and better-educated generations, the wife remains responsible for cooking, cleaning house, and washing and ironing clothes. Men's participation in family labor is more sporadic, often limited to weekends, vacations, or during a health emergency. When men are involved in domestic tasks, it is usually limited to the entertainment of children, housing repairs, and dealing with various administrative issues (see De Barbieri 1984; Sánchez Gómez 1989; García and Oliveira 1994, 2001; García 1995; Wainerman 2000; and Rendón 2000). The burdens borne by families, and by women in particular, have only increased in recent years as the state narrows the provision of social services.

Tension and Change in Gender Relations

Generally speaking, educational achievement, employment outside the home, and control over earned income enhance women's autonomy and self-esteem, as well as women's bargaining power within the domestic unit. Moreover, educated women with well-paid jobs and good employment benefits tend to be those most committed to gender equality and the struggle for women's rights (Blumberg 1991; Oropesa and Hogan 1994; García and Oliveira 1994; García 2000). Here again, social differentiation is important. If the relationship between outside employment and a more equitable division of labor within the home tends to characterize women in medium- and upper-income families, these relationships may not characterize poorer women. When women earn incomes that are similar to or higher than their male counterparts, the result can be a loss of male authority and self-esteem, which can frequently lead to domestic violence. This is particularly the case when married women are the main income earners (Safilios-Rothschild 1990; García and Oliveira 1994).

International migration has introduced further complications in family life, which vary according the kind of migration involved. The intrafamily consequences are different depending on whether migration involves an individual family member or the entire family unit. Similarly, the effects of migration are different when one compares families that remain in the place of origin to those reunited in the place of destination. A husband's absence does not necessarily imply long-lasting changes in the structure of authority within families that stay behind (Mummert 1992; Szasz 1999). However, when women migrate their departure is more likely to introduce tensions and doubts to the extent that their activities depart from their traditional domestic roles. Exposure to different experiences and cultures can promote changes that favor greater gender equality, although this process is slow and ambivalent, often charged with conflict and subject to reversals (Hondagneu-Sotelo 1994; Ariza 2000, 2002; Popkin and Andrade-Eekhoff 2000).

Critique of Concepts and Approaches

The conceptual approaches that analysts have relied on to explore the complex and multidirectional relationships between social change and family structure are currently in the process of being redefined. In this section we draw on a gender perspective to review some of the leading criticisms of the assumptions underlying theories of the family. In so doing we will note the conceptual revisions that have taken place during the last few decades, emphasizing the analytical value of concepts developed in other fields of research that have been applied in family studies.

Assumptions and Concepts

Skepticism concerning the public-private dichotomy that underpins many conventional approaches in family research has questioned the idea of the private sphere as a natural and apolitical domain. The dichotomy obscures key aspects of the internal dynamics of family behavior, as well as the strategic linkages that connect the family to other social arenas. Deemphasizing the public/private vision removes the family from the realm of nature, granting it a more realistic social character that highlights the central role of power in structuring intrafamily relations.

Focusing attention on gender and generational asymmetries has further called into question the ideological image of the family as a cohesive and harmonious unit, making it possible to give visibility to the different ways in which power can be exercised within the family. The revised approach has prompted an interest in analyzing intrahousehold dynamics based on cooperative arrangements, social exchanges, the deployment of power, and presence of conflict between men and women and between members of different generations. Problematizing the notion of "sex roles" made it easier to detect the presence of conflict and power differentials that otherwise remain hidden. Newer perspectives promoted a greater sensitivity to gender-delimited power domains and the processes by which intrafamily authority is exercised, negotiated, and legitimized. The intrahousehold approach similarly shed new light on family behavior, including domestic violence, which is seen as compelling evidence of the perverse consequences of the profound asymmetries within the family (M. Harris 1981; Thorne 1982; Collier and Yanagisako 1987; Oliveira 1989; González de la Rocha 1991; Jelin 1998; Oliveira, Eternod, and López 1999).

The effort to reconceptualize intrafamily relationships has called attention to how the traditional patterns of family authority have become more flexible, leading to the empowerment of women as well as changes in the domain of male authority (see Powell 1986; Benería and Roldán 1987; García and Oliveira 1994; Ariza and Oliveira 1999a; Jelin 1998; and Oliveira and Ariza 1997). The redistribution of power within the domestic unit has implications at the individual, familial, and social levels. The empowerment of women involves changes in the legislation and the ideologies that underpin gender inequalities, as well as changes in community-level decision making and the capacity for women to engage in the collective struggle for women's rights. At the individual and familial levels, the redistribution of power involves increased awareness of injustice, recognition of women's rights, greater participation in family decisions, and a questioning of the existing structure of family authority (Sen and Grown 1985; Batliwala 1994; García 2003).

At the same time, critical reassessments of the very concept of "work" have eroded the dichotomy between production on the one hand and reproduction on the other. By demonstrating the linkages between employment outside the home and the performance of domestic chores indispensable to the reproduction of the labor force, the notion of the "sexual division of labor" served to articulate family life and the world of work (for gender-based studies of female employment, see Bruschini 1994; García, Blanco, and Pacheco 1999; and Oliveira 1997). Analyses along these lines underscored two fundamental points. First, gender-based criteria determined both the organization of labor markets and the allocation of jobs within the family. Second, the two domains were related. The jobs women performed within the home influenced the possibilities available to them in the labor market, just as women's participation in the labor market conditioned the jobs they performed at home. Related approaches (such as the focus on "family survival" or "family reproduction" strategies) were similarly useful in showing how rational economic behavior within the family influenced, and in turn was influenced by, the dynamics of the labor market.

As a consequence of these conceptual reformulations, the family is no longer treated as an isolated and self-sufficient unit. The analytical focus turns, instead, to the relationships between the family, the economy, and the state, emphasizing the different ways and different levels that domestic and extra-domestic spheres permeate each other. Through studies of social networks and of the operation of neighborhood organizations that pressure the state for goods and services, analysts have illuminated the different types of linkages between the family and public institutions. Implementing family-related public policies is now a priority, as is the use of legal mechanisms to protect the rights of family members, including the prosecution of domestic violence (Rapp 1982; Jelin 1998; Oliveira, Eternod, and López 1999).

The emphasis on the plurality of family types has blurred the Parsonian image of the nuclear family as the social ideal. The idyllic model of the nuclear family that dominated the field of sociology until the 1960s was further undermined by the growing prevalence of two-income families and the increase in the number of female-headed households. Ideological notions that subordinated women within the family came under scrutiny, as did reductionist strategies that failed to account for the social construction of sexuality, reproduction, and the gendered division of domestic labor.

The revised analytical approaches in family research similarly highlighted the importance of the social construction of gender identity, parental roles, and family life (Palma, Moral, and Cabrera 1992; González Montes 1994; García and Oliveira 1994; Oliveira, Eternod, and López 1999). The new lines of investigation placed in bold relief the existing gap between sociostructural change and the subjective world of representations, prompting analysts to account for both dimensions in the study of families and households. There is a fundamental conceptual distinction between the family and the household (or domestic unit). The former refers solely to persons who are linked by kinship ties and affective relationships; the latter refers to individuals who share in consumption and reproduction within the same domicile but who are not necessarily joined by kinship ties (Jelin 1998).

Interrelated Social Inequities

A lasting methodological consequence of the conceptual reformulations just discussed is the recognized need to consider the superimposition of various forms of social inequality. This methodological exigency, which has assumed increasing importance in Latin American sociology, derives mainly from gender studies that have criticized traditional stratification approaches for their inability to identify and understand gender-based disparities.

Classical sociology, with its excessive preoccupation with the emergence of industrial society, gave inordinate importance to social classes as the primary units of analysis, thereby downplaying other forms of social differentiation. Current theorizing takes an opposite stance, contending that stratification studies should focus on the family as the initial source of many forms of inequality and social exclusion (Delphy and Leonard 1986).

Contemporary stratification research recognizes the multidimensional character of inequality (Grusky 1994). This approach owes much to the feminist critique of conventional perspectives, to the findings produced by gender studies, and to the more general decline in the significance of social class as the key element of social cohesion and identity in the modern world (Hobsbawm 1996; Touraine 1998; Beck 1998). An indispensable feature of the multidimensional perspective is the need to simultaneously take into account the various axes of differentiation. In addition to class and gender, the strategy encompasses age, ethnicity, and any other distinctions that provide the basis of identity and that enable a social group to recognize and to think of itself as different. The family itself is a prominent feature of social stratification inasmuch as kinship ties are the foundation of solidarity as well as the initial (and perhaps most durable) basis of hierarchy and reciprocity (Ariza and Oliveira 1999b).

It is the intersection of the various axes of social differentiation and subjective identity that inspires current research (see Wood in this volume). The results often lead to unexpected conclusions. The joint effects of class and gender, for example, can produce quite different outcomes. A particular country can have a relatively open class structure with a high degree of social mobility yet, at the same time, impose severe restrictions on women (as appears to be the case in countries where women are sequestered from public life). If we introduce race and ethnicity into the analysis, we confront a more complex mosaic of possibilities, ranging from highly segregated societies, to those which endorse affirmative actions to rectify social exclusion. The family plays a central role in terms of reproducing as well as compensating for the various form of inequality that characterize a society's stratification system (Jelin 1998).

Uncertainty, Vulnerability, and Risk

The observations noted in the previous sections reflect the expanding scope of stratification analyses that simultaneously encompass multiple dimensions of inequality without, at the same time, loosing sight of the strategic processes that occur within the family. Key concepts—such as the notions of uncertainty, risk, and vulnerability—have enhanced the capacity to comprehend the role of the family in terms of its ability to intensify or compensate for other dimensions of social inequality.

The uncertainty and risk characteristic of an increasingly globalized society renders it impossible for people to mobilize their resources to design a thoroughly predictable course of action (Beck 1998, 2000). Constant and unpredictable change requires a calculating vigilance that is alert to the emergence of different opportunities and constraints (Giddens 1991).

With respect to families, risk and uncertainty stem from three main sources. The first is associated with the limited employment possibilities caused by the fragmented and polarized character of the labor market (see Pérez Sáinz in this volume). The latter is an expression of the broader sociostructural changes under way, including a weakened relationship between educational credentials and access to good jobs, the inability to survive solely on the income provided by the head of the family, and the growing lack of standardized career paths necessary for social mobility. Factors such as these make it difficult for family members to formulate an effective socioeconomic strategy.

The second source of uncertainty and risk emanates from the inequalities that exist within the family itself in terms of the distribution of resources as well as the disparities linked to age and gender. In Mexico, analysts have shown that the subordination of women within the family, and culturally prescribed roles that restrict women to the domestic sphere, have prompted some parents in rural areas to deprive their daughters of higher levels of education (González Montes 1994). Other studies of children born to poor families suggest that the risk of being put out on the street varies according to the family's stage in the life cycle and the age and sex of the child. In this case, males are at higher risk than females, since the traits associated with masculinity are regarded as more compatible with those of the "street" (Ariza 1994). Similarly, domestic violence, adolescent pregnancy, malnutrition, and drug addiction are risks that vary by social status and the type of family, as well as by age and gender.

The third source of uncertainty can be traced to an increasingly individualistic social context and the family's growing inability to serve as a refuge of personal security (Cicchelli-Pugeault and Cicchelli 1999). The notion of the family as the locus of group solidarity and individual fulfillment has been undermined by the rise of values antithetical to the traditional family norm and by the emergence of alternative living arrangements. The result is increased tension between the notion that marriage, family formation, and procreation are the basis of individual fulfillment and the growing prevalence of life trajectories that do not follow the traditional family norm. The increase in the number of possible social itineraries is a source of uncertainty and doubt among those who are compelled to choose.

Closely related concepts are the notions of vulnerability and risk. Social groups that suffer exclusion or discrimination, or are subject to any form of unequal treatment, can be said to be vulnerable. Risk, in turn, is a measure of the magnitude or intensity of vulnerability. Pérez Sáinz (2000) treats the degree of vulnerability as a useful corrective to conceptual approaches that rely on such dichotomies as integration/exclusion and formal/informal sectors. He is thus able to conceptualize a range of inequalities that exists between the extremes, and to recognize those groups which are socially integrated to some degree, yet at the same time permanently subject to a high risk of impoverishment. Jelin (1998) further notes the irreversible human consequences that befall those who live under conditions of permanent vulnerability. The notion of "social harm" (*daño social*) is amply documented by life-course analyses that investigate the more or less permanent negative effects caused by early marriage and childbearing (Elder 1985). Similar studies point to the long-term consequences and the deep psychological (and physical) scars that are caused by domestic violence, a culture of behavior often passed on from one generation to the next within the same family.

These facets of family behavior underscore the sensitivity of domestic life to changes in the institutional context in which families are embedded and highlight the ways in which the family domain can enhance or attenuate the impact of external events. These relationships call attention to the need to reconceptualize how the quality of life is affected by factors that lie beyond the confines of the family. Such factors include the actions of the state, as well as other structural changes that directly or indirectly influence the patterns of consumption, production, and reproduction that take place within the family unit.

Continuity and Change

In this chapter we have noted how the socioeconomic, cultural, and demographic changes in Latin America have affected the structure, composition, and behavior of the family. Trends such as the increase in female headship, the rise in teenage pregnancy, and the growing frequency of separation, divorce, and cohabitation have undermined the social significance of the traditional family. The male-headed, single-earner model is partially giving way to novel forms of family organization and to new relationships between men and women and between younger and older generations.

Gender perspectives on the interplay between family life and structural change have prompted the development of new conceptual approaches in the field of family studies. Biological and functionalist assumptions have been discredited, along with conventional approaches that invoke a strict dichotomy between public and private spheres. New analytical strategies give priority to the complex relationships between family organization and other social domains. The notions of uncertainty, vulnerability, risk, and social harm are among the conceptual tools that have permitted a more nuanced understanding of the various ways that changes in the economic and institutional environment influence family life. The ability to capture the simultaneous effects of multiple dimensions of vulnerability and inequality has emerged as a leading methodological challenge.

It is worth noting that the trends we have identified in this chapter speak more to the increasing flexibility of the traditional family model than to a fundamental crisis in the family as an institution. Although the drift toward individualistic personal values works to undermine conventional patterns of authority, they have yet to replace the nuclear family as the main locus of social identity and the basis of economic and emotional support. Changes in family structure occur slowly, especially when it concerns male participation in domestic labor and child care. The independence of women and their participation in the economic maintenance of the family are limited primarily to the more educated sectors of the population. Moreover, the trend toward democratic intrahousehold relationships is fraught with tensions, conflict, and ambivalence. Egalitarian expectations coexist with rigid authoritarian practices, often imposed through violence against women and other family members, including children, adolescents, and the elderly. Similarly, new types of living arrangements have not been accepted as legitimate options. Laws, public policy, and the organization of the economy continue to be permeated by idealized conceptualizations of family life. Hence there is a need to propose alternative social policies that are more in tune with the slow but significance changes taking place in the Latin American family.

10 Population and Development: Then and Now

JOSEPH E. POTTER AND
RODOLFO A. TUIRÁN GUTIÉRREZ

In the context of this conference, perhaps all of us, as we review our assigned topics, have the sensation that the world has changed more than we had ever expected over the last three decades. Certainly there has been more demographic change than most of us expected, and the questions at the center of the debates related to population and population policy have also evolved in unanticipated directions. If this was not reason enough for our review, it could also be argued that the demographic changes we will point to have much to do with many of the other topics in this volume.

Thirty years ago, with exception of Argentina, Uruguay, Cuba, and Chile, most of Latin America was poised at the front end of the demographic transition. Mortality had declined considerably since the Second World War, but fertility had not fallen much, if at all, and population growth in the region was at its historical high point, and rivaled that to be found in any other part of the world. Today, the demographic transition is well advanced. Mortality continued to fall throughout the intervening decades and has reached levels much lower than the United Nations had projected in the 1970s. Even more surprising, fertility has fallen dramatically throughout the region and is now converging to near replacement level in most countries with no guarantee that it will not continue to fall to the very low levels now found in much of Europe. In part because of these trends, but also for other reasons connected to the rest of the agenda before us, the "population questions" or "issues" that are being discussed in international forums as well as in local political contexts are very different from those which were being debated twenty-five or thirty years ago. Many of the actors have changed, but much of the original cast is still in place. Indeed, population is an arena where academics or scholars have frequent interaction with the policy process and have often played the lead roles. As such, the issue of linking research with policy over these three decades has considerable potential.

In the following sections, we will summarize and characterize the population debate as it existed in the 1970s in the region, and then review the demographic change that occurred between 1970 and 2000, highlighting the experience of the five largest countries of Latin America: Brazil, Mexico, Colombia, Argentina, and Peru. We will then look at what were the major questions these trends generated for both research and policy. After reflecting on these questions and the extent to which they have been answered in the intervening years, we then turn to the contemporary debate. We will note how the questions have changed, how the new questions are being addressed, and how they might connect with other items on the conference agenda.

The Causes and Consequences of Rapid Population Growth (circa 1975)

During the 1950s and 1960s, awareness of the declines in mortality and the increases in the rate of population that were taking place in many parts of the developing world grew as data became available, and debates emerged on how these trends might affect the countries involved as well as the rest of the world. Foundations, principally Rockefeller, Ford, and the Population Council, provided support for study of the phenomenon, as well as for experimental efforts to establish family planning programs (Ford Foundation 1985). The United Nations took an increasingly greater interest in population and became an important source of information as well as an international forum for the discussion of global and national population policy.

By 1974, when the United Nations convened the World Population Conference in Bucharest, there was a considerable amount at stake. World population growth had reached two percent per annum (a doubling time of about thirty-five years), and there was little evidence for thinking that fertility in developing countries was about to fall of its own accord. In addition to foundations, NGOs, the United Nations, most European governments, and eventually, the United States had given priority to population on their development agenda. Last but not least, some poor countries had already adopted national policies to reduce population growth and promote family planning. On the other hand, the decade preceding the conference had witnessed the emergence of Third World solidarity, OPEC, the Group of 77, and a series of calls for New International Economic Order (NIEO). The socialist nations, especially the USSR and China, strongly supported the Third World position on the NIEO and were natural allies in any movement to oppose neomalthusian projects (Singh 1998).

The struggle that emerged at the 1974 World Population Conference was over a plan that would guide the world's nations over the next decade with respect to population policy and support for population programs. On the one hand, there was the proposal advanced by the United Nations Secretariat, the United States, and some but not all developed countries, which included a clear statement that population growth constituted a problem and considerable resources should be mobilized to control it. The opposing "redistributionist" proposal advanced by most developing and socialist countries was that population problems are not a cause but a consequence of underdevelopment, and that "development was the best contraceptive." The conference ended up adopting a compromise plan of action, which recognized the rights of couples to have the number of children that they desired, and the responsibility of governments to provide them with the means to do so, but which also recognized the role of development in determining population outcomes. The eventual document was certainly based more on political expediency than the results of scientific research, but there were two clear research questions that were central to the debate. The first concerned the implications of rapid population growth for a country's development prospects. The second concerned the conditions or measures required for fertility to fall.

Action, Reaction, and Social Science in Latin America

In Latin America, the debate regarding population in the 1960s and the first half of the 1970s was by turns, heated, awkward, and muted. Thanks to CELADE, the UN Latin American Demographic Center located in Santiago, and the tradition of certain government statistical offices, there was a considerable amount of information and analysis regarding demographic rates and population parameters. Much less effort was devoted to analyzing the determinants and consequences of these rates even though they revealed that many countries were experiencing population growth higher than had been observed anywhere else in the world, and which were the result of the combination of continuing high fertility with substantial declines in mortality. Why was this not a topic for concern and investigation?

We would highlight three complementary factors. One of them was the "development optimism" that was the legacy of the rapid economic growth based on import-substitution industrialization that many countries, but particularly Brazil and Mexico, had experienced in the 1960s and the beginning of the 1970s (Alba and Potter 1986). Population growth rates of 3 percent per

annum did not loom so large when the economy was growing at 10 percent per annum. Second and probably more important was that the central
questions that had been posed both by academics and organizations in
developed countries (principally the United States) were not attractive to
Latin American social scientists. Dependency theories placed the blame for
underdevelopment on exploitative trade relations between the center and the
periphery, as well as on the exploitation inherent in the domestic class structure and system of production. In this context, as at Bucharest, highlighting
the role of population growth in blocking development seemed like a highly
misguided attempt to blame the victim. Moreover, most formulations of
the question regarding the determinants of fertility seemed to be couched in
the language of the very modernization theories that dependency theorists
were seeking to overturn. There may well have been a third reason for the
lack of engagement having to do with the lack of a quantitative tradition in
the social sciences.

Considering the lack of research and writing on the consequences of rapid
population growth for national development being done in Latin America,
and the wide diversity of conclusions being offered on the subject by scholars in the United States and Europe, perhaps it is not surprising that government officials and academics in different countries came to widely varying
conclusions. To illustrate the point, we briefly review the experience of Mexico and Brazil. In Mexico, as in many other countries, the first people to
become involved with the population issue were the doctors who were
involved with the development and (later) the distribution of contraceptive
methods. There were several private family planning associations, one of
them affiliated with the International Planned Parenthood Federation. There
was also an appreciable community of researchers involved in reproductive
medicine. In addition to these researchers and clinicians, several prominent
social scientists (especially Victor Urquidi and Leopoldo Solis) eventually
began to consider the implications of the over three percent population
growth rate for economic development. In a context in which prominent
academics had considerable contact with (and some would say, dependency
on) government officials, when the president of Mexico began to take a personal interest in the population question, he was immediately able to initiate
a dialogue with interested individuals.

The origin of Luis Echevarría's interest in population growth remains
unknown, and may well have been influenced by World Bank president,
Robert McNamara, as well as his own ambitions in the international arena,
but to make a long story short, the outcome of this "conversation" was the

well-known reversal of Mexico's pronatalist population policy in 1973 (Alba and Potter 1986; Brambila 1998). In the following decade, the idea that it was in the national interest to bring down the birthrate became solidly entrenched in the cabinet of successive PRI governments, as well as in the public institutions responsible for delivering medical services. The wider community of social scientists was occasionally skeptical of the government's initiatives in this realm, but also seemed to appreciate the emphasis on human rights and the effort to include population in the broader context of development that were embodied in the constitutional amendment no. 23 and the National Population Law.

Brazil, like Mexico, had private family planning organizations and an important community of medical researchers involved in reproductive medicine and contraceptive development. The relationship of social science to the state, however, was quite different. Most leading social scientists had been forced out of their universities by the military government, and many were employed at private research institutions such as CEBRAP that were supported by foundations. These social scientists took a dim view of the private family planning organizations operating in the country, in part because they seemed to be only too willing to collaborate with the military. The latter, in turn, were divided on the population question. On the one hand, they viewed demographic size as a strategic advantage in terms of military strength and recruitment. On the other, there seemed to be a sense that, to the extent high fertility led to impoverishment in the North and Northeast, population growth was a liability to national security. In such a context, it is not surprising that what debates there were turned acrimonious, and the position that was most comfortable for social scientists was that rapid population growth did not constitute a pressing problem for Brazil (Martine and Faria 1988).

In comparison, there was somewhat more research and debate among social scientists in Latin America on the second question regarding the demographic transition—what would be required for fertility to decline? The most contentious issue at the international level concerned the possibility of substantial latent demand for fertility control and the role that family planning programs could play in meeting that demand. The main way to get at this issue was by way of surveys that included questions regarding ideal family size, desire for additional children, knowledge of contraception, and so on. In Latin America, these surveys (often referred to as KAP, or Knowledge, Attitude, and Practice surveys) were adapted and implemented by CELADE in collaboration with Donald Bogue and the University of

Chicago. The first round of surveys was conducted in 1964 in nine metropolitan cities (Buenos Aires, Rio de Janeiro, Bogota, San José, Mexico City,
Panama City, Caracas, Quito, and Guayaquil) (CELADE and CFSC 1972).
The second round was conducted in 1969 in the rural areas of some of the
larger countries, including Mexico and Colombia. These two rounds of surveys constituted a pioneering effort in survey research that achieved a level of
scientific rigor in terms of sampling, questionnaire design, and interviewing
procedures that would only be replicated in other regions of the developing
world more than a decade later. Although these data were extremely "well
collected," they were not extensively analyzed in Latin America. Among
the reasons might have been limitations on the funding available for analysis and researchers' limited access to mainframe computers and people who
could program them. But perhaps more important was the ambivalence that
derived from the heritage of these instruments in modernization theory, and
the emphasis they placed on assessing the potential demand for contraceptive methods.

Certainly one of the main findings of the second round of rural surveys
was the extremely high level of fertility that prevailed in rural areas, and the
corresponding near total absence of contraceptive practice in this population (e.g., García 1976). If anything, these surveys pointed less to the latent
demand for family planning that might exist in this segment of the population than to the predominance of women who fully expected to have large
numbers of children and could not readily conceive of an alternative trajectory. In these terms, the surveys served to reinforce the idea that poverty,
primitive living conditions, and low levels of education constituted a substantial impediment to fertility decline.

The Transition in Fertility (and the Continued Transition in Mortality)

Over the quarter century following the Bucharest conference, fertility declined in Latin America at a rate few people would have believed possible,
especially considering the difficult economic situations and sharp declines in
the rate of growth of GDP that were to be observed throughout the period.
A graph showing the path of the Total Fertility Rate (TFR) from 1950 to
the year 2000 for the five largest (most populous) countries may be found in
Figure 10.1. In this picture, Argentina is a notable outlier, since fertility had
declined there well before the Second World War. In the other countries, the

TFR was above six children per woman in 1960. By the year 2000 it was less than three children per woman in all five countries. While the graph shows declines in fertility in Brazil and Colombia that were quite well advanced by the time of the Bucharest conference, it bears mentioning that no one was aware of those declines until late in the 1970s.

Almost as surprising as the decline in fertility was the continued drop in mortality. Figure 10.2 shows the evolution of the Infant Mortality Rate (IMR) between 1950 and 2000, while Figure 10.3 shows life expectancy over the period. In 1974, the IMR appears to have been more than 70 per thousand in every country but Argentina, and over 100 per thousand in Peru. By 2000, it was below 40 per thousand in all five countries. There was a corresponding gain in life expectancy, with an increase of more than ten years during the last twenty-five years in all five countries. The net result of these mortality declines combined with still high but falling fertility was considerable population growth, as may be seen for these five countries in Figure 10.4.

Explaining the Transition

As evidence of the scope and magnitude of these transitions became available, attention turned to the question of what was responsible for this largely unexpected change in behavior. For social scientists, the fertility transition

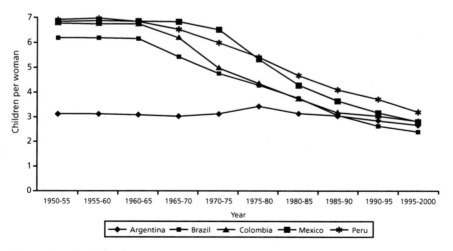

Fig 10.1 Total fertility rate, 1950–2000

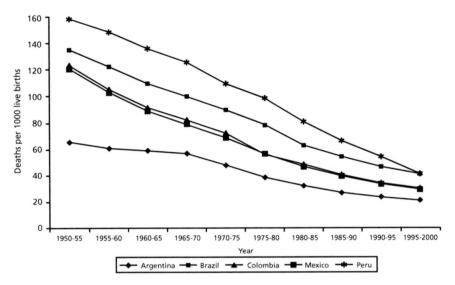

Fig 10.2 Infant mortality rate, 1950–2000

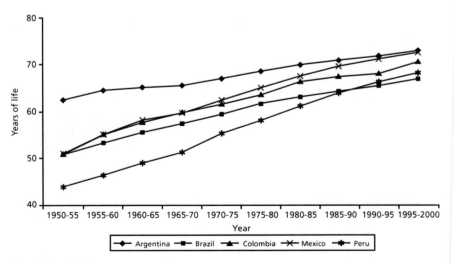

Fig 10.3 Life expectancy, 1950–2000

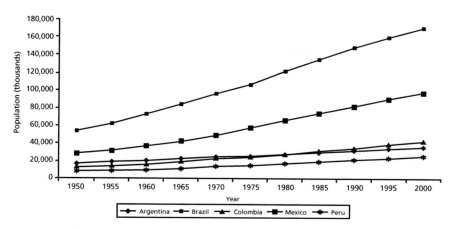

Fig 10.4 Population, 1950–2000

was the greatest draw.[1] The change was both more abrupt and more recent. Moreover, having children was more clearly a matter related to people's behavior and choices than was morbidity or mortality, or so it seemed at the time. Within the broad question concerning the factors underlying the fertility transition was the more specific issue of the role that family planning programs, either public or private, may have played in bringing about the increase in contraceptive use that was, by far, the dominant proximate determinant of the decline in fertility.

Research on these issues in Latin America was, not surprisingly, related to debates that were taking place in international forums and organizations, Europe, Australia, and the United States. Indeed, the debates within the region as well as internationally were frequently spurred by the rush of persons associated with internationally financed family planning programs to give these programs the credit for the uptake in contraceptive practice. Moreover, much but certainly not all of the data collection that was taking place was organized, shaped, and financed by international organizations such as the World Fertility Survey (Gille 1987).

While it would be difficult to argue that the work on these questions done in Latin America had a strong influence on the worldwide scientific consensus, it does seem to us in retrospect that the period from 1974 to 1989 or

---

1. It is worth noting that internal migration, urbanization, and labor force participation drew more attention than research on fertility or mortality.

so was a good, perhaps golden, moment for social science research on population and development. New methods and conceptualizations were developed, and debate that was often both energetic and stimulating took place. Although, the approaches taken or developed often drew on the frameworks employed in the sociology of the 1960s and early 1970s, they were not bound by it, and often involved an eclectic assimilation of other conceptual paradigms.

In his chapter, Vilmar Faria, speaking of the social sciences more generally, refers to the paralyzing embrace and insurmountable tension between positivistic modernization theory and scientific Marxism. In the population sphere, one might also think of a paralyzing embrace or insurmountable tension between progressive social scientists and *controlistas*, who zealously believed in the need for family planning, and in the appeal of the family planning message, and who had only instrumental use for social science (read survey research), of any stripe.[2] As mentioned earlier, one of the first reactions to the news of fertility decline in Colombia by the advocates of international family planning was the argument that since little else had changed in Colombia over the decade preceding the 1973 census, the fertility decline must have been the result of the programs introduced in that country by ASCOFAME and Profamilia. This argument and others like it that would continue to surface throughout this period were relatively easy to disprove, and did not require much imagination or new ways of thinking beyond those embodied in the early versions of demographic transition theory formulated with respect to the historical European experience (Potter, Ordoñez G., and Measham 1976). However, simply demonstrating fertility differentials or change in certain development indicators went only a small distance toward providing a comprehensive explanation of the phenomena.

The first notable attempt toward the latter was the project launched at CEBRAP in 1974 under the title "Pesquisa Nacional de Reprodução Humana" (hereafter PNRH). The conception and design of this study involved many of the leading social scientists in Brazil, a number of whom had little or no prior experience in studying human reproduction. Rather than implement a nationally representative sample of households, the CEBRAP researchers decided to undertake an in-depth study of nine strategically chosen municipalities.[3] In each municipality, before proceeding to draw a sample of households and individuals for interview, they gathered extensive background data

2. See Hodgson and Watkins (1997) for an illuminating essay on the relations between feminists and neomalthusians.

3. The criteria for selecting *municipios* emphasized economic criteria such as mode of production (see Lamounier 1981).

on the community and carried out extended structured interviews with agents and clients of a wide variety of institutions. They wanted to know if organizations such as churches, schools, private businesses, the media, and the medical community were attempting to influence reproductive behavior. Given that almost the entirety of fertility research elsewhere in the world had been based on surveys of individuals that took little or no account of the environments in which they were found, this was a revolutionary strategy.

The institutional component of the research yielded some strong and unexpected insights (Loyola and Quinteiro 1982; Potter 1983). In a country where, at least nominally, most of the population is Catholic, the church was expected to have an important influence on attitudes toward fertility limitation and modern contraception. The study found, however, that this was not the case. In addition to the apparent atrophy of the church itself, there was no uniformity of opinion among priests, many of whom seemed to have adopted a "hands-off" approach to the question of birth control and advocated "responsible parenthood," in which couples were to find a balance between their economic circumstances and their obligation to reproduce. Birth control methods were often seen as a question for doctors rather than clerics to address, and another finding of the research was the surprising readiness of the former to advocate the use of modern contraception. This finding was the initial basis for thinking that medicalization, quite apart from any connection to family planning programs, might constitute an important factor underlying the ongoing transition in fertility.

A second and related area in which Brazilian researchers made an important contribution was in terms of the impact that the changing labor relations might have on the prevalence and value of child labor and on the costs of children. The structure of the agricultural economy was changing rapidly and involved a dramatic increase in temporary wage labor (*boia fria*) at the expense of tenant farmers (*parceiros* and *moradores*), squatters, and small holders. Paiva (1987) argued that most tenant farming arrangements conferred advantages on large families, since income from the commercial harvest varied directly with the number of workers in the family, and there were economies of scale in domestic food production, and no disadvantage in terms of housing, which did not represent a financial cost. The novelty of the argument was considerable because the direction of the influence on fertility was exactly opposite that postulated in the voluminous literature on proletarianization in historical Europe.[4]

4. See also Carvalho, Paiva and Sawyer (1981), Almeida (n.d.), and Saint (1981).

In Mexico, as in many other countries, the staple of fertility research was the nationally representative survey. Yet within that format, there were some notable innovations that attempted to increase the social and economic content that international sponsored data collection efforts had been seriously criticized for lacking. One such was the inclusion in the 1982 National Demographic Survey, which was designed to yield an accurate and meaningful categorization according to social class, of questions designed to collect a wide variety of information on the economic insertion of different members of the household (Bronfman, López, and Tuirán 1986; Tuirán 1986). Another, following the lead of the PNRH, was to interview the medical practitioners who served a subset of the localities included as the primary sampling units for a survey of rural areas (Potter, Mojarro, and Nuñez 1987). In contrast to Brazil, where no nationally representative survey was undertaken until 1986, five such surveys were carried out in Mexico prior to that year, and all of them under the aegis of a government agency.

One of the most comprehensive statements regarding the factors underlying the fertility transition in Brazil was Vilmar Faria's seminal formulation regarding the entirely unintended and unanticipated role played by a series of policies adopted and implemented by the Brazilian government in the 1970s in bringing about a decline in fertility (Faria 1989). He drew attention to developments in three institutional realms that he believed deserved close attention in the Brazilian case. These developments were the spread of modern medicine, social security, and the mass media (particularly TV). His claim was that

> the expansion of medical coverage—and the consequent *medicalization* of sexual and reproductive behavior—the growth of publicly provided services of social security—and the resulting change in the value of offspring as a source of support in old age—and the expansion of exposure to the mass media, particularly TV, for reasons that we intend to outline in this paper, *converged* to institutionalize and diffuse new patterns of value orientation and behavioral norms leading to widespread change in family size preferences, on the one hand, and increasing the demand for fertility regulation, on the other. (Faria and Potter 1999)

Moreover, Faria stressed that "the mass media, or rather the centrality of TV for the functioning and reproduction of modern, contemporary Brazilian society, played a central and strategic role in this converging process, articulating, diffusing, reiterating and institutionalizing these new behavioral and attitudinal patterns" (Faria and Potter 1999). Finally, he emphasized the importance of consumption and provision of credit for purchasing consumer durables.

Alongside these and other efforts to delineate a coherent argument (rather than empirical demonstration) concerning the factors underlying the ongoing transition in fertility, many social scientists exhibited distrust of programs to deliver family planning services, whether these were operating in the private sector as in Brazil, or were sponsored by the government as in Mexico. The sharp increase in female sterilization drew the most criticism or queries about the conditions under which decisions were made and the agency of the women concerned. In contrast to the research agenda of most investigators observing the transition from North America, few investigators in Latin America were heavily invested in assessing the extent to which programs were responsible for the dramatic uptake in contraceptive practice. Rather, the question concerned the route by which programs achieved this result.

Shifts in the International Debate and the Emergence of Reproductive Health

Over the twenty years between the population conferences in Bucharest and Cairo, there were quite dramatic shifts in the international environment that bore on population issues (Singh 1998). By the time of the 1984 conference in Mexico City, the respective roles of the developed and developing countries had been reversed. With a Republican administration in Washington eager to please the religious Right (anti-abortionists) and set on advocating the benefits that were to be derived from economic liberalization and market forces, the United States found itself arguing that there was no need for nations to adopt population policies. On the other hand, at this conference the developing countries such as China and Mexico that had made substantial commitments to such policies would end up defending their right to adopt and implement population programs.

During the following decade, resistance to this conservative stance accumulated in both sets of countries. In the United States, as MacIntosh and Finkle (1995) note, "After twelve years in which the Reagan and Bush administrations had downplayed the effects of rapid population growth and had given only tepid support to population programs, the population community felt a need for political help" in both the environmental and feminist communities. The feminist movement, on the other hand, building on the experience gained during the UN Decade for the Advancement of Women, had mobilized a large number of grassroots organizations and gained ground within a wide range of international organizations, NGOs, and foundations. Moreover, it had developed a clear agenda regarding the kinds of reforms that needed to be implemented in population programs and policies (Correa and Reichman 1994).

The agenda or program that the feminist organizations and leaders, in alliance with a large part of the population community brought to the Cairo ICPD was titled "Reproductive Health," defined as an approach or perspective that recognized the right of all individuals (i) regulate their fertility safely and effectively; (ii) to have and raise healthy children; (iii) to understand and enjoy his or her own sexuality; and (iv) to remain free of sickness, incapacity, or death associated with sex or reproduction. It was based entirely on reproductive and sexual rights, and discarded any justification based on the societal gains that might result from reduced population growth, going so far as to condemn the practice of setting quantitative targets for either population growth or the adoption of methods of contraception. The emphasis was on providing a range of services in addition to family planning, and on addressing such issues as domestic violence, maternal mortality, and sexually transmitted diseases in addition to fertility. A central tenet was that enhancing the position of women should be a main policy goal, and that doing so would lead to lower fertility.

The reproductive health approach was well received by most social scientists who had been concerned with population issues. It appealed both to those who had been involved in research on gender, family, and sexuality, and to those who had always had a distaste for earlier pronouncements coming from the United States and international organizations regarding the need for family planning programs. Indeed, Latin American social scientists were well represented among those who played a prominent role in the ICPD and the various meetings leading up to and following this event, and at the subsequent Fourth World Conference on Women held in Beijing in 1995. The natural adversaries were, on the one hand, the Vatican and its alliances with conservative political elements or parties, and, on the other hand, anyone espousing or practicing population control.

There is no question that the new paradigm served to mobilize a wide range of academic discussions, research initiatives, and interactions between scholars and activists. While the concept of reproductive health is not per se theoretical, it certainly draws heavily on concepts related to gender and human rights, and created opportunities for those seeking to develop and apply feminist perspectives to population questions. Moreover, it provided the grounds for addressing issues that had been overlooked in earlier decades in which the emphasis was on household survival strategies rather than on the conflicts, domination, and exploitation that exist within households. Sexuality, domestic violence, maternal mortality, sexually transmitted diseases, adolescents, males, and abortion were among the topics that gained new prominence thanks to this change of perspective.

The initiative to discuss and investigate reproductive health in Latin America has led to a good number of conferences, the formation and consolidation of collaborative research groups across and within countries, and a considerable number of research projects and publications (e.g., Ramos et al. 2001). Among the more notable edited volumes are those by Parker and Barbosa (1996), Heilborn (1999), Pantelides and Bott (2000), Figueroa and Stern (2001), and Oliveira and da Rocha (2001). There were numerous contributions to the International Population Conference held in Salvador, Bahia, under the auspices of the International Union for the Study of Population (IUSSP), on reproductive health in Latin America, and Latin Americans have contributed regularly to *Reproductive Health Matters,* a journal launched in 1993 to address sexual and reproductive health and rights issues for a multidisciplinary, international audience.

While there is much to be applauded in the expansion of activity and scope that the adoption of reproductive health as a paradigm or organizing principle has generated, not all of its implications are positive. One drawback that has been noticed by several observers in the region, as well as elsewhere, is that reproductive health often seems to be a new dogma (Salles and Tuirán 2001). Some questions no longer seem to be politically correct, certainly any that would pertain to the social and economic consequences of persisting high fertility, or even of measures that might serve to accelerate fertility decline. Moreover, an additional danger is that of substituting words for action (Basu 1997), a phenomenon that arguably occurred in Brazil where the Cairo agenda was immediately incorporated into the structure and policy of the incoming Cardoso administration but with less than dramatic changes in the amount of resources and programs that were directed toward women's health in general and contraception in particular (Berquó 1999).

The Consequences of Demographic Change (ca. 2000): The Demographic Dividend

Remarkably enough, shortly after it was decided that inducing fertility decline was no longer an acceptable objective for population policy, researchers examining the experience of Asian countries between 1965 and 1990 found that a considerable portion of the economic success they had enjoyed during this period could be attributed to shifts in the age distribution and dependency ratio that were generated by the sharp decline in fertility that occurred during this period (Kelley and Schmidt 1995; Bloom and Williamson 1998; Bloom, Canning, and Malaney 2000; Higgins and Williamson 1997). These authors conclude that population age structure, more than size or growth per se, affects economic development, and that reducing high fertility can create opportunities for economic growth if the right kinds of educational, health, and labor-market policies are in place. Although their analyses of how differing policy environments have affected the relationship between population change and economic development often have the ring of an uncritical endorsement of neoliberal economic prescriptions, it clearly poses the question of whether Latin American countries will be able to reap the potential benefits of the shifts in the age distribution that are now unfolding as a result of the fertility declines that began in the mid-1970s and which are now proceeding toward near or below-replacement levels.

To illustrate these dynamics, we will present the case of Mexico, based on the official projections made by the National Population Council (CONAPO 2002). Figure 10.5 shows the projected the size of the total population over the first fifty years of the new millennium, along with per annum rate of growth. Assuming that fertility will continue to decline until the year 2030, when the Total Fertility Rate will reach the below-replacement level of 1.85 children per woman, the growth rate falls steadily while the total population size increases to a peak slightly above 130 million around 2040. The changing age distribution of the population is shown in Figure 10.6, which shows the population pyramids for the years 2000, 2015, 2025, and 2050. The dramatic evolution in the shape of the age distribution has been described in confectioner's terms as the shift from a "kiss" to a "bon bon."[5]

Figure 10.7 shows the ratio of the fraction of the population that is, at least in terms of age, dependent to the population of working age (15–64), distinguishing between persons under 15, and those 65 and over, for the century between 1950 and 2050. For the bulk of this period, the overall dependency ratio is driven by the fraction of the population under 15. This share rises between 1950 and 1970 as a result of declining child mortality, and then falls as a result of the onset of fertility decline in the mid 1970s. The

---

5. Virgilio Partida Bush, CONAPO's lead demographer and author of the national projections, coined this phrase.

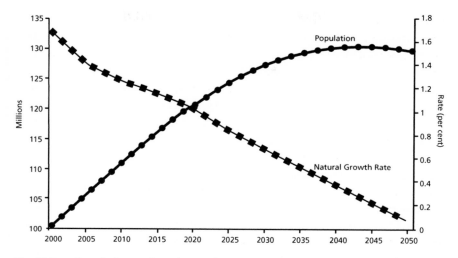

Fig 10.5 Population and total growth rates, 1950–2000

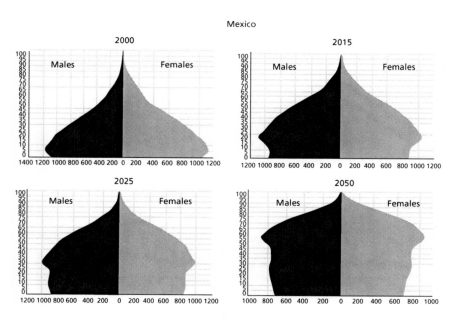

Fig 10.6 Age distribution of the population, 2000–2050 (Mexico)

plunge in youth age dependency proceeds unabated until after 2020 as fertility begins to stabilize. About a decade earlier, the old age dependency ratio begins a gradual ascent that becomes pronounced after 2030. From the point of view of the ability of individuals, families, and societies, the years when the total dependency ratio is low represent an opportunity. It is in these years that saving can occur as the ratio of production to consumption should be high. Figure 10.8 shows the same phenomenon by way of bar graph in which the total dependency ratio is decomposed into youth and old age dependency. As noted above, youth dependency drives the change in total dependency from 1930 onward, but after 2020 old age dependency becomes a much larger share as the large cohorts born in the 1960s and 1970s reach retirement age.

Whether or not Latin American countries such as Brazil, Colombia, and Mexico, which have all experienced rapid declines beginning in the 1970s, will reap the potential rewards of the reduced dependency burden that they are just beginning to "enjoy" is, of course, a very important and challenging question. An alternative view of the same dynamics that focused on the increase in the working age population might see the current period as being extremely difficult in terms of generating jobs that would provide productive

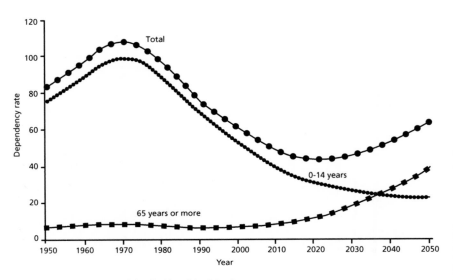

Fig 10.7   Demographic dividend in Mexico, 1950–2050

employment for a rapidly growing labor force. Moreover, since the fertility decline took place first among the more educated and better off, the demographic dividend is unlikely to affect all groups at the same time, and without sufficient redistributive policy might even serve to increase inequality. In Mexico, the size of the labor force is projected to grow from about 43 million workers in 2000 to about 69 million in 2030, requiring that more than 10 million jobs be created during each of the first two decades of the millennium.

Clearly, a research agenda with considerable relevance to policy can be derived from these questions. On the one hand, since taking advantage of the demographic dividend depends on investments in human capital, particularly in the areas of health, education, and job training, there is a need to evaluate both current and prospective policies in these realms with a view toward finding opportunities to better equip youth, particularly disadvantaged youth, to find productive employment. In addition, in many countries there is a considerable time series of census and survey data on labor force participation and earnings that could be exploited to learn more about the relationship between demographic dynamics and employment, as well as to diagnose those places and sectors where the imbalances are likely to be greatest.

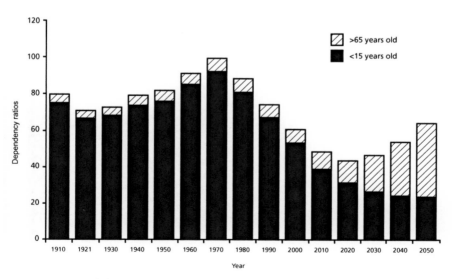

Fig 10.8   Total dependency ratios, 1930–2050 (Mexico)

Population Development and Inequality in the
New Millennium

The debates over population and development are clearly not over in Latin America; however, the questions are now much changed from what they were thirty or more years ago when they first engaged social scientists in the region. There are still questions regarding the future course of fertility, but the concern is fast moving toward a concern with the onset of very low levels of fertility and aging rather than with rapid population growth. Also, in this realm the central guiding framework of class seems to have given way to, or at least been complemented by frameworks based on gender and human rights. The threats to improved policy seem less likely to come from abroad, and more likely to come from conservative, often religiously based elements within the national society.

At the same time, the remarkable changes in birthrates and death rates, and the dynamic shifts in the age distribution that they have unleashed are casting a long shadow and seem to demand more attention than they have received in past decades. We are hopeful that the conjuncture of increased interest in the consequences of demographic change, the large accumulation of data, and the growing capacity for analysis will lead to creative attempts to make sense of what is going on. The most important fruits of such analyses will be suggestions that may improve the chances the societies of the region will, in some measure, overcome their legacy of social inequality and the perverse cycles of deprivation that seem to have trapped such a significant share of their populations.

PART V

Urban Settlements, Marginality, and Social Exclusion

11 The Lack of "Cursive Thinking" Within Social Theory and Public Policy: Four Decades of Marginality and Rationality in the So-Called Slum

PETER M. WARD

The topic that I propose to analyze in this chapter is one of human settlements, specifically the production of low-income housing and irregular settlement that, throughout the region, commonly makes up 30 to 60 percent of the built-up area of major cities (Gilbert 1996). By "irregular settlement" I mean that which usually develops informally (sometimes illegally) in which housing and land costs are reduced by a lack of legal title to the land and a lack of services, and by a process of self-built house construction and "consolidation" by households themselves over a period of time—usually ten to twenty-five years (Gilbert and Ward 1985). Ex-post "regularization," which as we shall see, has emerged as a principal policy plank since the late 1970s, can comprise the transfer of legal titles to de facto low-income owner/builders and the provision of basic services of electricity, water, drainage, street paving, and so on (UNCHS 1996).

This arena of housing production expanded dramatically during the rapid phase of urbanization that Latin America experienced, especially tied to import-substitution industrialization (ISI) strategies from the 1950s onward, fueling the in-migration of labor of young men and women, and generating city growth rates of 3 to 5 percent per annum. In the earlier periods especially, most governments were incapable or unwilling to produce worker housing on a scale necessary to meet the needs of this labor force, which, consequently, had to seek methods of reproducing itself socially through the private sector. Complicity between the state and private capital necessary for sustaining the rate of profit in this industrialization strategy meant keeping wage levels low. Thus, the costs of reproducing labor power socially (housing, medication, education, basic foodstuffs, etc.) also needed to be kept down,

A brief note to explain my title: Originally, "joined-up thinking" was a play on the English idiom "joined-up writing" (cursive), which describes the learning transition among young children as they move from single-letter to cursive writing. For a U.S. audience, however, "joined-up writing" has no similar embedded meaning, hence I am obliged to use the term "cursive."

and informally produced housing along the lines outlined above became the principal method to achieve this. The state learned to be pragmatic and turned a "blind eye" to illegal methods of land and housing development. Not only was this laissez-faire policy a principal route through which low-income households became home owners (de facto at least), but it also offered widespread opportunities for state-exercised social control and clientelist links to fledgling communities over issues of tenure irregularities and service provision, making low-income settlement the key arena for statecraft (A. Leeds 1969; E. Leeds 1972; Gilbert and Ward 1985; Ward 1986). Only later did the state become more interventionist, but even then it sought mostly to work inside the "box" of informally produced housing (through regularization), rather than outside it through massive formal housing programs.

Not everyone chose to live in self-built settlements. Many others rented, especially at the initial phases of adult participation in urban life and employment, living for the most part in shantytowns or in tenement slums in the downtown area. As irregular settlements expanded and consolidated physically, they became the loci of rental tenements embedded within them. But this private rental sector was also unregulated, informal, and affordable (but rarely cheap) to low-income workers in both the formal and so-called informal sectors of the labor market (Gilbert 1993).

Of course, both the process of housing development and the nature of public intervention and policy have changed significantly in the past two decades, and this will be the focus of further discussion throughout this chapter. But I hope that this overview, albeit broad brush, will provide the backdrop to my primary goal here, namely to examine the iterations between housing production processes and public policy in Latin America over the past four decades (i.e., since the 1960s), in order to unpack two important areas of sociological enquiry and understanding. The first is to document the major shifts that have occurred in the paradigms and principal disciplinary wellsprings that underpin our understanding of social processes in Latin America, particularly insofar as these relate to poverty and human settlements. Second, I want to tease out how these paradigms come to inform—often rather imperfectly and disjointedly—the emerging conventional wisdoms of public policy at different periods. Further, I will show how these "received" ideas can also take on lives of their own, reshaping the paradigms themselves.

To begin, I want to highlight some of the moments when social science disciplines—and particularly sociology—appear to have led the way. Living in Austin, home of Tour de France champion cyclist Lance Armstrong, I have come to enjoy the annual event, such that this chapter will draw upon a cycle race metaphor in which two groups may be identified. First, there is a small group of anointed stars who are "protected" by their respective teams, and who compete for the individual winner's prize; and second, is the group of regular team members—the *pelaton* as it is called—who guard, support, and inspire the stars, and who from time to time strike out and attack the star of another team. I argue that occasionally sociologists have been intellectual stars, but for the most part we have been part of the *pelaton;* and it would be misleading and disingenuous to pretend otherwise. Collectively, social scientists are usually in the *pelaton,* and it is interesting to observe that while our intellectual endeavor in the housing and urban development field has always been *multi*disciplinary, individual disciplines do appear to have had their moment in the limelight. Anthropology appears to have been especially influential in the 1950s and 1960s; social psychology emerged strongly during the mid-1960s and mid-1970s; sociologists made significant contributions from the mid-1970s through the mid-1980s; political scientists and economists came to the forefront in the mid-1980s to the mid-1990s. These have been the disciplines and periods during which intellectual leaders appear to have jumped out from the *pelaton* of their social science followers.

During the last decade, however, it seems to me that no single discipline has taken the lead; rather, there has been a concerted shift toward our becoming more *inter*disciplinary in approach, eschewing the sometimes limiting boundaries of any one disciplinary formation. Indeed, I suggest that most, if not all, of the authors represented in this volume, have become more interdisciplinary in their endeavors as their respective research careers have developed, and as paradigms have shifted. Some may even consider themselves to be *pan*-disciplinary. Whichever, my point is that we are at the intersection of disciplines where the new frontiers, leaders, and future "joined-up" thinking will emerge.

Periods of Not-So-Joined-Up Thinking

In looking back over research productivity and ideas in the housing and human settlements arena, one can observe five broad periods of endeavor or paradigm dominance that exemplify a lack of joined-up thinking over the past forty years, each of which has been typified by different forms of state action and inaction. Throughout these five periods, it has been the state's role as primary broker in reproducing the conditions for ongoing capital accumulation that has provided the "hidden hand" to guide and inform policy changes (see also Davis in this volume). Of course, various broader changes have strongly influenced the nature of state intervention in the region over the years, among them: democratization, privatization and the rolling back of the state, internationalization of orthodoxy, and globalization. At different times this has made for a highly interventionist state, while at other times the state has ceded control to the private sector. In essence this is a classic Poulantzas-style (1973) view of state intervention, in which the state brokers a series of pragmatic adjustments, the overarching rationality of which is to stave off breakdown and societal collapse and to ensure the maintenance of stability.[1] Having been through a period of relative withdrawal of the state, we now appear to be experiencing calls for a reinvigorated state to manage and direct if only as part of a "third way" of societal development. And even if the strong state is not completely "back in," the balance has been redressed somewhat.

The phases of thinking I describe run from the (exclusionary) marginality theories of the 1960s, through more inclusionary approaches predicated upon a more positive appreciation of the informal sector during the 1970s, into a "resources of poverty" model in the 1980s. In the latter, the poor were seen to be mobilizing their social capital, ingenuity, and household resources in order to articulate strategies that would allow them to survive the predations of structural adjustment and the new expectancies of urban sustainability rather than urban subsidization. In order for the state to maintain development and to mitigate the worst effects of urban breakdown, there was a greater recourse to principles of efficiency, technocracy, and urban management. The fourth phase (1990s) has been characterized by a recognition of the limits of centralized government and technocracy per se to overcome

1. I recognize the problems with Althussarian-inspired analysis—itself a paradigm of the 1970s—and in particular, the failure of such approaches to provide explanatory rigor, rationalizing as they do any form of state action as being necessary to reproduce the conditions of accumulation. In short, the "relative autonomy" of the state explains everything and nothing (Gilbert and Ward 1985). But in the drafting this chapter, the editors specifically requested that authors highlight the plot that runs through the analysis; and to seek to identify the guiding hand(s) that best account for the changes being tracked. Thus, in my case I go back to theories of the state, and in particular those that sought to analyze state action and how it served to maintain the social conditions of reproduction. This was the main thesis underlying my 1986 volume *Welfare Politics in Mexico: Papering Over the Cracks,* in which I trace social development policy changes over two decades and link specific policy shifts to changing imperatives required in Mexico in order to ensure overall stability. In this way, statecraft was built around patron-client linkages in the 1960s and 1970s and gave way to more rational and systematized policy approaches from the 1980s onward.

poverty and to provide sustainable housing solutions and an attempt to devolve and decentralize responsibility and powers upon local tiers of government and upon citizens themselves (see chapters by Davis and Roberts in this volume). This period continues today, but it is complicated by what is widely described as the "New Poverty" or the "New Marginality," in which there is an emerging underclass who are so poor, and so lacking in social capital, that they have no resources to mobilize in order to survive. Theirs is a total "poverty of resources." Contemporary analysis focuses upon the processes that underpin social exclusion, exploring not just economic factors, but also how ethnic, educational, and spatial disadvantage and inequality of access are reproduced, intensifying the exclusion of the poor and inhibiting their ability to escape from poverty (Roberts 2004).

Marginality Theory

There were two competing backdrops to marginality thinking during the 1960s. The first was modernization theory, in which it was believed that poverty would be overcome through social change, and through the diffusion and adoption of modern practices and strategies, as societies shifted from being traditional and underdeveloped, to being modern and developed. The second, dependency theory, was less sanguine about the prospects of development, predicated as it was on the asymmetry of trading and political relations between the developed and the less-developed worlds. Among others, development economists and sociologists such as Osvaldo Sunkel (1964, 1972) and Fernando Enrique Cardoso and Enzo Faletto (1969) sprinted away from the *pelaton* at that time and played an important role in shifting understanding away from "modernization school" explanations of social change, toward a more conflictual or dialectical model of society, with concomitantly greater emphasis upon structurally embedded causes of poverty.

Each of these paradigms dictates a different understanding of the nature of poverty—one *functionalist,* the other *Marxist.* Under modernization, poverty is understand in *functionalist* terms. Irregular or spontaneous settlements were the outcome of dysfunctional urbanization in which (largely) ill-prepared and rural populations were flocking into cities and recreating traditional housing and social relations that were familiar to them from their villages of origin. Allegedly, they lacked modern values; their housing structures were rural throwbacks (called *bohios, jacales, ranchos*) leading to a "ruralization" of the city (Juppenlatz 1970). Although this interpretation was largely erroneous—as subsequent research quickly revealed—the intellectual root of such approaches was clear, having been shaped by the sociological theory of *gemeinschaft* and *gesellschaft* of Tönnies, Durkheim, Parsons, and others. Similarly, in urban sociology there were influential parallels epitomized by Louis Wirth's classic paper "Urbanism as a Way of Life," published in 1938 in the *American Journal of Sociology*, which focused upon the ills of urbanization in the United States, and the underlying propensity of breakdown as the fabric of social relations shifted from rural, close-knit relations with overlapping roles and strong community bonds, to urban social relations typified by diffuse networks, singular roles, and associative rather than community patterns. Highly regarded anthropologists of this period, such as Robert Redfield and Sol Tax, working in rural contexts, appeared to be arriving at similar conclusions; namely, that as Latin American societies urbanized, so social changes were leading them toward instability and breakdown. Within this context, irregular settlements, now growing apace, were considered to be "marginal" in a number of ways: socially, physically, politically, and spatially (Nelson 1979). In short, these ideas from classic urban sociology and from cultural anthropology fueled the perceptions of dysfunctional and "parasitic" urbanization as enunciated in the work of Hoselitz (1956), Gino Germani (1962), and Phillip Hauser, whose edited volume *Urbanization in Latin America* (1967) is a classic representation of the state of the art of that period.

An important offshoot of this marginality thinking was Oscar Lewis's "culture of poverty" concept (Lewis 1966), which argued that the poor were steeped in a series of traits that impeded their development and ability to progress; indeed, that they were trapped in poverty, with little opportunity to escape. The diagnosis deriving from this view was that the *culture* needed attention and needed to be recast (rather than the *structures* of poverty). Thus, such views put the onus for poverty upon the poor themselves, and upon their inappropriate or traditional value systems, and this found resonance among policymaking circles both in institutions such as DESAL in Peru and among scholars (later politicians) such as Daniel P. Moynihan and Nathan Glazer in the United States (Valentine 1968). Notwithstanding widespread critique in the middle to late 1960s (see Safá 1970, Valentine 1968, and Leacock 1971), the culture of poverty and its residential characterization of life in inner-city tenement slums and peripheral squatter settlements of Mexico and Puerto Rico remained an important construction of Latin American urban poverty for over a decade (Perlman 1976).

Equally important was how such ideas translated into public policy. In large part stimulated by Alliance for Progress funding, social development funds were established throughout the region that fostered major programs, the most important of which was land reform. In the urban arena, national housing funds were established, sometimes creating influential agencies such as the ICT (Instituto de Credito Territorial) in Colombia, and the Instituto Nacional de Vivienda (INV) in Mexico. However, the reach of these funds proved to be relatively limited—providing what was called "social interest" ("soft" or noncommercial) loans to better-off workers and lower-middle-income groups. For the majority of the urban poor the policy was, de facto, one of blind neglect. Moreover, the negative image of the urban migrant poor, as rural and dysfunctional, served to justify 1960s policies of selective settlement eradication and housing eviction programs, sometimes rehousing the population in modern public housing projects such as Cidade Kennedy in northern Rio de Janeiro, clearing out *favelas* from the city's south side (Perlman 1976). Such projects, however, were superficial in their impact, affecting only a minimal part of the demand and invariably failing to understand, let alone meet, the needs of target populations (J. Turner 1976). Invariably those settlements slated for removal were chosen for political expediency or because they were seen as eyesores detracting from the construction of a new and modern urban landscape. These programs not only reinforced the dominant social constructions of poverty prevalent at the time but also justified policies that were fundamentally paternalistic in nature. Sometimes, too, this received wisdom had a kind of backwash effect, even shaping the negative self-image of the poor themselves as lazy or "backward" (Perlman 1976).

I dwell on this period of thinking, since the urgent need to challenge this cultural perspective of marginality is where several authors whose work appears in this volume and participants in the seminar at which these papers were originally presented began their careers. For example, Helen Safa's (1970) brilliantly evocative "The Poor Are Like Everyone Else, Oscar" (1970) was explicitly aimed at Oscar Lewis; Alejandro Portes's "Rationality in the Slum: An Essay in Interpretative Sociology," published in *Comparative Studies in Society and History* in 1972, took a similar tack. One of Portes's first major publications, it was a formative paper in shaping my own thinking at that time (Ward 1976). For a while, at least, he and a number of other then relatively young "upstarts" (many of them sociologists) broke out of the *pelaton*—for example, Bryan Roberts, with *Organizing Strangers: Poor Families in Guatemala City;* William Mangin (an anthropologist) working in Lima, with "Latin American Squatter Settlements: The Problem and the Solution"; and Tony Leeds, with "The Significant Variables Determining the Character of Squatter Settlements," also sought to debunk Lewis and others' stereotyping of a culture of poverty and the alleged hopelessness of shantytowns and tenement life.

On the physical status of squatter areas, probably no one did more at the time to reorient our way of looking at urban development and irregular settlement processes than John Turner, Pat Crooke, and other "barefoot" architects working in Lima and elsewhere. And from a parallel perspective, others began to focus upon the political ramifications of the settlement process, most notably Manuel Castells (1977), who in the late 1960s and early 1970s worked within the *campamentos* of Allende's Chile, and Alejandro Portes, in his article "Political Primitivism, Differential Socialization and Lower-class Leftist Radicalism." The thrust of these studies, together with parallel work by political scientists, demonstrated quite unequivocally that so-called slum areas often demonstrated high levels of organization, great capacity, and if left to themselves, considerable ability for local development initiatives. Their research showed that rarely did the empirical reality correspond to the views of helplessness and dependency promulgated by the culture of poverty thesis.

In the normative field, this was also a period of imminent change arising from the growing disillusionment with the failures of modernism and social engineering, analyzed in Faber and Seers's 1972 *Crisis in Planning* and graphically related in Peter Hall's *Great Planning Disasters of the 1960s* (Hall 1982). Anthropologists such as Herbert Gans (1962) in Boston and Gerald Suttles in Chicago (1968) had begun to challenge many of the policy prescriptions derived from the intellectual threads that unraveled from Wirth and others' work some two decades earlier. Indeed, my own early research in the early 1970s was in no small measure inspired by Michael Young and Peter Willmott's (1957) *Family and Kinship in East London,* which demonstrated the negative social impacts and destruction of "community" wrought by the well-intentioned, large-scale urban clearance projects in the East End of London. Prompted precisely by their comparative analysis of family and kinship in Bethnall Green and the new municipal housing estates of Woodfood, Essex, I aspired to examine squatter settlements from the inside out, with a view to placing, if not a more positive spin on poverty, then at least to achieving a better understanding of the informal responses that poverty generates. Indeed, the idea of analyzing social networks in urban situations was developed in J. Clyde Mitchell's *Social Networks in Social Situations* (1969), which was an important early reference point for many of us working in Latin America (Roberts 1973; Lomnitz 1975; Ward 1978). Much later, similar ideas were recast in the "resources of poverty" and "social capital" literature of the 1980s and 1990s. And significantly, even at that time some of the disadvantages of social capital were presaged. Robert van Kemper (1974), working among Tzintzuntzán migrants from Michoacán in Mexico City, showed that would-be socially mobile households had to physically move away from their kin-anchored neighborhoods in order to remove themselves from local kinship obligations that resulted in a sharing (and therefore equalizing) of resources across the larger group.

By the late 1960s, and throughout the 1970s, these theories were challenged, not only by empirical evidence and new interpretations, but also by a fundamentally different theoretical paradigm. Unlike the functionalist theories, these structural interpretations of poverty argued that poverty was an inevitable outcome of asymmetrical relations between the "metropolitan" core (read "advanced industrial") and "periphery" (less developed countries), as well as internal "colonial" and unequal relations within Latin American societies (Frank 1967; Stavenhagen 1965). The marginality associated with the urban poor was viewed in a number of sometimes contradictory ways. For example, sociologist José Nun (1967) and his colleagues saw the poor as a marginal "mass" whose existence had little impact upon capital accumulation processes from which they were largely excluded; others viewed them as an industrial reserve army that depressed wages and provided cheap labor and services. Irrespective of the relative merits of this polemic, it was clear that the majority of these workers were increasingly likely to be housed in irregular settlements of one form or another.

But while these overarching paradigms challenged the way we sought to analyze social phenomena, they did little to shake the underpinnings of public policy approaches, predicated as these were upon trickle-down economics, rather than on structural change. What we had begun to achieve, however, was a clearer understanding of the nature of the housing problem: namely, that it was structural rather than cultural; and that it was a functional and logical outcome of capitalism, rather than a dysfunctional and aberrational one. Although it might be argued that we were sometimes in danger of looking at poverty through rose-colored spectacles, we did manage to place a more positive spin on the opportunities for socioeconomic mobility brought about by migration, by self-help housing, and by leveraging access to public goods that were previously denied to such populations. And even if income profiles remained low and relatively "flat," it was apparent that there was widespread access to the formal sector tied to the ISI expansion of the 1950s and 1960s (Safá 1974). For this new and rapidly expanding population, poverty derived not from marginality and being outside the economic system, but from being closely tied into it—as underpaid workers.

Informal Sector: The "Problem" Is the Solution

These development debates continued in the 1970s and became polarized between the advocates of dependency on the one hand, and those who increasingly took a more nuanced and less overarchingly deterministic viewpoint associated with interdependent development schools of thinking. This was a segue to a new stream of thinking about the urban poor and about labor market behavior in general. I have already observed how researchers working out of Latin America were beginning to challenge some of the stereotypical views of poverty and spontaneous settlements, and this work dovetailed well with the challenges of dualist economic theory being made by Keith Hart working in Ghana in the early 1970s, which demonstrated that the formal and informal economic and labor sectors were, in fact, highly interdependent. Neither transitional nor aberrational, the "informal sector" as it became known had a life and vitality of its own, was capable of expansion, and was "benign" and nonthreatening to broader capitalist development. Social geographers, sociologists, and social anthropologists such as Birkbeck (1978), Bromley (1978), Bromley and Gerry (1979), and Moser (1978)—for a while in the late 1970s—burst away from the *pelaton,* offering fascinating Latin American case studies that showed the complex and highly functional interrelationships between the two sectors. Indeed, they showed how both directly and indirectly the formal sector often relied heavily upon the informal one for cheap services and inputs.

Policymaking also did a double take. Now the aim was not so much as to drive the informal sector to the margins and out of existence, but to work with it, recognizing its "unending virtuosity" and capacity for absorbing labor and for producing cheap services. The informal sector was part of the solution—and not in and of itself, the problem. The parallels of this late 1970s work are clearly seen in the earlier shift in thinking about low-income social organization and the nature of irregular settlement and self-help housing arena—which preceded it by a few years. In reality, though, we formed part of the same *pelaton,* all of us seeking to better understand and to theorize out of what were often small-scale case studies. Here is not the moment to dwell upon changing labor policies, since my primary concern in this chapter is with housing and settlement policy changes where several major shifts took place. First, we began to view the rapid growth of irregular settlements, if not in positive terms, at least more realistically as a rational housing response by low-income homesteaders who could not acquire shelter formally. There were no mortgage markets to speak of, and anyway they would be largely irrelevant given that incomes were too low to sustain any supply by the formal sector. Nor were governments willing or able to provide housing, since the demand (numbers) was overwhelmingly large, and the costs of providing such housing were prohibitive. Therefore, government attention focused upon occasional emergency housing and selective redevelopment projects, on the one hand, and on providing some housing in lower middle-income projects, on the other. The poor were left to fend for themselves, and this they did more or less successfully. Other things being equal, squatter and other self-help areas were gradually upgraded by individual self-help and by collective mutual aid of the residents themselves. The conventional wisdom emerged that this was "an architecture that works" (J. Turner 1968), and that informal systems of self-help housing were not only pragmatic but were also more desirable, given people's needs and aspirations (J. Turner 1976).

Nor were these informal and spontaneous settlements found to be radical and system-threatening. This fear remained widespread (for governments at least), predicated upon the writings of Frantz Fanon (Gerassi 1963); and among intellectuals and radicals of the period there was indeed a quickening of interest in the opportunities that irregular settlements offered as crucibles for radical social transformation. Indeed, this was sometimes the case—as among the settlements in Allende's Chile that supported the Movement of the Revolutionary Left (MIR), for example. But these were generally the exceptions; as a rule, these settlements, far from being a vehicle to foment mobilization and social change, actually served to draw out the radical sting. Sociologist Manuel Castells broke away from the *pelaton* and led the way for several years, pretty much single-handedly developing a theory about urban change and social movements at the beginning of the 1970s. His work raised high expectations about the potential of what he called secondary (class) conflicts being articulated through residentially based social movements to generate effective mobilization and social change and attaining a "qualitative new effect in power relations"—his criterion for a social movement (Castells 1977; see also Castells 1979 and 1983 and Lowe 1986). Very influential at the time, Castells's thesis about the potential strength of social mobilization around the means of collective consumption, and its capacity to transcend the labor relation as a means to develop class consciousness, became more diluted with each theoretical iteration that he developed. By 1983, while he continued to view social movements as important in their own right for defense of community and for interest-group articulation, he no longer saw them as a viable means for changing power relations in society. Now more interested in high-tech change and other urban environments, Castells had given up the race leader's yellow jersey. But throughout the 1980s and 1990s others continued to explore social movements, new social movements, and even "new new" social movements (Foweraker 1995; Assies 1990; Salman 1990; Escobar and Alvarez 1992).

One of the reasons why Castells was obliged to step back from the radical mobilization thesis was that political scientists were showing that just as these urban residents were part of an informal-formal sector continuum in their employment structures, so, too, these settlements were integrative—providing opportunities for employment creation and marketing, for home-based production, and for social reproduction generally—raising and sustaining a family. Although at considerable social cost and sacrifice, residents continued to enter the housing market as stakeholders and as homeowners, and were actually quite conservative, and not radical at all. As de facto homeowners, they were increasingly tied into the political and governmental system, albeit embedded in clientelistic networks with politicians and local authorities (Cornelius 1973; Leeds 1972). Thus, far from being radical and system-threatening, irregular settlements were a way for governments to integrate (or at least to control) the urban poor (Perlman 1976). Moreover, although cooptation was the name of the game, as Tony and Elizabeth Leeds were showing in their work, it was a two-way process, one in which residents "sold" their political support and vote in exchange for not being evicted, and in exchange for the gradual extension of basic infrastructure and services. Politically, too, this was an informal "architecture" that worked.

Although not without its critics (Ward 1982), state policy had begun to shift from one of laissez-faire to being more interventionist and supportive of informal sector initiatives. It fell to governments to intervene and regularize this informality by providing basic infrastructure, and sometimes to regularize the housing tenure from de facto to de jure ownership, usually through expropriation. Indeed, this is precisely what architects and planners such as Turner (1968) and Abrams (1966) had advocated in the late 1960s. By the late 1970s, as the informal sector theory took hold and entered conventional wisdom, so new policy approaches emerged, arguing that governments should seek to harness—not obstruct—the informal sector initiatives of self build and mutual aid that many of us had described in detail in our studies. Rather than invest in large-scale housing projects that society could ill afford, governments were urged to focus those same resources upon providing services, tenure regularization, technical support, and so on, to existing irregular settlements (J. Turner 1976). The call went out for government to become more interventionist, but in ways that would help to incorporate these marginal settlements and to quicken their physical integration into the urban fabric. Pragmatic and realistic, this more supportive policy approach recognized the need to invert the normal settlement logic of Planning-Infrastructure-Building-Settlement (PIBS) to that of SBIP (Baross 1990). Although some scholars advised caution (Ward 1982), drawing attention to the important linkages between successful self-help in irregular settlements and the dynamics of the wider economy, earning capacity, and real wages, most of us nevertheless thought that we were, at last, on the cusp of achieving a major shift in urban policy direction, and that it would be one for the better.

And so it proved, in part at least. Key to the changes at this time were international agencies, and in particular the World Bank. From pursuing a macrolevel, development-oriented, and largely rural-focused role in the 1950s and 1960s, the Bank was beginning to change, also embracing urban and microproject approaches (World Bank 1972). Impressed by the research of Turner, Abrams, and others, the Bank actively promoted a series of urban programs that took account of the principles of informal sector understanding and self-build. Most significant among these were (1) upgrading (provision of services to existing settlements), and (2) sites-and-services in which planned settlements with (usually) serviced lots would be offered to self-builder homesteaders (PISB in the aforementioned sequencing), and sometimes including "wet-cores" of bathrooms and kitchens that could be "added-to." Principles of individual "sweat equity" and community mutual aid sat comfortably with the emerging expectancy of greater popular participation and a "bootstraps" (self-help) orthodoxy that was emerging from informal sector theorists. Demonstration projects were established in an attempt to stimulate adoption (Harth, Deneke, and Silva 1982). However, it was more the simple fact that the Bank had indicated its recognition of the shortcomings of the earlier 1960s policies and that it was embracing self-build and informal sector policy that encouraged many Latin American countries do the same. In 1976 the United Nations created a new institution, the Center for Human Settlements, and a World Habitat conference in Vancouver that same year set the seal on the policy change.

Although timely, it was probably already a decade late. By the end of the 1970s and early 1980s important changes were afoot: intellectual, political, and economic. Intellectually, many of us were beginning to adopt more of a political economy approach to urbanization, no longer just looking sectorally at housing and employment, but instead, examining in a more holistic way the interaction between economy, politics, and societal development and change (Roberts 1978; Portes and Walton 1976; Gilbert and Ward 1985). We recognized the driving importance of the economy in shaping urban development and the overarching role that the state played in that process. By this time, of course, the state apparatus had become very large and often unwieldy, and that, too, was about to change.

Latin America was about to be reshaped by two driving forces: economic austerity on the one hand, and democratization on the other. In 1979 two-thirds of the countries in the region were under military control, yet by 1985, all were democracies except Chile, which held out until 1990. This fact alone registers that a momentous shift was taking place in opportunities for *representative* democracy associated with elections and regime change in the 1980s, and which would also lead to opportunities and demands for more *participatory* democracy. In the 1990s, the latter would be closely associated with decentralization and governance (to be discussed). But it was economic crisis that precipitated most of these political changes. By 1980 import-substitution industrialization strategies and protection policies were exhausted, and a different orthodoxy of export-oriented growth for global markets was fast becoming the new currency. This required macroeconomic restructuring; new investment; a more competitive, free-market-oriented economic environment; and a slimmer and less interventionist state.

The economic crisis that many countries confronted through the 1980s is frequently referred to as the "lost decade," since social development programs were so badly eroded by the combination of political and economic restructuring that took place. While it is not the point here to elaborate upon what is already well documented and understood, for the purposes of this chapter, I wish to underscore how these processes, and the austerity of the 1980s that accompanied them, helped to usher in a new period of thinking about state intervention in general, and about housing and urban development in particular.

The 1980s: Resources of Poverty, the Rise of Technocracy, and "Urban Management"

The stuttering macroeconomic performance in many countries, together with the IMF-driven obligations to engage in market and structural adjustments, had a generally negative (and sometimes disastrous) effect upon employment and incomes (Portes 1985). Earning opportunities and real wages declined, and social development programs were severely reduced, prompting public policy in countries like Mexico to become more effective and efficient in managing scarce resources (Ward 1986). States were obliged to downsize, and decentralization began to be pursued as means of distributing responsibility more widely, not least under a less patrimonialist and now more democratic state. As the decade advanced, the private sector was encouraged to play a fuller role, by making new investments in now privatized activities. Nongovernmental organizations (NGOs) also began to discover newfound spaces of activity and responsibility as the state showed some willingness to hand off social provision responsibility to them—a trend that would intensify a decade later.

Against this backdrop, housing, household, and employment survival strategies became the high ground of academic endeavor. Once again sociology and sister disciplinary areas jumped out from the *pelaton,* offering insight into how populations were managing to cope with such a disastrous scenario. Understanding the informal sector allowed us to examine multisourcing income-earning strategies (Escobar and González de la Rocha 1991); household extension organization arrangements (Safá 1995; Chant 1991); the rise of renting and sharing and the declining access to land for self-help (Gilbert and Ward 1985; Gilbert 1993); and the sharp decline in housing and employment opportunities for "second generation" migrants whose parents had successfully ridden the ISI expansion phase of the previous two to three decades. No longer were large cities in Latin America cities of (former) peasants; they were now cities of urbanites, many of whom faced dire prospects, at least over the short term. But a common feature of all of these studies was the way in which poor people adjusted to austerity by, for example, extending the working day, moving into the informal sector, increasing participation in the economic active population (especially women), extending their households, sharing dwellings, and so forth. In short, how the poor mobilized the resources of poverty to reasonably good effect in order to survive (Chant 1991; González de la Rocha 1994; Moser 1998).

Faced with this scenario, it really became "Thank Heavens for the Informal Sector," perceived now as offering an important cushion that would absorb and sustain households against the crisis. Indeed, by the late 1980s researchers elsewhere were discovering the informal sector anew—in sweatshops in New York and in outwork or in factories targeting the global marketplace associated with restructuring and flexible accumulation (D. Harvey 1989).[2] In Peru

2. There is a recent resurgence of interest in the informal sector and related activities in the context of globalization—see Roy and Alsayyad 2003.

in 1986, Hernando de Soto picked up the ideas of informal sector analysts of a decade earlier and (often without attribution) made them his own. He argued persuasively for the need for governments to allow this informal sector to thrive, and not to seek to regulate it out existence (Soto 1986).

In the housing and public policy field from the early 1980s on we see a policy response that is quite consistent with the macrolevel economic changes that were being entrained. The World Bank recognized that the urban projects approach they had advanced in the late 1970s would no longer be appropriate in an urban environment that eschewed subsidies and direct public expenditure from a slimmer state. Also, there was a growing awareness that the affordability of self-help was declining (as wages were eroded). Governments also realized the need to achieve greater efficacy in social development through streamlining and programs, cutting out waste and duplication, and improving policy approaches, such as primary health care, and the beginnings of social targeting to specific populations. Another characteristic of this greater routinization and systematization of delivery of public goods was the marked decline of overt clientelism. However, an outcome of this heavier emphasis upon a more systematic approach was an increased segmentation and stratification into constituencies eligible to receive those goods, and to the extent that this occurred, it acted to reproduce stratification patterns— for example, in access to health-care benefits, social insurance, and even housing (Ward 1986). In some respects the drive to greater efficiency observed in the 1980s was a precursor to the unintended consequences borne of structures that appear to be intensifying social exclusion today.

Another factor informing these changes was the declining margin for error faced by politicians. The sharpening of potential and more articulated unrest, flushed with incipient democratization challenges, meant that parties and political groups needed to win friends and convince people, and to do so less with pork and patronage, and more by winning confidence and votes at the ballot box. Above all, the 1980s required solutions that would be fiscally responsible and sustainable. "Sustainability" emerged as a watchword, and one that should no longer be predicated upon strong infusion of state and central resources. In short, there was a need to prime the marketplace to generate provision and expansion of social goods.

Returning to the housing policy arena, we see a withdrawal from urban housing projects advocated in the 1970s, toward approaches that would make the private housing market system work more smoothly. Inter alia this included, first, removing the impediments to the housing and land supply system that made for scarcity and for higher prices—namely, policies to reduce monopolies, to open up competition, to regularize "clouded" titles to foster a sense of full ownership, and to provide infrastructure in order to reduce the scarcity of serviced land and thereby lower overall prices. A second feature was to predicate all investment upon the principle of full cost recovery and minimal subsidies, or where these were required, to ensure full transparency of those supports. A third was to encourage private sector housing production by offering guarantees to existing and newly created housing finance programs. A fourth was to develop mechanisms that would allow for the inclusion of the informal sector residents into the formal sector—especially insofar as they entered the formal land registry and subsequently became contributors to the fiscal base of the city—as de jure property owners. The concepts of sustainability and citizenship (responsibility) became intertwined.

Sociologists had had their day during the 1970s; now it was the turn of the economists. A good example of this new thinking was Johannes Linn's 1982 *Cities in the Developing World: Policies for Their Equitable and Efficient Growth,* which although independently authored, comprised the early 1980s blueprint for World Bank thinking at the time (Linn was a consultant to the Bank). The effects of this new approach are not always easy to gauge and to disaggregate from the impacts of wider austerity programs. Certainly, however, there does seem to have been a sharp quickening and improved public policy responsiveness in the servicing arena, as well as in greater viability of private sector production of housing for the lower middle income end of the market. Also, greater land-use and planning controls were reducing the land available for self-help, and some densification was being achieved in existing irregular settlements. But densification was also an outcome of the vise effect that increasing costs of self-help construction and home improvement were having, given the declining and truncated wages. The so-called Resources of Poverty were not limitless; indeed, in the late 1980s they became extremely hard pressed.

This palpable shift away from direct government intervention in urban projects toward an agenda that privileged the market, seeking to ensure administrative and market performance reforms, was a clear precursor of the shape of things to come. From the late 1980s the World Bank sought to focus increasingly upon "urban operations on city-wide policy reform, institutional development, and high priority investments—and to put the development assistance in the urban sector in the context of broader objectives of economic development and macroeconomic performance" (World Bank 1991, 4). By the late 1980s this neoliberal philosophy was being firmly translated into urban policy embodied in the New Urban Management Program (NUMP) that had been elaborated in conjunction with the United Nations Development Programme (UNDP). In essence, this philosophy argues for urban "management" over urban "administration," in order to free housing and land markets from constraints and to formalize their operations. Table 11.1 provides a snapshot of the priority issues defined by the Bank under the land management section of the NUMP. Significantly, the first subject area is municipal finance, and three of the four categories of municipal finance issues deal directly with finance and institution building, while a fourth identifies community participation, the informal sector, and the need for urban managers to respond to public needs. The second subject area outlines the linkages between the macroeconomy, urban infrastructure, and service performance and the need for effective administration to improve infrastructure maintenance (read sustainability). The third subject area seeks to remove "constraints" from the land market and to improve land use control and to formalize property rights. The fourth subject area is environmental management, where the Bank prioritizes the need for more regulation and control (Jones and Ward 1994; see also Zanetta 2003).

Here, rather than focus upon the "Resources of Poverty" literature and responses with which most of us are already familiar and which grew out of the informal sector research of the 1970s, I seek to describe the dramatic urban policy changes during the 1980s. I have already alluded to the clear convergence between the wider macroeconomic orthodoxy that came to the forefront in the 1980s and the growing emphasis upon administration and urban management and upon technocratic approaches that took off in the 1990s. And the aim has been to give the reader a sense of how we got to where we are today from the "there" of the early 1980s. These changes have taken place in Latin America against a backdrop of profound political change and democratization. Ultimately, this intersection between neoliberal reforms, democratic opening, and political accountability has led to the major paradigm shift experienced since the 1990s.

Decentralization, Institutional Strengthening, and Good Governance

Decentralization has been on the policy agenda for many years, albeit largely rhetorically and almost always ineffectually. Yet democratization appears to have changed that, and decentralization has been described as the "quiet revolution" of the 1990s (Campbell 2003). Decentralization has indeed changed—and is changing—how housing, urban policy, and social policy generally are

Table 11.1 Priority issues in land management under the New Urban Management Program

UMP subject area	Emerging "priority" issues
Municipal finance	Central-local relationships (allocations and functions, financial flows, access to credit)
	Assignment and administration of revenue sources (including user charges)
	Municipal organization and administration
	Community participation, the informal sector, and responsive urban management
Infrastructure	The linkages between urban infrastructure and service performance and the macroeconomy
	Administrative, financial, and technical means to improve infrastructure maintenance
Urban land management	Urban land and related markets: identifying and rectifying constraints
	Institutions and instruments to support land markets: the role of land registration, information management, urban planning, and informal land management and administrative practices
	Urban land tenure and property rights
The urban environment	Improving urban waste-management capacity and operational efficiency
	The legal and regulatory framework for environmental protection: the assignment of jurisdiction for legislation, monitoring, and enforcement
	Use of economic instruments as alternatives to command and control
	Environmental implications of land-use control and property rights

SOURCE: World Bank 1990.

being conducted today, particularly if we conceive decentralization in both its vertical and horizontal dimensions.

The vertical dimension is most familiar to us, and in Latin America its most salient characteristic in the 1990s is that it is no longer largely nominal, but embraces genuine decentralization and devolution to lower levels of government. This change has occurred for two reasons: first, power has been wrested from the center by political parties coming to power in the periphery, sometimes combined with beleaguered power holders in the center having a genuine sense that they can hold onto power only by releasing some of the reins (Rodríguez 1997). Second, decentralization has found some strong policy advocates and has received positive encouragement from international organizations since the early 1990s (Zanetta 2003). Prime examples of this opening and decentralization are Bolivia's Participation Law of 1992, and the decentralization of public education and health care to the states in Mexico. So widespread and fast is this process of devolution and decentralization that today there are some calls to recentralize, at least in certain arenas of activity. Indeed, in 1998 the World Bank in its *World Development Report* also argued in favor of redressing the imbalance, and to bring the central state back in— at least a little. Although less well analyzed, when looking at large cities it is important also to consider decentralization *within* urban areas themselves, and not just within the national hierarchy. Specifically, to examine how social policy is apportioned through different levels of city government (metropolitan, borough or district, settlement, and so on). For the most part, cities, especially large ones in Latin America, remain heavily centralized in their power and governance structures.

The horizontal dimension of decentralization is less frequently considered, despite its growing importance, embracing as it does the space between the branches of government— executive, legislative, and judicial. Traditionally, in Latin America all eyes were focused upon the executive branch— presidents, governors, and municipal leaders. But in today's newfound political space, legislative and judicial policymakers are increasingly the subjects of study, witnessed in a spate of scholarly texts and analyses on legislatures. Similarly, as participatory democracy (in contrast to representative democracy) becomes an important dimension, the manner in which civil society participates and influences the process of governance is an increasingly important issue.

As I have already suggested, decentralization increasingly intersects with good governance, and how one seeks to strengthen the capacity of the responsible state authority to govern, in order to provide for urban sustainability, has become an important challenge. Thus, there is a growing and systematic emphasis in decentralized governments and agencies on bureaucratic stream-lining, modernization, transparency, sustainability, reform, "re-engineering," and so on, and on the application of new techniques such as total quality management, zero-based budgeting, participatory budgeting, and the sharing of best practices and innovations (Spink 2001). Sometimes, too, this obses-sion with technocratic administration and efficiency at the local city-wide level threatens to overwhelm principles of good government (understood as the capacity of political leaders to foster participation and democratic partic-ipation and awareness). Good administration it may be, but it can also be at the cost of dreadful government (Ward 1998).

As the principles of the NUMP begin to be systematically implemented within these participatory spaces, a growing responsibility has been placed upon individuals, households, and citizens. Within the housing policy arena, therefore, there has been a dramatic withdrawal of the central state and an increasing responsibility of local government. States and cities are expected to take primary responsibility for housing, for urban development planning, and for policy implementation. No longer are almost all major programs generalized and run by the central government, but instead they are decen-tralized to state and city departments, or to public-private partnerships. Statewide housing agencies have become far more common, albeit largely targeting the better-off working classes.

Cities, too, are expected to develop regularization programs, usually tied to property register modernization and to more systematic fiscal recovery through property and other valorization taxes. To the extent that they can leverage major funding from international agencies, federal, state, and local governments are developing major upgrading schemes such as the $300 million IDB *favela bairro* program in Rio de Janeiro, and its counterparts in Chile, Argentina, and Uruguay. Moreover, there is emphasis on (1) indi-vidual—rather than group or collective—contracting and bargaining; (2) physical regularization (upgrading) usually tied to cost recovery; (3) tenure regularization, no longer primarily an end in itself (that is, to give people secure titles), but more as a means to integrate irregular settlement popula-tions into the planning and fiscal base of the city; (4) integration as citizens; and (5) public participation. At the city-wide level housing policies are ori-ented at restricting unregulated growth and making land markets work more efficiently; at raising densities and greater efficiency of land use; at promoting what the World Bank calls "urban productivity" (the use of land and hous-ing to generate income); and above all, to cultivate sustainability, specifically a policy of "pay-as-you-go." In short, the housing and urban development agenda has been created endogenously through the internationalization of conventional wisdom (see also Sunkel in this volume), and it is being applied across the region. It is important to recognize that this broadening of orthodoxy is less a by-product of *globalization,* and more an *internationalization* process—in this context administration, management, and microplanning. Today, while no single discipline leads the *pelaton,* the international recipe of received wisdoms and the so-called Washington consensus does appear to be having an lasting impact upon housing and urban development orthodoxy in Latin America, although some authors argue that receptivity and implementation are driven less by individual government's agendas, and more by that of the World Bank (Zanetta 2003).

The Current Challenge—From the "Resources of Poverty," to a "Poverty of Resources," to Social Exclusion

Despite these attempts to enhance efficiency and to husband urban resources, the Latin American reality of today appears to be one of growing segregation and exclusion. If structural readjustment and austerity had a major impact upon the Latin American class and social structures of the 1980s, then neoliberalism in the 1990s has intensified many of those changes, throwing more people into unemployment and self-employment (Portes and Hoffman 2003). If in the 1980s the poor appeared to have been able to mobilize certain social capital and assets with some success, that is, the resources of poverty model, by the end of that decade this no longer appeared to be the case. Since that time there is an emerging body of the population who are unable to mobilize such assets, either because they are isolated (sometimes abandoned children or elderly), or because they are no longer embedded in networks of reciprocity (since they cannot themselves offer to reciprocate), or because they cannot raise even the minimal resources to allow them to provision their petty production for sale in the informal sector. This is the "poverty of resources" model in which disadvantages accumulate (González de la Rocha 2001, 2004). Perhaps paradoxically, although classic marginality may have lacked empirical veracity in its earliest iteration, the changes outlined above do appear to be creating the very conditions and cultural constructions conceived and predicted by Nun, Quijano, and Lewis from their different perspectives in the 1960s. Rising unemployment, declining opportunities in even informal sector activities, a rise of private provisioning within a barter economy (the *trueque* system in Argentina), social exclusion and new dimensions of marginalization, rising violence and insecurity, and so on, are all frequent features of the contemporary urban scene and not just in Latin America, but also in the United States and Western Europe (Wacquant 1997).

Nevertheless, while these trends suggest the past, the political and public policy architectures are very different today, and this so-called new poverty is embedded within a framework of democratization, a smaller, less centralized state, and a new intermediate "third sector" of nongovernmental organizations with increasing responsibility for the delivery of social goods. In order to offset some of the negative and unintended consequences of neoliberal reform, "targeting" has become the order of the day—directing scarce resources at the most vulnerable populations. In this context, the Solidarity Program in Mexico (1989–94), and its later iterations as Progresa (1994–2001) and *Oportunidades,* have become models that are being replicated in various Latin American countries. Since the mid-1990s these schemes have targeted women and children, paying the household "scholarships" to keep the children in school and to ensure that families get basic medical attention. Successful though they are, these are emergency schemes that target the desperately poor, usually (though no longer exclusively) in rural areas.

Elsewhere in society at large and especially in cities there is an increasing formalization and technocratization of the urban environment. And tied to democratic opening and a more participatory democracy, a general broadening of citizenship rights has empowered the poor to claim and assert those rights, or as Jelin (2004) describes it, "afirmar el derecho a afirmar."[3] Moreover, the broadening of social development and social development programs through state and especially nongovernmental agencies is creating a raft of differential levels of coverage and access. As Roberts points out (2004), no one leaves the poor alone any more. Moreover, given that the nature, access, and quality of the benefits leveraged are themselves highly segmented, this is creating new arenas of social exclusion with those less able to take advantage being left further behind.

Today sociologists have a number of challenges to investigate: the threat of urban breakdown from rising violence; the new dimensions of poverty and social exclusion; and the need to develop new traditions of participating within the spaces of administration and local governance that have opened up, but which, having been denied for so long, were never part of the agenda.

3. See the research note in *Latin American Research Review* 39, no. 1 (2004): 183–203, for an overview of these changes from several authors whose work spans the period from the 1960s to the present.

Gender issues remain an important dimension for analysis, and increasingly we are looking more systematically at male roles, behaviors, and constructions, not just female ones: gender *qua* gender, not gender *qua* women. Many cities are no longer growing fast, and urban analysis will need to focus upon consolidation and renovation rather than growth. The Latin American population is no longer overwhelmingly youthful, but is increasingly "young-middle-aged" such that aging will become a key dimension of analysis in the next decade or two. That is, how will Latin American populations care for their elderly (Varley and Blasco 2000), many of whom were the successful urbanizing poor migrants of the 1960s, and whose children and grandchildren are all too often not experiencing the same relative socioeconomic mobility, and whose expectations, as urban dwellers all their lives, remain high? As Sunkel and others have observed in this volume, the parents and grandparents of today's young adults appear to have lived better in the past.

Within these broad-brush challenges I would like to conclude this overview of marginality and rationality in the so-called slum by examining the current challenges facing us in the housing and human settlements arena, and to point toward what I consider will be the next (third) generation of housing analysis and public policy. In the previous sections of this essay I have described two earlier generations; namely, (1) the rise of spontaneous settlement and the gradual shift in attitudes and policy approaches to support and integrate de facto land occupations and enhance do-it-yourself construction; and (2) the decentralization of such programs to the city level within a context of greater efficiency, planning, and fiscal sustainability. Today, servicing provisions, tenure regularization, and government intervention in recently formed areas, often at the distant periphery, remains a high priority, and these services generally come "on line" more quickly and more systematically than in the past. This is laudable and commendable, but it should also be recognized that the capacity to successfully consolidate and improve one's dwelling has been seriously eroded by the declining economic opportunities and real wages on the one hand, and by the rising costs caused in part by the withdrawal of subsidies, the requirement of cost recovery, and so on, on the other. To the extent that these self-help alternatives are no longer working anywhere near as well as in previous generations, then these may indeed be contemporary "slums." Certainly one sees less evidence of optimism; the residents consolidate and improve their dwellings much more slowly than in the past, notwithstanding the "supportive" policies.

And what of those settlements that began thirty to forty years ago as shanties and have been through the full cycle of "consolidation" and integration within the fabric of the city? Today these areas form the majority working-class districts in the old suburbs, now located in the intermediate ring of the city, and even close to downtown in some cases. Yet no one appears to be taking an inventory or an account of their social structure, or recognizing their increasingly dilapidated nature. Although not yet analyzed, there are numerous factors at work here. The first is the age of such homes—now thirty or more years old, which were self-built accretively as resources permitted, and without an integral dwelling plan for the long term. Although they have generally served the original families well in the past, it is highly unlikely that, without substantial remodeling, the same housing structure and plan will work well today. Second, the family structure has changed—first expanding as a nuclear household, and then later either contracting or, more usually, being extended laterally or vertically to accommodate two or more households in the same lot, even if not necessarily under the same roof. Third, and related, lot densities have increased. Moreover in these new shared lot arrangements there may be considerable uncertainty about which sibling (now adult) will ultimately inherit, and what will happen to the other lesser stakeholders also involved. Densities have also risen because of the expansion of low-cost rental housing—tenements or apartments that offer accommodation to the second- and third-generation households who wish to continue living in their *barrio* but are unable or unwilling to share with close kinsmen. Oftentimes, it is those living in the "new poverty" that today rent or share with kin (*arrimados*) in these inner and intermediate old neighborhoods. Fourth, the neighborhood itself is distressed physically, having been intensively used and yet neglected by municipal government, since it is no longer without services. If they weren't the slums of the past, they are fast becoming the slums of the future.

What is required, therefore, is a more nuanced analysis of the second- and third-generation living arrangements, a systematic policy agenda for in-situ renovation and re-accommodation to contemporary household dwelling needs, and flexible stakeholder tenure arrangements that will reduce the new-found insecurity borne of intestacy. Thus far, however, no one appears to be looking at the contemporary "rationalities" of the slum, or to be seeking to understand the interaction between the processes of social exclusion and their spatial and residential outcomes. In part this is further evidence of the lack of "joined-up-thinking" between social theory and public policy presaged in the title of this chapter. And it appears to have emerged as a disjuncture between the socioeconomic reality of Latin American material conditions under neoliberalism and the wishful thinking that administrative and urban management reforms will ultimately overcome. Whether these areas remain slums will in part depend upon the emergence of creative and effective housing policies—hopefully crafted by sociologists who are able to jump from the *pelaton*—but that alone will not be sufficient. Unless Latin American societies, parties, and governments can make real inroads against joblessness, reduce the segmented structures that exacerbate social exclusion, and offer protection for the most vulnerable (the elderly, street kids, and the infirm) who are trapped in the new poverty, then I cannot be especially sanguine either for those people's future or for the potential adequacy of their dwelling environments. On the housing front the trajectory is downward, and there is very little that is rational in that.

12 Social Exclusion

CHARLES H. WOOD

During the past decade or so, the concept "social exclusion" steadily made its way from its home ground in Western Europe to the lexicon of academic research and social policy in Latin America. Initially in France and later in England the concept was invoked to help explain the paradoxical persistence of poverty and vulnerability in the presence of Europe's elaborate welfare system (Hills, Le Grand, and Piachaud 2002; Aggleton and Parker 2003, 2; Byrne 1999). Analysts turned attention to immigration and the globalizing forces that have promoted a qualitative change in the character of advanced industrial societies (Byrne 1999, 5), and to the mechanisms of the modern state, which, for all of its sophistication, fosters dependency and denies substantial numbers of people citizenship rights and access to opportunities (Roberts 2002, 115–16).

In light of the distant realities to which the concept was originally applied, we might do well to ask whether social exclusion, even properly adapted, can deepen our understanding of contemporary Latin America, or if it can only blur the focus on underemployment and poverty, which many analysts consider the fundamental causes of the inequalities that plague the region. The assessment that follows remains agnostic inasmuch as the concept's utility has only begun to be tested. If social exclusion holds the promise of novel insights and innovative social action, the fact remains that the promise has not yet been kept.

The first section of this chapter summarizes the events that promoted the application of the concept of social exclusion in the Latin American context. The second specifies the various meanings of the term, the distinctive features of which come into relief when compared and contrasted to the notion of "marginality" that mobilized so much research in Latin America during the 1960s and 1970s. The last explores the implications of the social exclusion framework with respect to the methodological advances it demands and the data collection efforts it requires. The degree to which the social sciences advance in these respects will ultimately determine whether the concept of social exclusion lives up to its potential as a new way of looking at, responding to, and resolving social inequality in Latin America.

Social Exclusion in Latin America

Beginning in the early 1990s, the International Labour Office (ILO) began applying and adapting the concept of social exclusion to the Latin American context using regional case studies (see Faria 1994). Two major United Nations conferences—the United Nations Social Summit in 1996 and the United Nations Conference Against Racism in 2001—further crystallized awareness of social inclusion as a policy priority in Latin America and the Caribbean (Buvinic 2003, 1). In preparation for the Conference Against Racism, the Inter-American Development Bank (IDB) adopted an "action plan" designed to address the social inclusion of racial and ethnic populations within the Bank's policies, projects, and practices (IDB 2002). In 2001 the United Nations Research Institute for Social Development (UNRISD) also held a conference titled "Racism and Public Policy" to deal with the construction of race and citizenship, the dynamics of racism and inequality, and the impact of public policies on race relations (Bangura 2002). Similarly, the Santiago Consensus of the second (1998) Summit of the Americas underscored equity and social justice as priority issues of the twenty-first century. Soon thereafter the World Bank commissioned position papers with the objective of advancing a definition of a conceptual and methodological framework for the analysis of social exclusion (see Gacitúa, Sojo, and Davis 2001).

Conferences and workshops alone could not have had a significant effect had they not occurred in the context of the broader social and economic changes that have taken place in Latin America over the last several decades, such as the "new" union movement and the student mobilizations in Brazil and in Mexico in the late 1960s, the rise of international human rights networks in the 1970s, and the emergence in the 1980s of new forms of protest and social activism among women's groups, neighborhood organizations, and other social actors who previously had little voice within existing institutional channels (see Jelin in this volume). Among the consequences of these events was an erosion of macrolevel economic models that once dominated earlier research traditions (see Portes in this volume). More recent perspectives have become less abstract, and more focused on rights and citizenship, and concerned with subjective processes, both individual and collective, involved in the mobilization of new social actors (see Foweraker in this volume). Underlying the diversity of demands is the more fundamental commitment to the "right to have rights" and the assumed prerogative to debate the content of laws and public policy (Jelin, in this volume).

What emerged from these events is a growing consensus regarding the social and economic significance of human rights and citizenship, as well as racial, ethnic, and gender disparities in Latin America and the Caribbean. The new approach treats the social exclusion of population subgroups as a persistent, sometimes intensified, feature that poses a threat to social development, a risk to democratization, and a drag on economic growth (Deutsch and Reichmann 2001; Flórez, Medina, and Urrea 2001; Zoninsein 2001).

Social Exclusion Defined

Social exclusion refers to the mechanisms by which people are denied social rights and access to economic and social benefits. Social exclusion pays attention to complex political, economic, and cultural practices by which certain populations are excluded from the rewards of social change and the benefits of economic growth, based on their race, gender, ethnicity, physical disability, or sexual preference. It refers to the process of being "shut out" of the opportunity structures that determine a person's life chances. In contrast to older societal divisions, which set those "above" against those "below," Alain Touraine, speaking of the European context, described the new arrangement that sets those on the "outside" against those on the "inside" (cited in Faria 1994).

Membership in social networks is thought to be an important, perhaps decisive, asset, especially in the context of economic transactions that require an endorsement in the workplace, or in the pursuit of benefits and services provided by the state, or in the signing of binding contracts and agreements. Social networks may also influence the scope of citizenship rights and the application of the law (Figueroa, Altamirano, and Sulmont 1996, 6).

Social exclusion represents a phenomenon that emanates from concrete practices that take place within economic, political, and cultural institutions (Gacitúa and Davis 2001, 13). Proponents of the social exclusion framework draw distinctions between three areas of social interaction. Economic exclusion is in relation to a dominant mode of productive organization and refers to material deprivation and access to markets and services that satisfy basic needs. Political exclusion occurs when the rights of citizenship are not guaranteed, and people are denied participation in decision making. Cultural exclusion occurs when social groups are marginalized because they do not share the basic codes required to communicate and interact with the community (through language abilities, reading and writing skills, education levels, or adherence to religious or ethical values) or can be viewed by others as being inferior, and therefore subject to discrimination and humiliating treatment (Gacitúa and Davis 2001; Figueroa, Altamirano, and Sulmont 1996, 4).

The multidimensionality of exclusion implies that exclusion in one dimension can be countered by integration in another. Political integration can, to some extent, counteract both economic exclusion and ethnic or racial exclusion. Ethnic or racial exclusion may be counteracted by economic success. In effect, all three forms of integration/exclusion should be seen in their mutual relationships, the outcome of which may be positive or negative. "Hard social exclusion," for example, is a term that Figueroa, Altamirano, and Sulmont (1996, 4) use to refer to the process by which various forms of exclusion are subject to negative feedbacks that, in the end, can produce *"a perverse process of cumulative disadvantage"* (emphasis in original). Social exclusion is therefore a complex and multilayered process that can be intensified when the same individual simultaneously belongs to multiple excluded groups (Buvinic 2003, 4).

The term "social exclusion" is, therefore, broader than, but does not replace, the notion of poverty. The concept allows the analysis of "mechanisms leading to poverty that are not derived from the lack of income" (Gacitúa and Davis 2001, 13). If poverty is the most visible expression of exclusion, the poor are not necessarily excluded from everything, as they may involved in production, they may be recognized as citizens, and they may identify themselves with the cultural values of the nation (Figueroa, Altamirano, and Sulmont 1996, 7).

Rather than treat exclusion as a static outcome, we should understand the concept as a dynamic process that implies agency on the part of individuals, groups, or powerful classes. Exclusion can occur at different levels, affecting individuals, families, and communities, just as it can occur in different sites, ranging from neighborhoods to formal institutions, such as schools, factories, and hospitals (Aggleton and Parker 2003, 3). Each domain of exclusion calls forth different intervention strategies and can be resisted with different forms of mobilization.

Indicators of Exclusion

In Latin America and the Caribbean it is predominantly indigenous peoples, people of African descent, women, the disabled, and those living with HIV/AIDS that most suffer the consequences of exclusion. Housewives, single mothers, widows, and female household heads also suffer one form of exclusion or another (see Ariza and Oliveira in this volume). The "excluded," therefore, constitute no small proportion of the population in the region, where, in some places, they actually comprise the numerical majority. Preliminary estimates put people of African descent at around 30 percent of the region's population, with the largest concentrations found in Brazil, Colombia, Venezuela, and Haiti. Indigenous people also number some 40 million people, comprising 10 percent of the region's population, but 25 percent of the total poor. In Brazil, Peru, Bolivia, and Guatemala, ethnic groups, defined as indigenous groups and people of African descent, constitute the majority of the population and 60 percent of the poor (IDB 2003).

In many Latin American countries, indigenous women face multiple exclusions for being poor, for being of indigenous origin, and for being women. Indigenous women in Guatemala are reported to receive less schooling and to earn salaries that are 36 percent below that of nonindigenous women. The most disadvantaged are probably the women indigenous to Amazonia who are geographically isolated, cut off from health-care infrastructure, and suffer from social and political exclusion (Aggleton and Parker 2003, 12).

In Brazil, simple geography is partly to blame for racial inequality inasmuch as a majority of Afro-Brazilians lives in the poverty-stricken Northeast, while whites are concentrated in the more prosperous Southeast (Lovell 1994; Andrews 1991). But wage discrimination in the labor market is also at work. In 1980, discrimination accounted for 24 percent of the wage gap between white and Afro-Brazilian men, and 51 percent of the wage gap between white and Afro-Brazilian women (Lovell 1994, table 7; also, N. Silva 1978, 1985). Other studies further document the disadvantages that afflict the Afro-Brazilian population in terms of a wide range of indicators of social exclusion, including residential segregation (Telles 1992, 1995), child mortality (Wood and Carvalho 1988; Wood and Lovell 1992), police brutality (Mitchell and Wood 1999), social mobility (Hasenbalg 1988b), and educational and occupational opportunities (Hasenbalg 1988a; Hasenbalg and Silva 1992).

Although the inventory of the various forms of inequality in Latin America and the Caribbean is far from complete, disparate observations imply that the various dimensions of social exclusion have deep roots, many of which can be traced to the colonial period, to slavery, to the subjugation of indigenous populations, and to varied historical processes. Today it is understood that global transformations in the world economy both intensify some longstanding inequalities and bring others to life—a phenomenon that appears to be under way in nearly all countries, both North and South. Castells (1996, 1998) describes the globalization process as a shift from a Fordist regime of industrial accumulation to a new system of "informational capitalism." In Castells's view, informational capitalism is responsible for the emergence of what he calls the "Fourth World," referring to major segments of the population in almost all societies—even entire continents, as in the case of sub-Saharan Africa—that have become largely irrelevant to global production and consumption (Aggleton and Parker 2003, 5).

From Marginality to Social Exclusion

The list of population groups to which the concept of social exclusion has been applied—migrants, women, indigenous groups, Latin Americans of African descent, the disabled, the homeless, the jobless, the powerless, and the penniless—will remind most readers of the attention once lavished on the concept of "marginality" in the field of Latin American studies. Although the term has long been present in sociology (see Germani 1980), it was not until the 1960s and 1970s that marginality assumed special significance in the Latin American context, presumably in response to the far-reaching changes under way in the region in the decades immediately following World War II. The combined effects of urban-based import-substitution industrialization, the prolonged neglect of the rural sector, and the population explosion caused by the rapid decline in the mortality rate contributed to rural out-migration and the sudden expansion of displaced peoples to the "margins" of central cities, in teeming urban slums, variously called *pueblos jovenes, barriadas,* or *favelas.*

A variety of descriptive terms were invoked to characterize different forms of marginality (Germani 1973). Urban immigrants were not just poor, but incompletely assimilated along more than one dimension. Marginality could be economic, political, cultural, or psychological (see Perlman 1976 and Germani 1973 and 1980). Yet the degree of marginality was not necessarily total for any individual or social group. A person could be marginal in one respect and not in another, as in the case of someone who works as a street peddler but belongs to the same ethnic group as the ruling class (Worsley 1984, 184). Like many others, Gino Germani's (1973, 87–88) approach to the problem of multidimensionality was to measure each attribute separately, then combine the results into a summary profile of marginality, asserting, all the while, that the various dimensions were, in reality, associated with one another, directly or otherwise.

Advocates of Lewis's (1954) "two-sector model," like proponents of Rostow's (1960) "stages of growth," envisioned the marginal poor as a transitory stage along the road to modernization, a temporal bottleneck to be over-come through economic growth. Rather than target specific groups or social processes (as we shall see in the case of social exclusion), they proposed solutions to marginality that were societal in scope and holistic in orienta-tion. When the patience of urban planners ran thin, a quick solution to the unsightly blemishes on the urban landscape was to deploy a battalion of bull-dozers to make short order of entire neighborhoods handcrafted out of scraps of wood, cardboard, and tarpaper.

Intense debates hinged on the functionality of marginal groups to the process of accumulation in the capitalist sector. The notion of marginality as a condition of separateness from the dominant society and economy was vig-orously challenged by Janice Perlman in her book *The Myth of Marginality*. On the basis of in-depth interviews in poor neighborhoods in Brazil, Perlman (1976, 243) showed that *favela* dwellers in Rio not only engaged in manu-facturing, transportation, and construction but also had the "aspirations of the bourgeoisie, the perseverance of pioneers, and the values of patriots." Others, such as José Nun (1969), held a different view. Nun proposed the concept of a "marginal mass" (*masa marginal*) to declare that, under the con-ditions of dependent capitalism, entire population groups were simply irrel-evant to the dominant sectors of the economy. Fernando Henrique Cardoso (1970) took issue with Nun, largely with respect to what he considered Nun's misreading of Marx. Lengthy polemics ensued, often turning on com-peting exegeses of Marx, as scholars assiduously scoured the ancient texts for "some hitherto overlooked passage, usually in the *Grundrisse* or Volume 3 of *Capital,* which might provide the required revelation" (Worsley 1984, 189).

While debates of this nature have not disappeared (see Nun 2001, chap. 5), they typified the kind of theoretical arguments that predominated in the 1960s and 1970s as researchers scrambled for concepts that could situate the reality of persistent poverty within a larger conceptualization of Latin Amer-ican economies. In their emphasis on macrolevel processes, it can arguably be concluded that the Marxist theoretical ruminations of the day were not wholly inconsistent with the modernization nemesis, at least insofar as both neglected concrete analyses of the historically situated actors, institutions, and processes that generated one or another type of marginality, and inasmuch as both discourses resided at the level of holistic abstractions. As Worsley (1984, 189) put it, "One hunts in vain through such texts for anything so mundane as a fact—or even a datum."

It is against this background that the concept of social exclusion may have found a footing, although the distinctiveness of the social exclusion agenda is easily obscured by its many similarities to marginality research, now four decades old. In keeping with the marginality literature, the social exclusion approach points to economic, political, and sociocultural arrangements that lead to material deprivation, the lack of citizenship participation, the denial of cultural rights, and the deficit of needs, associated with gender, age, ethnic identity, and religious beliefs (Gacitúa and Davis 2001, 14). As the list implies, the social exclusion agenda—like marginality studies before it—embraces a multidimensional approach and is alert to the cumulative effects of simulta-neous exclusion/marginality along more than one dimension.

These similarities notwithstanding, the social exclusion approach has fea-tures that set it apart from the theory and methods of marginality. If earlier research treated marginality as the composite of more or less separate dimen-sions, the "social exclusion framework" seeks to understand the linkages and interactions between the different risk factors that generate poverty and inequality, acknowledging that these factors are "not linked through linear causality but rather in a complex process of reciprocal causation and inter-actions" (Clert and Wodon 2001, 3).

Resonating with many of the same issues as marginality, yet offering a different approach, the social exclusion approach aspires to an empirical agenda that focuses on the institutional, cultural, and behavioral processes that produce social exclusion. Social exclusion thus gives greater attention to the mechanisms by which people are excluded from the standards of their society, whereas marginality was more concerned with the situation of exclu-sion (Roberts 2002, 115). Put another way, "marginality viewed lack of par-ticipation in the institutions of the modern state, such as the formal labor market, health and human services, as the reason for poverty. In contrast, the exclusion and vulnerability focuses warn that it is the way in which these institutions now operate that poses the real threat to equality" (Roberts 2002, 116).

Exclusion is therefore understood as a process, situated in time and place, and caused by initiatives taken by some people that redound to the detri-ment of others. The social exclusion framework thus invokes the notion of social agency, inasmuch as exclusion points to active processes by which certain groups deny equal access to services and opportunities (Buvinic 2003, 2). "Social exclusion does not just happen," as Angleton and Parker (2003, 3, emphasis in original) note, "it has to be *made to happen*."

Social agency is further attributed to, or expected of, the excluded them-selves. Resuscitating Paulo Freire's (1982) pedagogical principles, authors commonly invoke the notion of "popular education" as a way to unleash the power of resistance on the part of excluded social groups and communities (e.g., Byrne 1999, 133–34; Aggleton and Parker 2003, 14). Empowerment is presumed to promote social solidarity, and to increase the voice and policy influence of excluded groups in local and national agendas (Buvinic 2003, 10). The process of empowerment relies on structures that people themselves produce by getting together and getting organized. In keeping with the literature on community-based conservation efforts (see Agrawal 1997), mobilization can involve voluntary organizations, neighborhood associations, NGOs, and so on (Gacitúa, Sojo, and Davis 2001, 4). Skeptics of empowerment contend that "techniques of this kind may prove to be more beneficial to facilitators and educators who wish to cling to the vestiges of a personally rewarding form of 'radical' practice rather than to those disadvantaged members of the community for whom the promise of a better tomorrow appears to be as far away as ever" (Page 1992, 92).

The emphasis on community organization establishes an affinity between the social exclusion framework and the concept of social capital (Putnam 1993a, 1995). A good stock of social capital—that is, well-developed norms of trust, reciprocity, and cooperation—is considered a necessary foundation for the creation of networks that promote collective action, peaceful politics, and the ability to effectively shape public institutions. Accumulated social capital is presumed to reduce transactions costs and facilitate people working together (Roberts 2002, 117), enabling them collectively to pressure for their greater inclusion within society. Social capital thus "enables individuals in society to cooperate, to take risks and short cuts in social relations, and to achieve social goals collectively that could not be achieved individually" (Newton 2001, 657).

Not all social networks and voluntary organizations promote harmony or common interests, as in the case of the Mafia, or extremist political or sectarian religious groups. The "downside of social capital" can therefore promote social exclusion by limiting personal freedom, denying access to certain occupations or industries, and by exerting downward leveling pressures that impede participants from rising above their situation of exclusion (Portes and Landolt 1996).

It thus appears that social capital and social exclusion intersect in two ways, at least at the community level. When collective action is proposed as a solution to social exclusion, the strategy relies on the "bridging associations" that social capital theory sees as necessary for transcending social divisions. When the social exclusion framework laments the cultural, political, and institutional networks that deny people full participation in society, the analytical focus points to the "exclusive associations" that social capital theory sees as promoting differences, divisions, and discrimination.

As these observations suggest, the issues called to mind by the social exclusion framework resonate with many of the topics once studied under the heading of marginality. Yet it is the fusion of processes (not outcomes) under a single umbrella that imparts a certain novelty to the concept of social exclusion, offering the potential of a fresh approach to long-standing problems. The image of overlapping exclusions, each with their own dynamic, yet interacting with the others in complex and cumulative ways, is a compelling one that potentially takes us beyond the limits of marginality. Devising a method and generating the data capable of living up to the ambitious vision is another matter.

Methods, Design, and the Social Exclusion Agenda

Even staunch proponents of quantitative methods recognize the need for broader approaches to data collection and interpretation. The World Bank, for one, has enriched its quantitative tradition with participatory research and qualitative approaches that range from key informant interviews to focus groups (Gacitúa-Marió and Wodon 2001). Examples of attempts to integrate various methods include studies of reproductive health in Argentina (Gacitúa-Marió, Sians, and Wodon 2001), research on social programs in Chile (Clert and Wodon 2001), analyses of social exclusion in urban Uruguay (Baker 2001), and multidimensional studies of social exclusion and inequality in Peru (Figueroa, Altamirano, and Sulmont 1996).

Yet for all their ambitious intentions, such initiatives remain hamstrung by the lack of clear rules for integrating quantitative and qualitative methods. As a result, even notable efforts to bridge the quantitative/qualitative divide tend to fall short of truly coming to grips with the core insight of the social exclusion perspective. More generally, the limitations inherent to the methods and materials at hand whittle flights of conceptual fancy down to manageable levels, ultimately resulting in analyses that much resemble the "same old thing."

The emphasis on social agency—central to the social exclusion framework, and quite different from marginality—further demands novel approaches to research design and data collection that, for the most part, remain esoteric to mainstream social science and inconsistent with conventional strategies of data collection and interpretation. By invoking agency, social exclusion necessarily delves into the interactions of at least two social actors—the "excluder(s)" on the one side, and the "excluded" on the other. The agents may be individuals, domestic units, ethnic groups, or social classes that interact with one another, often within the confines of some institutional structure. Between the two extremes, there are social networks, intermediate institutions, and cultural agents that can avoid, reduce, increase, or accelerate the interactions between the excluders and the excluded (Figueroa, Altamirano, and Sulmont 1996, 23).

By giving priority to social agency, the analyst is thrust into "actor-oriented" perspectives developed by the likes of anthropologist Norman Long (2001) and sociologists Jaber Gubrium and James Holstein (1997). Long's (2001, 71–92, 240) notion of analyses at the "interface" is particularly promising because it focuses on at least four relevant dimensions: (1) the ordering processes—rather than "order" *per se*—relevant to different institutional domains; (2) the social relations and networks, as well as meanings and values, that are generated within different arenas; (3) the critical interfaces that depict points of contradiction or discontinuity between different, often incompatible, interests, including not only "local" actors but also "intervening" institutional actors; and (4) the social construction, and continuous reconstruction, of the knowledge and power structures that govern the interaction between actors, thereby determining the outcome of those interactions. The perspective is compelling and eminently pertinent to the conceptual issues called into play by the social exclusion framework. At the same time, the approach demands skills that are hard to come by and requires an epistemological stance that is fundamentally counterintuitive to conventional positivist perspectives.

Further appreciation of the social exclusion challenge is enhanced by the daunting realization that each of the economic, political, and cultural contexts to which the framework refers differs in terms of the respective processes at work, the variables at hand, and the temporal rhythms in which events play themselves out. Common sense may be quite comfortable with the idea that one form of integration can offset another form of exclusion. Or that multiple forms of exclusion can have perverse and cumulative negative feedbacks. However, the task of demonstrating the magnitude of such effects and the possibility of garnering a practical understanding of the underlying processes—and their multiple interactions—push available methods and accessible data to the limits of existing practice. Waxing eloquent about the need to "go dynamic" and "nonlinear" in order to deal with "emergence, bifurcation, complexity and the possibility of willed alternatives" (Byrne 1995, 5) may stir one's conceptual imagination, only to find those imaginings frustrated by the stubborn limitations of data collection and analysis.

In a more positive vein, it is worth noting that some forms of exclusion—especially those associated with race, ethnicity, and perhaps sexual preference—lend themselves to direct intervention via legislative action. Laws against discrimination have been passed in a number of countries in Latin America, prohibiting discrimination against minorities of every sort. Associated initiatives recommend the strengthening of the rights of victims to sue employers and others through the institution of contingency fee arrangements that would provide the incentive for private attorneys to represent victims of discrimination (Cottrol and Hernandez 2001). Affirmative action programs often accompany legislative efforts, such as the largely successful initiatives to increase women's participation in legislatures, which rose during the 1990s by more than 50 percent (Buvinic 2003, 10; see also Rohter 2003). It can be argued that such targeted approaches represent an advance over the tendency of marginality analyses to passively await macroeconomic growth for eventual redress. Nonetheless, there remains in nearly every country a deep chasm between the enactment of noble laws on the one hand and effective enforcement on the other.

Attempts to develop policies and programs to overcome social exclusion necessarily highlight the priority given to the collection of accurate data on such characteristics as the population's ethnic and racial composition (among other attributes, such as disability). At a minimum, the demand for information requires that census bureaus develop meaningful indicators of minority identity and generate a stable classification system—in order to estimate the magnitude of exclusion that may exist and assess the effectiveness over time of intervention policies. Both objectives appear relatively straightforward, yet a closer look at racial classification in Brazil amply demonstrates the difficulties involved.

Measuring Racial and Ethnic Exclusion

Improving the quality of censuses and household surveys to include information disaggregated by gender, race and ethnicity, disability, age, and other features associated with exclusion is considered a basic step that governments can take to promote inclusion (Buvinic 2003; Aggleton and Parker 2003; Zoninsein 2001). Information of this kind is deemed critical for the allocation of public resources, the targeting of intervention initiatives, and the assessment of program success. At present, twelve countries in the region included questions on ethnicity and race in the 2000 round of census enumerations, many for the first time, such as Honduras and Peru (Buvinic 2003, 7).

The task of devising a valid and reliable typology of majority/minority status is especially challenging in Latin America and the Caribbean, where the subjective differentiations that produce significant material consequences in daily life are culturally blurred, covertly practiced, and officially denied. Indicative of the difficulties ahead are the problems that beset the collection of data on skin color in Brazil.

Putting aside any pretense of measuring "race" in the genetic sense of the word, the Brazilian census bureau simply asks respondents to choose their own identity among pre-coded options: white (*branco*), black (*preto*), brown (*pardo*), yellow (*amarelo*), and "Indian" (*indígena*). This method of data collection is subject to three major caveats that apply not only to Brazil but also to other countries whose populations include a significant number of people of indigenous or African descent.

The first issue pits the simplified typology of surveys and censuses against the extraordinary complexity of the system of color classification that Brazilians commonly use in their daily lives. Anthropological research on race relations in Brazil amply documents the fine distinctions Brazilians make when asked to identify a person's skin color. Armed with a set of portrait drawings, Marvin Harris (1964) was among the first to inventory the range of terms applied to people who varied with respect to hair texture, skin tone, and various facial markers. The pictures elicited forty different racial types that "grade into each other like the colors of the spectrum and no one category stands significantly isolated from all the rest" (M. Harris 1964, 57). More recently, an open-ended question on racial self-identification included in the 1976 National Household Survey (PNAD) elicited nearly two hundred different terms (N. Silva 1988, 38). The subtle and fluid character of the subjective identification of race in Brazil questions the validity of the simplified census scheme.

A second caveat concerns the conflation of class and color, and the associated mutability of skin color identity. As in many other countries in the region, a dark-skinned Brazilian who is also poor is likely to be thought of, and to classify him- or herself, as black (*preto*). On the other hand, a high-status person of the same dark tone is more likely to be thought of, and to classify him or herself, as brown (*pardo* or *moreno*), or some other term closer to the white end of the color continuum (see Telles and Lim 1998).

Subjective identity in Brazil is therefore based on physical appearance in combination with other factors, such as income, education, and related insignias of social rank.

The multidimensional basis of racial identity suggests the possibility that an upwardly mobile individual who identifies him- or herself as black at one point in time may, after rising in socioeconomic status, reclassify him- or herself as brown later on. To estimate the mobility of people from one color category to another, one study measured the magnitude of color reclassification between the 1950 and 1980 census by applying the forward survival technique demographers commonly use to estimate net rural migration (Wood and Carvalho 1994). The findings showed that over the thirty-year period, the black color category experienced a loss of around 38 percent; the intermediate brown category experienced a net gain of 36 percent; and the white color category remained comparatively stable over time (with a net loss of 9 percent among men). The magnitude of "migration" across color categories clearly indicated that a large number of people who identified themselves as black in 1950 reclassified themselves as brown in 1980. Estimates for the 1980/1990 period, adjusted for the effects of international migration, reveal the same pattern, although the magnitude of color reclassification may have declined somewhat during the 1980s (Carvalho, Wood, and Andrade 2004).

If color reclassification is prevalent, and if it is selective of upwardly mobile individuals, the instability of skin color identity over time has critical methodological implications for any study that uses census data (or their equivalent) to investigate changes in the exclusion of Brazil's black and brown populations. Among other things, the selective "outmigration" of upwardly mobile individuals from the black category introduces a downward bias in analyses that seek to track the progress of blacks over time.

The selectivity bias, together with the relative small percentage of people who declare themselves black in Brazil (5.9 percent in 1980), has prompted researchers to merge the black and brown designations into a single Afro-Brazilian category (e.g., Lovell 1994; Wood and Carvalho 1988; Wood and Lovell 1992), or to use both the aggregated and separated versions in the same study (e.g., Lovell 2000a and 2000b). It is not surprising that the strategy of converting the already simplified census typology to a white/Afro-Brazilian dichotomy has been criticized for imposing an inappropriate bipolar racial scheme on Brazil (Harris et al. 1993). Others contend that, regardless of the profusion of linguistic terms that apply to gradations of skin color, in the practice of daily interactions, the great divide is nonetheless between white and nonwhite (Andrews 1991; Sheriff 2001).

The Brazilian case advises caution with respect to any attempt to objectively and reliably classify people by race, skin color, ethnicity, or other contested identities. The fear is to implicitly endorse an unwarranted "essentialist" stance that presumes to identify and record some immutable core quality (e.g., the state of being "black," or "Indian"), and then proceed to associate that essential quality with a presumably independent social attribute (e.g., being poor). Reasoning of this kind runs counter to the recognition that social identities are constructed (and continuously reconstructed) within a fluid economic and political context, manipulated by members of both dominant and excluded groups, often in consciously strategic ways. The dynamic interplay between subjective experiences and ascriptive differences imbues a shifting quality to social identities that are thoroughly embedded in the very contexts of exclusion that are the object of concern. Ignoring these dilemmas is to run the risk of falling into circular logic, where the classification of particular individuals is, itself, a function of their degree of exclusion.

The formidable problem of devising a valid and reliable method of producing an accurate typology of the racial and ethnic composition of populations in Latin America and the Caribbean is further exacerbated by hegemonic national self-images that deny the existence and severity of prejudice and discrimination on home ground. People in the region are justifiably proud of the absence of officially condoned forms of outright racism associated with the U.S. South during the Jim Crow era or South Africa during apartheid. Yet notions of "social democracy," and the surface "cordiality" characteristic of intergroup relations, so thoroughly mask the prevalence of less obvious (but no less insidious) forms of inequality and discrimination that it is often difficult to persuade public officials to take effective action, even when the data reveal systematic patterns of social exclusion.

In contrast to the marginality perspective, the promise of the social exclusion approach lies in (1) its emphasis on process, rather than a focus on outcomes; (2) its attention to human agency, rather than a reliance on structural mechanisms that operate "without subjects"; (3) its attempt to conceptualize the offsetting and amplifying interconnections between different axes of exclusion, rather than aggregating the various domains of exclusion; (4) its promotion of targeted proposals that promote legal protections and opportunities for particular individuals and groups, rather than relying on the redemptive qualities of macroeconomic growth; and (5) its commitment to social networks and mobilization in the struggle for visibility and rights, rather treating marginal groups a passive victims of impersonal forces.

For some (see Hills 2002, 240), the concept of social exclusion diverts attention toward "softer and fuzzier" issues, and away from the more difficult—and more expensive—issues of deprivation and inequality. Others (see Hills, Le Grand, and Piachaud 2002) are more optimistic, concluding that the social exclusion framework can significantly change how we think about poverty, deprivation, and disadvantage, and can contribute to the formulation of effective policy interventions. Whether its potential is realized will largely depend on developing the methods and data required to address the conceptual issues at its heart.

References

Abers, Rebecca. 1998. "Learning Democratic Practice: Distributing Government Resources Through Popular Participation in Porto Alegre, Brazil." In *Cities for Citizens: Planning and the Rise of Civil Society in a Global Age,* ed. Mike Douglas and John Friedmann. Chichester: John Wiley and Sons

Abrams, C. 1966. *Squatter Settlements, the Problem and the Opportunity.* Washington, D.C.: Department of Housing and Urban Development.

Aggleton, Peter, and Richard Parker. 2003. "Understanding and Countering Social Exclusion in the Americas: A Conceptual Framework and Implications for Action." Paper prepared for the seminar "Good Practices in Social Inclusion: A Dialogue Between Europe and Latin America and the Caribbean," Milan, Italy, March 21–22.

Agrawal, Arun. 1997. *Community in Conservation: Beyond Enchantment and Disenchantment.* CDF Discussion Paper. Gainesville, Fla.: Conservation and Development Forum.

Aguilar Camin, Hector. 2000. *Mexico: la ceniza y la semilla.* Mexico City: Cal y Arena.

Aguirre, Carlos, and Robert Buffington. 2000. *Reconstructing Criminality in Latin America.* Wilmington, Del.: Scholarly Resources.

Alba, Francisco, and Joseph E. Potter. 1986. "Population and Development in Mexico Since 1940: An Interpretation." *Population and Development Review* 12:47–75.

Alexander, Jeffrey. 1995. *Fin de Siècle Social Theory. Relativism, Reduction, and the Problem of Reason.* London: Verso Books.

Alexander, J., and Philip Smith. 2000. "Ciencias Sociales y Salvación: Sociedad del Riesgo como Discurso Mítico." In *Sociologia Cultural. Formas de Clasificiación en las Sociedades Complejas,* ed. Jeffrey Alexander. Mexico City: Anthropos-FLACSO-Mexico.

Almeida, A.L.O. de. n.d. *Share Tenancy and Family Size in the Brazilian Northeast.* Rio de Janeiro: Instituto de Planeamiento Economico e Social.

ALOP (Associación Latinoamericana de Organizaciones de Promoción). 1999. *¿Que rol cabe a ALOP y a las ONG en la América Latina de hoy? Retos y perspectivas.* Informe sobre el estudio "Cambios institucionales de las ONG de A. Latina." San José, Costa Rica.

Alvarez, Artuor, and Sonia Escobar, eds. 1992. *The Making of Social Movements in Latin America: Identity, Strategy, and Democracy.* Boulder, Colo.: Westview Press.

Alvarez, Sonia E., Evelina Dagnino, and Arturo Escobar, eds. 1998. *Cultures of Politics, Politics of Cultures: Re-visioning Latin American Social Movements.* Boulder, Colo.: Westview Press.

Andrade-Eckhoff, Katharine. 1997. "Asociaciones salvadoreñas en Los Angeles y las posibilidades de desarrollo en El Salvador." In *Migración y Desarrollo Internacional,* vol. 2, ed. M. Lungo. San Salvador: FUNDE.

Andrews, George Reid. 1991. *Blacks and Whites in São Paulo, Brazil, 1888–1998*. Madison: University of Wisconsin Press.

Angell, Alan, and Carol Graham. 1995. "Can Social Sector Reform Make Adjustment Sustainable and Equitable? Lessons from Chile and Venezuela." *Journal of Latin American Studies* 27 (February): 189–219.

Arendt, Hannah. 1973. *The Origins of Totalitarianism*. New York: Harcourt, Brace, and World.

Ariza, Marina. 1994. "Familias y pobreza, menores deambulantes en República Dominicana." *Nueva Sociedad* 129 (January-February): 90–103.

———. 2000. *Ya no soy la que deje atrás . . . Mujeres migrantes en República Dominicana*. Mexico City: Instituto de Investigaciones Sociales/UNAM/Plaza Valdez.

———. 2002. "Migración, familia y transnacionalidad en el contexto de la globalización: Algunos puntos de reflexión." *Revista Mexicana de Sociología* 64, no. 4:53–84.

Ariza, Marina, and Orlandina de Oliveira. 1999a. "Formación y dinámica familiar en México, Centroamérica y el Caribe." In *México diverso y desigual: Enfoques sociodemográficos*, ed. Beatriz Figueroa. Mexico City: El Colegio de México / Somete.

———. 1999b. "Escenarios contrastantes: Patrones de formación familiar en el Caribe y Europa Occidental." *Estudios Sociológicos* 17, no. 51:815–36.

———. 1999c. "Género y clase como ejes de inequidad: Una mirada metodológica." Paper presented at the *Primer Congreso de Ciencias Sociales, Consejo Mexicano de Ciencias Sociales* A.C. México, Mexico City, April 2.

Arriagada, Irma. 1994. "Transformaciones del trabajo femenino urbano." *Revista de la CEPAL* 53 (August): 91–110.

———. 1997. *Políticas sociales, familia y trabajo en la América Latina de fin de siglo*. Santiago: ECLA-U.N.

———. 1998. "Familias Latinoamericanas: Convergencias y divergencias de modelos y políticas." *Revista de la CEPAL* 65 (August): 85–102.

Arrighi, Giovanni. 1994. *The Long Twentieth Century: Money, Power, and the Origins of Our Times*. London: Verso Books.

Arrighi, Giovanni, and Beverly Silver. 1999. *Chaos and Governance in the Modern World System*. Minneapolis: University of Minnesota Press.

Assies, Willem. 1990. *Structures of Power, Movements of Resistance: An Introduction to the Theories of Urban Movements in Latin America*. Edited by Willem Assies, Gerrit Burgwal, and Ton Salman. Amsterdam: CEDLA.

Auyero, Javier. 2001. *La política de los pobres. Las prácticas clientelistas del peronismo*. Buenos Aires: Manantial. Published in English under the title *Poor People's Politics* (Durham: Duke University Press).

Babb, Sarah. 2001. *Managing Mexico: Economists from Nationalism to Neoliberalism*. New York: Routledge.

Baiocchi, Gianpaolo. 2000. "Participation, Activism, and Politics: The Porto Alegre Experiment and Deliberative Democratic Theory." Paper delivered at the Experiments for Deliberative Democracy Conference, Madison, Wis., January.

———. 2003. "Participation, Activism, and Politics: The Porto Alegre Experiment in Participatory Governance." In *Deepening Democracy: Institutional Innovations in*

Empowered Participatory Governance, ed. Archon Fung and Erik Olin Wright. London: Verso Books.

Bair, Jennifer, and Gary Gereffi. 1999. "Industrial Upgrading, Networks, and Employment in Global Industries." Paper presented to IILS/CAMAT Regional Workshop, "Decent Work and Global Competition: New Roles for Enterprises and Their Organization," Port of Spain, Trinidad and Tobago, October.

Bairoch, Paul, and Richard Kozul-Wright. 1998. "Globalization and Its Limits." In *Transnational Corporations and the Global Economy,* ed. Richard Kozul-Wright and Robert Rowthorn. New York: St. Martin's Press.

Baker, Judy L. 2001. "Social Exclusion in Urban Uruguay." In *Measurement and Meaning: Combining Quantitative and Qualitative Methods for the Analysis of Poverty and Social Exclusion in Latin America,* ed. Estanislao Gacitúa-Marió and Quentin Wodon. Washington, D.C.: The World Bank.

Balan, Jorge, Harley Browning, and Elizabeth Jelin. 1973. *Men in a Developing Society: Geographic and Social Mobility in Monterrey, Mexico.* Austin: University of Texas Press.

Banco Interamericano de Desarrollo. 1997. "América Latina tras una década de reformas progreso económico y social en América Latina, informe 1997." Bulletin. Washington, D.C.: IADB.

———. 2000. "Desarrollo: Más allá de la economía—Informe 2000." Bulletin. Washington, D.C.: IADB.

Banco Mundial. 2000. "Lucha contra la pobreza: Informe sobre el desarrollo mundial 2000/2001." Bulletin. New York: The World Bank, September.

Bangura, Yusuf. 2002. "Racism, Citizenship and Social Justice." *UNISRD News* 25:1–3.

Barbalet, J. M. 1988. *Citizenship: Rights, Struggle and Class Inequality.* Milton Keynes, U.K.: Open University Press.

Barkey, Karen, and Sunita Parikh. 1991. "Comparative Perspectives on the State." *Annual Review of Sociology* 17:523–49.

Baross, Paul. 1990. "Sequencing Land Development: The Price Implication of Legal and Illegal Settlement Growth." In *The Transformation of Land Supply Systems in Third World Cities,* ed. P. Baross and J. van der Linden. Aldershot: Avebury.

Barreto, Maria Inés. 1998. "Las organizaciones sociales en la reforma del estado Brasileño." In *Lo público no estatal en la reforma del estado,* ed. Luiz Carlos Bresser Pereira and Nuria Cunill Grau. Buenos Aires: Paidós.

Barrios, Alicia, and Jose Joaquin Brunner. 1988. *La Sociologia en Chile.* Santiago: FLACSO.

Basu, Alaka M. 1997. "The New International Population Movement: A Framework for a Constructive Critique." In "Cairo's Legacy: Where Is the International Population Movement Going?" Special issue, *Health Transition Review* 7:7–31.

Batliwala, Srilatha. 1994. "The Meaning of Women's Empowerment: New Concepts from Action." In *Population Politics Reconsidered. Health, Empowerment, and Rights,* ed. Sen Gita, Adrienne Germain, and Lincoln C. Chen. Boston: Harvard Center for Population and Development Studies / International Women's Health Coalition.

Beck, S. H., and K. Mijeski. 2001. "Barricades and Ballots: Ecuador's Indians and the Pachacutik Political Movement." *Ecuadorian Studies/Estudios Ecuatorianos* 1, http://www.yachana.org/ecuatorianistas/journal/1/1.html.

Beck, Ulrich. 1998. *La sociedad del riesgo*. Barcelona: Piados Básica.

———. 2000. *Un nuevo mundo feliz. La precariedad del trabajo en la era de la globalización*. Barcelona: Piados Básica.

———. 2001. "Vivir nuestra propia vida en un mundo desbocado: individuación, globalización y política." In *En el límite. La vida en el capitalismo global*, ed. A. Giddens and W. Hutton. Madrid: Tusquets Editores.

Bell, Daniel. 1978. *The Cultural Contradictions of Capitalism*. New York: Basic Books.

Bendix, Reinhard. 1962. *From Max Weber: An Intellectual Portrait*. Part 2. Garden City, N.Y.: Anchor Books.

Benería, Lourdes. 1992. "The Mexican Debt Crisis: Restructuring the Economy and the Household." In *Unequal Burden: Economic Crises, Persistent Poverty, and Women's Work*, ed. Lourdes Benería and Shelley Feldman. Boulder, Colo.: Westview Press.

Benería, Lourdes, and Marta Roldán. 1987. *The Crossroads of Class and Gender. Industrial Homework, Subcontracting and Household Dynamics in Mexico City*. Chicago: University of Chicago Press.

Berquo, Elsa. 1999. "The ICPD Programme of Action and Reproductive Health Policy Development in Brazil." *Reproductive Health: Programme and Policy*, 24–41.

Biaocchi, Gianpaolo. 2003. "Participation, Activism, and Politics: The Porto Alegre Experiment and Democratic Theory." In *The Real Utopia Project: Deepening Democracy—Institutional Innovations in Empowered Participatory Governance*, ed. Archon Fung and Erik Olin Wright. London: Verso Books.

Birkbeck, C. 1978. "Self-employed Proletariats in an Informal Factory: The Case of Cali's Garbage Dump." *World Development* 6:1173–85.

Birou, A. 1997. "Las fuerzas hegemónicas de la mundialización." *Estudios Sociales* 90:9–28.

Bloom, D., D. Canning, and P. Malaney. 2000. "Demographic Change and Economic Growth in Asia." *Population and Development Review* 26:257–90.

Bloom, D., and J. Williamson. 1998. "Demographic Transitions and Economic Miracles in Emerging Asia." *World Bank Economics Review* 12:419–56.

Blumberg, Rae Lesser. 1991. "Introduction: The Triple Overlap of Gender, Stratification, Economy and the Family." In *Gender, Family and Economy: The Triple Overlap*, ed. Rae Lesser Blumberg. Newbury Park, Calif.: Sage Publications.

Boschi, Renato. 1987. "Social Movements and the New Political Order in Brazil." In *State and Society in Brazil*, ed. John D. Wirth, Edson de Oliveira Nunes, and Thomas E. Bogenschild. Boulder, Colo.: Westview Press.

Bourdieu, Pierre.1980. "Le capital social: Notes provisoires." *Actes de la Recherche en Sciences Sociales* 31:2–3.

———. 1985. "The Forms of Capital." In *Handbook of Theory and Research for the Sociology of Education*, ed. J. G. Richardson. New York: Greenwood Press.

Brachet-Márquez, Viviane. 1994. *The Dynamics of Domination: State, Class and Social Reform in Mexico, 1910–1990*. Pittsburgh: University of Pittsburgh Press.

Brambila, Carlos. 1998. "Mexico's Population Policy and Demographic Dynamics:

The Record of Three Decades." In *Do Population Policies Matter? Fertility and Politics in Egypt, India, Kenya, and Mexico,* ed. Anrudh Jain. New York: Population Council.

Bresser Pereira, Luis Carlos. 1993. "Economic Reforms and Economic Growth: Efficiency and Politics in Latin America." In *Economic Reform in New Democracies: A Social Democratic Approach,* ed. L. C. Bresser Pereira, J. M. Maravall, and A. Przeworski. Cambridge: Cambridge University Press.

———. 1997. *Cidadania e res publica: a emergência dos dereitos republicanos.* Texto para Discussâo 15. Brasilia: ENAP.

———. 1999. "Managerial Public Administration: Strategy and Structure for a New State." In *Reforming the State: Managerial Public Administration in Latin America,* ed. L. Bresser Pereira and P. Spink. Boulder, Colo.: Lynne Rienner.

Bresser Pereira, Luis Carlos, and Nuria Cunill Grau, eds. 1998. "Entre el estado y el mercado: lo público no estatal." In *Lo público no estatal en la reforma del estado,* ed. Luiz Carlos Bresser Pereira and Nuria Cunill Grau. Buenos Aires: Paidós.

Bresser Pereira, Luis Carlos, and P. Spink, eds. 1999. *Reforming the State: Managerial Public Administration in Latin America.* Boulder, Colo.: Lynne Rienner.

Briceño-Leon, Roberto, and Heinz R. Sonntag. 1998. "La sociología de América Latina entre pueblo, época y desarrollo." In *Pueblo, época y desarrollo: La sociología de América Latina,* ed. R. Briceño-León and H. R. Sonntag. Caracas: Nueva Sociedad.

Bromley, Ray. 1978. "The Urban Informal Sector: Why Is It Worth Discussing?" *World Development* 6:1033–39.

———. 1994. "Informality, de Soto Style: From Concept to Policy." In *Contrapunto: The Informal Sector Debate in Latin America,* ed. C. A. Rakowski. Albany: SUNY Press.

———, ed. 1979. *The Urban Informal Sector: Critical Perspectives on Employment and Housing Policies.* Oxford: Pergamon Press.

Bromley, R., and C. Gerry, eds. 1979. *Casual Work and Poverty in Third World Cities.* London: John Wiley and Sons.

Bronfman, M., E. López, and R. Tuirán. 1986. "Práctica anticonceptiva y clases sociales en México: La experiencia reciente." *Estudios Demográficos y Urbanos* 1, no. 2.

Brubaker, Rogers. 1992. *Citizenship and Nationhood in France and Germany.* Cambridge: Harvard University Press.

Brunner, José Joaquin. 1988. *El Modo de Hacer Sociología en Chile.* Santiago: FLACSO.

Bruschini, Cristina. 1994. "Trabalho femenino: Trajetória de um tema, perspectivas para o futuro." *Estudios Feministas* 1:17–33.

Bulmer-Thomas, Victor. 1997. Introduction to *El nuevo modelo económico en América Latina. Su efecto en la distribución del ingreso y en la pobreza,* ed. V. Bulmer-Thomas. Mexico City: Fondo de Cultura Económica.

Burki, Shahid Javed, and Guillermo Perry. 1997. *The Long March: A Reform Agenda for Latin America and the Caribbean in the Next Decade.* Washington, D.C.: The World Bank.

Buvinic, Mayra. 2003. "Social Inclusion in Latin America and the Caribbean: Experience and Lessons." Paper prepared for the seminar "Good Practices in Social

Inclusion: A Dialogue Between Europe and Latin America and the Caribbean," Milan, Italy, March 21–22.

Byrne, David. 1999. *Social Exclusion.* Buckingham: Open University Press.

Caldeira, Teresa Pires de Rio. 1990. "Women, Daily Life, and Politics." In *Women and Social Change in Latin America,* ed. Elizabeth Jelin. London: UNRISD / Zed Books.

———. 1996. "La delincuencia y los derechos individuales: redefiniendo la violencia en América Latina." In *Construir la democracia: derechos humanos, ciudadanía y sociedad en América Latina,* ed. Elizabeth Jelin and Eric Hershberg. Caracas: Nueva Sociedad.

Calderón, Fernando, ed. 1986. *Los Movimientos sociales ante la crisis.* Buenos Aires: CLACSO.

Calderón, Fernando, and Elizabeth Jelin, eds. 1987. *Clases y movimientos sociales en América Latina: perspectivas y realidades.* Buenos Aires: CEDES.

Calderón, Fernando and Norberto Lechner, 1998. "Más allá del estado, más allá del mercado, la democracia. La Paz, Bolivia. Plural Editores.

Camargo, Candido Procopio Ferreira de. 1976. *São Paulo, Crescimento e Pobreza.* São Paulo: Edições Loyola.

Camdessus, Michel. 1997. "Reglas, instituciones y estrategias para el bien común en una economía global." *Estudios Sociales* 88:9–28.

Campbell, T. 2003. *The Quiet Revolution: Decentralization and the Rise of Political Participation in Latin American Cities.* Pittsburgh: University of Pittsburgh Press.

Candina Palomer, Azun. 2002. "El día interminable. Memoria e instalación del 11 de septiembre de 1973 en Chile." In *Las conmemoraciones: las disputas en las fechas "in-felices,"* ed. Elizabeth Jelin. Madrid: Siglo XXI de España Editores; Buenos Aires: Siglo XXI de Argentina Editores.

Cardoso, Fernando Henrique. 1964. *Empresario industrial e desenvolvimento econômico no Brasil.* São Paulo: Difusão Europeia do Livro.

———. 1970. "Comentario sobre los conceptos de Sobrepopulación relativa y marginalidad." *Revista Latinoamericana de Ciencias Sociales.* Santiago: ELAS-ICIS.

———. 1971a. "Comentários sobre os conceitos de superpopulação relative e marginalidade." *Estudios CEBRAP* 1: 99–130.

———. 1971b. *Ideologías de la burguesía industrial en sociedades dependientes (Argentina y Brasil).* Mexico City: Siglo Veintiuno Editores.

———. 1999. Foreword to *Reforming the State: Managerial Public Administration in Latin America,* ed. L. Bresser Pereira and P. Spink. Boulder, Colo.: Lynne Rienner.

Cardoso, Fernando H., and Enzo Faletto. 1967. *Dependencia y desarrollo en América Latina.* Mexico City: Fondo de Cultura Económica.

———. 1969. *Dependencia y desarrollo en América Latina.* Mexico City: Siglo Veintiuno Editores.

———. 1970. *Dependência e desenvolvimento en America Latina: ensaio de interpretação sociológica.* Rio de Janeiro: Jorge Zahar.

———. 1979. *Dependency and Development in Latin America.* Berkeley and Los Angeles: University of California Press.

Cardoso, Ruth Corrêa Leite. 1992. "Popular Movements in the Context of the Consolidation of Democracy in Brazil." In *The Making of Social Movements in Latin America: Identity, Strategy, and Democracy,* ed. Arturo Escobar and Sonia E. Alvarez. Boulder, Colo.: Westview Press.

Carrillo, Jorge. 1995. "La experiencia latinoamericana del justo a tiempo y del control total de calidad." *Revista Latinoamericana de Estudios del Trabajo* 1:193–205.

Carrillo, Jorge, and Alfredo Hualde. 1998. "Third Generation Maquiladoras? The Delphi-General Motors Case." *Journal of Borderlands Studies* 8, no. 1:79–97.

Carrillo, Jorge, and Consuelo Iranzo. 2000. "Calificación y competencias laborales en América Latina." In *Tratado latinoamericano de sociología del trabajo,* ed. E. de la Garza. Mexico City: El Colegio de México / FLACSO / UAM / Fondo de Cultura Económica.

Carvalho, J.A.M. de, P. de T. A. Paiva, and D. R. Sawyer. 1981. "The Recent Sharp Decline in Fertility in Brazil: Economic Boom, Social Inequality and Baby Bust." Population Council Working Paper no. 8. Mexico City.

Carvalho, José Alberto, Charles H. Wood, and Flávia Cristina Drummond Andrade. 2004. "Estimating the Stability of Census-based Racial/Ethnic Classifications: The Case of Brazil." *Population Studies* 58(3): 331–43.

Castañeda, Jorge. 1993. *Utopia Unarmed.* New York: Knopf.

Castel, Robert. 1997. *La metamorfosis de la cuestión social. Una crónica del salariado.* Buenos Aires: Paidós.

Castells, M. 1977. *The Urban Question: A Marxist Approach.* London: Edward Arnold.

———. 1979. *City, Class and Power.* London: Macmillan.

———. 1983. *The City and Grassroots.* London: Edward Arnold.

———. 1996. *The Rise of Network Society.* Vol. 1 of *The Information Age: Economy, Society, and Culture.* Oxford: Basil Blackwell.

———. 1998. *End of Millennium.* Vol. 3 of *The Information Age: Economy, Society, and Culture.* Oxford: Basil Blackwell.

Catela, Ludmila da Silva, and Elizabeth Jelin, eds. 2002. *Los archivos de la represión: Documentos, memoria y verdad.* Madrid: Siglo XXI de España Editores; Buenos Aires: Siglo XXI de Argentina Editores.

CELADE (Centro Latinoamericano de Demografía, and Community and Family Study Center [CFSC]). 1972. *Fertility and Family Planning in Metropolitan Latin America.* Chicago: University of Chicago Press.

Centeno, Miguel Angel. 1994. *Democracy Within Reason.* University Park: Pennsylvania State University Press.

———. 2002. *Blood and Debt: War and the Nation-State in Latin America.* University Park: Pennsylvania State University Press.

Centeno, Miguel, and Fernando Lopes-Alves, eds. 2001. *The Other Mirror: Grand Theory Through the Lens of Latin America.* Princeton: Princeton University Press.

CEPAL. 1990. *Transformación productiva con equidad.* Santiago: CEPAL.

———. 1994. *Panorama Social de América Latina.* Santiago: CEPAL.

———. 1995. *Panorama Social de América Latina.* Santiago: CEPAL.

———. 2000. *Equidad, desarrollo y ciudadanía.* (LC/G.2071/Rev.1-P). Santiago: CEPAL.

———. 2001. "Una década de luces y sombras: América Latina y el Caribe en los años noventa." Alfaomega, Colombia: CEPAL.

Cerrutti, Marcela. 2000. "El problema del desempleo: el caso argentino en el contexto latinoamericano." Paper presented to the workshop "Latin American
Labor and Globalization: Trends Following a Decade of Economic Adjustment," organized by the Social Science Research Council and FLACSO-Costa
Rica, San José, Costa Rica, July 10 and 11.

Chant, Sylvia. 1991. *Women and Survival in Mexican Cities: Perspectives on Gender,
Labour Markets and Low-income Households.* Manchester: Manchester University Press.

———. 1994. "Women and Poverty in Urban Latin America: Mexican and Costa
Rican Experiences." In *Poverty in the 1990s: The Responses of Urban Women,* ed.
Fatima Meer. Paris: UNESCO/ International Social Science Council.

Charlton, Sue Ellen M., Jana Matson Everett, and Kathleen A. Staudt. 1989. *Women,
the State, and Development.* Albany: SUNY Press.

Chevigny, Paul. 1995. *The Edge of the Knife: Police Violence in the Americas.* New York:
The New Press.

Cicchelli-Pugeault, Catherine, and Vincezo Cicchelli. 1999. *Las teorías sociológicas de la
familia.* Buenos Aires: Nueva Visión.

CIM (Consejo Inter-regional Mapuche). 1998. *Mapuche Nation; Mapuches Denounced
Chilean Government at the UN.* Statement before the United Nations Commission on Human Rights, 54th sess., Geneva, March 30.

Cimillo, Elsa. 1999. "Empleo e ingresos en el sector informal en una economía
abierta: El caso Argentino." In *Informalidad y exclusión social,* ed. J. Carpio,
E. Klein, and I. Novacovsky. Buenos Aires and Santiago: Siempro/OIT.

Clark, Colin. 1940. *The Conditions of Economic Progress.* London: Macmillan.

Clert, Carine, and Quentin Wodon. 2001. "The Targeting of Government Programs
in Chile." In *Measurement and Meaning: Combining Quantitative and Qualitative Methods for the Analysis of Poverty and Social Exclusion in Latin America,* ed.
Estanislao Gacitúa-Marió and Quentin Wodon. Washington, D.C.: The World
Bank.

Coleman, James, S. 1988. "Social Capital in the Creation of Human Capital." *American Journal of Sociology* 94 (Supplement): S95–S120.

Collier, David S., and Ruth B. Collier. 1991. *Shaping the Political Arena: Critical Junc-
tures, the Labor Movement, and Regime Dynamics.* Princeton: Princeton University Press.

Collier, Jane Fishburne, and Sylvia Junko Yanagisako, eds. 1987. *Gender and Kinship.
Essays Toward a Unified Analysis.* Stanford: Stanford University Press.

Collins, Randall. 1994. *Four Sociological Traditions.* New York: Oxford University
Press.

Conan, Eric, and Henry Rousso. 1994. *Vicy, un passé que ne passe pas.* Paris: Fayard.

CONAPO. 2002. "Proyecciones de la población de México, 2000–2050." Mexico City:
CONAPO.

Coriat, Benjamin. 1993. *Pensar al revés. Trabajo y organización en la empresa japonesa.*
Madrid: Siglo XXI de España Editores.

Cornelius, Wayne A. 1973. "The Impact of Governmental Performance on Political
Attitudes and Behavior: The Case of the Urban Poor in Mexico." *Latin American Urban Research* 3:217–55.

———. 1975. *Politics and Migrant Poor in Mexico City*. Stanford: Stanford University Press.

Cornia, Giovanni Andrea. 1999. "Liberalization, Globalization and Income Distribution." Working Paper 157, Universidad de las Naciones Unidas (UNU) / Instituto Mundial de Investigaciones de Economía del Desarrollo (WIDER), Helsinki, March.

Correa, S., and R. Reichman. 1994. *Population and Reproductive Rights: Feminist Perspectives from the South*. Atlantic Highlands, N.J.: Zed Books.

Cortázar, René. 1997. "Chile: The Evolution and Reform of the Labor Market." In *Labor Markets in Latin America: Combining Social Protection with Market Flexibility*, ed. S. Edwards and N. Lustig. Washington, D.C.: Brookings Institution Press.

Cottrol, Robert J., and Tanya Kateri Hernandez. 2001. "The Role of Law and Legal Institutions in Combating Social Exclusion in Latin American Countries: Afro-American Populations." In *Dialogue on Race, Ethnicity and Inclusion,* ed. Inter-American Development Bank. Washington, D.C.: Inter-American Development Bank. CD-ROM.

Couriel, Alberto. 1999. "De la democracia política a la democracia económica y social." In *América Latina en el siglo XXI: De la esperanza a la equidad,* ed. Carlos Contreras. Mexico City: Fondo de Cultura Económica / Universidad de Guadalajara.

Dagnino, Evelina. 2003. "Confluéncia perversa, deslocamentos de sentido, crise discursiva." Paper presented in the meeting of the Cultura y Poder working group of CLACSO, Buenos Aires, 5–6 June.

———, ed. 2002. *Sociedad civil, espacios públicos y democratización: Brasil*. Mexico City: Fondo de Cultura Económica.

Dahl, Robert A. 1971. *Polyarchy: Participation and Opposition*. New Haven: Yale University Press.

Dandler, Jorge. 1999. "Indigenous Peoples and the Rule of Law in Latin America: Do They Have a Chance?" In *The (Un)Rule of Law and the Underprivileged in Latin America,* ed. Juan E. Mendez, Guillermo O'Donnell, and Paulo Sergio Pinheiro. Notre Dame: University of Notre Dame Press.

Davis, Diane E. 1989. Review of *Power and Popular Protest: Latin American Social Movements,* edited by Susan E. Eckstein. *Journal of InterAmerican Studies and World Affairs* 30, no.4:225–34.

———. 1992. "The Sociology of Mexico: Stalking the Path Not Taken." *Annual Review of Sociology* 18:395–417.

———. 1993. "The Dialectic of Autonomy: State Actors, Class Actors, and the Roots of Economic Crisis in Mexico, 1964–1983." *Latin American Perspectives* 20, no. 3 (summer): 46–76.

———. 1994. "Failed Urban Democratic Reform: From Social Movements to the State and Back Again." *Journal of Latin American Studies* 26, no. 2 (May): 1–34.

———. 1999. "The Power of Distance: Re-theorizing Social Movements in Latin America." *Theory and Society* 28, no. 4:585–638.

———. 2004. *Discipline and Development: Middle Classes and Prosperity in East Asia and Latin America*. Cambridge: Cambridge University Press.

Davis, Diane E., and Arturo Alvarado. 1999. "Liberalization, Public Insecurity, and Deteriorating Rule of Law in Mexico City." *Working Papers in Local Governance and Democracy* 99, no. 1:95–107.

Davis, Diane E., and Anthony W. Pereira. 2003. *Irregular Armed Forces and Their Role in Politics and State Formation*. Cambridge: Cambridge University Press.

De Barbieri, Teresita. 1984. *Mujeres y vida cotidiana*. Mexico City: Instituto de Investigaciones Sociales, Fondo de Cultura Económica (FCE) / UNAM.

Degregori, Carlos Ivan, Cecilia Blondet, and Nicolas Lynch. 1986. *Conquistadores de un nuevo mundo*. Lima: Instituto de Estudios Peruanos.

De Janvry, Alain. 1981. *The Agrarian Question and Reformism in Latin America*. Baltimore: Johns Hopkins University Press.

Delphy, Christine, and Diana Leonard. 1986. "Class Analysis, Gender Analysis, and the Family." In *Gender and Stratification*, ed. Rosemary Crompton and Michael Mann. Cambridge: Polity Press.

Deutsch, Ruthanne, and Rebecca Reichmann. 2001. "Costs of Racial Exclusion Reported at IDB Conference." *Social Development*, July.

Dezalay, Yves, and Bryant G. Garth. 2002. *The Internationalization of Palace Wars: Lawyers, Economists, and the Contest to Transform Latin American States*. Chicago: University of Chicago Press.

Diamond, Larry. 1999. *Developing Democracy: Toward Consolidation*. Baltimore: Johns Hopkins University Press.

Di Tella, Torcuato S. 1965. "Populism and Reform in Latin America." In *Obstacles to Change in Latin America*, ed. Claudio Véliz. New York: Oxford University Press.

———. 1966. *Argentina, sociedad de masas*. Buenos Aires: Editorial Universitaria de Buenos Aires.

———. 1967. *Sindicato y comunidad: Dos tipos de estructura sindical latinoamericana*. Buenos Aires: Editorial del Instituto.

———. 1990. *Latin American Politics: A Theoretical Framework*. Austin: University of Texas (published in Spanish in 1985).

Dos Santos, Theotonio. 1970. "La crisis de la teoría del desarrollo y las relaciones de dependencia en América Latina." In *La dependencia politico-economica de America Latina*, ed. Helio Jaguaribe, Aldo Ferrer, Miguel S. Wionczek, and Theotonio dos Santos. Mexico City: Siglo Veintiuno Editores.

Dos Santos, Wanderley Guilherme. 1979. *Cidadania e justiça. A política social na ordem brasileira*. Rio de Janeiro: Campos.

Douglas, Mary, and Aaron Wildavsky. 1983. *Risk and Culture*. Berkeley and Los Angeles: University of California Press.

Draibe, Sonia. 1985. *Relatório sobre a situação social do país*. Campinas: Editora da Unicamp.

Dubar, Claude. 1991. *La socialisation. Construction des identités sociales et professionnelles*. Paris: Armand Collin.

———. 2001. "El trabajo y las identidades profesionales y personales." *Revista Latinoamericana de Estudios del Trabajo*, no. 13:5–16.

Durkheim, Emile. [1912] 1961. *The Elementary Forms of the Religious Life*. New York: Macmillan.

——. [1893] 1984. *The Division of Labor in Society.* New York: The Free Press.

Durston, John. 1999a. "Building Community Social Capital." *CEPAL Review* 69:103–18.

——. 1999b. "Construyendo capital social comunitario. Una experiencia de empoderamiento rural en Guatemala." Serie Políticas Sociales, 30. Santiago: CEPAL.

——. 2000. "Qué es el capital social comunitario?" Serie Políticas Sociales, 38. Santiago: CEPAL/ECLAC.

Eckstein, Susan. 1977. *The Poverty of Revolution: The State and the Urban Poor in Mexico.* New Jersey: Princeton University Press. (A revised edition of this work was published in 1988.)

——. 1989. *Power and Popular Protest: Latin American Social Movements.* Berkeley and Los Angeles: University of California Press.

ECLAC. *See* Economic Commission for Latin American.

Economic Commission for Latin American and the Caribbean (ECLAC). 1990. *Changing Production Patterns with Social Equity: The Prime Task of Latin American and Caribbean Development in the 1990s.* Santiago: ECLAC.

——. 2000. *Equity, Development and Citizenship.* Santiago: ECLAC.

——. 2001. *ECLAC Notes,* 15. Santiago: ECLAC.

——. 2002. *Foreign Investment in Latin America and the Caribbean, 2001.* Santiago: ECLAC.

Elder, Glen H., Jr. 1985. "Perspectives on the Life Course." In *Life Course Dynamics, Trajectories and Transitions, 1968–1990,* ed. Glen H. Elder, Jr. Ithaca: Cornell University Press.

Emmerij, L. 1997. *Economic and Social Development into the XXI Century.* Washington, D.C.: Inter-American Development Bank.

Ensalaco, Mark. 1994. "In with the New, Out with the Old? The Democratizing Impact of Constitutional Reform in Chile." *Journal of Latin American Studies* 26, no. 2:409–30.

Escobar, Agustín, and Mercedes González de la Rocha. 1991. "Family Well-Being, Food Consumption, and Survival Strategies During Mexico's Economic Crisis." In *Social Responses to Mexico's Economic Crisis of the 1980s,* ed. Mercedes González de la Rocha and Agustín Escobar Latapí. La Jolla, Calif.: Center for U.S.-Mexican Studies.

Escobar, Agustín, and Bryan Roberts. 1991. "Urban Stratification, the Middle Classes, and Economic Change in Mexico." In *Social Responses to Mexico's Economic Crises of the 1980s,* ed. M. González de la Rocha and A. Escobar. San Diego, Calif.: Center for U.S.-Mexican Studies, UCSD.

Escobar, Arturo. 1999. "An Ecology of Difference: Equality and Conflict in a Globalized World." In *World Culture Report,* vol. 2, ed. Lourdes Arizpe. Paris: UNESCO.

Escobar, Arturo, and Sonia E. Alvarez, eds. 1992. *The Making of New Social Movements in Latin America: Identity, Strategy, and Democracy.* Boulder, Colo.: Westview Press.

Espinoza, Vicente. 1998. "Social Networks Among the Urban Poor: Inequality and Integration in a Latin American City." In *Networking in the Global Village,* ed. Barry Wellman. Boulder, Colo.: Westview Press.

Etzioni, Amitai. 1988. *The Moral Dimension: Toward a New Economics*. New York: The Free Press.

Evans, Peter. 1979. *Dependent Development: The Alliance of Multinational, State, and Local Capital in Brazil*. Princeton: Princeton University Press.

———. 1989. "Predatory, Developmental, and Other Apparatuses: A Comparative Political Economy Perspective on the Third World State." *Sociological Forum* 4:561–87.

———. 1992. "The State as Problem and Solution: Predation, Embedded Autonomy, and Structural Change." In *The Politics of Economic Adjustment*, ed. Stephan Haggard and Robert R. Kaufman. Princeton: Princeton University Press.

———. 1995. *Embedded Autonomy: States and Industrial Transformation*. Princeton: Princeton University Press.

———. 1996. "Government Action, Social Capital and Development: Reviewing the Evidence on Synergy." *World Development* 24, no. 6:1119–32.

———, ed. 2002. *Livable Cities*. Berkeley and Los Angeles: University of California Press.

Evans, Peter, and James E. Rauch. 1999. "Bureaucracy and Growth: A Cross-National Analysis of the Effects of 'Weberian' State Structures on Economic Growth." *American Sociological Review* 64:748–65.

Evans, Peter, Dietrich Rueschemeyer, and Theda Skocpol. 1985. *Bringing the State Back In*. Cambridge: Cambridge University Press.

Evans, Peter, Dietrich Rueschemeyer, and Evelyne Huber Stephens, eds. 1995. *States Versus Markets in the World System*. Beverly Hills, Calif.: Sage Publications.

Evers, Tilman. 1985. "Identidad: la faz oculta de los nuevos movimientos sociales." *Punto de vista* 25:31–41.

Faber, M., and D. Seers, eds. 1972. *The Crisis in Planning*. London: Chatto and Windus for Sussex University Press.

Fanon, Frantz. 1963. *The Wretched of the Earth*. New York: Grove Press.

Faria, Vilmar. 1976. "Occupational Marginality, Employment and Poverty in Urban Brazil." Ph.D. diss., Department of Sociology, Harvard University.

———. 1989. "Políticas de governo e regulação da fecundidade: Consequencias nao antecipadas e efeitos perversos." *Ciencias Sociais Hoje* 5:62–103.

———. 1992. *A conjuntura social brasileira: Dilemas e perspectivas*. Novos Estudos CEBRAP no. 33. São Paulo: CEBRAP.

———. 1994. *Social Exclusion in Latin America: An Annotated Bibliography*. Geneva: ILO, Labour Institutions and Development Programme DP/70/1994.

———. 1995. "Strengthening Democracy, Accelerating Economic Growth, and Promoting Equality: The Changing Role of Brazilian Scholars." In *Beyond Government. Extending the Public Policy Debate in Emerging Democracies*, ed. Crawford D. Goodwin and Michael Nacht. Boulder, Colo.: Westview Press.

Faria, Vilmar E., and Joseph E. Potter. 1999. "Television, Telenovelas, and Fertility Change in Northeast Brazil." In *Dynamics of Values in Fertility Change*, ed. R. Leete. Oxford: Oxford University Press.

Fausto, Boris. 1976. *Trábalho urbano e conflito social*. San Pablo and Río de Janeiro: Difel.

Feld, Claudia. 2002. *Del estrado a la pantalla: Las imágenes del juicio a los ex comandantes*.

Madrid: Siglo XXI de España Editores; Buenos Aires: Siglo XXI de Argentina Editores.

Ferrer, Aldo. 1996. *Historia de la globalización: Orígenes del orden económico mundial.* Mexico City: Fondo de Cultura Económica.

Ffrench-Davis, Ricardo. 1999. *Macroeconomía, comercio y finanzas para reformar las reformas en América Latina.* Santiago: McGraw-Hill Interamericana.

Ffrench-Davis, Ricardo, Oscar Muñoz, and José Gabriel Palma. 1994. "The Latin American Economies, 1950–1990." In *The Cambridge History of Latin America,* vol. 4, part 1, ed. Leslie Bethell. Cambridge: Cambridge University Press.

Figueroa, Adolfo, Teofilo Altamirano, and Denis Sulmont. 1996. *Social Exclusion and Inequality in Peru.* Geneva: International Institute for Labour Studies, United Nations Development Programme.

Figueroa Perea, Juan G. 1994. "Anticoncepción Quirúrgica, educación y elección anticonceptiva." In *Memorias de la IV reunión nacional de investigación demográfica en México,* vol. 1. Mexico City: Instituto Nacional de Estadística, Geografía e Informática (INEGI).

Figueroa, Juan G., and C. Stern, eds. 2001. *Sexualidad y salud reproductiva: Avances y retos para la investigación.* Mexico City: El Colegio de México.

Filgueira, Carlos. 1996. "Estado y sociedad civil: Politicas de ajuste estructural y estabilizacion en America Latina." Paper presented at the Conference on "Responses by Civil Society to Neoliberal Adjustment," University of Texas, Austin.

———. 1999. "Bienestar y ciudadanía. Viejas y nueva vulnerabilidades." In *Pobreza y desigualdad en América latina. Temas y nuevos desafíos,* ed. V. E. Tokman and G. O'Donnell. Buenos Aires: Paidós.

———. 2002. "Estructura de oportunidades, activos de los hogares y movilización de activos en Montevide (1991–1998)." In *Trabajo y ciudadanía,* ed. Rubén Kaztman and Guillermo Wormald. Montevideo: Cedra.

Filgueira, Carlos, and Carlo Geneletti. 1981. *Estratificación y movilidad ocupacional en América Latina.* Santiago: United Nations.

Fitzgerald, David. 2000. *Negotiating Extra-Territorial Citizenship.* Monograph no. 2. La Jolla, Calif.: Center for Comparative Immigration Studies, University of California-San Diego.

Flores, Julia Isabel. 1998. "Persistencia y cambios en algunos valores de la familia Mexicana de los noventa." In *Vida familiar y cultura contemporánea,* ed. José Manuel Valenzuela and Vania Salles. Mexico City: CONACULTA.

Flórez, Carmen Elisa, Carlos Medina, and Fernando Urrea. 2001. "Understanding the Cost of Social Exclusion due to Race or Ethnic Background in Latin American and Caribbean Countries." Paper presented at the conference Todos Contamos: Los Grupos Étnicos en los Censos, Cartagena de Indias, Colombia.

Ford Foundation. 1985. "Ford Foundation's Work in Population: A Review of Past and Present Emphases and a Discussion of Plans to Expand the Foundation's Population Programs Based on Current Work." In *Ford Foundation Working Papers.* New York: Ford Foundation.

Foweraker, Joe. 1989. *Making Democracy in Spain: Grass-Roots Struggle in the South, 1955–1975.* Cambridge: Cambridge University Press.

——. 1993. *Popular Mobilization in Mexico: The Teacher's Movement, 1977–1987.* Cambridge: Cambridge University Press.

——. 1995. *Theorizing Social Movements.* London: Pluto Press.

Foweraker, Joe, and Ann Craig. 1990. *Popular Movements and Political Change in Mexico* Boulder Colo.: Lynne Rienner.

Foweraker, Joe, and Todd Landman. 1997. *Citizenship Rights and Social Movements: A Comparative and Statistical Analysis.* Oxford: Oxford University Press.

Fox, Jonathan. 1996. "How Does Civil Society Thicken? The Political Construction of Social Capital in Rural Mexico." *World Development* 24, no. 6:1089–1103.

Foxley, Alejandro. 1997. *Chile en la nueva etapa: Repensando el país desde los ciudadanos.* Santiago: Editorial Dolmen.

Frank, A. G. 1967. "The Development of Underdevelopment in Brazil." In *Capitalism and Underdevelopment in Latin America.* New York: Monthly Review Press.

Freire, Paulo. 1982. *The Pedagogy of the Oppressed.* Harmondsworth: Penguin.

French, John D. 1998. "Drowning in Laws but Starving (for Justice?): Brazilian Labor Law and the Workers' Quest to Realize the Imaginary." *Political Power and Social Theory* 12:181–221.

Fukuyama, Francis. 1992. *The End of History and the Last Man.* New York: The Free Press.

Gacitúa, Estanislao, with Shelton Davis. 2001. "Poverty and Social Exclusion in Latin America and the Caribbean." In *Social Exclusion and Poverty Reduction in Latin America and the Caribbean,* ed. Estanislao Gacitúa and Carlos Sojo, with Shelton Davis. Washington, D.C.: The World Bank.

Gacitúa, Estanislao, and Carlos Sojo, with Shelton Davis, eds. 2001. *Social Exclusion and Poverty Reduction in Latin America and the Caribbean.* Washington, D.C.: The World Bank.

Gacitúa-Marió, Estanislao, Corinne Sians, and Quentin Wodon. 2001. "Reproductive Health in Argentina's Poor Rural Area." In *Measurement and Meaning: Combining Quantitative and Qualitative Methods for the Analysis of Poverty and Social Exclusion in Latin America,* ed. Estanislao Gacitúa-Marió and Quentin Wodon. Washington, D.C.: The World Bank.

Gacitúa-Marió, Estanislao, and Quentin Wodon, eds. 2001. *Measurement and Meaning: Combining Quantitative and Qualitative Methods for the Analysis of Poverty and Social Exclusion in Latin America.* Washington, D.C.: The World Bank.

Gans, H. 1962. *The Urban Villagers: Group and Class in the Life of Italian-Americans.* New York: The Free Press of Glencoe.

García, Brígida. 1976. "Anticoncepción en el México rural, 1969." *Demografía y Economía* 10:297–351.

——. 1995. "Dinámica familiar, pobreza y calidad de vida: Una perspectiva Mexicana y latinoamericana." In *Familias y relaciones de género en transformación. Cambios trascendentales en América Latina y el Caribe,* ed. Beatríz Schmuckler. Mexico City: Population Council/Edamex.

——. 2003. "Empoderamiento y autonomía de las mujeres en la investigación demográfica actual." *Estudios Demográficos y Urbanos* 18, no. 2 (May–August): 221–53.

———, ed. 2000. *Women, Poverty and Demographic Change.* New York: Oxford University Press.

García, Brígida, Mercedes Blanco, and Enith Pacheco. 1999. "Género y trabajo extradoméstico." In *Mujer, género y población en México,* ed. Brígida García. Mexico City: El Colegio de México.

García, Brígida, and Orlandina de Oliveira. 1994. *Trabajo femenino y vida familiar en México.* Mexico City: El Colegio de México.

———. 2001. "Cambios socioeconómicos y división del trabajo en las familias mexicana." *Investigación Económica* 51, no. 236 (March-April): 137–62.

García, Brígida, and Olga Lorena Rojas. 2002. "Cambios en la formación y disolución de las uniones en América Latina." *Papeles de Población, Nueva Epoca* 8, no. 32 (April–June): 11–29.

———. 2003. "Las uniones conyugales en América Latina: Transiciones en un marco de desigualdad social y de género." Paper presented at the meeting "La Fecundidad en América Latina: ¿Transición o revolución?" organized by ECLA, Santiago, Chile, June 9–11.

García Delgado, Daniel. 1998. *Estado-nación y globalización. Fortalezas y debilidades en el umbral del tercer milenio.* Buenos Aires: Ariel.

Geddes, Barbara. 1994. *Politician's Dilemma: Building State Capacity in Latin America.* Berkeley and Los Angeles: University of California Press.

Gerassi, John. 1963. *The Great Fear: The Reconquest of Latin America by Latin Americans.* New York: Macmillan.

Gereffi, Gary. 1989. "Rethinking Development Theory: Insights from East Asia and Latin America." *Sociological Forum* 4:505–33.

———. 1999. "International Trade and Industrial Upgrading in the Apparel Commodity Chain." *Journal of International Economics* 48:37–70.

———. 2001. "Shifting Governance Structures in Global Commodity Chains, with Special Reference to the Internet." *American Behavioral Scientist* 44:1616–37.

Gereffi, Gary, and Stephanie Fonda. 1992. "Regional Paths of Development." *Annual Review of Sociology* 18:419–48.

Gereffi, Gary, John Humphrey, Raphael Kaplinsky, and Timothy Sturgeon. 2001. "Introduction: Globalisation, Value Chains and Development." *IDS Bulletin* 32, no. 3.

Gereffi, Gary, and Miguel Korzeniewicz. 1994. *Commodity Chains and Global Capitalism.* Westport, Conn.: Praeger.

Gereffi, Gary, and Donald Wyman. 1990. *Manufacturing Miracles: Paths of Industrialization.* Princeton: Princeton University Press.

Germani, Gino. 1955. *Estructura social de la Argentina: Análisis estadístico.* Buenos Aires: Editorial Raigal.

———. 1962. *Política y sociedad en una época de transición. De la sociedad tradicional a la sociedad de masas.* Buenos Aires: Paidós.

———. 1969. *Sociología de la modernización: Estudios teóricos, metodológicos, y aplicados a América Latina.* Buenos Aires: Paidós.

———. 1973. *El concepto de marginalidad.* Buenos Aires: Nueva Visión.

———. 1978. *Authoritarianism, Fascism, and National Populism.* New Brunswick, N.J.: Transaction Books.

——. 1980. *Marginality*. New Brunswick, N.J.: Transaction Books.

——. 1985. *Los Limites de la Democracia*. Buenos Aires: CLACSO.

Gerstenfeld, Pascual. 2002. "Social Policy Delivery: The New Economic Model and the Reform of the State in Latin America." In *Exclusion and Engagement: Social Policy in Latin America*, ed. Christopher Abel and Colin M. Lewis. London: Institute of Latin American Studies.

Giddens, Anthony. 1991. *Modernity and Self-identity. Self and Society in the Modern Age*. Stanford: Stanford University Press.

——. 2000. *The Third Way and Its Critics*. Cambridge: Polity Press.

Gilbert, Alan. 1993. *In Search of a Home*. Tucson: Arizona University Press.

——, ed. 1996. *The Mega-City in Latin America*. New York: United Nations University Press.

Gilbert, Alan, and Peter Ward. 1985. *Housing, the State and the Poor: Policy and Practice in Three Latin American Cities*. Cambridge: Cambridge University Press.

Gille, H. 1987. "Origins and Nature of the World Fertility Survey." In *The World Fertility Survey: An Assessment*, ed. J. Cleland and C. Scott. Oxford: Oxford University Press.

Glaser, William A., and Christopher Habers. 1974. "The Migration and Return of Professionals." *International Migration Review* 8:227–44.

Gledhill, John. 1997. "Liberalism, Socio-Economic Rights and the Politics of Identity: From Moral Economy to Indigenous Rights." In *Human Rights, Culture and Context: Anthropological Approaches*, ed. R. Wilson. London: Pluto Press.

——. 2002. "Some Conceptual and Substantive Limitations of Contemporary Western (Global) Discourses of Rights and Social Justice." In *Exclusion and Engagement: Social Policy in Latin America*, ed. Christopher Abel and Colin M. Lewis. London: Institute of Latin American Studies.

Glick Schiller, N., L. Bash, and C. Blanc-Szanton. 1992. *Towards a Transnational Perspective on Migration. Race, Class, Ethnicity and Nationalism Reconsidered*. New York: Academy of Sciences.

Godio, Julio. 1972. *El movimiento obrero y la cuestión nacional. Argentina: Inmigrantes asalariados y lucha de clases, 1880–1910*. Buenos Aires: Erasmo.

Gómez, Sergio, and Emilio Klein, eds. 1993. *Los pobres del campo. El trabajador eventual*. Santiago: FLACSO/PREALC.

González Casanova, Pablo. 1965. "Internal Colonialism and National Development." *Studies in Comparative International Development* 1:27–47.

——. 1970. *Democracy in Mexico*. Oxford: Oxford University Press.

——. 1998. "Restructuración de las ciencias sociales: Hacia un nuevo paradigma." In *Pueblo, época y desarrollo: La sociología de América Latina*, ed. R. Briceño-León and H. R. Sonntag. Caracas: Nueva Sociedad.

González de la Rocha, Mercedes. 1991. "Violence and Gender in the Context of Urban Working Class Households." Paper prepared for the Seminar "Gender, Violence and Society in Mexico and Latin America," University of Texas at Austin, April 11–12.

——. 1994. *The Resources of Poverty: Women and Survival in a Mexican City*. Oxford: Basil Blackwell.

——. 1995. "Social Restructuring in Two Mexican Cities: An Analysis of Domestic

Groups in Guadalajara and Monterrey." *European Journal of Development Research* 7, no. 2:389–406.

——. 1999a. "La reciprocidad amenazada: un costo más de la pobreza urbana." *Revista Latinoamericana de Estudios del Trabajo* 5, no. 9:33–50.

——. 2001. "From the Resources of Poverty to the Poverty of Resources? The Erosion of a Survival Model." *Latin American Perspectives* 28, no. 4:72–100.

——. 2004. "De los 'recursos de la pobreza' a la 'pobreza de recursos' y a las 'desventajas acumuladas.'" In "From the Marginality of the 1960s to the 'New Poverty' of Today." *Latin American Research Review* 39 (1): 192–94.

——, ed. 1999b. *Divergencias del modelo tradicional: Hogares de jefatura femenina en América Latina.* Mexico City: Centro de Investigaciones y Estudios Superiores en Antropología Social (CIESAS) / Plaza y Valdés.

González Montes, Soledad. 1994. "La maternidad en la construcción de la identidad femenina. Una experiencia de investigación participativa con mujeres rurales." In *Neuvos textos y renovados pre-textos,* ed. Vania Salles and Elsie McPhail. Mexico City: El Colegio de México.

González Pérez, M. 1997. *Gobiernos pluriétnicos: La constitución de regiones autónomas en Nicaragua.* Mexico City: Editorial Plaza y Valdés.

Gordon, Colin. 1991. "Governmental Rationality: An Introduction." In *Notes on Foucault: The Foucault Effect,* ed. Graham Burchell, Colin Gordon, and Peter Miller. Chicago: University of Chicago Press.

Gough, Ian. 1979. *The Political Economy of the Welfare State.* London: Macmillan.

Grandin, Greg. 2000. *The Blood of Guatemala: A History of Race and Nation.* Durham: Duke University Press.

Granovetter, Mark. 1973. "The Strength of Weak Ties." *American Journal of Sociology* 78:1360–80.

——. 1985. "Economic Action and Social Structure: The Problem of Embeddedness." *American Journal of Sociology* 91:481–510.

——. 1992. "The Sociological and Economic Approaches to Labor Market Analysis: A Social Structural View." In *The Sociology of Economic Life,* ed. M. Granovetter and R. Swedberg. Boulder, Colo.: Westview Press.

Griffith-Jones, Stephanie, and Osvaldo Sunkel. 1986. *Debt and Development Crises in Latin America: The End of an Illusion.* Oxford: Clarendon Press.

Grindle, Merilee. 2002. "Despite the Odds: The Political Economy of Social Sector Reform in Latin America." In *Exclusion and Engagement: Social Policy in Latin America,* ed. Christopher Abel and Colin M. Lewis. London: Institute of Latin American Studies.

Grusky, David B. 1994. *The Contours of Social Stratification. Class, Race, and Gender in Sociological Perspective.* Boulder, Colo.: Westview Press.

——. 2001. *Social Stratification: Class, Race, and Gender in Sociological Perspective.* Boulder, Colo.: Westview Press.

Guarnizo, Luis. 1995. "Regresando a casa. Clase, género y transformación del hogar entre migrantes dominicanos/as." *Género y Sociedad* 2, no. 3 (January–April): 53–127.

——. 1998. "The Rise of Transnational Social Formations: Mexican and Dominican State Responses to Transnational Migration." *Political Power and Social Theory* 12:45–95.

Guarnizo, Luis E., and Alejandro Portes. 2001. "From Assimilation to Transnationalism." Working Paper Series, Center for Migration and Development, Princeton University.

Guarnizo, Luis E., and Michael Peter Smith. 1998. "The Locations of Transnationalism." In *Transnationalism from Below*, ed. M. P. Smith and L. E. Guarnizo. New Brunswick, N.J.: Transaction Publishers.

Gubrium, Jaber F., and James A. Holstein. 1997. *The New Language of the Qualitative Method*. New York: Oxford University Press.

Guillén, Mauro. 2001. *The Limits of Convergence: Globalization and Organizational Change in Argentina, South Korea, and Spain*. Princeton: Princeton University Press.

Guttman, Mathew. 1993. "Los hombres cambiantes, los machos impenitentes y las relaciones de género en México en los noventa." *Estudios Sociológicos* 11, no. 33 (September–December): 725–40.

Habermas, Jürgen. 1991. *Escritos sobre moralidad y etnicidad*. Barcelona: Paidós.

———. 1998. *Between Facts and Norms*. Cambridge: The MIT Press.

Hall, Peter. 1982. *Great Planning Disasters*. Berkeley and Los Angeles: University of California Press.

Hamilton, Nora. 1982. *The Limits to State Autonomy*. Princeton: Princeton University Press.

Harris, Marvin. 1964. *Patterns of Race in the Americas*. New York: Walker.

Harris, Marvin, Josildeth G. Consorte, Joseph Lang, and Bryan Byrne. 1993. "Who Are the Whites? Imposed Census Categories and the Racial Demography of Brazil." *Social Forces* 72:451–62.

Harris, Olivia. 1981. "Household as Natural Units." In *Of Marriage and the Market: Women's Subordination in International Perspective*, ed. Kate Young, Carol Wolkowitz, and Roslyn McCullagh. London: CSE Books.

Harth Deneke, A., and M. Silva. 1982. "Mutual Help and Progressive Development Housing: For What Purpose? Notes on the Salvadorean Experience." In *Self-help Housing: A Critique*, ed. P. Ward. London: Mansell.

Hart, Keith. 1973. "Informal Income Opportunities and Urban Employment in Ghana." *Journal of Modern African Studies* 11:61–89.

Harvey, D. 1985. *The Urbanization of Capital*. Oxford: Basil Blackwell.

———. 1989. *The Condition of Postmodernity: An Enquiry into the Origins of Cultural Change*. Oxford: Basil Blackwell.

Harvey, Neil. 1998. *The Chiapas Rebellion: The Struggle for Land and Democracy*. Durham: Duke University Press.

———. 2001. "Rights, Minority and Indigenous." In *Encyclopedia of Democratic Thought*, ed. Joe Foweraker and Paul Barry Clarke. London: Routledge.

Hasenbalg, Carlos A. 1988a. "Desigualdades raciais no Brasil." In *Estrutura social, mobilidade, e raça*, ed. Carlos Hasenbalg and Nelson do Valle Silva. Rio de Janiero: Vertice.

———. 1988b. "Raça e mobilidade social." In *Estrutura social, mobilidade, e raça*, ed. Carlos Hasenbalg and Nelson do Valle Silva. Rio de Janiero: Vertice.

Hasenbalg, Carlos A., and Nelson do Valle Silva. 1992. "Raça e oportunidades educacionais no Brasil." In *Relações raciais no Brasil contemporâneo*, ed. Nelson do Valle Silva and Carlos A. Hasenbalg. Rio de Janeiro: Rio Fundo.

Hauser, Phillip, ed. 1967. *Urbanization in Latin America.* New York: Columbia University Press.

Heilborn, M., ed. 1999. *Sexualidade: O olhar das ciencias sociais.* Rio de Janeiro: Jorge Zahar.

Heilbronner, Robert. 2000. *The Worldly Philosophers: The Lives, Times, and Ideas of the Great Economic Thinkers.* Seventh edition. London: Penguin.

Helleiner, Gerald K. 2000. "Markets, Politics and Globalization: Can the Global Economy Be Civilized?" The Tenth Raúl Prebisch Lecture, Geneva, December 11.

Hershberg, Eric. 1998. "Industrial Upgrading and Development: Workshops Notes." *Items* 52, no. 4:96.

Higgins, M., and J. G. Williamson. 1997. "Age Dynamics in Asia and Dependence on Foreign Capital." *Population and Development Review* 23:261–93.

Hills, John. 2002. "Does a Focus on 'Social Exclusion' Change the Policy Response?" In *Understanding Social Exclusion,* ed. John Hills, Julian Le Grand, and David Piachaud. New York: Oxford University Press.

Hills, John, Julian Le Grand, and David Piachaud, eds. 2002. *Understanding Social Exclusion.* New York: Oxford University Press.

Hirata, Helena. 1997. "Os mundos do trabalho: Consequencias e diversidada num contexto de mudança dos paradigmas productivos." In *Empregabilidade y educaçao: Novos caminhos no mundo de trabalho,* ed. A. Casali, J. E. Texeira, and M. A. Cortella. São Paulo: Editora da PUC-SP, EDUC.

Hirsch, Paul, Stuart Michaels, and Ray Friedman. 1990. "Clean Models vs. Dirty Hands: Why Economics Is Different from Sociology." In *Structures of Capital: The Social Organization of the Economy,* ed. Sharon Zukin and Paul DiMaggio. New York: Cambridge University Press.

Hirschman, Albert O. 1981. *Essays in Trespassing: Economics to Politics and Beyond.* Cambridge: Cambridge University Press.

Hobsbawm, E. 1994. *The Age of Extremes: A History of the World, 1914–1991.* New York: Pantheon Books.

———. 1996. *Historia del siglo XX.* Barcelona: Grijalbo.

Hodgson, Dennis, and Susan Cotts Watkins. 1997. "Feminists and Neo-Malthusians: Past and Present Alliances." *Population and Development Review* 23:469–523.

Hojman, David E. 1994. "The Political Economy of Recent Conversions to Market Economics in Latin America." *Journal of Latin American Studies* 26, no. 1:191–219.

Hondagneu-Sotelo, Pierrette. 1994. *Gendered Transitions. Mexican Experiences of Immigration.* Berkeley and Los Angeles: University of California Press.

Hopenhayn, M. 1998. "Identidad diseminada—identidad desintegrada: Opciones abiertas." *Revista Cultura Secretaría de Comunicación y Cultura.* Santiago, Chile.

Hoselitz, B., ed. 1956. *Agrarian Societies in Transition.* Philadelphia: Annals of the American Academy of Political and Social Sciences.

Hualde, Alfredo. 2001. *Aprendizaje industrial en la fronteira norte de México.* Mexico City: Norte-Plaza y Valdéz Editores.

Huber, Evelyne. 2002. *Models of Capitalism: Experiences from Latin America.* University Park: Pennsylvania State University Press.

Huber, Evelyne, and John D. Stephens. 2000. *The Political Economy of Pension Reform: Latin America in Comparative Perspective*. Geneva: United Nations Research Institute for Social Development.

———. 2001. *Development and Crisis of the Welfare State: Parties and Policies in Global Context*. Chicago: University of Chicago Press.

Huggins, Martha K. 1991. *Vigilantism and the State in Modern Latin America: Essays on Extra-legal Violence*. New York: Praeger.

———. 1998. *Political Policing: The United States and Latin America*. Durham: Duke University Press.

Huggins, Martha K., M. Haritos-Fatouros, and P. Zimbardo. 2002. *Violence Workers: Police Torturers and Murderers Reconstruct Brazilian Atrocities*. Berkeley and Los Angeles: University of California Press.

Huyssen, Andreas. 2003. *Present Pasts: Urban and Palimpsests and the Politics of Memory*. Stanford: Stanford University Press.

Ianni, Octavio. 1996. *Teorías de la globalización*. Mexico City: Siglo Veintiuno Editores.

IDB. *See* Inter-American Development Bank.

Infante, Ricardo, and Emilio Klein. 1991. "Mercado latinoamericano del trabajo en 1950–1990." *Revista de la CEPAL* 45:129–44.

Instituto Nacional de Pesquisas Educacionais (INEP). 2001. *Sinope Estatística da educaçao superior 2000*. Brasília: Ministerio de Educação.

Inter-American Development Bank (IDB). 2002. *Action Plan for Combating Social Exclusion due to Race or Ethnic Background*. Washington, D.C.: Inter-American Development Bank.

———. 2003. "About social exclusion: mission statement." http://www.iadb.org/sds/soc/site_3094_e.htm.

Itzigsohn, José. 2000. *Developing Poverty. The State, Labor Market Deregulation, and the Informal Sector in Costa Rica and the Dominican Republic*. University Park: Pennsylvania State University Press.

Itzigsohn, José, Carlos Dore, Esther Hernandez, and Obed Vazquez. 1999. "Mapping Dominican Transnationalism: Narrow and Broad Transnational Practices." *Ethnic and Racial Studies* 22:316–39.

Jaguaribe, Helio, Aldo Ferrer, Miguel S. Wionczek, and Theotonio dos Santos. 1970. *La dependencia politico-economica de America Latina*. Mexico City: Siglo Veintiuno Editores.

Jaquette, Jane, ed. 1989. *The Women's Movement in Latin America: Feminism and the Transition to Democracy*. Winchester, Mass.: Unwin Hyman.

Jelin, Elizabeth. 1984. *Familia y unidad doméstica: Mundo público y vida privada*. Buenos Aires: Centro de Estudios de Estado y Sociedad.

———. 1990. *Women and Social Change in Latin America*. London: UNRISD / Zed Books.

———. 1993. *¿Ante, de, en, y? Mujeres y derechos humanos*. Lima: Entre Mujeres.

———. 1994. "Las relaciones intrafamiliares en América Latina." In *Familia y futuro. Un programa regional en América Latina y El Caribe*. Santiago: CEPAL / UNICEF.

———. 1995. "La política de la memoria: El movimiento de derechos humanos y la construcción democrática en la Argentina." In C. H. Acuña et al., *Juicio, casti-gos y memoria: Derechos humanos y justicia en la política argentina.* Buenos Aires: Nueva Visión.

———. 1996a. "La construcción de la ciudadanía: Entre la solidaridad y la respons-abilidad." In *Construir la democracia: Derechos humanos, ciudadanía y sociedad en América Latina,* ed. Elizabeth Jelin and Eric Hershberg. Caracas: Nueva Sociedad.

———. 1996b. "Citizenship Revisited: Solidarity, Responsibility and Rights." In *Con-structing Democracy,* ed. Elizabeth Jelin and Eric Hershberg. Boulder, Colo.: Westview Press.

———. 1996c. "Women, Gender and Human Rights." In *Constructing Democracy,* ed. Elizabeth Jelin and Eric Hershberg. Boulder, Colo.: Westview Press.

———. 1998. *Pan y afectos. La transformación de las familias.* Mexico City: Fondo de Cultura Económica.

———. 2002a. *Los trabajos de la memoria.* Madrid: Siglo XXI de España Editores; Buenos Aires: Siglo XXI de Argentina Editores. A revised edition has been published in English under the title *State Repression and the Labors of Memory* (Minneapolis: University of Minnesota Press, 2003).

———. 2004. "Ciudadanía, derechos e identidad." In "From Marginality of the 1960s to the 'New Poverty' of Today." *Latin American Research Review* 39, no. 1:197–201.

———, ed. 1985. *Los Nuevos movimientos sociales.* Buenos Aires: Centro Editor de América Latina.

———, ed. 1987. *Ciudadanía e identidad: Las mujeres en los movimientos sociales latino-americanos.* Geneva: Instituto de Investigaciones de las Naciones Unidas para el Desarrollo Social.

———, ed. 2002b. *Las conmemoraciones: las disputas en las fechas "in-felices."* Madrid: Siglo XXI de España Editores; Buenos Aires: Siglo XXI de Argentina Editores.

Jelin, Elizabeth, and Eric Hershberg, eds. 1996. *Construir la democracia: Derechos humanos, ciudadanía y sociedad en América Latina.* Caracas: Nueva Sociedad.

Jelin, Elizabeth, and Victoria Langland, eds. 2003. *Monumentos, memoriales y marcas territoriales.* Madrid: Siglo XXI de España Editores; Buenos Aires: Siglo XXI de Argentina Editores.

Jones, G., and P. Ward. 1994. *Methodology for Land and Housing Market Analysis.* Lon-don: University College London.

Joseph, Gilbert M., and Daniel Nugent, eds. 1994. *Everyday Forms of State Formation: Revolution and the Negotiation of Rule in Modern Mexico.* Durham: Duke Uni-versity Press.

Joseph, Jaime. 1999. *Organizaciones sociales de base y gobiernos locales.* Lima: Centro Alternativa, UNRISD-UNV, June.

Juppenlatz, Morris. 1970. *Cities in Transformation: The Urban Squatter Problem of the Developing World.* Brisbane: University of Queensland Press.

Kalmanowiecki, Laura. 2000. "Police, Politics, and Repression in Modern Argentina." In *Reconstructing Criminality in Latin America,* ed. Carlos and Robert Buffington. Wilmington, Del.: Scholarly Resources.

———. 2003. "Policing the People, Building the State: The Police-Military Nexus in

Argentina." In *Irregular Armed Forces and the Role in Politics and State Formation,* ed. Diane E. Davis and Anthony W. Pereira. Cambridge: Cambridge University Press.

Katz, Jorge. 2000. *Reformas estructurales, productividad y conducta tecnológica en América Latina.* Santiago: Fondo de Cultura Económica / CEPAL Chile.

Kaufman, Robert R. 1999. "Approaches to the Study of State Reform in Latin American and Post-socialist Countries." *Comparative Politics* 31, no. 3 (April): 357–75.

Kaul, Inge, Isabelle Grunberg, and Marc A. Stern, eds. 1999. *Global Public Goods. International Cooperation in the 21st Century.* New York: Oxford University Press.

Kay, Cristobal, and Patricio Silva, eds. 1992. *Development and Social Change in the Chilean Countryside.* Amsterdam: CEDLA.

Kay, Stephen J. 1999. "Unexpected Privatizations: Politics and Social Security Reform in the Southern Cone." *Comparative Politics* 31, no. 4 (July): 403–22.

Kaztman, Rubén. 1999. *Activos y estructuras de oportunidades: Estudios sobre las raíces de la vulnerabilidad social en Uruguay.* Montevideo: PNUD / CEPAL.

Kaztman, Rubén, Luis Beccaria, Fernando Filgueira, Laura Golbert, and Gabriel Kessler. 1999. *Vulnerabilidad, activos y exclusión social en Argentina y Uruguay.* Santiago: OIT.

Kaztman, Rubén, and Guillermo Wormald, eds. 2002. *Trabajo y ciudadanía.* Montevideo: Cebra.

Kearney, Michael. 2000. "Transnational Oaxacan Indigenous Identity: The Case of Mixtecs and Zapotecs." *Identities* 7, no. 2 (June): 173–95.

Keck, Margaret, and Kathryn Sikkink. 1998a. *Activists Beyond Borders: Advocacy Networks in International Politics.* Ithaca: Cornell University Press.

———. 1998b. "Transnational Advocacy Networks in the Movement Society." In *The Social Movement Society: Contentious Politics for a New Century,* ed. David S. Meyer and Sidney Tarrow. Lanham, Md.: Rowman and Littlefield.

Kelley, A., and R. Schmidt. 1995. "Aggregate Population and Economic Growth Correlations: The Role of the Components of Demographic Change." *Demography* 32:543–55.

Kemper, R. van. 1974. "Family and Household Organization Among Tzintzuntzán Migrants in Mexico City: A Proposal and a Case Study." In *Latin American Urban Research, volume 4,* ed. W. Cornelius and F. Trueblood. Beverly Hills, Calif.: Sage Publications.

Keynes, John Maynard. 1920. *The Economic Consequences of the Peace.* New York: Harcourt, Brace and Howe.

Kingdom, John W. 1993. "How Do Issues Get on Public Policy Agendas?" In *Sociology and Public Agenda,* ed. William Julius Wilson. Newbury Park: Sage Publications.

Kirby, Peadar. 1996. *The Impact of Neo-liberalism on Chilean Society: A Report for Trócaire School of Communications.* Dublin: Dublin City University. http://www.dcu.ie/~comms/pkirby/chile.htm.

Kitschelt, H. 1986. "Political Opportunity Structures and Political Protest: Anti-Nuclear Movements in Four Democracies." *British Journal of Political Science* 16:58–95.

Koonings, Kees, and Dirk Kruijt. 1999. *Societies of Fear: The Legacy of Civil War, Violence, and Terror in Latin America*. London and New York: Zed Books.

Koonings, Kees, Dirk Kruijt, and Fritx Wils. 1995. "The Very Long March of History." In *Globalization and Third World Trade Unions*, ed. H. Thomas. London: Zed Books.

Koselleck, Reinhart. 1993. *Futuro Pasado: para una semántica de los tiempos históricos*. Barcelona: Paidós.

Kuhn, Thomas. 1970. *The Structure of Scientific Revolutions*. Chicago: University of Chicago Press.

Kurtz, Marcus J. 1999. "Chile's Neoliberal Revolution: Incremental Decisions and Structural Transformation, 1973–89." *Journal of Latin American Studies* 31, no. 2 (May): 399–427.

Kyle, David. 1999. "The Otavalo Trade Diaspora: Social Capital and Transnational Entrepreneurship." *Ethnic and Racial Studies* 22:422–46.

LaCapra, Dominick. 2001. *Writing History, Writing Trauma*. Baltimore: Johns Hopkins University Press.

Laclau, Ernesto. 1977. *Politics and Ideology in Marxist Theory: Capitalism, Fascism, and Populism*. London: Verso Books.

La Garza, Enrique de. 2000. "La flexibilidad del trabajo en América Latina." In *Tratado latinoamericano de sociología del trabajo*, ed. E. de la Garza. 2000. Mexico City: El Colegio de México / FLACSO / UAM / Fondo de Cultura Económica.

Lakatos, Imre. 1978. *The Methodology of Scientific Research Programmes*. Cambridge: Cambridge University Press.

Lamounier, B. 1981. *Instituções e comportamento reprodutivo: O caso de Recife*. São Paulo: CEBRAP.

Lander, Edgardo. 1998. "Límites Actuales del Potencial Democratizador de la Esfera Pública no Estatal." In *Lo público no estatal en la reforma del Estado*, ed. Luiz Carlos Bresser Pereira and Nuria Cunill Grau. Buenos Aires: Paidós.

Landes, D. 1969. *The Unbound Prometheus. Technological Change and Industrial Development in Western Europe from 1750 to the Present*. Cambridge: Cambridge University Press.

Landim, Leilah, and Neide Beres. 1999. *As organizações sem fins lucrativos no Brasil: Ocupacções, despesas e recursos*. Rio de Janeiro: Universidade de Johns Hopkins / Instituto de Estudos da Religião.

Landolt, Patricia. 2000. "The Causes and Consequences of Transnational Migration: Salvadorans in Los Angeles and Washington, D.C." Ph.D. diss., Department of Sociology, Johns Hopkins University.

Landolt, Patricia, Lilian Autler, and Sonia Baires. 1999. "From 'Hermano Lejano' to 'Hermano Mayor': The Dialectics of Salvadoran Transnationalism." *Ethnic and Racial Studies* 22:290–315.

Lasch, Christopher. 1978. *The Culture of Narcissism*. New York: Norton.

Leacock, E. 1971. *The Culture of Poverty: A Critique*. New York: Simon and Schuster.

Lechner, Norbert. 1982. "¿Qué significa hacer política?" In *¿Qué significa hacer política?* ed. Norbert Lechner. Lima: DESCO.

———. 1986. "Los derechos humanos como categoría política." In *La ética de la democracia*, ed. Waldo Ansaldi. Buenos Aires: CLACSO.

———. 2000. "Desafíos de un desarrollo humano: individualización y capital social." *Instituciones y Desarrollo* 7. Barcelona: Instituto Internacional de Gobernabilidad.

Leeds, A. 1969. "The Significant Variables Determining the Character of Squatter Settlements." *America Latina* 12:44–86.

———. 1971. "The Concept of the 'Culture of Poverty': Conceptual, Logical, and Empirical Problems, with Perspectives from Brazil and Peru." In *The Culture of Poverty: A Critique,* ed. E. B. Leacock. New York: Simon and Schuster.

Leeds, Elizabeth. 1972. "Forms of Squatment Political Organization: The Politics of Control in Brazil." Master's thesis, University of Texas at Austin.

Lefort, Claude. 1987. "Los derechos del hombre y el Estado benefactor." *Revista Vuelta Sudamericana* 12 (July).

Leite, Marcia. 1999. "Nuevos desafíos en el mundo del trabajo." *Sociología del Trabajo* 36:3–31.

Le Monde Diplomatique. 1998. Spanish Edition. April 15–June 15.

Lentner, Howard H. 1993. *State Formation in Central America: The Struggle for Autonomy, Development, and Democracy.* Westport, Conn.: Greenwood Press.

León, Magdalena, ed. 1997. *Poder y empoderamiento de las mujeres.* Bogotá: Tercer Mundo y Facultad de Ciencias Humanas.

Lesgart, Cecilia. 2003. *Usos de la transición a la democracia. Ensayo, ciencia y política en la década del ochenta.* Rosario, Argentina: Homo Sapiens.

Lesthaeghe, Ron. 1998. "On Theory Development and Applications to the Study of Family Formation." *Population and Development Review* 24, no. 1 (March): 1–14.

Levitt, Peggy. 2000. "Transnational Migration and Development: A Case of Two for the Price of One?" Working Paper, Center for Migration and Development, Princeton University.

Lewis, Oscar. 1966. *La Vida.* New York: Random House.

Lewis, W. Arthur. 1954. "Economic Development with Unlimited Supplies of Labor." *Manchester School* 22 (May): 139–91.

Lim, Lin Lean. 1993. "Effects of Women's Positions on Their Migration." In *Women's Position and Demographic Change,* ed. Nora Federici, Karen Oppenheim Mason, and Solvi Sogner. Oxford: Unión Internacional para el Estudio Científico de la Población (IUSSP) / Oxford University Press.

Lloyd-Sherlock, Peter. 1997. "Models of Public Sector Intervention: Providing for the Elderly in Argentina (c.1890–1994)." *Journal of Latin American Studies* 29, no. 1 (February).

Lomnitz, Larissa. 1975. *Como sobreviven los marginados.* Mexico City: Siglo Veintiuno Editores. Published in English in 1977 under the title *Networks and Marginality: Life in a Mexican Shantytown.*

———. 1977. *Networks and Marginality: Life in a Mexican Shantytown.* New York: Academic Press.

Long, Norman. 2001. *Development Sociology: Actor Perspectives.* London: Routledge.

López Barajas, María de la Paz. 1998. "Composición de las Unidades Domésticas: Revisión de los cambios recientes." In *Vida familiar y cultura contemporánea,* ed. José M. Valenzuela and Vania Salles. Mexico City: CONACULTA / Culturas Populares.

Lovell, Peggy A. 1994. "Race, Gender and Development in Brazil." *Latin American Research Review* 29, no. 3:7–35.

——. 2000a. "Gender, Race and the Struggle for Social Justice in Brazil." *Latin American Perspectives* 27, no. 6:85–103.

——. 2000b. "Race, Gender and Regional Labor Market Inequalities in Brazil." *Review of Social Economy* 62, no. 3:277–93.

Lowe, Stuart. 1986. *Urban Social Movements: The City After Castells.* New York: St. Martin's Press.

Loyola, M. A., and M. de Conceição Quinteiro. 1982. *Instituções e reprodução.* São Paulo: CEBRAP.

Lozano, Wilfredo. 1998. "Desregulación laboral, estado y mercado en América Latina: Balance y retos sociopolíticos." *Perfiles Latinoamericanos* 13:113–52.

Lucena, Hector. 2000. "El cambio en las relaciones industriales en América Latina." Paper presented at the conference "New Directions for Union Organizing in Mexico." Organized by Enrique de la Garza for the Center for Latin American Studies at the University of California, Berkeley, September 28.

Maddison, A. 1991. *Dynamic Forces in Capitalist Development. A Long-Run Comparative View.* Oxford: Oxford University Press.

Madrid, Raul. 2003. *Retiring the State: The Politics of Pension Privatization in Latin America and Beyond.* Stanford: Stanford University Press.

Mander, J., and E. Goldsmith. 1996. *The Case Against the Global Economy.* San Francisco: Sierra Club Books.

Mangin, William. 1967. "The Latin American Squatter Settlements: A Problem and a Solution." *Latin American Research Review* 2 (3):65–98.

Mann, M. 1987. "Ruling Class Strategies and Citizenship." *Sociology* 21, no. 3:339–54.

Mares, David R. 1993. "State Leadership in Economic Policy: A Collective Action Framework with a Colombian Case." *Comparative Politics* 25, no. 4 (July): 454–74.

Markarian, Vania. 2003. "Uruguayan Exiles and the Latin American Human Rights Networks, 1967–1984." Ph.D. diss., Columbia University.

Mars, J. R. 2002. *Deadly Force, Colonialism, and the Rule of Law: Police Violence in Guyana.* Westport, Conn.: Greenwood Press.

Marshall, Adriana. 1996. "Empleo público en América Latina." *Revista Latinoamericana de Estudios del Trabajo* 2:49–78.

Marshall, T. H. [1949] 1964. "Citizenship and Social Class." In T. H. Marshall, *Class, Citizenship, and Social Development.* Chicago: University of Chicago Press.

——. 1964. *Citizenship and Social Democracy.* New York: Doubleday.

——. 1981. *The Right to Welfare.* New York: The Free Press.

Martine, G., and V. E. Faria. 1988. "Impacts of Social Research on Policy Formulation: Lessons from the Brazilian Experience in the Population Field." *Journal of Developing Areas* 23:43–61.

Marx, Karl. [1867] 1967. *Capital: A Critique of Political Economy, Volume I. A Critical Analysis of Capitalist Production.* Edited by Frederick Engels. New York: International Publishers.

Massey, D., R. Alarcón, J. Durand, and H. González. 1987. *Return to Aztlan: The*

Social Process of International Migration from Western Mexico. Berkeley and Los Angeles: University of California Press.

Massiah, Jocelyn. 1983. *Women as Heads of Households in the Caribbean: Family Structure Statues.* Organización para las Naciones Unidas para la Educación, la Ciencia y la Cultura. Colchester: Essex.

Mauceri, Philip. 1995. "State Reform, Coalitions, and the Neoliberal Autogolpe in Peru." *Latin American Research Review* 30, no. 1:7–38.

Maxfield, Sylvia. 1997. *Gatekeepers of Growth: The International Political Economy of Central Banking in Developing Countries.* Princeton: Princeton University Press.

McAdam, Doug, John McCarthy, and Mayer Zald. 1988. "Social Movements." In *Handbook of Sociology,* ed. Neil Smelser. Newbury Park, Calif.: Sage Publications.

McIntosh, G., and J. J. Finkle. 1995. "The Cairo Conference on Population and Development." *Population and Development Review* 21:223–60.

Mello Lemos, Maria Carmen. 1998. "The Politics of Pollution Control in Brazil: State Actors and Social Movements Cleaning up Cubatão." *World Development* 26, no. 1:75–88.

Melo, Marcus. 1996. "Crise federativa, guerra fiscal e 'hobbesianismo municipal': Efeitos perversos da descentralização?" *São Paulo em Perspectiva* 10, no. 3:11–20.

Melucci, Alberto. 1989. *Nomads of the Present: Social Movements and Individual Needs in Contemporary Society.* London: Hutchinson Radius.

Mendez, Juan, Guillermo O'Donnell, and Paolo Sergio Pinheiro, eds. 1999. *The (un)Rule of Law and the Underprivileged in Latin America.* Notre Dame: University of Notre Dame Press.

Merkel, Wolfgang. 1999. "Defective Democracies." Estudio/Working Paper 132, Centro de Estudios Avanzandos en Ciencias Sociales, Instituto Juan March de Estudios e Investigaciones, Madrid, March.

Mertens, Leonard. 1996. *Competencia laboral: Sistemas, surgimiento y modelos.* Montevideo: Cintefor/OIT.

Merton, Robert K. [1949] 1968. *Social Theory and Social Structure.* Part 1. New York: The Free Press.

———. 1984. "Socially Expected Durations: A Case Study of Concept Formation in Sociology." In *Conflict and Consensus,* ed. W. W. Powell and R. Robbins. New York: The Free Press.

Mesa-Lago, Carmelo. 1978. *Social Security in Latin America: Pressure Groups, Stratification and Inequality.* Pittsburgh: University of Pittsburgh Press.

———. 1994. *Changing Social Security in Latin America. Towards Alleviating the Social Costs of Economic Reform.* Boulder, Colo.: Lynne Rienner.

Mezzera, Jaime. 1987. "Notas sobre la segmentación de los mercados laborales urbanos." *Documentos de trabajo* 289. Santiago: PREALC.

Mills, C. Wright. 1959. *The Sociological Imagination.* London: Oxford University Press.

Minujin, Antonio. 1998. "Vulnerabilidad y exclusión en América Latina." In *Todos entran. Propuesta para sociedades influyentes,* ed. E. Bustelo and A. Minujin. Bogotá: UNICEF/Santillana.

Mishra, Ramesh. 1981. *Society and Social Policy.* London: Macmillan.

Mitchell, J. Clyde. 1969. "The Concept and Use of Social Networks." In *Social Networks in Social Situations,* ed. J. Clyde Mitchell. Manchester: Manchester University Press.

Mitchell, Michael, and Charles H. Wood. 1999. "Ironies of Citizenship in Brazil: Skin Color, Police Brutality, and the Challenge to Democracy in Brazil." *Social Forces* 77, no. 3:1001–20.

Moguillansky, Graciela, and Ricardo Bielschowsky. 2000. *Inversión y reformas económicas en América Latina fondo de cultura económica.* Santiago: CEPAL Chile.

Moisés, José Alvaro. 1981. "O estado, as contradições urbanas e os movimentos sociais." In *Cidade, Povo e Poder,* ed. Moisés et al. Rio de Janeiro: Paz e Terra.

Molyneux, Maxine. 2000a. "Comparative Perspectives on Gender and Citizenship." In *Towards a Gendered Political Economy,* ed. Joanne Cook, Jennifer Roberts, and Georgina Waylen. London: Macmillan; New York: St. Martin's Press.

———. 2000b. "Ciudadanía y política social en perspectiva comparada." In *Política social: Vínculo entre estado y sociedad,* ed. Sergio Reuben Soto. San José, Costa Rica: Editorial de la Universidad de Costa Rica.

Monsiváis, Carlos. 1987. *Entrada libre: Crónicas de la sociedad que se organiza.* Mexico City: ERA.

Mora, Mainor. 2000. "Tendencias de precarización de empleo en América Latina." Paper presented to the workshop "Latin American Labor and Globalization: Trends Following a Decade of Economic Adjustment," organized by the Social Science Research Council and FLACSO-Costa Rica, San José, Costa Rica, July 10 and 11.

Moreno, José Antonio. 1970. *Barrios in Arms; Revolution in Santo Domingo.* Pittsburgh: University of Pittsburgh Press.

Moser, C.O.N. 1978. "Informal Sector of Petty Commodity Production: Dualism or Dependence in Urban Development?" *World Development* 6:1041–64.

———. 1998. "The Asset Vulnerability Framework: Reassessing Urban Poverty Reduction Strategies." *World Development* 26:1–19.

Mummert, Gail. 1992. "Mexican Rural Women's Struggle for Family Livelihood: Case Study of Working Daughters and Working Wives in a Migrant Village." Paper presented at the conference "Learning from Latin America: Women's Struggles for Livelihood," University of California at Los Angeles, February.

Muñoz, Humberto, Orlandina de Oliveira, and Claudio Stern. 1982. *Mexico City: Industrialization, Migration, and the Labour Force, 1930–1970.* Paris: UNESCO.

Murillo, María Victoria. 2000. "From Populism to Neoliberalism: Labor Unions and Market Reforms in Latin America." *World Politics* 52, no. 2:135–74.

———. 2001. "La encrucijada del sindicalismo latinoamericano." *Política y Gobierno* 8, no. 2:315–46.

Murray, Charles. 1984. *Losing Ground: American Social Policy, 1950–1980.* New York: Basic Books.

Nagel, Ernest. 1961. *The Structure of Science.* New York: Harcourt, Brace, and World.

Nassuno, Marianne. 1998. "El control social en las organizaciones sociales en el Brasil." In *Lo público no estatal en la reforma del estado,* ed. Luiz Carlos Bresser Pereira and Nuria Cunill Grau. Buenos Aires: Paidós.

Navarro, Juan Carlos. 1998. "Las ONGs y la prestación de servicios sociales en América Latina: El aprendizaje ha comenzado." In *Lo público no estatal en la reforma del estado,* ed. Luiz Carlos Bresser Pereira and Nuria Cunill Grau. Buenos Aires: Paidós.

Navarro, Zander. 1998. "Democracia y control social de fondos públicos. El caso del "presupuesto participativo" de Porto Alegre (Brasil)." In *Lo público no estatal en la reforma del estado,* ed. Luiz Carlos Bresser Pereira and Nuria Cunill Grau. Buenos Aires: Paidós.

Nayyar, Deepak. 2002. *Governing Globalization: Issues and Institutions.* New York: Oxford University Press.

Negretto, Gabriel L., and Jose Antonio Aguilar-Rivera. 2000. "Rethinking the Legacy of the Liberal State in Latin America: The Cases of Argentina and Mexico." *Journal of Latin American Studies* 32, no. 2 (May): 361–97.

Nelson, Joan. 1979. *Access to Power: Politics and the Urban Poor in Developing Nations.* Princeton: Princeton University Press.

Newton, Ken. 2001. "Social Capital." In *Encyclopedia of Democratic Thought,* ed. Joe Foweraker and Paul Barry Clarke. New York: Routledge.

Nun, José. 1967. "The Middle Class Military Coup." In *The Politics of Conformity in Latin America,* ed. Claudio Véliz. New York: Oxford University Press.

———. 1969. "Superpoblación relativa, ejército industrial de reserva y masa marginal." *Revista Latinoamericana de Sociología* 5, no. 2:178–236.

———. 2001. *Marginalidad y exclusión social.* Buenos Aires: Fondo de Cultura Económica.

———. 2003. *Democracy: Government of the People, or Government of the Politicians.* Lanham, Md.: Rowman and Littlefield.

Nylen, William R. 1993. "Selling Neoliberalism: Brazil? Instituto Liberal." *Journal of Latin American Studies* 25, no. 2:301–11.

Oberschall, Anthony. 1973. *Social Conflict and Social Movements.* Englewood Cliffs, N.J.: Prentice Hall.

Ocampo, José Antonio. 2000. *Developing Countries Anti-Cyclical Policies in a Globalized World.* Temas de Coyuntura series, no. 13. Santiago: CEPAL.

———. 2001. "Recasting the International Financial Agenda." In *External Liberalization, Economic Performance, and Social Policy,* ed. John Eatwell and Lance Taylor. New York: Oxford University Press.

O'Connor, James. 1973. *The Fiscal Crisis of the State.* New York: St. Martin's Press.

O'Donnell, Guillermo. 1973. *Modernization and Bureaucratic-Authoritarianism: Studies in South American Politics.* Berkeley: Institute for International Studies, University of California.

———. 1988. *Bureaucratic Authoritarianism: Argentina, 1966–1973, in Comparative Perspective.* Berkeley and Los Angeles: University of California Press.

———. 1999. *Counterpoints: Selected Essays on Authoritarianism and Democratization.* Notre Dame: University of Notre Dame Press.

Offe, Claus. 1984. *Contradictions of the Welfare State.* London: Hutchinson.

OIT. 2000. "La reforma laboral en América Latina. Un análisis comparado." *Documentos de Trabajo* 123. Lima: OIT.

———. 2001. *Panorama laboral 2001.* Lima: OIT.

Oliveira, Maria Coleta, and Maria Isabel Baltar da Rocha, eds. 2001. *Saude reprodutiva na esfera pública e política.* Campinas, Brasil: Editora da Unicamp.

Oliveira, Orlandina de. 1997. "Multiple Analytic Perspectives on Women's Labor in Latin America." *Current Sociology* 45, no. 1:109–19.

——. 1998. "Familia y relaciones de género en México." In *Familias y relaciones de género en transformación. Cambios trascendentales en América Latina y el Caribe,* ed. Beatríz Schmuckler. Mexico City: Population Council-Edamex.

——. 1999. "Políticas económicas, arreglos familiares y perceptores de ingresos." *Demos. Carta Demográfica de México* 12:32–33.

——, ed. 1989. *Trabajo, poder y sexualidad.* Mexico City: Programa Interdisciplinario de Estudios de la Mujer, El Colegio de México.

Oliveira, Orlandina de, and Marina Ariza. 1997. "División sexual del trabajo y exclusión social." *Revista Latinoamericana de Estudios del Trabajo* 3, no. 5:183–202.

Oliveira, Orlandina de, Marina Ariza, and Marcela Eternod. 1996. "Trabajo e inequidad de género." In *La condición femenina: Una propuesta de indicadores. informe final.* Mexico City: Sociedad Mexicana de Demografía (Somede) / Consejo Nacional de Población (Conapo).

——. 2001. "La fuerza del trabajo en México: Un siglo de cambios." In *La población de México. Tendencias y perspectivas sociodemográficas hacia el siglo XXI,* ed. Gómez De León and Cecilia Rabell. Mexico City: Consejo Nacional de Población / Fondo de Cultura Económica.

Oliveira, Orlandina de, Marcela Eternod, and Paz López. 1999. "Familia y género en el análisis sociodemográfico." In *Mujer, género y población,* ed. Brígida García. Mexico City: El Colegio de México.

Oliveira, Orlandina de, and Bryan Roberts. 1994. "Urban Growth and Urban Social Structure in Latin America, 1930–1990." In *The Cambridge History of Latin America,* vol. 6, ed. Lesley Bethell. Cambridge: Cambridge University Press.

Oquist, Paul H. 1980. *Violence, Conflict, and Politics in Colombia.* New York: Academic Press.

Oropesa, R. S., and Dennis Hogan. 1994. "The Status of Women in Mexico: An Analysis of Marital Power Dynamics." Working Papers Series, Population Research Institute, Pennsylvania State University.

Ostrom, Edward. 1996. "Crossing the Great Divide: Co-production, Synergy and Development." *World Development* 24, no. 6:1073–88.

Oteiza, Enrique. 1971. "La migración de profesionales, técnicos y obreros calificados Argentinos a los estados unidos." *Desarrollo Económico* 10:429–54.

Oved, Jaâcov. 1978. *El anarquismo y el movimiento obrero en Argentina.* Mexico City: Siglo Veintiuno Editores.

Oxhorn, Philip. 1994. "Understanding Political Change after Authoritarian Rule." *Journal of Latin American Studies* 26 (October): 737–59.

——. 1995. *Organizing Civil Society: The Popular Sectors and the Struggle for Democracy in Chile.* University Park: Pennsylvania State University Press.

Page, R. 1992. "Empowerment, Oppression and Beyond: A Coherent Strategy?" *Critical Social Policy* 35:89–92.

Paiva, Paulo de Tarso A. 1987. "O proceso de proletarização como fator de destabilização dos niveis de fecundidade no Brasil." *Revista Brasileira de Economia* 41, no. 4:383–414.

Paley, Julia. 2001. *Marketing Democracy: Power and Social Movements in Post-dictatorship Chile.* Berkeley and Los Angeles: University of California Press.

Palma, Yolanda, Teresa Jácome del Moral, and José Luis Palma Cabrera. 1992. "Percepción del valor de los hijos en tres regiones de México." Paper presented at the conference "El Poblamiento de las Américas: Actas," Veracruz, May.

Pantelides, E. A., and S. Bott, eds. 2000. *Reproducción, salud y sexualidad en América Latina.* Buenos Aires: Editorial Biblos / OMS.

Parker, R. G., and R. Barbosa, eds. 1996. *Sexualidades brasileiras.* Rio de Janeiro: Relume-Dumará Ann.

Pastor, Manuel, and Carol Wise. 1997. "State Policy, Distribution, and Neoliberal Reform in Mexico." *Journal of Latin American Studies* 29, no. 2:419–52.

Pastore, José, and Nelson do Valle e Silva. 2000. *Mobilidade social no Brasil.* São Paulo: Makron Books.

Patrón, Pepi. 1998. "Peru: Civil Society and the Autocratic Challenge." In *Civil Society and the Aid Industry,* ed. Alison Van Rooy. London: Earthscan.

Payne, Leigh. 2000. *Uncivil Movements: The Armed Right-Wing and Democracy in Latin America.* Baltimore: John Hopkins University Press.

Paz, P. 1970. *El subdesarrollo latinoamericano y la teoría del desarrollo.* Mexico City: Siglo Veintiuno Editores.

Pereira, Anthony W. 2001. "Virtual Legality: Authoritarian Legacies and the Reform of Military Justice in Brazil, the Southern Cone, and Mexico." *Comparative Political Studies* 34, no. 5 (June): 555–74.

——. Forthcoming. *Political (In)justice: National Security Legality in Brazil and the Southern Cone.* Pittsburgh: Pittsburgh University Press.

Pereira, Anthony W., and Diane E. Davis. 2000. "New Patterns of Militarized Violence and Coercion in the America." In "Violence, Coercion and Rights in the America." Special issue, *Latin American Perspectives* 27, no. 2:3–17.

Pérez Sáinz, Juan Pablo. 1994. *El dilema del nahual.* San Jose: FLACSO Editores.

——. 1996. "Apatia y esperanzas: Las dos caras del area metropolitana de Guatemala." In *Ciudades del Caribe: En el umbral del nuevo siglo,* ed. A. Portes and C. Dore. Caracas: Nueva Sociedad.

——. 1998. "¿Es necesario aún el concepto de informalidad?" *Perfiles Latinoamericanos* 13:55–72.

——. 1999. "Mercado laboral, integración social y modernización globalizada en Centroamérica." *Nueva Sociedad* 164 (November-December): 106–21.

——. 2000. "Labor Market Transformations in Latin America." Paper presented at the workshop "Latin America Labor and Globalization Trends Following a Decade of Economic Adjustment," organized by the Social Science Research Council (SSRC) and FLACSO-Costa Rica, San José, July 10–11.

——. 2002. "Globalización, *upgrading* y pequeña empresa: algunas notas analíticas." In *Encadenamientos globales y pequeña empresa en Centroamérica,* ed. J. P. Pérez Sáinz. San José: FLACSO.

——. 2003a "Exclusión laboral en América Latina: viejas y nuevas tendencias." *Sociología del Trabajo* 47:107–38.

———. 2003b "Globalización, riesgo y empleabilidad. Algunas hipótesis." *Nueva Sociedad* 184:68–85.

Pérez Sáinz, Juan Pablo, and Katharine Andrade-Eekhoff. 2003. *Communities in Globalization. The Invisible Mayan Nahual.* Lanham, Md.: Rowman and Littlefield.

Pérez Sáinz, Juan Pablo, and Mainor Mora. 2001. "El riesgo de pobreza. Una propuesta analítica desde la evidencia costaricense." *Estudos Sociológicos* 57:747–68.

Perlman, Janice E. 1976. *The Myth of Marginality: Urban Poverty and Politics in Rio de Janeiro.* Berkeley and Los Angeles: University of California Press.

Peruzzotti, Enrique. 1999. "Constitucionalismo, populismo y sociedad civil. Lecciones del caso argentino." *Revista Mexicana de Sociología* 61, no. 4 (October–December): 149–72.

Petras, James F., and Maurice Zeitlin, eds. 1968. *Latin America, Reform or Revolution?* Greenwich, Conn.: Fawcett Publications.

del Pino, Ponciano, and Elizabeth Jelin, eds. 2003. *Luchas locales, comunidades e identidades.* Buenos Aires: Siglo XXI de Argentina Editores; Madrid: Siglo XXI de España Editores.

PNUD (Programa de las Naciones Unidas para el Desarrollo). 1999. *Informe sobre desarrollo humano.* New York: United Nations.

Polanyi, K. 1957. *The Great Transformation.* Boston: Beacon Press.

Popkin, Eric. 1999. "Guatemalan Mayan Migration to Los Angeles: Constructing Transnational Linkages in the Context of the Settlement Process." *Ethnic and Racial Studies* 22:267–84.

Popkin, Eric, and Katharine Andrade-Eekhoff. 2000. "The Construction of Household Labor Market Strategies in Central American Transnational Migrant Communities." Paper presented to the workshop "Latin American Labor and Globalization: Trends Following a Decade of Economic Adjustment," organized by the Social Science Research Council and FLACSO-Costa Rica, San José, Costa Rica, July 10 and 11.

Popper, Karl. 1959. *The Logic of Scientific Discovery.* London: Hutchinson.

Population Division of the Department of Social and Economic Affairs of the United Nations Secretariat. 2003. *World Population Prospects: The 2002 Revision.* New York: United Nations.

Portantiero, Juan Carlos. 1981. *Los usos de gramsci.* Mexico City: Pasado y Presente.

Portes, Alejandro. 1970. "Los grupos urbanos marginados: Nuevo intento de explicación." *Aportes* 18:131–47.

———. 1971. "Political Primitivism, Differential Socialization and Lower-class Leftist Radicalism." *American Sociological Review* 36:820–35.

———. 1972. "Rationality in the Slums: An Essay in Interpretive Sociology." *Comparative Studies in Society and History* 14, no. 3:268–86.

———. 1985. "Latin American Class Structures: Their Composition and Change During the Lost Decade." *Latin American Research Review* 20:7–39.

———. 1994. "When More Can Be Less: Labor Standards, Development, and the Informal Economy." In *Contrapunto: The Informal Sector Debate in Latin America,* ed. Cathy Rakowski. Albany: SUNY Press.

———. 1995a. "Economic Sociology and the Sociology of Immigration: A Conceptual Overview." In *The Economic Sociology of Immigration, Essays on Networks, Ethnicity, and Entrepreneurship,* ed. Alejandro Portes. New York: Russell Sage Foundation.

——. 1995b. *En torno a la informalidad: ensayos sobre teoría y medición de la economía no regulada*. Mexico City: Porrúa.

——. 1996a. "Global Villages: The Rise of Transnational Communities." *American Prospect* 25:74–77.

——. 1996b. "Transnational Communities: Their Emergence and Significance in the Contemporary World-System. In *Latin America in the World-Economy*, ed. Roberto P. Korzeniewicz. Westport, Conn.: Greenwood Press.

——. 1997. "Neoliberalism and the Sociology of Development: Emerging Trends and Unanticipated Facts." *Population and Development Review* 23:229–59.

——. 1998a. "Like Phoenix from the Ashes: Cuban Sociology Is Back." *Footnotes* 2 (November).

——. 1998b. "Social Capital: Its Origins and Applications in Modern Sociology." *Annual Review of Sociology* 24:1–24.

——. 1999. "Globalization from Below: The Rise of Transnational Communities." In *The Ends of Globalization: Bringing Society Back In*, ed. M. van der Land, D. Kalb, and R. Staring. Lanham, Md.: Rowman and Littlefield.

——. 2000a. "The Hidden Abode: Sociology as Analysis of the Unexpected." *American Sociological Review* 65:1–18.

——. 2000b. "The Resilient Significance of Class: A Nominalist Interpretation." *Political Power and Social Theory* 14:249–84.

Portes, Alejandro, Manuel Castells, and Lauren A. Benton. 1989. *The Informal Economy: Studies in Advanced and Less-Developed Countries*. Baltimore: Johns Hopkins University Press.

Portes, A., and C. Dore, eds. 1996. *Ciudades del Caribe: En el umbral del nuevo siglo*. Caracas: Nueva Sociedad.

Portes, Alejandro, Luis Guarnizo, and Patricia Landolt. 1999. "The Study of Transnationalism: Pitfalls and Promises of an Emergent Research Field." *Ethnic and Racial Studies* 22, no. 2 (March): 217–37.

Portes, Alejandro, and Kelly Hoffman. 2003. "Latin American Class Structures: Their Composition and Change During the Neoliberal Era." *Latin American Research Review* 38, no. 1:41–82.

Portes, Alejandro, and Douglas Kincaid. 1989. "Sociology and Development in the 1990s: Critical Challenges and Empirical Trends." *Sociological Forum* 4:479–503.

Portes, Alejandro, and Patricia Landolt. 1996. "The Downside of Social Capital." *American Prospect* 26:18–22.

Portes, Alejandro, and Julia Sensenbrenner. 1993. "Embeddedness and Immigration: Notes on the Social Determinants of Economic Action." *American Journal of Sociology* 98:1320–50.

Portes, Alejandro, and John Walton. 1976. *Urban Latin America: The Political Condition from Above and Below*. Austin: University of Texas Press.

——. 1981. *Labor, Class and the International System*. New York: Academic Press.

Potter, Joseph E. 1983. "Effects of Societal and Community Institutions on Fertility." In *Determinants of Fertility in Less Developed Countries*, ed. R. D. Lee and R. Bulatao. New York: Academic Press.

Potter, Joseph E., Octavio Mojarro, and Leopoldo Nunez. 1987. "The Influence of Health Care on Contraceptive Acceptance in Rural Mexico." *Studies in Family Planning* 18:144–56.

Potter, Joseph E., Myriam Ordoñez G., and Anthony R. Measham. 1976. "The Rapid Decline in Colombian Fertility." *Population and Development Review* 2:509–28.

Poulantzas, N. 1973. *Political Power and Social Classes*. London: New Left Books.

Powell, Dorian. 1986. "Caribbean Women and Their Response to Familial Experiences." *Social and Economic Studies* 35, no. 2:83–130.

PREALC. 1991. *Empleo y equidad: el desafío de los 90*. Santiago: PREALC.

Prebisch, Raul. 1950. *The Economic Development of Latin America and Its Principal Problems*. New York: United Nations.

———. 1964. *The Economic Development of Latin America in the Post-War Period*. New York: United Nations.

———. 1986. "Notes on Trade from the Standpoint of the Periphery." *CEPAL Review* 28:203–16.

———. 2001. "Canada and U.S. Taken to WTO." *Latin American Weekly Report*, February 6, p. 65.

Pries, Ludwig. 2000. "Una nueva cara de la migración globalizada: El surgimiento de nuevos espacios sociales transnacionales y plurilocales." *Trabajo* 3.

Przeworski, Adam. 1986. "Some Problems in the Study of the Transition to Democracy." In *Transitions from Authoritarian Rule: Comparative Perspectives*, ed. G. O'Donnell, P. Schmitter, and L. Whitehead. Baltimore: Johns Hopkins University Press.

Psacharapoulos, George, and Zafiris Tzannatos, eds. 1992. *Case Studies on Women's Employment and Pay in Latin America*. Washington, D.C.: The World Bank.

Putnam, Robert. 1993a. *Making Democracy Work: Civic Traditions in Modern Italy*. Princeton: Princeton University Press.

———. 1993b. "The Prosperous Community: Social Capital and Public Life." *American Prospect* 13:35–42.

———. 1995. "Bowling Alone: America's Decline of Social Capital." *Journal of Democracy* 6, no. 1:65–78.

Quijano, Anibal. 1966. *Notas sobre el concepto de marginalidad social*. Report, División de Asuntos Sociales. Santiago, Chile: Economic Comission for Latin America y el Caribe.

———. 1973. "Redifinicion de la dependencia y proceso de marginalización en América Latina." In *Populismo, marginalización y dependencia*, ed. F. Weffort and A. Quijano. San José, Costa Rica: Editorial Universitaria Centroamericana.

———. 1974. "The Marginal Pole of the Economy and the Marginalized Labor Force." *Economy and Society* 3, no. 4:393–428.

Quilodrán, Julieta. 2000. "Atisbos de cambios en la formación de las parejas conyugales a fines del milenio." *Papeles de Población* 6, no. 25.

Quinteros, Carolina. 2000. "Acciones y actores no sindicales para causas sindicales. El caso del monitoreo independiente en Centroamérica." *Nueva Sociedad* 169.

Radcliffe, Sarah, and Sallie Westwood. 1996. *Remaking the Nation: Place, Identity, and Politics in Latin America*. London: Routledge.

Ramos, S., M. Gogna, M. Petracci, and D. Szulik. 2001. *Los médicos frente a la anticoncepción y el aborto: Una transición ideológica?* Buenos Aires: CEDES.

Randall, Vicky, and Georgina Waylen, eds. 1998. *Gender, Politics and the State*. London and New York: Routledge.

Rapp, Rayna. 1982. "Family and Class in Contemporary America: Notes Toward an

Understanding of Ideology." In *Rethinking the Family. Some Feminist Questions*, ed. Barrie Thorne and Marilyn Yalom. New York: Longman.

Ray, Talton. 1969. *The Politics of the Barrios*. Berkeley and Los Angeles: University of California Press.

Reilly, Charles A. 1998. "Redistribución de derechos y responsabilidades: Ciudadanía y capital social." In *Lo público no estatal en la reforma del estado*, ed. Luiz Carlos Bresser Pereira and Nuria Cunill Grau. Buenos Aires: Paidós.

Reis, Fabio Wanderly. 1996. "The State, the Market and Democratic Citizenship." In *Constructing Democracy*, ed. Elizabeth Jelin and Eric Hershberg. Boulder, Colo.: Westview Press.

Rendón, María Teresa. 2000. "Trabajo de hombres y trabajo de mujeres en México durante el siglo XX." Ph.D. diss., Facultad de Economía, Universidad Autónoma de México.

Richards, Patricia. 2004. *Pobladoras, Indígenas, and the State*. New Brunswick: Rutgers University Press.

Ricoeur, Paul. 1999. *La lectura del tiempo pasado: memoria y olvido*. Madrid: Arrecife-Universidad Autónoma de Madrid.

Rifkin, J. 1996. *The End of Work: The Decline of the Global Labor Force and the Dawn of the Post-Market Era*. New York: Tarcher/Putnam.

Risse, T., S. C. Ropp, and K. Sikkink. 1999. *The Power of Human Rights: International Norms and Domestic Change*. Cambridge: Cambridge University Press.

Rivera, Marcia. 1998. "Reinventando el oficio: El desafío de reconstruir la investigacion en ciencias sociales en el proximo milenio." In *Pueblo, época y desarrollo: La sociología de América Latina*, ed. R. Briceño-León and H. R. Sonntag, 119–33. Caracas: Nueva Sociedad / LACSO.

Roberts, Bryan. 1968. "Protestant Groups and Coping with Urban Life in Guatemala." *American Journal of Sociology* 73, no. 6:753–67.

———. 1973. *Organizing Strangers: Poor Families in Guatemala City*. Austin: University of Texas Press.

———. 1978. *Cities of Peasants: The Political Economy of Urbanization in the Third World*. London: Edward Arnold; Beverly Hills, Calif.: Sage Publications.

———. 1995. *The Making of Citizens*. London: Edward Arnold.

———. 1996. "The Social Context of Citizenship in Latin America." *International Journal of Urban and Regional Research* 20:38–65.

———. 2002. "Citizenship, Social Policy and Population Change." In *Exclusion and Engagement: Social Policy in Latin America*, ed. Christopher Abel and Colin M. Lewis. London: Institute of Latin American Studies.

———. 2004. "From Marginality to Social Exclusion: From Laissez Faire to Pervasive Engagement." In "From the Marginality of the 1960s to the 'New Poverty' of Today." *Latin American Research Review* 39 (1): 195–97.

Roberts, Bryan R., Reanne Frank, and Fernando Lozano-Ascencio.1999. "Transnational Migrant Communities and Mexican Migration to the United States." *Ethnic and Racial Studies* 22:238–66.

Robinson, William I. 1998a. "Beyond Nation-state Paradigms: Globalization, Sociology, and the Challenge of Transnational Studies." *Sociological Forum* 13, no. 4:561–94.

———. 1998b. "Latin America and Global Capitalism." *Race & Class* 2, no. 3:111–31.

———. 1999. "The Fin de Siecle Debate: Globalization as Epochal Shift." *Science and Society* 63, no. 1:10–39.

———. 2004. *A Theory of Global Capitalism: Production, Class, and State in a Transnational World*. Baltimore: Johns Hopkins University Press.

Rodríguez, V. E. 1997. *Decentralization in Mexico: From Reforma Municipal to Solidaridad to Nuevo Federalismo*. Boulder, Colo.: Westview Press.

Rodrik, Dani. 1997. *Has Globalization Gone Too Far?* Washington, D.C.: Institute for International Economics.

Rohter, Larry. 2003. "Racial Quotas in Brazil Touch Off Fierce Debate." *New York Times*, April 8.

Rojas, Olga. 2002. "Paternidad y vida familiar en la ciudad de México: Un acercamiento cualitativo al papel desempeñado por los varones en los ambitos doméstico y reproductivo." Ph.D. diss., Estudios de Población, El Colegio de México.

Roncagliolo, R. 1998. "¿Integración Cultural versus Globalización?" *Revista Cultura Secretaría Comunicación y Cultura*. Santiago.

Rosanvallon, Pierre. 2000. *The New Social Question: Rethinking the Welfare State*. Princeton: Princeton University Press.

Rostow, W.W. 1960. *The Stages of Economic Growth: A Non-Communist Manifesto*. New York: Cambridge University Press.

Roussel, Loues. 1987. "Deux décennies de mutations démographiques (1965–1985) dans les pays industrailisés." *Population* 42, no. 3.

Roxborough, Ian. 1984a. "Unity and Diversity in Latin American History." *Journal of Latin American Studies* 16, no. 1:1–26.

———. 1984b. *Unions and Politics in Mexico*. New York: Cambridge University Press.

———. 1989. "Organized Labor: A Major Victim of the Debt Crisis. In *Debt and Democracy in Latin America*, ed. Barbara Stallings and R. Kaufman. Boulder, Colo.: Westview Press.

Roy, Ananya, and Nezar Alsayyad, eds. 2003. *Urban Informality: A Transnational Perspective—Latin America to the Middle East and South Asia*. Lanham, Md.: Lexington Books.

Rubin, Jeffrey. 1997. *Decentering the Regime: Ethnicity, Radicalism and Democracy in Juchitán, Mexico*. Durham: Duke University Press.

———. 2002. "The State as Subject." *Political Power and Social Theory* 15:107–34.

Rueschemeyer, Dietrich, Peter Evans, and Theda Skocpol. 1985. *Bringing the State Back In*. New York: Cambridge University Press.

Rustow, Dankwart A. 1970. "Transitions to Democracy: Toward a Dynamic Model." *Comparative Politics* 2:337–63.

Sabatini, Francisco, Gonzalo Cáceres, and Jorge Cerda. 2001. "Residential Segregation Pattern Changes in Main Chilean Cities." International Seminar on Segregation and the City, Lincoln Institute of Land Policy Web Site. http://www.lincolninst.edu/pubs/d1/615_sabatini_caceres_cerda.pdf.

Safá, Helen. 1970. "The Poor Are Like Everyone Else, Oscar." *Psychology Today* 4, no. 4:26–32.

———. 1974. *Urban Poor of Puerto Rico: A Study in Development and Inequality.* New York: Holt, Rinehart, and Winston.

———. 1995. *The Myth of the Male Breadwinner: Women and Industrialization in the Caribbean.* Boulder, Colo.: Westview Press.

Safilios-Rothschild, Constantina. 1990. "Socio-economic Determinants of the Outcomes of Women's Income-Generation in Developing Countries." In *Women, Employment and the Family in the International Division of Labor,* ed. Sharon Stichter and Jane L. Parpart. Philadelphia: Temple University Press.

Saint, W. S. 1981. "The Wages of Modernization: A Review of the Literature on Temporary Labor Arrangements in Brazilian Agriculture." *Latin American Research Review* 16:91–110.

Salles, Vania, and Elsie McPhail, eds. 1994. *Nuevos textos y renovados pre-textos.* Mexico City: El Colegio de México.

Salles, Vania, and Rodolfo Tuirán. 1998. "Cambios demográficos y socioculturales: Familias contemporáneas en México." In *Familias y relaciones de género en transformación. Cambios trascendentales en América Latina y el Caribe,* ed. Beatríz Schmuckler. Mexico City: Population Council / Edamex.

———. 2001. "El discurso de la salud reproductiva: un Nuevo dogma?" In *Sexualidad y salud reproductiva. Avances y retos para la investigación,* ed. J. Figueroa and C. Stern. Mexico City: El Colegio de México.

Salman, T. 1990. "Between Orthodoxy and Euphoria, Research Strategies on Social Movement: A Comparative Perspective." In *Structures of Power, Movements of Resistance: An Introduction to the Theories of Urban Movements in Latin America,* ed. Willem Assies, Gerrit Burgwal, and Ton Salman. Amsterdam: CEDLA.

Sánchez Gómez, Martha Judith. 1989. "Consideraciones teórico-metodológicas en el estudio del trabajo doméstico en México. In *Trabajo, poder y sexualidad,* ed. Orlandina de Oliveira. Mexico City: Programa Interdisciplinario de Estudios de la Mujer (PIEM) / El Colegio de México.

Sassen, Saskia. 1998. *Globalization and Its Discontents.* New York: The New Press.

———. 2000. "Spatialities and Temporalities of the Global: Elements for a Theorization." *Public Culture* 12, no. 1:215–32.

———. 2001. Public Lecture, Graduate Faculty of Political and Social Science, New School for Social Research, New York, April.

Schild, Verónica. 2000. "Neo-liberalism's New Gendered Market Citizens: The 'Civilizing' Dimension of Social Programmes in Chile." *Citizenship Studies* 4, no. 3:275–305.

Schneider, Cathy. 1995. *Shantytown Protest in Pinochet's Chile.* Philadelphia: Temple University Press.

Schulz, Marcus. 1998. "Collective Action Across Borders: Opportunity Structures, Network Capacities, and Communicative Praxis in the Age of Advanced Globalization." *Sociological Perspectives* 41, no. 3:587–616.

Schumpeter, Joseph Alois. 1939. *Business Cycles: A Theoretical, Historical, and Statistical Analysis of the Capitalist Process.* New York: McGraw-Hill.

Scott, James C. 1998. *Seeing like a State: How Certain Schemes to Improve the Human Condition Have Failed.* New Haven: Yale University Press.

Selby, Henry A., Arthur D. Murphy, and Stephen A. Lorenzen. 1990. *The Mexican Urban Households Organizing for Self Defense.* Austin: University of Texas Press.

Sen, Gita, and Caren Grown. 1985. *Development Alternatives with Women for a New Era: Crises and Alternative Visions*. London: Earthscan.

Sennett, Robert. 2000. "La calle y la oficina: Dos fuentes de identidad." In *En el límite: La vida en el capitalismo global*, ed. Anthony Giddens and William Hutton. Barcelona: Tusquets Editores.

Share, Donald, and Scott Mainwaring. 1986. "Transitions Through Transaction: Democratization in Brazil and Spain." *Political Liberalization in Brazil*, ed. W. Selcher. Boulder, Colo.: Westview Press.

Sheriff, Robin E. 2001. *Dreaming Equality: Color, Race and Racism in Urban Brazil*. New Brunswick: Rutgers University Press.

Silva, Eduardo. 1996. "From Dictatorship to Democracy: The Business-State Nexus in Chile? Economic Transformation, 1975–1994." *Comparative Politics* 28, no. 3.

Silva, Nelson do Valle. 1978. "Black-White Income Differentials in Brazil." Ph.D. diss., University of Michigan.

———. 1985. "Updating the Cost of Not Being White in Brazil." In *Race, Class and Power in Brazil*, ed. Pierre-Michel Fontaine. Los Angeles: Center for Afro-American Studies, UCLA.

———. 1988. "Cor e o processo de realização sócio-econômica." In *Estrutura social, mobilidade e raça*, ed. Carlos Hasenbalg and Nelson do Valle Silva. Rio de Janeiro: Vertice.

Singer, Paul. 1973. *Economía política da urbanizaçao*. São Paulo: CEBRAP / Editora Brasiliense.

Singh, Jyoti Shankar. 1998. *Creating a New Consensus on Population: The International Conference on Population and Development*. London: Earthscan.

Sklair, Leslie. 2002. *Globalization: Capitalism and Its Alternatives*. New York: Oxford University Press.

Skocpol, Theda. 1979. *States and Social Revolutions*. Princeton: Princeton University Press.

Smith, Gavin. 1989. *Livelihood and Resistance: Peasants and the Politics of Land in Peru*. Berkeley and Los Angeles: University of California Press.

Smith, Jackie G., Charles Chatfield, and Ron Pagnucco. 1997. *Transnational Social Movements and Global Politics: Solidarity Beyond the State*. Syracuse: Syracuse University Press.

Smith, Robert C. 1998. "Mexican Immigrants, the Mexican State, and the Transnational Practice of Mexican Politics and Membership." *LASA Forum* 24:19–24.

Smith, William, and Carlos Acuña. 1994. "Future Politico-Economic Scenarios for Latin America." In *Democracy, Markets and Structural Reform in Latin America: Argentina, Bolivia, Brazil, Chile and Mexico*, ed. William Smith, Carlos Acuña, and Eduardo Gamarra. New Brunswick, N.J.: Transaction Publishers.

Sojo, Carlos, and Juan Pablo Pérez Sáinz. 2002. "Reinvertar lo social en América Latina." In *Desarrollo social en América Latina: temas y desafíos para las políticas públicas*, ed. C. Sojo. San José: FLASCO / Banco Mundial.

Sorj, Bernado. 2000. *A nova sociedade Brasileira*. Rio de Janeiro: Jorge Zahar.

Soros, George. 1998. *The Crisis of Global Capitalism: Open Society Endangered*. London: Little, Brown.

Soto, Hernando de. 1986. *El otro sendero: La revolución informal*. Lima: El Barranco.

——. 2000. *The Mystery of Capital: Why Capitalism Triumphs in the West and Fails Everywhere Else*. New York: Basic Books.

Souza, Paulo, and Victor Tokman. 1976. "El sector informal urbano." In *El empleo en América Latina,* ed. P. R. Souza and V. E. Tokman. Mexico City: Siglo Veintiuno Editores.

Spink, Peter. 1999. "Possibilities and Political Imperatives: Seventy Years of Administrative Reform in Latin America." In *Reforming the State: Managerial Public Administration in Latin America,* ed. L. Bresser Pereira and P. Spink. Boulder, Colo.: Lynne Rienner.

——. 2000. "The Rights Approach to Local Public Management: Experiences from Brazil." *Revista da Administração de Empresas* (São Paulo) 40, no. 3:45–65.

——. 2001. *Reforming the Reformers: The Saga of Public Administration Reform in Latin America*. Stockholm: Sida.

Spulber, Nicholas. 1997. *Redefining the State in Latin America: Privatization and Welfare Reform in Industrializing and Transitional Economies*. Cambridge: Cambridge University Press.

Stallings, Barbara, and Wilson Peres. 2000. *Growth, Employment and Equity: The Impact of Economic Reforms in Latin America and the Caribbean*. Washington, D.C.: The Brookings Institution / ECLAC. Also published in Spanish as *Crecimiento, empleo y equidad: El impacto de las reformas económicas en América Latina y el Caribe*. Santiago: Fondo de Cultura Económica / CEPAL Chile.

Standing, Guy. 1999. "Global Feminization Through Flexible Labor: A Theme Revisited." *World Development* (Oxford) 27, no. 3:583–602.

Stavenhagen, Rodolfo. 1965. "Classes, Colonialism, and Acculturation." *Studies in Comparative International Development* 1, no. 6:53–77.

——. 1996. "Los derechos indígenas: Algunos problemas conceptuales." In *Construir la democracia: Derechos humanos, ciudadanía y sociedad en América Latina,* ed. Elizabeth Jelin and Eric Hershberg. Caracas: Nueva Sociedad.

Steris, Dimitris, and Stephen P Mumme. 1991. "Nuclear Power, Technological Autonomy, and the State in Mexico." *Latin American Research Review* 26, no. 3:55–82.

Stiglitz, Joseph. 1998. *More Instruments and Broader Goals. Moving Towards the Post-Washington Consensus*. Helsinki: World Institute for Development and Economic Research, United Nations University.

——. 1999. "Knowledge as a Global Public Good." In *Global Public Goods,* ed. I. Kaul, I. Grunberg, and M. A. Stein. Oxford: Oxford University Press.

Sunkel, Osvaldo. 1964. *Desarrollo económico*. Santiago: Instituto Latinoamericano de Planificación Económica y Social.

——. 1971. *Capitalismo transnacional y disintegración nacional en América Latina*. Mexico: El Trimestre Económico.

——. 1973. "Transnational Capitalism and National Disintegration in Latin America." *Social and Economic Studies* (University of the West Indies, Jamaica) 22, no. 1 (March): 132–71.

——. 1992. "The Consolidation of Democracy and Development in Chile." *CEPAL Review* 47.

——. 1993. "Contemporary Economic Reform in Historical Perspective." In *Rebuilding Capitalism: Alternative Roads after Socialism and Dirigisme,* ed. A.

Solimano, O. Sunkel, and M. Blejer. Ann Arbor: University of Michigan Press.

———. 1994. "La Crisis social en América Latina. Una perspectiva neoestructuralista." In *El Desarrollo Social: Tarea de Todos*, ed. Carlos Contreras. Santiago: Comisión Sudamericana de Paz, Seguridad y Democracia.

———. 1995. "Poverty and Development: From Economic Reform to Social Reform." In *Issues in Global Governance: Papers Written for the Commission on Global Governance*. London: Kluwer Law International.

———. 2001. "The Unbearable Lightness of Neoliberalism." Paper presented at the conference "Latin American Sociology," University of Florida, Gainesville.

———, ed. 1993b. *Development from Within: Toward a Neostructuralist Approach for Latin America*. Boulder, Colo.: Lynne Rienner.

Sunkel, O., and N. Gligo. 1981. *Estilos de desarrollo y medio ambiente*. Vols. 1 and 2. Mexico City: Fondo de Cultura Económica.

Sunkel, O., and M. Mortimore. 2001. "Transnational Integration and National Disintegration in Latin America and Asia Revisited." In *Comparing Regionalisms: Implications for Global Development*, ed. B. Hettne, A. Inotai, and O. Sunkel. London: Macmillan.

Sunkel, O., and Pedro Paz. 1970. El subdesarrolo Latinoamericano la teoría del desarroio. Mexico: Siglo XXI Editores.

Sunkel, O., and G. Zuleta. 1990. "Neo-structuralism versus neo-liberalism in the 1990s." *CEPAL Review*, no. 42 (December).

Suttles, Gerald. 1968. *The Social Order of the Slum: Ethnicity and Territory in the Inner City*. Chicago: University of Chicago Press.

Szasz Pianata, Ivonne. 1999. "La perspectiva de género en los estudios de migración." In *Mujer, género y población en México*, ed. Brígida García. Mexico City: El Colegio de México / Sociedad Mexicana de Demografía (Somede).

Székely, Miguel, Nora Lustig, Martin Cumpa, and José Antonio Mejía. 2000. "Do We Know How Much Poverty There Is?" Inter-American Development Bank Working Paper Series 437, IADB, Washington, D.C.

Tardanico, Richard, and Rafael Menjívar, eds. 1997. *Global Restructuring, Employment, and Social Inequality in Urban Latin America*. Miami: North-South Center Press.

Tarrow, Sidney. 1994. *Power in Movement: Social Movements, Collective Action and Politics*. Cambridge: Cambridge University Press.

Teivaninen, Teivo. 2002. *Enter Economism, Exit Politics: Experts, Economic Policy, and the Damage to Democracy*. London: Zed Books.

Telles, Edward E. 1992. "Residential Segregation by Skin Color in Brazil." *American Sociological Review* 57:186–97.

———. 1995. "Structural Sources of Socioeconomic Segregation in Brazilian Metropolitan Areas." *American Journal of Sociology* 5:1199–223.

Telles, E., and N. Lim. 1998. "Does It Matter Who Answers the Race Question? Racial Classification and Income Inequality in Brazil." *Demography* 35, no. 4:465–74.

Tendler, Judith. 1997. *Good Government in the Tropics*. Baltimore: Johns Hopkins University Press.

Tendler, Judith, and S. Freedheim. 1994. "Trust in a Rent-seeking World: Health and Government Transformed in Northeast Brazil." *World Development* 21, no.12:1771–92.

Thomas, Jim. 1997. "El nuevo modelo económico y los mercados laborales en América Latina." In *El nuevo modelo económico en América Latina. Su efecto en la distribución del ingreso y en la pobreza,* ed. V. Bulmer-Thomas. Mexico City: Fondo de Cultura Económica.

Thorne, Barrie. 1982. "Feminist Rethinking of the Family: An Overview." In *Rethinking the Family. Some Feminist Questions,* ed. Barrie Thorne and Marilyn Yalom. New York: Longman.

Thorp, Rosemary. 1998. *Progress, Poverty and Exclusion: An Economic History of Latin America in the Twentieth Century.* Baltimore: John Hopkins University Press.

Tilly, Charles. 1978. *From Mobilisation to Revolution.* Reading, Mass.: Addison-Wesley.

———. 1984. "Social Movements and National Politics." In *State Building and Social Movements,* ed. W. Bright and S. Harding. Ann Arbor: University of Michigan Press.

———. 1990. *Coercion, Capital and the European States, A.D. 990–1990.* Oxford: Blackwell.

———. 1996. "Invisible Elbow." *Sociological Forum* 11:589–601.

Todorov, Tzvetan. 1998. *La conquista de América. El problema del otro.* Mexico City: Siglo Veintiuno Editores.

Tokman, Victor. 1998. "Empleo y seguridad: Demandas de fin de siglo." *Anuario Social y Político de América Latina y El Caribe* (Caracas) 2:123–135.

Touraine, Alain. 1987. *Actores sociales y sistemas políticos en América.* Santiago: PREALC.

———. 1988a. *The Return of the Actor: Social Theory in Post-Industrial Society.* Minneapolis: University of Minnesota Press.

———. 1988b. *La parole et le sang. Politique et societé en Amérique Latine.* Paris: Odile Jacob.

———. 1988c. *¿Podremos vivir juntos?* Mexico City: Fondo de Cultura Económica.

———. 1989. *Palavra e sangue: Política e sociedade na América Latina.* São Paulo: Universidade Estadual de Campinas.

Tuirán, R. 1986. "Reproducción social y reproducción demográfica: Una relación por descifrar." In *Memorias de la III Reunión Nacional de Investigación Demográfica en México.* Mexico City: SOMEDE.

Turner, Bryan S. 1990. "Outline of a Theory of Citizenship." *Sociology* 24, no. 2 (May): 189–217.

Turner, J.F.C. 1966. "Uncontrolled Urban Settlements: Problems and Solutions." Paper presented to United Nations Conference, Pittsburgh. Subsequently published in *The City in Newly Developed Countries,* ed. G. Breese (Englewood Cliffs, N.J.: Prentice Hall, 1969).

———. 1968. "Housing Priorities, Settlement Patterns and Urban Development in Modernizing Countries." *Journal of the American Institute of Planners* 34:354–63.

———. 1976. *Housing by People: Towards Autonomy in Building Environments.* London: Marion Boyars.

UNCHS (United Nations Center for Human Settlements). 1996. *An Urbanizing World: Global Report on Human Settlements, 1996.* Oxford: Oxford University Press.

UNDP. 1992. *Human Development Report.* New York: UNDP.

UNEP (United Nations Environment Program). 1999. *GEO-2000: Global Environment Outlook.* London: Earthscan Publications.

Ungar, Mark. 2002. *Elusive Reform: Democracy and the Rule of Law in Latin America.* Boulder, Colo.: Lynne Rienner.

Valderrama, Mariano. 1998. *El fortalecimiento institucional y los acelerados cambios en las ONG Latinoamericanas.* Lima: ALOP-CEPES.

Valentine, C. 1968. *Culture and Poverty.* Chicago: University of Chicago Press.

Valenzuela, Arturo. 1993. "Latin America: Presidentialism in Crisis." *Journal of Democracy* 4, no. 4:3–16.

Van Alphen, Ernst. 1997. *Caught by History. Holocaust Effects in Contemporary Art, Literature and Theory.* Stanford: Stanford University Press.

Van Cott, D. L. 2000. *The Friendly Liquidation of the Past: The Politics of Diversity in Latin America.* Pittsburgh: University of Pittsburgh Press.

Van der Kaa, D. 1987. "Europe Second Demographic Transition." *Population Bulletin* 42, no. 1.

Van Gunsteren, Herman. 1978. "Notes on a Theory of Citizenship." In *Democracy, Consensus, and Social Contract,* ed. Pierre Birnbaum, Jack Lively, and Geraint Parry. London: Sage Publications.

———. 1994. "Four Conceptions of Citizenship." In *The Condition of Citizenship,* ed. B. van Steenbergen. London: Sage Publications.

Varley, Ann. 2002. "Private to Public: Debating the Meaning of Tenure Legalization." *International Journal of Urban and Regional Research* 26, no. 3:449–61.

Varley, Ann, and Maribel Blasco. 2000. "Intact or in Tatters? Family Care of Older Women and Men in Urban Mexico." *Gender and Development* 8:47–55.

Vetter, Stephen. n.d. *Mobilizing Resources: The Business of Grassroots Development.* http://www.iaf.gov/jrnl19-2/vetter.htm.

Wacquant, Loïc. 1996. "The Rise of Advanced Marginality: Notes on Its Nature and Implications." *Acta Sociológica* 39, no. 2:121 n. 40.

———. 1997. "Three Pernicious Premises in the Study of the American Ghetto." *International Journal of Urban and Regional Research* 21, no. 2:341–57.

———. 2000. "Durkheim and Bourdieu: The Common Plinth and Its Cracks." In *Reading Bourdieu on Society and Culture,* ed. B. Fowler. Oxford: Basil Blackwell.

Wainerman, Catalina. 2000. "División del trabajo en familias de dos proveedores. Relatos desde ambos géneros y dos generaciones." *Estudios Demográficos y Urbanos* 15, no. 1 (January-April): 149–84.

Wallerstein, Immanuel. 1976. *The Modern World-System: Capitalist Agriculture and the Origins of the European World-Economy in the Sixteenth Century.* New York: Academic Press.

———. 1995. *Open the Social Sciences.* Report to the Gulbenkian Commission, Lisbon.

Ward, Peter M. 1976. "The Squatter Settlements as Slum or Housing Solutions: Evidence from Mexico City." *Land Economics* 2, no. 3:330–46.

———. 1978. "Social Interaction Patterns in Squatter Settlements in Mexico City." *Geoforum* 9, no. 94/95: 235–43.

———. 1986. *Welfare Politics in Mexico: Papering over the Cracks.* London: Allen and Unwin.

———. 1993. "Social Welfare Policy and Political Opening in Mexico." *Journal of Latin American Studies* 25, no. 3 (October).

———. 1998. "From Machine Politics to the Politics of Technocracy: Charting

Changes in Governance in the Mexican Municipality." *Bulletin of Latin American Research* 17, no. 3:341–65.

———, ed. 1982. *Self-Help Housing: A Critique*. London: Mansell.

Ward, Peter, 2004. "Marginality then and now." In "From the Marginality of the 1960s to the 'New Poverty' of Today." *Latin American Research Review* 39, no. 1: 183–87.

Ward, Peter M., Victoria E. Rodríguez, and Enrique Cabrero Mendoza. 1999. "New Federalism and State Government in Mexico." U.S.-Mexican Policy Report # 9, Lyndon B. Johnson School of Public and Public Affairs, University of Texas at Austin.

Weber, Max. 1930. *The Protestant Ethic and the Spirit of Capitalism*. London: Unwin University Books.

———. 1947. *The Theory of Social and Economic Organization*. New York: The Free Press.

———. [1904] 1949. *The Methodology of the Social Sciences*, trans. E. A. Shils and H. A. Finch. New York: The Free Press.

———. 1963. *The Sociology of Religion*. Translated by E. Fischoff. Boston: Beacon Press.

Weffort, Francisco. 1976. "Clases populares y desarrollo social." In *Populismo, marginalización y dependencia,* ed. Francisco Weffort and Anibal Quijano. San José, Costa Rica: Editorial Universitaria Centroamericana.

Weiss, Carol. 1993. "The Interaction of the Sociological Agenda and Public Policy." In *Sociology and Public Agenda,* ed. William Julius Wilson. Newbury Park, Calif.: Sage Publications.

Welch, John H. 1993. "The New Face of Latin America: Financial Flows, Markets and Institutions in the 1990s." *Journal of Latin American Studies* 25, no. 1 (February): 1–24.

Weller, Jurgen. 2000a. *Reformas económicas, crecimiento y empleo: Los mercados de trabajo en América Latina y el Caribe*. Santiago: Fondo de Cultura Económica / CEPAL Chile.

———. 2000b. "Tendencias del empleo en los años noventa en América Latina y el Caribe." *Revista de la CEPAL* 72.

Weyland, Kurt. 1995. "Social Movements and the State: The Politics of Health Reform in Brazil." *World Development* 23, no. 10:1699–713.

———. 1996. *Democracy Without Equity: Failures of Reform in Brazil*. Pittsburgh: University of Pittsburgh Press.

Whitehead, Laurence. 1992. "The Alternatives to Liberal Democracy: A Latin American Perspective." In "Prospects for Democracy," ed. D. Held. Special issue, *Political Studies* 40.

Whyte, William F. 1943. *Street Corner Society*. Chicago: University of Chicago Press.

Wickham-Crowley, Timothy. 1992. *Guerrillas and Revolution in Latin America*. Princeton: Princeton University Press.

Wilenski, Harold L. 1975. *The Welfare State and Equality*. Berkeley and Los Angeles: University of California Press.

Williamson, John. 1997. "The Washington Consensus Revisited." In *Economic and Social Development into the XXI Century*, ed. Louis Emmerij. Washington, D.C.: Johns Hopkins University Press / IDB.

Willis, Eliza, Christopher Garman, and Stephen Haggard. 1999. "The Politics of Decentralization in Latin America." *Latin American Research Review* 34, no.1:7–56.

Wirth, Louis. 1938. "Urbanism as a Way of Life." *American Journal of Sociology* 44, no. 1:1–24.

Wood, Charles H., and José Alberto Magno de Carvalho. 1988. *The Demography of Inequality in Brazil*. London: Cambridge University Press.

———. 1994. "Categorias do Censo e Classificação Subjetive de Cor no Brasil." *Revista Brasileira de Estudos Populacionais* 11, no. 1.

Wood, Charles H., and Peggy A. Lovell. 1992. "Racial Inequality and Child Mortality in Brazil." *Social Forces* 70, no. 3:703–24.

World Bank. 1972. *Urbanization* (Sector Policy Paper). Washington, D.C.: The World Bank.

———. 1990. *Urban Management Program: Phase 2. Capacity Building for Urban Management in the 1990s*. Washington, D.C.: The World Bank with UNDP, UNCHS.

———. 1991. *Urban Policy and Economic Development: An Agenda for the 1990s*. Washington, D.C.: The World Bank.

———. 1999. *World Development Report 1999/2000: Entering the 21st Century: The Changing Development Landscape*. New York: Oxford University Press.

World Commission on Environment and Development. 1987. *Our Common Future*. Oxford: Oxford University Press.

Worsley, Peter. 1984. *The Three Worlds: Culture and World Development*. Chicago: University of Chicago Press.

Yashar, Deborah. 1999. "Democracy, Indigenous Movements, and the Postliberal Challenge in Latin America." *World Politics* 52, no. 1:76–104.

Young, M., and P. Willmott. 1957. *Family and Kinship in East London*. London: Routledge and Kegan Paul.

Zakaria, Fareed. 1997. "The Rise of Illiberal Democracy." *Foreign Affairs*, November-December: 22–43.

Zanetta, C. 2003. *The Influence of the World Bank on National Housing and Urban Polices: The Case of Mexico and Argentina During the 1990s*. Aldershot, U.K.: Ashgate.

Zapata, Francisco. 1993. *Autonomía y subordinación en el sindicalismo latinoamericano*. Mexico City: Fondo de Cultura Económica / El Colegio de Cultura Económica.

Zaverucha, Jorge. 1993. "The Degree of Military Political Autonomy During the Spanish, Argentine, and Brazilian Transitions." *Journal of Latin American Studies* 25, no. 2 (May).

Zeitlin, Maurice. 1984. *The Civil Wars in Chile: or, the Bourgeois Revolutions That Never Were*. Princeton: Princeton University Press.

Zoninsein, Jonas. 2001. "The Economic Case for Combating Racial and Ethnic Exclusion in Latin American and Caribbean Countries." Unpublished paper written for the Inter-American Development Bank, Combating Social Exclusion in LAC.

Zuleta, Gustavo. 1992. "El desarrollo desde dentro: Un enfoque neoestructuralista para América Latina." In *Pensamiento Iberoamericano. Revista de economía política* (Madrid) 21 (January-June).

———. 2000. "'Civilizing' Dimension of Social Programmes in Chile." *Citizenship Studies* 4, no. 3:275–305.

Contributors

MARINA ARIZA is a tenured researcher at the Universidad Nacional Autónoma de México. She received her doctorate in sociology from El Colegio de México. Her publications include *Yo no soy la que dejé atrás: Mujeres Migrantesen la Republica Dominicana* (Plaza y Valdés / UNAM, 2001), "Migración, familia, y transnacionalidad en el contexto de la globalización. Algunos puntos de reflexión" (*Revista Mexicana de Sociología*, 2002), and "Obreras, sirvientas y prostitutas. Globalización, familia y mercados de trabajo en la República Dominicana" (forthcoming in *Estudios Sociológicos*). Her areas of interests include urban migration, the family, and labor markets.

DIANE DAVIS is professor of political sociology in the Department of Urban Studies and Planning at the Massachusetts Institute of Technology. She is the author of *Urban Leviathan: Mexico City in the Twentieth Century* (Temple University Press, 1994; Spanish edition, 1998) and *Discipline and Development: Middle Classes and Prosperity in East Asia and Latin America* (Cambridge University Press, 2004). She edited *Violence, Coercion, and Rights in the Americas* (Sage Publications, 2000, with Anthony W. Pereira) and *Irregular Armed Forces and Their Role in Politics and State Formation* (Cambridge University Press, 2003). For the past fourteen years she has served as editor of *Political Power and Social Theory: A Research Annual,* published by Elsevier Science. Her research interests include late development, urban sociology, comparative-historical sociology, and states and social movements. She is currently examining the police and rule of law in Latin America and other "posttransition" regions of the world.

VILMAR FARIA, at the time of the conference that produced this volume, was Executive Secretary of the Brazilian Government Chamber for Social Policy, where he was responsible for coordinating the policies of the administration of President Fernando Henrique Cardoso. His obtained his doctorate in sociology from Harvard University and subsequently held a number of distinguished positions throughout his career. He was a professor at the University of São Paulo and the University of Campinas, visiting professor at the University of Texas, and Rio Branco Chair at the University of California, Berkeley. He served as the executive director of FUNDAP and was president of the Brazilian Center for Analysis and Planning (CEBRAP). His published articles and presentations include "Government policy and fertility regulation: unintended consequences and perverse effects" (*Brazilian Journal of Population Studies*, 1997–1998), "Brasil: compatibilidade entre a estabiliçazão e o resgate da dívida social" (*Cadernos Adenauer*, 2000), and "Uma agenda social para o Brasil" (*Encontro 2000,* with R. Brant, D. Perriera, and C. Buarque).

ELIZABETH JELIN is a senior researcher at the National Council of Scientific Research, Argentina (CONICET). She received her doctorate in sociology from the University of Texas at Austin. She is research director at IDES (Instituto de Desarrollo Económico y Social), and director of the doctoral program in the social sciences developed jointly at the Universidad Nacional de General Sarmiento (UNGS) and IDES. She is the author of numerous publications, including *State Repression and the Labors of Memory* (University of Minnesota Press, 2003) and editor of several volumes in the series "Memorias de la represión," published by Siglo XXI Editores in Madrid and Buenos Aires. She is author and editor of *Más Allá de la Nación: las Eescalas Múltiples de los Movimientos Sociales* (Buenos Aires: Libros del Zorzal, 2003). Her research interests are in human rights, the family, citizenship, and social movements.

JOE FOWERAKER is professor of government at the University of Essex and former executive director of the European Consortium for Political Research. He has authored a number of books, including of *The Struggle for Land: A Political Economy of the Pioneer Frontier in Brazil from 1930 to the Present Day* (Cambridge University Press, 1981), *Making Democracy in Spain: Grass-roots Struggles in the South, 1955–1975* (Cambridge University Press, 1989), *Popular Mobilization in Mexico: The Teachers' Movement 1977–87* (Cambridge University Press, 1993), *Theorizing Social Movements* (Pluto, 1995), and *Citizenship Rights and Social Movements: A Comparative and Statistical Analysis* (Oxford University Press, 2000, with Todd Landman). He is also the editor of the *Encyclopaedia of Democratic Thought* (Routledge, 2001) and has recently published *Governing Latin America* (Polity, 2003).

ORLANDINA DE OLIVEIRA earned a master's degree in sociology from the Latin American Faculty of Social Sciences (FLACSO) and a doctorate in sociology from the University of Texas at Austin. She is professor and researcher at the Center for Sociological Studies at El Colegio de México.

Her main research topics concern labor markets and family and gender studies. Her recent publications include "Quality of life and marital experiences in Mexico" (in *Women, Poverty and Demographic Change*, edited by Brígida García, Oxford University Press, 2000), "Contrasting scenarios: non-residential family formation patterns in the Caribbean and Europe" (*International Review of Sociology*, University of Roma, La Sapienza, 2001), and "Mujer y legislación social mexicana" (*Estudios Sociológicos* 20, no. 60 [2003], with Viviane Brachet).

JUAN PABLO PÉREZ SÁINZ is a senior researcher at FLACSO in Costa Rica. His recent publications include *From the Finca to the Maquila: Labor and Capitalist Development in Central America* (Westview Press, 1999), "The new faces of informality in Central America" (*Journal of Latin American Studies* 30 [1998]), "Between the global and the local: community economies in Latin America" (in *The Revival of Civil Society: Global and Comparative Perspectives*, ed. Michael Schecter [London: Macmillan, 1999]), and *Communities in Globalization: The Invisible Mayan Nahual* (Rowman and Littlefield, 2003, with Catherine Andrade-Eekhoff).

ALEJANDRO PORTES received his master's degree and his doctorate from the University of Wisconsin at Madison. He is chair of the Department of Sociology at Princeton University, where he is also Howard Harrison and Gabrielle Snyder Beck Professor of Sociology and director of the Center for Migration and Development. In 1997, he was elected president of the American Sociological Association and served in that capacity in 1998–99. He is the author of over two hundred articles and chapters on national development, international migration, Latin American and Caribbean urbanization, and economic sociology. His books include *City on the Edge—The Transformation of Miami* (California University Press, 1993), coauthored with Alex Stepick and winner of the Robert Park Award for best book in urban sociology and the Anthony Leeds Award for best book in urban anthropology in 1995. His current research is on the adaptation process of the immigrant second generation and the rise of transnational immigrant communities in the United States. His most recent books, coauthored with Rubén G. Rumbaut, are *Legacies: The Story of the Immigrant Second Generation* and *Ethnicities: Children of Immigrants in America* (California University Press, 2001). *Legacies* is the winner of the 2002 Distinguished Scholarship Award from the American Sociological Association (ASA) and of the 2002 W. I. Thomas and Florian Znaniecki Award for best book from the International Migration

Section of the ASA. He is a fellow of the American Academy of Arts and Sciences and a member of the National Academy of Sciences.

JOE POTTER is an economist-demographer in the Department of Sociology at the University of Texas at Austin. Before joining the University of Texas in the fall of 1989, he spent six years in Mexico City at the Colegio de México, and then moved to the Harvard School of Public Health, where he continued his research on the fertility transition in Mexico. He is the director of the Vilmar Faria Fellowship in Quantitative Analysis and Public Policy, a program dedicated to building the quantitative analytical capacity of Brazilian social scientists. His current research focuses on the demography of the U.S.-Mexico Border region, the fertility transition in Brazil, and the influence of doctors and medicalization on reproductive behavior.

BRYAN ROBERTS is the C. B. Smith Sr. Centennial Chair in U.S.-Mexico Relations in the Department of Sociology at the University of Texas at Austin and director of the Center for Latin American Social Policy of the Teresa Lozano Long Institute of Latin American Studies. He has a doctorate in sociology from the University of Chicago. He taught at the University of Manchester from 1964 to 1986 where he held a professorship in the Department of Sociology. He has published numerous books, including *Organizing Strangers* (1973), *Cities of Peasants* (1978), *Miners, Peasants and Entrepreneurs* (1984), and *The Making of Citizens* (1995). His activities encompass a Ford Foundation funded research and training project on Self-sustaining Community Development in Argentina, Chile, Colombia, and Peru and two projects on urbanization in Latin America, supported by the Andrew W. Mellon Foundation. One of these, jointly sponsored by the Urban Affairs Institute at the University of Texas, is on urban governance and intra-urban population differentials in six countries of Latin America (Argentina, Brazil, Chile, Mexico, Peru, and Uruguay). The other, jointly with the Center for Migration and Development of Princeton University, concerns Latin American urbanization in the late twentieth century.

OSVALDO SUNKEL is an internationally acclaimed economist from Chile who has written extensively on Latin American development and on development and the environment. He has served as a special adviser to the United Nations Economic Commission for Latin America and president of the Corporación de Investigaciones del Desarrollo Económico (CINDE) in Santiago, Chile. He has been a visiting professor in a number of universities, including the Institute of Development Studies at the University of Sussex, the Center for International Studies at Duke University, and Graduate Program in Urban Planning at UCLA. In 1993, he was the Bacardi Eminent Scholar at the University of Florida. His recent books include *Comparing Regionalisms: Implications for Global Development* (Palgrave Macmillan, 2001, with Bjorn Hettne and Andras Inotai), *The Sustainability of Long-term Growth: Socioeconomic and Ecological Perspectives* (Edward Elgar, 2001, with Mohan Munasinghe and Carlos de Miguel), and *Debt and Development Crises in Latin America* (Oxford University Press, 1995, with Stephanie Griffith-Jones).

RODOLFO TUIRÁN is undersecretary for urban development and planning in the Ministry of Social Development, Mexico. He has a doctorate in sociology and demography from the University of Texas at Austin. He has been the secretary general of the National Population Council in Mexico and was on the Committee for the International Conference on Population and Development. He has also served as a member of CEPAL, vice president of a forum for the UN, and visiting professor in several universities in Mexico. His many articles have been published in both English and Spanish, and he is the coordinator of *La migración mexicana hacia Estados Unidos-Presente y Futuro* (Consejo Nacional de Población, Mexico 2000).

PETER WARD is the C. B. Smith Sr. Centennial Chair in U.S.-Mexico Relations and professor of sociology and public affairs at the University of Texas at Austin. He has a doctorate in geography from the University of Liverpool. He previously taught at University College, London, and at the University of Cambridge. He is executive editor of the *Latin American Research Review* and author of fourteen books and seventy articles dealing with low-cost housing, land markets, social policy, local government, Mexican politics, and megacities. Among his most recent publications are *Mexico City* (second edition), *New Federalism and State Government in Mexico: Bringing the States Back In* (with Victoria Rodríguez), *Colonias and Public Policy in Texas: Urbanization by Stealth*, and *Common Origins, Segmented Futures: Mexican and Mexican American Households in Transnational and Border Contexts* (forthcoming). His principal research interests are Latin American urbanization, contemporary Mexican politics, housing policy and planning, Mexico City, and colonia-type housing in the United States.

CHARLES H. WOOD is the director of the Center for Latin American Studies at the University of Florida in Gainesville. He received his doctorate in sociology from the University of Texas at Austin. He specializes in population studies, the sociology of development, population and the environment, and the comparative study of race and ethnic relations. His books include the *Demography of Inequality in Brazil* (Cambridge University Press, 1988, with José Alberto de Carvalho), *Contested Frontiers in Amazonia* (Columbia University Press, 1992, with Marianne Schmink), and *Deforestation and Land Use in the Amazon* (University Presses of Florida, 2002, with Roberto Porro). Recent articles include "Ironies of citizenship in Brazil: skin color, police brutality, and the challenge to democracy in Brazil" (*Social Forces*, 1999, with Michael Mitchell) and "Estimating the stability of census-based racial/ethnic classifications: the case of Brazil" (forthcoming in *Population Studies*, with José Alberto Magno de Carvalho and Flávia Cristina Drummond Andrade).

Index

Lightning Source UK Ltd.
Milton Keynes UK
22 September 2009

144029UK00001B/303/P